THE PROCEDURE OF THE UN SECURITY COUNCIL

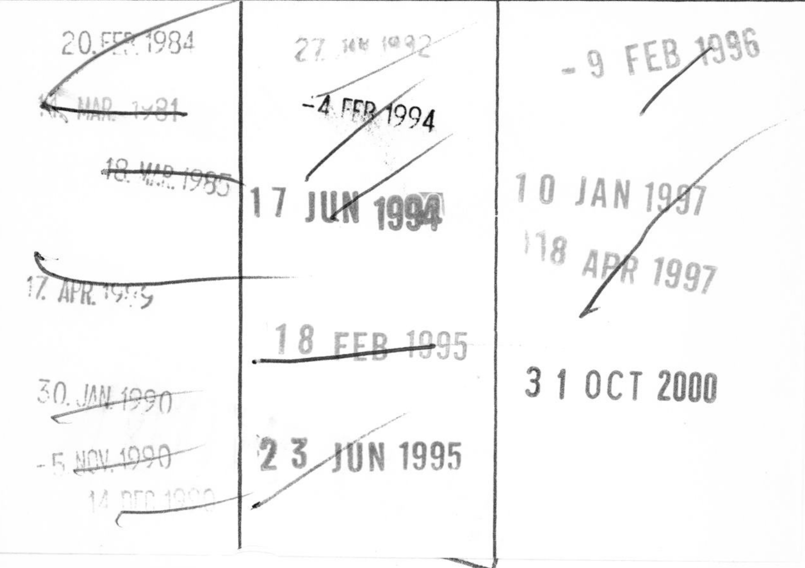

THE PROCEDURE OF THE UN SECURITY COUNCIL

Sydney D. Bailey

Clarendon Press · Oxford
1975

Oxford University Press, Ely House, London W.1

GLASGOW NEW YORK TORONTO MELBOURNE WELLINGTON
CAPE TOWN IBADAN NAIROBI DAR ES SALAAM LUSAKA ADDIS ABABA
DELHI BOMBAY CALCUTTA MADRAS KARACHI LAHORE DACCA
KUALA LUMPUR SINGAPORE HONG KONG TOKYO

ISBN 0 19 827199 9

Printed in Great Britain by
Richard Clay (The Chaucer Press), Ltd.,
Bungay, Suffolk

PREFACE

*Every Christian prince must take as his chief maxim not to employ arms to support or vindicate his rights until he has employed and exhausted the way of reason and persuasion.**

In an earlier volume I have reviewed the practice of the UN Security Council with regard to voting. This book examines other aspects of the procedure and practice of the Council. I hope to complete the trilogy with a further volume which will deal with aspects of the Council's primary responsibility for peace-making and peace-keeping.

It is usually only the casual reviewer who starts reading a book at the last chapter, but some who read this book may be unfamiliar with the working of the Security Council. I suggest that they read pages 290–308 of Chapter 7.

A number of diplomats and international officials were good enough to advise me on various factual points while I was writing this book. I have drawn fully on their experience, and in a couple of cases on their indiscretions, but not in a way that will embarrass any of them or enable the reader to identify the source of any particular item of information. I would like to express my appreciation to some who cannot be mentioned by name, and to the following: Sir Harold Beeley, Lord Caradon, F. Y. Chai, Sir Colin Crowe, Sir Patrick Dean, Lord Gladwyn, Sir Leslie Glass, Rosalyn Higgins, James N. Hyde, Sir Roger Jackling, Alan G. James, Gunnar Jarring, Judge Philip Jessup, Ismat Kittani, Sir Donald Maitland, Anthony Parsons, Oscar Schachter, Brian E. Urquhart, and Charles W. Yost.

It goes without saying that I alone am responsible for any factual mistakes or faulty judgments.

I am grateful for the consistent and friendly help I have received from several libraries, especially those at the London Office of the United Nations, the Royal Institute of International Affairs, and the Carnegie Endowment for International Peace in New York.

S.D.B.

1 March 1974

* This and the other epigraphs are taken from *On the manner of negotiating with Princes*, by François de Callières, first published in 1716.

CONTENTS

APPENDICES

List of Tables

List of Charts

CHAPTER 1

THE INSTITUTIONAL FRAMEWORK

> There is no durable treaty which is not founded on reciprocal advantage, and indeed a treaty which does not satisfy this condition is no treaty at all and is apt to contain the seeds of its own dissolution.

WHEN a new body meets for the first time, it usually has a clean procedural slate, except for the rules which customarily govern bodies of that kind, be it a political party, a religious congregation, or a golf club. But when the Security Council met for the first time just after 3 p.m. on Thursday 17 January 1946, the procedural slate was not clean. The Council had to operate within the framework of the UN Charter, which had been approved at San Francisco seven months previously. Moreover, the UN Preparatory Commission had drafted some tentative rules of procedure for the Council and had drawn up a provisional agenda of thirteen items for the first meeting, which the Secretariat placed before the Council after making some slight adjustments in the order of items.[1]

The Security Council met in Church House, London, close to Westminster Abbey and the bomb-scarred Houses of Parliament. The Council's membership included, as it still does, five permanent members:* the Republic of China, France, the Soviet Union, the United Kingdom, and the United States, represented respectively by K. V. Wellington Koo, Vincent Auriol, Andrei A. Gromyko, Ernest Bevin, and Edward R. Stettinius Jr. (see pp. 114–15 and 124–5). The previous Saturday, the General Assembly had added six non-permanent members: Australia, Brazil, Egypt, Mexico, Netherlands, and Poland.

* In this book, I refer to members of the Security Council, but Members (with a capital M) of the United Nations.

It was a distinguished company. Paul-Boncour was a former Prime Minister and veteran of French public life. Vincent Auriol was to become President of the Fourth French Republic. Wellington Koo (China), Badawi (Egypt), Cordova (Mexico), and Padilla Nervo (Mexico) were to become members of the International Court of Justice. Padilla Nervo and van Kleffens (Netherlands) were to become Presidents of the General Assembly. Modzelewski (Poland) was in 1950 to be the Soviet candidate to succeed Trygve Lie as Secretary-General. Bidault (France) was to become Prime Minister; Bevin (United Kingdom) was Foreign Minister, and Cyro de Freitas-Valle (Brazil), Andrei Gromyko (Soviet Union), van Kleffens (Netherlands), and Andrei Y. Vyshinsky (Soviet Union) were later to reach that rank; Massigli (France) was a future Secretary-General at the Quai d'Orsay; Cadogan (United Kingdom) and Stettinius (U.S.A.) (Table pp. 118–19 and 124–5) were their countries' first ambassadors at the United Nations. Abdel Fattah Amr (Egypt), Foo Ping-sheung (China), W. R. Hodgson (Australia), Alfonso de Rosenzweig Diaz (Mexico), Henrique R. Valle (Brazil), and Jonkheer Michiels van Verduynen (Netherlands) were or were soon to become senior diplomats. Philip Noel-Baker (United Kingdom) was to be awarded the Nobel Peace Prize for 1959. Of those twenty-five men from eleven countries who were accredited to the Security Council during its first month, Gromyko is still active in international diplomacy and serves as Soviet Foreign Minister.

But it was Norman Makin, a former Australian Minister for Navy and Munitions, who by the accident of the alphabet was to become the Security Council's first presiding officer. The Council established a tradition, which it has respected ever since, by starting late. Modzelewski presented part of the report of the Preparatory Commission (item 2 of the agenda), after which the Council adopted a rule by which the presidency was to rotate on a monthly basis in the English alphabetical order of the names of the Council's members. Makin then changed from being 'temporary chairman' to becoming President, and addressed the Council briefly about the political and organizational tasks which lay ahead and the need to base the work of the Council on the Charter. Other members of the Council then made remarks appropriate to a formal historic occasion,

Bevin taking special pride in the fact that a British Dominion (as the jargon then was) had been called upon to preside. The Council approved the provisional agenda, adopted the remaining rules of procedure on an interim basis, and appointed a committee of experts to consider procedural matters. At 4.15 p.m., Stettinius moved that the Council adjourn, and one minute later the motion was approved. The Council had disposed of six of its first thirteen items.

By the time the Council met again eight days later, substantive problems had started to accumulate. Iran had complained of Soviet interference in its internal affairs. The Soviet Union alleged that the presence of British troops in Greece endangered world peace. The Ukrainian Soviet Socialist Republic drew attention to military operations against the people of Indonesia. Albania had applied for UN Membership. The Council was thus faced at an early date with some of the issues of the Cold War.

1. THE ROLE OF THE SECURITY COUNCIL

The United Nations was created to advance human welfare; in particular, by the avoidance of war through co-operative efforts among sovereign States. But the avoidance of war is a negative goal, and in positive terms the United Nations devotes its efforts, or should devote them, to creating the conditions of peace in which disputes do not arise or, if they do, are resolved without recourse to armed force; in which human rights are protected on a non-discriminatory basis, economic and social advancement for all is promoted, international law is respected, and nations co-operate in those technical matters which affect the universal common good.

It is sometimes said that the United Nations has had more success in dealing with economic and social problems than in the field of peace and security. This is a judgment which it is difficult to substantiate in a scientific way, but it may be doubted whether the Organization will have a useful future in the long term if it is manifestly failing to do what it should to preserve world peace. It is on the Security Council that this primary responsibility rests.

Five facts about the Security Council are especially relevant to this study.

First, although the Council consists of only a limited number of UN Members (originally eleven, now fifteen), it acts on behalf of them all (Article 24(1) of the Charter).

Second, the Council has the authority to take decisions which bind not only its own members but all the Members of the Organization (Articles 25 and 49) and, to some extent, even non-Members (Article 2(6)).

Third, this right of decision is limited by the rule of unanimity, or veto, by which all five permanent members have the right to block non-procedural proposals in the Security Council and amendments to the Charter (Articles 27(3) and 108). I would interject at this point that Article 27(3) is concerned with non-procedural decisions ('. . . all other matters . . .'), but I will in this book often use the more handy terms 'substantive proposals' or 'substantive decisions'.*

Fourth, the Council must be able to function at all times (Article 28(1)). Other UN organs, such as the General Assembly, meet at prescribed times of the year, and the machinery for calling emergency or special sessions is relatively cumbersome. The Security Council can and does meet at only an hour or two's notice.

Fifth, the Charter gives to the Council the right to adopt its own rules of procedure (Article 30) subject, of course, to the Charter itself.

The Charter, like any basic constitutional document, expresses the views and expectations of the founders at a particular point in time. The long process of planning an international organization to keep the peace began in national capitals more than thirty years ago, leading to the Dumbarton Oaks meetings in 1944, the summit consultations in Malta and Yalta in 1945, and culminating in the San Francisco Conference in 1945 and the formal signing of the Charter on 26 June.

The Charter consists of 111 Articles divided into 19 Chapters, occupying about fourteen pages of medium octavo text. Attached to the Charter and integral to it is the Statute of the International Court of Justice (Article 92). Relevant articles from the two documents are reproduced in Appendix 1.

* It may be noted that in the General Assembly the distinction is not between procedure and substance but between 'important' and 'other' questions, the former requiring a two-thirds majority (Article 18(2)).

Throughout this book, references to the Charter are given in parentheses, as in the citing of Article 92 earlier in this paragraph.

It is possible to rank the issues which come before the Security Council according to their gravity, beginning with those which are described as matters, questions, or situations, and proceeding through disputes, to threats to or breaches of the peace, and (most serious of all) acts of aggression. The more threatening the issue, the more likely it is that the Security Council will be involved (see Table 1).

Some of these semantic differences are not of great importance, but parties to a 'dispute' must abstain from voting on substantive proposals in the Security Council (Article 27(3)), and measures under Chapter VII can be taken only if world peace is seriously endangered.* In this book I use the full Charter expression 'the maintenance of international peace and security' only when a shorter expression might be misleading or cause confusion; in other cases, I do not hesitate to use more crisp wording such as 'Members look especially to the Security Council to preserve world peace', whereas the full wording of the Charter is 'Members confer on the Security Council primary responsibility for the maintenance of international peace and security' (Article 24(1)).

2. THE CHARTER

All constitutions are imperfect, but some are more imperfect than others. The UN Charter was based on some assumptions in 1945 which are not valid thirty years later. As Secretary-General Waldheim has put it,

> some of the assumptions on which the United Nations was based have proved unfounded . . . The Organization has, for example, proved to be of limited value as an instrument of collective security . . . The idea of maintaining peace and security in the world through a concert of great Powers . . . would seem to belond to the nineteenth rather than to the twentieth century . . .[2]

Secretary-General Thant said much the same thing.[3]

* By 'measures', I include provisional measures referred to in Article 40 of the Charter, preventive or enforcement measures in Articles 5 and 50, enforcement measures in Article 2(7), enforcement action in Article 53(1), measures or military measures in Articles 39, 41, 45, 49, 51, 53(1), and 94(2), and action in Articles 11(2), 42, and 106.

TABLE I

UN peace-making and peace-keeping: Charter responsibilities

	Articles of the Charter		
	General	*Security Council*	*General Assembly*
any questions or any matters within the scope of the . . . Charter or relating to the powers and functions of any organ provided for in the . . . Charter			10
general principles of co-operation in the maintenance of international peace and security			11(1)
to maintain [or restore] international peace and security, [establishment and]maintenance of international peace and security, [matters relative to the maintenance of] international peace and security	Preamble, 1(1), 2(3) and (6), 73, 76, 84, 106	12(2), 24(1), 26, 33(1), 37(2), 42, 43(1), 47(1), 48(1), 51, 54	18(2), 23(1)
any matter which in [the Secretary-General's] opinion may threaten the maintenance of international peace and security		99	
any question		31	
any question relating to the maintenance of international peace and security			11(2)
situation		12(1), 36(1)	12(1)
any situation which might lead to international friction or give rise to a dispute, situation(s) . . . likely to endanger [the maintenance of] international peace and security		34, 35(1)	11(3), 35(1)
situations which might lead to a breach of the peace	1(1)		
dispute(s)	1(1), 2(3)	12(1), 32, 34, 35(1) and (2), 38	12(1), 35(1) and (2)
dispute the continuance of which is likely to endanger the maintenance of international peace and security, or a situation of like nature	33(1)	33(2), 36, 37	
threat(s) to the peace	1(1)	39	
breach(es) of the peace	1(1)	39	
aggression, act(s) of aggression	1(1)	39, 53(1)	

This imperfect UN Charter contains contradictions, such as its assertion of the equality of States (Preamble and Article 2(1)) while at the same time conferring on five Members the right to veto substantive proposals in the Security Council and amendments to the Charter (Articles 27(3) and 108), as well as giving one State three seats in the General Assembly (the Soviet Union and the Byelorussian and Ukrainian Soviet Socialist Republics); or the ban on intervening in matters which are essentially within the domestic jurisdiction of any State (Article 2(7)) while at the same time requiring Members to take joint action to achieve universal observance of human rights and fundamental freedoms for all (Articles 55–6). There are expressions in the Charter which are ambiguous, or the meaning of which is not absolutely clear, such as 'the expenses of the Organization' in Article 17(2), or the relationship between Articles 25 and 49 regarding the obligation of UN Members to implement resolutions of the Security Council. Some provisions of the Charter are out of date, such as the references to 'any state which during the Second World War has been an enemy of any signatory of the present Charter' (Articles 53 and 107). There have been some *de facto* amendments to the Charter, such as the interpretation of Article 12(1) so as to permit the General Assembly to make recommendations about matters of which the Security Council is seized; or the practice whereby an abstention by a permanent member of the Security Council on a substantive proposal is not regarded as a veto, which is inconsistent with the natural meaning and intention of Article 27(3).

It is, however, the only UN Charter we have, and none of the Members which can veto proposals to amend the Charter (Article 108) has given any encouragement to the idea that major amendments are within the bounds of possibility. The challenge, then, is to use whatever flexibility the Charter allows so as to adapt the Organization to a world which differs greatly from that of 1942–5, when statesmen were taking their minds momentarily off the prosecution of war in order to speculate about the hazards of world politics once victory had been achieved. A Hungarian scholar has described the Security Council as 'a living organism'[4]—an expression which would have appealed to Dag Hammarskjold. The fault (and the

United Nations has more than its share of faults) is not primarily in the Charter: Charles Yost (see p. 132), a man of vast experience and wise judgment, has exonerated the Charter and blamed the Members. 'I do not think the fault really lies primarily in the Charter. I think it lies in the policies of the various governments . . .'[5]

Whether or not one is now disenchanted with the United Nations depends to some extent on how enchanted one was in the first place. Robert E. Riggs has conducted a rigorous examination of whether the United Nations was 'oversold' in the United States, and he found that a close examination of statements by U.S. supporters of the United Nations in the early days 'belies the allegation that the campaign was based on unrealistic promises of a brave new world'.[6] My own examination of public governmental statements, as well as the recently published documents on U.S. Foreign Relations for 1946 and 1947, points in the same direction. In March 1946, Adlai Stevenson wrote:

> The atmosphere of the General Assembly . . . was one of sobriety, of relentless realism, in marked contrast with the boundless optimism that prevailed after the last war, at the time of the League's birth . . . There were no illusions, no slap-happy optimism. There was just sober restraint, not melancholy pessimism. On balance, I think it was generally agreed . . . that the startling candor and vigor of the debates in the Security Council was wholesome . . .[7]

At private meetings of the five permanent members of the Security Council later in 1946, British Foreign Minister Ernest Bevin said bluntly that something must be done to increase confidence in the United Nations 'as, quite frankly, we haven't much confidence now'; Paul-Henri Spaak noted that 'the atmosphere . . . fell far short of our hopes'; and Senator Warren Austin told a meeting of the U.S. delegation that an effort was needed 'to revive the spirit of our people with regard to the United Nations'.[8] A year later, a U.S. State Department official was expressing 'serious concern . . . as to whether the Organization will survive'.

It was those with less information or less experience or less contact with the realities of the embryonic Organization who were most bemused in the early days and who by now have either abandoned their faith in or support for an Organization which has proved such a bitter disappointment to them, or who are wilfully blind to its palpable defects and failures. The fact is that peace is a process to engage in, not a goal to be reached.

I have noted above how the Cold War intruded itself into the work of the Security Council almost from the word 'go', but it is interesting that the one thing on which the major powers were agreed was that the Charter must be upheld. This did not guarantee that they agreed on what the Charter meant or intended. 'When we are translating paper documents into living institutions,' said Philip Noel-Baker of the United Kingdom three weeks after the Council had begun work, 'difficulties in interpretation and procedure must inevitably arise.' [9]

I have remarked elsewhere that most diplomats enjoy arguing about procedure, for a time at least, because it is the one subject on which they are on their own, as it were. Once a UN organ becomes involved in a procedural discussion, representatives are able to free-wheel.

> One can sense the atmosphere of liberation which sweeps over a meeting when debate on the substance of a question is temporarily put aside so that some knotty procedural point can be resolved. One observes representatives closing their folders of papers and lighting cigarettes so as to deal in a thoroughly relaxed and level-headed way with a matter which requires initiative, tact, and imagination rather than fidelity to official instructions.[10]

Resolving procedural questions can be very time-consuming, but 'sometimes procedure is more important than time, especially when you are creating precedents . . .' [11]

Not that the distinction between procedure and substance is always clear and unambiguous.[12] If it were, Article 27(3) of the Charter would doubtless read 'Decisions of the Security Council on substantive matters shall be made . . .', and the problem of the double veto would never have arisen. Canada has recently pointed out that 'procedural problems cannot be pursued very far before they encounter political and substantive difficulties . . .' [13]

3. THE RULES OF PROCEDURE[14]

The Executive Committee of the Preparatory Commission had prepared a first draft of thirty-four of procedure, plus nine supplementary rules on the conduct of debate which had the support of a majority of the Committee but not the requisite two-thirds majority. There had been a division of opinion in the Committee, some members believing that 'the Council would have mainly to operate in the light of its own day-to-day experience and of certain guiding principles', while others favoured 'a complete set of rules of procedure and other detailed guidance . . .' Neither school of thought prevailed, and the rules drafted by the Committee were a 'not entirely satisfactory' compromise.

The Committee reported that the draft rule to the effect that the President would represent the Council 'in its corporate capacity' was intended to allow the President 'to nominate committees and to conclude agreements on behalf of the Council.' The presidency was 'deemed to attach to the member state concerned and not to the person of its representative . . .' In special circumstances, the President should be able to cede his office to 'the representative whose State is next in the alphabetical line of succession', a matter which is now covered by Rule 20. Australia reserved the right to reopen the discussion of the method of selecting the President, and France thought that rotating the presidency in French alphabetical order, or even drawing lots, would be preferable to using English alphabetical order. Yugoslavia considered that applicants for UN Membership should indicate the constitutional organ which would have to consent to ratification.[15]

The Preparatory Commission dropped most of the rules drafted by its Executive Committee on languages (now Rules 42 to 47) and one rule about verbatim records, as well as the proposed rules for the conduct of debate,[16] and then got completely bogged down in the question whether a rule providing for private (closed) meetings of the Security Council was or was not a reversion to the discredited idea of secret diplomacy. As so often happens in matters of this kind, the positions became more extreme, even more absurd, the longer the debate continued.

The matter was first raised by Syria, which considered that all UN Members should have the right to be acquainted with the Council's proceedings. The proposal that the Council could meet in private was 'unconstitutional and contrary to the provisions of the Charter.' Cuba insisted that 'the United Nations should have no secret documents', adding the curious suggestion that the Council might well be permitted to reach private *decisions* so long as the *debates* which preceded those decisions were open. Another member, unidentified in the summary record, said that the whole purpose of the United Nations was to minimize secret diplomacy: States making honest and sincere decisions had no reason to be afraid of publicity. Another unidentified member said, with doubtful relevance, that if enemy States were to be admitted to UN Membership, it was important that they should not have equal status with the others.

The United Kingdom was surprised at the fuss over 'a routine article of rather minor importance'. The Soviet Union said that there was no implication of secret diplomacy in the draft rule, adding that if a member of the Council should choose not to attend a Council meeting which was private, it should clearly have the right to see the record. Norway thought that if the Council could not hold closed meetings, informal meetings would be held, and this would tend to even greater secrecy.

The Preparatory Commission appended a summary of its somewhat heated debates to the draft rules.[17] These rules were then adopted on a provisional basis at the first meeting of the Council, and a Committee of Experts consisting of all members of the Council was asked to review the draft rules.[18]

Within three weeks, the Committee had done as it was asked. Many draft rules were revised, one (no. 23) was divided into two (becoming nos. 32 and 36), and fourteen new rules were added: one (no. 2) stated the right of the President to call a meeting of the Council at the request of any member; four (nos. 9–12) dealt with representation and credentials; two (nos. 37–8) required the President to approve and sign the records of meetings; and the rules about languages which had been proposed by the Executive Committee but dropped by the Preparatory Commission itself (nos. 18–25) were revised along lines decided upon by the First Committee of the General Assembly and reinstated (nos. 22–9).[19]

The rules thus revised were issued on 5 February 1946, but the Council was too preoccupied with substantive business to

Table 2

The Evolution of the Rules of Procedure

Draft of Executive Committee of Preparatory Commission, PC/EX/113/Rev. 1, 12 Nov. 1945: rule no.	*Draft of Preparatory Commission, PC/20, 23 Dec. 1945 (also issued as SCOR, 1st year, 1st series, Supplement no. 1, pp. 3–6, S/28): rule no.*	*First revision by Committee of Experts, SCOR, 1st year, 1st series, Supplement no. 2, pp. 3–8, S/6, 5 Feb. 1946: rule no.*	*Second revision by Committee of Experts, SCOR, 1st year, 1st series, 31st meeting (9 April 1946), pp. 103–18, S/29, and Supplement no. 2, pp. 25–30, S/57 (13 May 1946): rule no.*	*Further revisions by the Committee of Experts, SCOR, 1st year, 1st series, Supplement no. 20, pp. 40, 42–3, S/71, S/88: rule no.*	*Present rule adopted, SCOR, meeting and page no.*	*Present rule no.*
1	1	1	1		31, pp. 103–7	1
		2	2		31, pp. 103–7	2
3, 15	3, 15	3	3		31, pp. 103–7	3
2	2	5	4		31, pp. 103–7	4
			5		21, pp. 103–7	5
			6		31, pp. 108–11	6
4	4	7	7		31, pp. 108–11	7
5	5	4	8		31, pp. 108–11	8
8	8	8	9		31, pp. 108–11	9
			10		31, pp. 108–11	10
			11		31, pp. 108–11	11
6, 7	6, 7	6	12		31, pp. 108–11	12
		9	13		468, pp. 9–11	13
			14		31, pp. 111–15	14
		10	15		31, pp. 111–15	15
		11	16		31, pp. 111–15	16
		12	17		31, pp. 111–15	17
9	9	13	18		31, pp. 115–16	18
10	10	14	19		31, pp. 115–16	19
				20	48, p. 382	20
11	11	15	20		44, pp. 310–11	21
				21		22
				22	44, pp. 310–11	23
12	12	16	21		31, p. 116	24

13	13	17	22	31, p. 116	25
14	14	18	23	31, p. 116	26
A			24	41, pp. 254–60	27
B			25	41, pp. 254–60	28
			26	41, pp. 254–60	29
C			27	41, pp. 254–60	30
D			28	41, pp. 254–60	31
E			29	41, pp. 254–60	32
			30	41, pp. 254–60	33
			31	41, pp. 254–60	34
			32	41, pp. 254–60	35
F, H			33	41, pp. 254–60	36
			34	41, pp. 254–60	37
			35	41, pp. 254–60	38
I	17	20	36	41, pp. 254–60	39
26	19	30	37	41, pp. 260–1	40
17	18	21	38	1761, p. 6	41
18		22	39	1761, p. 6	42
19		23	40	deleted	43
20		24	41	1761, p. 6	44
22		25	42	1761, p. 6	45
24		28	43	1761, p. 6	46
21, 25		29	44	1761, p. 6	47
16, 27	16, 20	19, 31	45	41, p. 261	48
30	23	32	46	1761, p. 6	49
		36	47	41, p. 261	50
31	24	35	48	41, p. 261	51
		37	49	41, p. 261	52
		36, 38	50	41, p. 261	53
29	22	33	51	41, p. 261	54
28	21	34	52	41, p. 261	55
			53	41, p. 261	56
			54	41, p. 261	57
32	25	39	55	222, p. 2771	58
33	26	40	56	42, p. 278	59
34	27	41	57	222, p. 2771	60
				138, pp. 949–52	61
			Annex A	31, pp. 117–18	Appendix

examine the draft with the necessary care. On 18 March, the Secretariat issued a working paper drawing attention to a number of new procedural problems which had arisen,[20] as a result of which the Committee of Experts prepared a fresh draft. Two rules relating to the languages of summary records (nos. 26 and 27) were dropped, twenty-seven rules were retained unchanged or with only minor textual amendments, eleven rules were considerably revised, nineteen further rules were added (twelve of them dealing with the conduct of business and being very much like the rules originally considered by the Executive Committee of the Preparatory Commission), and an annex was added setting out a procedure for dealing with communications from non-governmental organizations. On 9 April, the Council turned its attention to the first twenty-three of the new draft rules as well as the proposed annex.

The debate was surprisingly low-keyed. The Committee of Experts had been unable to agree how often there should be high-level 'periodic' meetings under Article 28(2) of the Charter (rule 4, present Rule 4), and the Council decided that the number should be two a year. The chairman of the Committee of Experts was asked to clarify the difference between the Council's agenda and the matters of which it was seized, and the word 'also' was inserted in the last sentence of rule 12 (present Rule 12). In rule 13 on credentials (present Rule 13) 'Prime Minister' was changed to 'Head of Government'.[21]

The Committee of Experts then encountered serious difficulties over the rule or rules about voting. The rule on voting provisionally approved in February (rule 30, now Rule 40) had read:

> Voting in the Security Council shall be in accordance with the relevant Articles of the Charter and of the Statute of the International Court of Justice.

The Soviet Union wanted a more precise rule for applying Article 27(3) of the Charter, which deals with the veto and the obligation of parties to a dispute to abstain from voting. The Soviet Union proposed that:

1. a distinction should be made between a dispute within the scope of Article 33 'the continuance of which is likely to

endanger the maintenance of international peace and security' and disputes and situations under Article 34 or other Articles of the Charter;

2. the veto should apply when the Council had to decide (a) whether a question was procedural or substantive, (b) whether the question was a dispute or a situation, and (c) in the event that it was a dispute, whether or not it was 'of the nature referred to in Article 33 of the Charter' in which case a party would have to abstain from voting.

This proposal caused consternation in Washington, and the U.S. representative on the Committee of Experts, Joseph E. Johnson, was instructed to stall. On 13 April, the U.S. delegation received from Washington the text of three draft rules on voting 'to promote discussion' but not representing a firm U.S. position. The debate continued in the Committee of Experts until 25 April. On 13 May, the Committee reported that 'certain members' took the view that the rules should contain 'detailed provisions covering both the mechanics of the vote and the majorities by which the various decisions of the Council should be taken'. The Committee recommended to the Council that the provisional rule should be retained for the time being, pending further study. This further study is still pending, because the matter was soon submerged by the General Assembly's concern about the veto. John Ross, Alger Hiss's deputy in the State Department, was later to comment that the United States had perhaps been indulging in 'a large amount of shadow-boxing with the technicalities of rules of procedure without having first formulated our broad policies with regard to the veto . . .'[22]

The Council considered the remaining thirty-seven rules at four further meetings between 16 May and 24 June. The United Kingdom proposed, and the Council agreed, to bring the wording of draft rule 25 (present Rule 28) into line with draft rule 26 (present Rule 29). Following proposals of Netherlands, Poland, the United Kingdom, and China, the last five words of present Rule 32 were added. The United Kingdom wanted to know the difference between substantive motions, principal motions, proposed resolutions, and draft resolutions in draft rules 28 and 29 (present Rules 31 and 32), and was given contradictory explanations. Two new rules were adopted on the rights of the Secretary-General (present Rules 22 and 23) and one on the cession of the presidency (present Rule 20). The United States expressed a wish to have a rule providing for the closure of debate, and Australia repeated the objections to holding private (closed) meetings of the Council. Australia also made an impassioned speech about the procedure for admitting new Members, arguing that 'the General Assembly is the only body which . . . can make the final and binding decisions on the subject of admission'; but an Australian proposal to defer the adoption of rules 55–7 (present Rules 58–60) was defeated by ten votes to one.[23] After five months' work, the Council had adopted sixty Provisional Rules of Procedure and a short Appendix, and these were issued shortly thereafter under the symbol S/96.

Only minor changes in the Rules have been made since 24 June 1946. A new Rule (61) was added in 1947 to clarify the procedure for electing members of the International Court of Justice, and Rules 58 and 60 concerning the admission of new Members were also revised in 1947.[24] Rule 13 regarding credentials was revised in 1950 following disagreements about the seating of China.[25] Russian and Spanish were added to the Council's working languages in 1969, and Chinese in 1974.[26] The Rules thus amended are issued under the symbol S/96/Rev.6.

The Rules are still only Provisional, but it would be tedious to remind the reader of this fact every time one of the Rules is cited. I have therefore omitted 'Provisional' and refer to particular Rules parenthetically.

The Charter refers to 'members of the Security Council'. Some of the Rules of Procedure do the same, especially where the Rule is based on a provision of the Charter and also in connection with the rotation of the presidency in the alphabetical order of members (Rules 2, 5, 12–14, 18, 20, 37, 59): in other Rules, the words 'representative(s) on' are used rather than 'member(s) of' (Rules 8, 11, 15–17, 27, 30–2, 34, 35, 44–6, 49, 50, 52, 59, and Appendix).

There are thus three ways in which one can refer to the people who comprise the Council. One can use the name of the State—Afghanistan, say, or Zambia; one can write each time 'the representative of Afghanistan' or 'the representative of

Zambia'; or one can be even more personal and refer to 'Ambassador Pazhwak' or 'Ambassador Lusaka'.

It has not been possible to be completely consistent in this book, but I usually use the name of the State only. Table 10 on page 110 lists the names of the permanent representatives of the five permanent members of the Security Council between 1946 and 1973, and this Table is followed by brief biographical sketches. Occasionally in the text I cross-refer to Table 10 and the appropriate sketch. Thus, in sections (4) (d) and (6) of Chapter 4, I mention the first Chinese representative, Quo Tai-chi, and add in parentheses (see pp. 109–110) so that those readers who think that, on that particular occasion, the personality of the man may have been as important as the policy of the country which he represented, may refer to the sketch of Ambassador Quo in Chapter 3.

4. CUSTOM

Any committee or similar body soon begins to adopt habits, and in due course habits become customs, and customs become traditions, traditions become rules, and rules become law. Nowhere in the Charter or the Rules of Procedure is it decreed that the Secretary-General shall sit at the right of the President at Council meetings. Nowhere is it specified that the Council shall hold closed (private) meetings when considering its draft report to the General Assembly. Nowhere is it stipulated that the President shall, or indeed shall not, thank the President for the previous month for discharging his responsibilities in so exemplary a manner. There is no Rule which states where a non-member of the Council invited to participate in the discussion of any matter shall be seated. There is not even a Rule requiring members of the Council to refrain from physically assaulting each other: the Charter prohibition of the threat or use of force applies only if the victim is a State (Article 2(4)).

There are, to be sure, general customs governing the conduct of diplomatic business, and there are special customs dealing with conference diplomacy. Much of the practice of the Security Council is based on custom, some of it so deeply rooted and generally respected as to have the force of law. But just as statute law can be changed by constitutional means, so can custom so long as those affected agree to, or at least acquiesce in, the change. Sometimes a change is accepted implicitly rather than explicitly, as when the Council during the course of 1972 gave up what had been the almost invariable practice of consecutive interpretation of speeches into all the working languages.

A living institution is always in course of development. I have tried in this book to examine the prodecure and practice of the Security Council as it was at a particular point in time: 1 March 1974. It would be astonishing if the Council were to have stopped evolving on that date. This, therefore, is a provisional book about an organ of the United Nations which still conducts its work according to Provisional Rules of Procedure. Perhaps *Il n'y a que le provisoire qui dure*.

CHAPTER 2

THE MEETING

> Most men in handling public affairs pay more attention to what they themselves say than what is said to them . . . Menaces always do harm to negotiations, and they frequently push one party to extremities to which they would not have resorted without provocation.

1. CONVENING A MEETING

ALL Members of the United Nations, by virtue of Article 24(1) of the Charter, have conferred on the Security Council primary responsibility for the maintenance of international peace and security and have agreed that, in carrying out this responsibility, the Council 'acts on their behalf'. The Security Council does not act simply on behalf of its fifteen (originally eleven) members; it acts for the whole Membership of the United Nations. Moreover, all UN Members have agreed 'to accept and carry out the decisions of the Security Council in accordance with the . . . Charter' (Article 25). If world peace is threatened or breached, or if an act of aggression occurs, UN Members *shall* (not 'may') join in affording mutual assistance in carrying out the measures decided upon by the Council (Article 49). That, at any rate, is what the Charter says. I discuss this matter further in section (7) of Chapter 4.

In order to discharge its primary responsibility for world peace and security, the Council must be ready to meet at short notice—or, to use the words of the Charter, 'shall be so organized as to be able to function continuously'. All members of the Council must be represented at all times at the seat of the Organization (Article 28(1)), that is to say, New York,* and it

* From time to time, suggestions have been made to transfer the Headquarters from New York because of the difficulty of ensuring the security of diplomatic missions and their personnel, but these suggestions have not been pressed.[1]

is this requirement which first led to the establishment of permanent diplomatic missions at the Headquarters of the United Nations.[2]

The responsibility for convening a meeting of the Council is laid upon the President for the time being (Rules 1–3), the presidency rotating monthly in English alphabetical order of the Council's members (Rule 18). The formal procedure for calling meetings is laid down in the Rules of Procedure, but in practice the President's decisions are normally taken after informal consultations. The Rules provide that ordinary meetings of the Council shall be held at any time deemed necessary by the President, 'but the interval between meetings shall not exceed fourteen days' (Rule 1). The *Repertoire* of Security Council practice states that when no particular item on the Council's agenda requires immediate consideration, it has become customary for the President to consult representatives regarding the waiver of the fourteen-day requirement.[3] Only one case has occurred which, by implication, challenged the practice of regularly waiving the fourteen-day requirement. The matter at issue concerned the appointment of a Governor for Trieste (a matter which in 1949 had been before the Council for more than two years and is still one of the items of which the Council is formally seized). The Soviet representative pointed out that it was 'more than a month now' since the Council had met. The Soviet representative did not expressly cite the fourteen-day Rule, but rather the Charter requirement that the Council should be in a position to function continuously. The Egyptian President for the previous month stated that he had been in constant touch with the Council's members and that no one had asked for a meeting. As for continuous functioning, the Egyptian representative added sardonically, 'I imagine that no one assumes that we sit here day and night.'[4] The Soviet representative did not press his point.

Rule 1 states that the President calls a meeting of the Council 'at any time he deems necessary . . .' Rules 2 and 3 state that he 'shall' call a meeting:

1. At the request of any member of the Council (Rule 2);
2. If the General Assembly makes recommendations to the Council or refers to it any question relating to the maintenance

of international peace and security under Article 11(2) of the Charter (Rule 3);

3. If the Secretary-General brings to the attention of the Council any matter which in his opinion may threaten the maintenance of international peace and security under Article 99 of the Charter (Rule 3);
4. If a dispute or situation is brought to the attention of the Council under Article 35 of the Charter (disputes, or situations which might lead to international friction or give rise to disputes) or Article 11(3) of the Charter (situations which are likely to endanger international peace and security) (Rule 3).

If the matter were not serious, one might be inclined to think that Rules 1–3 had been deliberately drafted so as to give rise to misunderstanding and confusion. Does Rule 1 empower the President to call a meeting of the Council simply when the fancy takes him, or only when he deems that one of the requirements of Rules 2 and 3 have been met? If there were only Rule 1 to go by, it might be argued that complete discretion to call meetings had been conferred on the President. Were Rules 2 and 3 added, then, to limit or to extend the President's discretion? If the second interpretation is accepted, does that mean that if any of the requirements are met, the President *must* call a meeting, even if he deems such an action to be unnecessary? Are there any contingencies not covered by Rules 2 and 3 which would fall within the scope of Rule 1? Is the crux of Rule 1 the words 'at any *time*' (my italics), so that the discretion granted to the President relates only to the precise timing of the meeting?

All this may seem typical UN niggling; and so it is. But lack of clarity about Rules 1–3 provides a convenient device for filibustering if a Council member has not yet received instructions from his capital, or is feeling annoyed because the President has fixed the meeting on an afternoon when he had planned to play golf, or if he wishes to delay Security Council debate and decision until anticipated events have become *faits accomplis*.

In an emergency, the President sometimes convenes a meeting even if he has not been able to consult all the members, and if the emergency is real, this normally gives rise to no difficulty.[5] But if a member, or indeed the President, wishes for substantive political reasons to have a meeting of the Council either sooner or later than other members desire, the Council can be prevented from getting down to business by a discussion about the President's discretion and, in particular, the relationship between Rule 1 and Rules 2–3.

In September 1959, Italy was the President for the month, and he received from Secretary-General Hammarskjold a request to 'convene urgently' a meeting of the Council to consider Hammarskjold's report on a request for the dispatch to Laos of 'an emergency force . . . to halt an aggression'. Hammarskjold had deliberately not cited in his request Article 99 of the Charter, which empowers the Secretary-General to bring to the attention of the Council any matter which in his opinion may threaten the maintenance of international peace and security. The President convened a meeting, claiming to be acting under the discretionary Rule 1.

The Soviet representative had apparently been kept in the dark as to the full purpose of the meeting, and probably did not know that his attempt to exercise a double veto was about to be thwarted by a presidential ruling. Be that as it may, he took the first opportunity to challenge what he called 'a number of irregularities' in the convening of the meeting.

> It is quite obvious that it is not rule 1 of the Council's rules of procedure that is applicable in the present case, but rules 2 and 3 . . .

The President replied that his decision was based on the rule which 'gives to the President of the Security Council complete discretion in calling meetings at any time he deems necessary'.[6] The Soviet representative did not persist in his objection, and the matter was allowed to lapse.

A similar situation arose in 1965, when the President (the United States) called a meeting to consider the fighting which had broken out between India and Pakistan in Kashmir. The President distinguished between the practice of the Council and the Rules of Procedure There had, he said, been 'extensive consultations', and he had been in touch personally with 'most' members of the Council. In view of the urgency of the situation, and simply citing Rules 1–3, he had felt justified in calling a meeting. The Soviet representative, as in 1959, challenged the attempt to separate Rule 1 from Rules 2 and 3. Before a meeting could be called, he said, there had to be a specific request as provided in Rules 2 and 3; 'meetings of the Council cannot be called as it were "anonymously"'. There followed an inconclusive discussion, but there was a general wish to proceed with the business of the Council, and the Soviet representative did not persist with his objection.[7]

The practice of the Council, as the President hinted in September 1965, is clearer than the wording of the Rules of Procedure. If the Council has not itself decided on the date and time of its next meeting, an agreed decision is usually reached, on the initiative of the President for the month, by informal consultation among the members of the Council. If agreement by this means is not possible, the President acts in accordance with the wishes of the majority and, in any public reference to his decision, uses some such wording as that he has met the wishes of 'some members' or 'most members' of the Council.[8] Often in such cases the minority is not unconditionally opposed to the calling of a meeting, but is in favour of its being held later or earlier than the time favoured by the majority.

Two other types of difficulty can theoretically arise. The first would be if a non-member of the Council were to desire a meeting to consider a matter not qualifying as a dispute or situation under Articles 11(3) or 35 of the Charter, and if no member of the Council, nor the Secretary-General, were to request a meeting to consider the matter, and if the President for the month did not deem it necessary to convene a meeting under his discretionary powers (Rule 1) It is, however, difficult to imagine such a situation arising: some means would surely be found to call a meeting, even if in the end the Council should not place the matter on its agenda—as, indeed, happened in the case of Ireland's request in August 1969 for an urgent meeting of the Council in connection with 'the situation in the six counties of Northern Ireland'.[9]

The other kind of difficulty would arise if one or more members of the Council were to consider that there has been an unreasonable delay in convening a meeting. The Australian representative made such a charge in 1948 in connection with the Indonesian question, but the response of the President (Belgium) suggested that the charge could not be substantiated.[10]

A more serious case arose in 1966 when a new member of the Council, Ambassador Keita of Mali, was President for the month of April. At 10 a.m. on 7 April 1966, the United Kingdom requested an urgent meeting to consider the question of Rhodesia and, in particular, the possibility that the tanker *Joanna V* might try to discharge oil at Beira in Mozambique for transmission to Rhodesia, contrary to the Council's sanctions policy. A majority of the Council's members were prepared to meet that day and, indeed, assembled in the Council chamber. The representative of Mali, who alone could call a meeting of the Council, could not be found, although there was reason to think that he was closeted with some of his colleagues from the African Group. Members of the Council were notified that the Council would meet at 5 p.m., but later, without consultation, were told that the meeting had been cancelled. A confused situation then ensued, and some members of the Council were under the impression that the meeting had been reinstated. At 7.20 p.m., eight members of the Council requested Secretary-General Thant to inform the Ambassador of Mali 'formally and urgently' that they were holding themselves ready to meet, and two other members of the Council had separately informed U Thant that they agreed that a meeting of the Council should be held that day. More than forty-eight hours were in fact to elapse between the request for an emergency meeting and the actual opening of the meeting (which, as it happened, was on Easter Saturday).

The representative of New Zealand described the situation as follows:

Under Rule 2, the President is obliged to call a meeting at the request of any Council member. The obligation is mandatory, not permissive. The one element of discretion given to the President is the precise timing . . .

In this instance . . . a request was made for the Council to meet urgently on Thursday afternoon . . . Almost all members of the Council were willing to meet at the time requested. They were unable to do so despite repeated efforts and the assistance, at the request of a majority of Council members, of the Secretary-General. Yet a meeting was fixed much later for another time upon which most members . . . were not consulted at all.

The explanation given by the Ambassador of Mali and his supporters was not very convincing. The representative of Uganda, for example, referring to the Charter requirement that the Security Council should be so organized as to function continuously, had this to say:

> The word 'continuously' . . . does not really mean 'continuously' in the usual sense. The Security Council does not sit or function without stop: it does stop from time to time . . .

The Soviet representative simply said that the representative of Mali had acted 'absolutely correctly and effectively, in full conformity with the rules of procedure and in observance of all necessary standards'. The representative of Mali, in a telephone message to an official in the UN Secretariat, the substance of which was circulated as an official document of the Security Council, said he was following 'the customary procedure by engaging in consultations', that he hoped to conclude these the following day (Good Friday), and that he would then 'announce a time and date for the Security Council meeting'.[11]

This unhappy (and, fortunately, unprecedented) incident led to a sharp exchange of written communications between the United States and Mali.[12]

The U.S. representative emphasized that Rule 2 is mandatory, and that even if a majority of the Council members are opposed to a meeting, it must nevertheless be held. The President's discretion under Rule 1 is simply 'to set the time of a meeting', but, in so doing, he acts as a servant of the Council. The President customarily consults the members, but in urgent circumstances, he may convene the Council without consultation when failure to consult might entail an inadvisable delay. The President may 'receive' the views of non-members of the Council, but the views of the Council's members must guide him. The United States did not believe that the proper practice had been followed, nor did it regard the incident as a precedent. The United States requested that its letter to the President of the Council be incorporated in the next edition of the official *Repertoire* of Security Council practice.[13]

The representative of Mali, as President, was the only Council member to submit a written reply to the United States, and it is therefore a fair assumption that the other members of the Council accepted that the U.S. letter accurately described what had been the practice of the Council. The representative of Mali said that he had acted entirely in accordance with the Rules of Procedure. Consultations with members of the Council had been held, he noted. Having sought to justify the course he had followed, the representative of Mali added, somewhat confusingly: 'Consequently, the President cannot think that the procedure followed at the latest meeting of the Security Council can be regarded as setting a precedent.'

Western members of the Council were inclined to attribute Ambassador Keita's behaviour to inexperience and concluded that no useful purpose would be served by revising the Rules of Procedure. What happened in April 1966 was an unfortunate departure from established practice, but one which was unlikely to recur. It was clear that the work of the Council would be brought to a halt if the President for the month were capriciously to flout the wishes of his colleagues.

The Council has, on average, held just over sixty meetings a year. At one period, it seemed to be in danger of running out of business, and one scholar has noted that, without Palestine and Kashmir, 'the Council would have been practically moribund throughout most of the 1950s'.[14]

Meetings rarely begin on time. Ambassador Farah of Somalia commented in 1961:

> I doubt whether the Security Council has ever met on time since it was established, and if we set the meeting for 10.30 a.m. we can be pretty sure that we shall not begin until 11.30 a.m. So for that reason I would suggest that we maintain our traditions of the past 25 years, schedule the meeting for 10.30, and begin at 11.30.[15]

It is interesting to recall here that in 1947 the United Kingdom proposed that the Rules of Procedure should be amended so as to provide that morning meetings of the Council should not continue beyond 1.00 p.m. and afternoon meetings beyond 6.30 p.m., except by express decision of the Council; and, further, that the Council should 'endeavour, so far as may be possible, so to arrange its business as to provide that for two periods of the year, of three weeks each, it shall not occupy itself with important business . . . It would be an advantage if one of those periods could be in the month of August.'[16]

TABLE 3

Number of meetings of the Security Council, 17 January 1946 to 31 December 1973

Year	*No. of meetings*
1946	88
7	137
8	171
9	62
1950	72
1	39
2	42
3	43
4	32
5	23
6	50
7	49
8	36
9	5
1960	71
1	68
2	38
3	59
4	104
5	81
6	70
7	46
8	76
9	64*
1970	38
1	59
2	61
3	76
	1,760

* This excludes the special meeting held on 16 June 1969 to hear an address by the President of Colombia.

Unfortunately, international politics do not arrange themselves in such a way as to suit the convenience of grouse-shooting diplomats, and no formal action was taken on the proposal.

2. NOTICE OF MEETINGS

Once a decision to convene a meeting has been taken, and the date and time fixed by the President, a notice of the meeting is sent to 'representatives on the Security Council . . .' The responsibility for this falls on the Secretary-General (Rule 25).

The Secretary-General is also required to communicate to representatives the Provisional Agenda. This shall be done at least three days before the meeting, although, in urgent circumstances, the Provisional Agenda may be communicated simultaneously with the notice of the meeting (Rule 8).

By the very nature of the Council's primary responsibility for world peace and security, 'circumstances' are frequently 'urgent', and the Council has usually been willing to dispense with the 'three days' notice' requirement. In the first twenty-four years of its existence, the Security Council met 1,526 times. On only six occasions did the Council fail to accept the item proposed in the Provisional Agenda or decide to adjourn without adopting the agenda. Four of these six instances took place during the early years, when the Council was almost continuously facing procedural or substantive difficulties. In the first of the six cases, the Council's decision to restrict the agenda did not prevent members from discussing the excluded item; and the sixth case was almost certainly pre-arranged.

The six cases were as follows:

1. The Council met on 9 January 1947 to consider the question of disarmament, and the Provisional Agenda included two resolutions of the General Assembly and proposals for the implementation of one of the resolutions, together with a letter from the Chairman of the Atomic Energy Commission transmitting the Commission's first report. This letter was not included in the Agenda because it had not been circulated in sufficient time, but this did not prevent members of the Council (who were members of the Atomic Energy Commission anyway) from referring to the contents of the Commission's report. The letter transmitting the Commission's report was included in the agenda of a later meeting (see pages 268–71 of Chapter 6).[17]

2. The Council met on 30 August 1948 under the presidency of the Soviet Union, the Provisional Agenda including both the India-Pakistan question and the Palestine question. The United States objected to the Provisional Agenda on the ground that it had been agreed that no further meetings would be held in New York (the General Assembly was due to convene in Paris on 21 September) unless an emergency arose, and he did not regard either of the items in question as constituting an

emergency. Two other members considered it inexpedient to discuss the Palestine question at that time. The Council rejected the Provisional Agenda (2 votes in favour, 9 abstentions).[18]

3. The Council had agreed informally that there would be no meetings during the second half of December 1948 unless urgent problems arose. The Council met, nevertheless, on 17 December to consider Israel's application for UN Membership. Syria proposed that an additional item be added to the agenda concerning attacks by Israel on Egyptian forces in the Faluja area. The Soviet representative said he did not object in principle to the Syrian proposal, but that advance notice was required, and it would be premature to include the matter in the agenda of that meeting. The Syrian proposal was put to the vote but was not adopted (2 in favour, 9 abstentions). At the end of the meeting, the Soviet representative asked the President of the Council for 'three days' notice in the event of an extraordinary meeting being called during the next few days'.[19]

4. The Council met on 18 November 1949 to consider the Indonesian question. The Ukrainian representative pointed out that he had received the documents for the meeting only that day, and he required time to study them. Other members expressed similar views, and the Council adjourned without adopting an agenda.[20]

5. The Council had been called to meet on the evening of 3 December 1960 under the presidency of the Soviet Union to consider Mauritania's application for UN Membership, dated 28 November 1960. Just before the meeting, a revised Provisional Agenda was circulated containing, as an additional sub-item, a letter from the Soviet Union proposing that the Council consider also Mongolia's application for UN Membership, which had been first submitted in 1946. When the Council met, the Soviet representative, speaking in that capacity and not as President, proposed that the Mongolian application should be considered first. Several representatives opposed this proposal, and Italy pointed out that the Provisional Agenda had to be circulated at least three days before the meeting, except in urgent circumstances. The Soviet proposal was rejected (4 votes in favour, 5 against, 2 abstentions).[21]

6. On 20 August 1969, Ireland requested an urgent meeting to

consider 'the situation in the six counties of Northern Ireland'. The United Kingdom maintained that the matter was one of domestic jurisdiction. Ireland then addressed the Council. Britain replied, whereupon Zambia proposed that the Council adjourn, and the Council approved the proposal unanimously.[22]

I recall only one occasion when a member has complained about the lack of three days' notice and been outvoted. This was on 14 October 1948, when Syria objected to the adoption of the agenda (the Palestine question) on the ground that he had received the notice of the meeting only the previous evening, and that no emergency had arisen to justify abandoning the requirement of three days' notice. The agenda was, nevertheless, approved (8 votes in favour, 3 abstentions).[23]

The 'three days' notice' requirement arose by implication on one other occasion. The Council had met to consider two complaints by Israel against Egypt (4 February 1954). Lebanon suggested that an Egyptian complaint that Israel was violating the General Armistice Agreement should be added as a sub-item. The Soviet Union stressed that the Council had the right to deal with urgent matters without the usual notice. The sub-item proposed by Lebanon was approved on the understanding that the two complaints would not be discussed simultaneously. But the discussion about the agenda had lasted more than two hours, and no sooner had the agenda been adopted than the Council decided to adjourn.[24]

3. PLACE OF MEETING

The Charter and Rules of Procedure provide that:

1. Meetings of the Council shall normally be held at the seat of the United Nations (Rule 5);
2. The Council may decide to meet elsewhere if to do so will 'facilitate its work' (Article 28(3) and Rule 5);
3. A proposal to meet other than at United Nations Headquarters may be made by any member of the Council or by the Secretary-General (Rule 5).

Five groups of meetings have been held away from New York. Meetings were held in London in 1946 and in Paris in 1948 and 1951–2, where the General Assembly was in session, the decision to meet in Paris being taken informally. Meetings 1627–39 (1972) were held in Addis Ababa, to give special attention to African questions. Meetings 1695–1704 (1973) were held in Panama City, ostensibly to consider peace and security in Latin America but in reality to enable Panama to ask for a new Canal treaty with the United States.

There had previously been a number of proposals that the Council should meet in cities away from Headquarters. On 8 September 1960, the Government of the Congo (Leopoldville), now Zaire, invited the Security Council to meet in the Congo so that the members could 'see for themselves . . . the United Nations authorities' interference in the Congo's domestic problems . . .' This proposal was supported by the Soviet Union and Poland and—with reservations—by Ceylon, but was rejected by the Council. In February 1961, Liberia also suggested that the Council should meet in the Congo, but the idea was not pressed.[25]

In 1965, the Soviet Union proposed that the Council should meet in Santo Domingo to consider the situation in the Dominican Republic, but the United States thought the proposal frivolous and mischievous, and Jordan wanted more time to consider the idea. The proposal was not put to a vote.[26]

The initiative for the meetings held in Africa in 1972 came from thirty-six African States and was considered by the General Assembly in 1971. By a vote of 113 to 2, the Assembly invited the Security Council 'to consider the request of the Organization of African Unity concerning the holding of meetings of the Council in an African capital'. There were reservations about this proposal on the part of some Western delegations, partly on grounds of expense; partly because the Council might find it difficult to 'function continuously' if a crisis erupted while the Council and its staff were *en route* to Africa or while returning to New York; and partly because to meet in Africa might increase anti-Western sentiment.

In the event, neither the hopes of the African States nor the fears of the Western countries were fully realized. The Council considered the proposal received from the General Assembly and decided to meet in Addis Ababa from 28 January to 4 February, at an estimated cost of $144,000. The meetings would be devoted to 'Consideration of questions relating to

Africa with which the Security Council is currently seized and the implementation of the Council's relevant resolutions.'[27]

Pakistan almost succeeded in throwing a spanner into the works by asking, on 24 January, for 'an urgent meeting' of the Council to discuss alleged violations of the cease-fire by India, but nobody seemed to take this ploy very seriously, and no meeting was held.[28]

The Security Council held thirteen meetings in the space of a week. The Council was addressed by Emperor Haile Selassie of Ethiopia, President Ould Daddah of Mauritania (Chairman of the O.A.U. Assembly), and UN Secretary-General Waldheim. The Council also heard representatives of nine liberation movements, two spokesmen for the O.A.U., a representative of the International Defence and Aid Fund, and the General Secretary of the All Africa Conference of Churches, all under Rule 39, which permits the Council to invite competent persons to supply it with information or to give other assistance.[29] Perhaps the most impressive statement was that made by the late Amilcar Cabral, President of the African Party for the Independence of Guinea Bissau and the Cape Verde Islands (PAIGC).

The Council adopted resolutions concerning Namibia (South West Africa), apartheid in South Africa, and Portugal's African territories, and a statement of consensus expressing gratitude to the host country.[30] The United Kingdom vetoed a draft resolution on Rhodesia which had been sponsored by Guinea, Somalia, and Yugoslavia.[31]

Opinions about the usefulness of the Addis Ababa meetings varied. Austria, Mongolia, Tunisia, and Yugoslavia (among others) considered that the experiment had been a success, and Secretary-General Waldheim commented that the meetings had been 'a useful and positive experience'.[32] During the course of the meetings, Panama said that the time had come for the Council to meet in Latin America, 'and for this purpose we would offer as a site the capital of Panama'. This enabled the representative of Panama to expatiate on Latin America's important role in securing the decolonization of the African continent, and to complain that Panama was divided into two parts by the Panama Canal, 'a veritable foreign enclave . . .'[33]

It was to be Panama's turn to preside over the Council in

March 1973, and in January Panama issued a formal invitation to the Council to meet in Panama City from 15 to 21 March in order to consider 'measures for the strengthening of international peace and security and the promotion of international co-operation in Latin America, in accordance with the provisions and principles of the Charter and the resolutions relating to the right of self-determination of peoples and strict respect for the sovereignty and independence of States'. The proposal of Panama was formally supported by the Latin American, Arab, and African Groups.[34] On 16 January, the Council agreed in principle to meet in Panama City at the time suggested and asked a Committee composed of all Council members to report on the necessary arrangements (see pages 277–8 in Chapter 6). The Committee reported in favour of the Panamanian proposal, but with a shorter agenda, and the Committee's report was endorsed by the Council.[35]

Ten meetings were duly held. Twenty-three non-members of the Council and the presiding officers of two UN organs took part, and invitations to participate were also issued to the Secretary-General of the Agency for the Prohibition of Nuclear Weapons in Latin America, the Executive Secretary of the Organization of African Unity in New York, and the Observer of the League of Arab States at the United Nations. At the end of a rather diffuse debate, the United States vetoed a resolution which would have invited the United States and Panama to conclude a new treaty guaranteeing 'full respect for Panama's effective sovereignty over all of its territory', but the Council approved a resolution urging States not to use or encourage coercion against Latin American countries, and a statement of consensus expressing gratitude to the host country.[36]

I refer on pages 145–52 in Chapter 3 to the Council's use of Rule 39, by which it may invite persons to supply it with information or to give other assistance. It is only necessary to note here that States are not the only entities which engage in international politics. When the Council met in Addis Ababa, for example, those who took part in its proceedings included the UN Secretary-General, representatives of an all-purpose regional inter-governmental organization (the O.A.U.), a limited-purpose regional non-governmental organization (the All Africa Conference of Churches), a number of political parties or liberation movements, and a quasi-charitable agency (the International Defence and Aid Fund). Entities other than States also participated in the meetings in Panama City.

When the Council convenes at UN Headquarters, it meets in a chamber set aside for its use at the south end of the Conference Building, lying between 43rd and 44th Streets in Manhattan, and overlooking the East River. The Security Council chamber was designed by Arnstein Arneberg of Norway, and the Norwegian Government supplied the marble, inlaid doors, blue and gold tapestry for the walls, curtains, railings, and the main chairs. The outstanding feature of the chamber is a large mural by Per Krohg which, with Nordic allegory, depicts man's struggle to rise from the sinister present to a warless world of freedom and brotherhood.[37]

The President of the Council for the month sits below the mural at the centre of the horseshoe-shaped table, with the Secretary-General or his representative on the right and the secretary of the Council on the left. The other delegates sit in English alphabetical order around the horseshoe, with their deputies and assistants behind them. Verbatim reporters are at tables in the centre of the horseshoe, and booths for interpreters are ranged on either side of the chamber. There are a few seats for non-members of the Council on the main floor of the chamber, but on important occasions all the seats are soon taken, and many diplomats and officials have to stand. There are raised tiers of seats for the news media, representatives of non-governmental organizations, and members of the public. A few security guards are on hand to deal with possible disturbances and to deter violent assaults on UN diplomats or officials.

4. 'PERIODIC' MEETINGS[38]

Whenever there is a period of special crisis in international politics, ordinary people, and sometimes diplomats and politicians and scholars also, seek for a scapegoat. For most people, a favourite scapegoat is 'the enemy', who (or which) is responsible for the disasters and is almost certainly benefiting from them—the 'conspiracy' explanation of politics. A minority, especially in democratic countries, invert the more popular explanation and consider that their own country is to be blamed for the world's ills—a kind of guilt complex which can, none the less, sometimes be put to constructive uses. But there are always a few who blame some aspect of 'the system': the weakness or strength of alliances, the absence or presence of China at the United Nations, the excess or paucity of multilateral aid, the personality (or impersonality) of the Secretary-General, the need to amend the UN Charter, the improper use of the veto in the Security Council, the failure to add to the number of the Council's permanent members, and so on.

The difficulty about assessing explanations of the latter kind is that it is often not clear whether those who propagate them believe that they are causes or only symptoms of a malady. There is no better illustration of the confusion between cause and effect than some widely held views about the Security Council veto. How often has it been said that the Security Council has been paralysed by the veto or, as Harold Macmillan once put it, 'the Russian veto'. I have examined elsewhere the use of the veto during the period 1946–67 and have suggested that it has proved less of a barrier to effective action than is often claimed;[39] and the fifteen or more vetoes which have been cast since 1967 have not caused me to modify the views I expressed earlier. The veto is a consequence rather than a cause of disagreement.[40]

Another example of the confusion between cause and effect concerns the holding of what the Charter calls 'periodic' meetings of the Security Council. It was hoped when the Charter was drafted that the United Nations would provide a suitable framework for what has come to be called summit diplomacy, and the Charter provides for periodic meetings 'at which each of its members may, if it so desires, be represented by a member of the Government or by some other specially designated representative' (Article 28(2)). The Rules of Procedure provide that such periodic meetings 'shall be held twice a year, at such times as the Security Council may decide' (Rule 4), a Rule which the Council has cheerfully disregarded. The Provisional Agenda for a periodic meeting is to be circulated to Council members at least twenty-one days before the opening of the meeting (Rule 12).

The first three Secretaries-General were in favour of holding periodic high-level Council meetings, and the General Assembly endorsed the idea on a number of occasions.[41] Without express recourse to Article 28(2), members of the Council have from time to time been represented at foreign minister or higher level. In 1965, Pakistan was represented in the Council by her Prime Minister: the provisional record of the meeting quotes the President as calling on 'the Prime Minister of Pakistan', but the official printed record changes this to 'the representative of Pakistan'.[42] Shortly after this, following the illegal declaration of independence by Rhodesia, Michael Stewart, the British Foreign Secretary, attended a number of meetings of the Council, even though Britain's permanent representative at UN Headquarters, Lord Caradon, was a Minister of State in the British Government.[43] In 1969, the President of Colombia addressed a special meeting of the Council without an agenda and convened for the sole purpose of hearing him.[44] In 1958, the United States, Britain, France, and Canada had proposed that the Security Council should be convened under the terms of Article 28(2) to consider the situation in Lebanon and Jordan, but before arrangements for calling a meeting had been completed, the Soviet Government requested that an emergency session of the General Assembly be held.[45] In the circumstances, the proposal for a 'periodic' meeting was dropped.

In 1969, in connection with a proposal to the General Assembly on strengthening international security, the Soviet Union included the convening of 'periodic' meetings of the Council among its specific proposals, and the Assembly, in a preambular paragraph of its subsequent resolution, recalled the terms of Article 28(2).[46] The following year, Finland's permanent representative to the United Nations actively promoted the idea of a 'periodic' meeting of the Council under Article 28(2),[47] with the support or at least acquiescence of a number of countries, including Belgium, Burma, Nationalist China, France, Ireland, Luxembourg, Pakistan, Poland, the Soviet Union, Spain, Syria, the United Kingdom, and the United States.[48] On 12 June 1970, the Security Council approved the following cautious consensus:

> The members of the Security Council have considered the question of initiating periodic meetings in accordance with Article 28(2) of the Charter. They consider that the holding of periodic meetings, at which each member of the Council would be represented by a member of the Government or by some other specially

designated representative, could enhance the authority of the Security Council and make it a more effective instrument for the maintenance of international peace and security. As to the date and other practical aspects of the first such meeting, these will be considered later in consultations.

It is understood that periodic meetings, the purpose of which would be to enable the Security Council to discharge more effectively its responsibilities under the Charter, would provide members with an opportunity for a general exchange of views on the international situation, rather than for dealing with any particular question, and that such meetings would normally be held in private, unless it were otherwise decided.

The provisional agenda of periodic meetings shall be drawn up by the Secretary-General in consultation with the members of the Council and in accordance with the relevant provisions of the provisional rules of procedure.[49]

After further consultation, it was decided to hold the first periodic meeting on 21 October 1970, as part of the twenty-fifth anniversary celebrations of the United Nations, and to direct the discussion to a general review of the international situation.

The Security Council duly convened and, as suggested in the consensus quoted above, decided that its meeting should be private (closed). As a result of this decision, no record of the meeting has been made public. But a *communiqué* was published in accordance with Rule 55, and accounts of the meeting were soon circulating in the corridors. If these are to be relied on, it was not a very inspiring or useful occasion. Speeches were delivered by the eminent statesmen meeting under the presidency of Sr. Lopez-Bravo, the Spanish Foreign Minister, after which a soporific *communiqué* was made public.[50] Four points about the meeting may be noted.

First, if corridor gossip is to be believed, the meeting was not so much 'a general exchange of views' (para. 2 of the *communiqué*) as a series of speeches along much the same lines as those delivered during the General Assembly's annual general debate. Second, the three African members of the Council 'reserved their position' (para. 8 of the *communiqué*) on the platitudes contained in the *communiqué* regarding Southern Africa. Third, the Deputy Foreign Minister of Syria stated that his Government's position was 'reflected in his delegation's statement at the meeting' (para. 8 of the *communiqué*), which hardly enlightened those diplomats who took the trouble to read the *communiqué* precisely because they had not been present at the meeting. Fourth, the members of the Council declared that they would determine the date of the next periodic meeting 'through consultations' (para. 7 of the *communiqué*).

To give the fifteen Council members a measure of encouragement, the other Members of the United Nations proceeded a couple of months later to welcome the decision of the Security Council to hold further periodic meetings in accordance with Article 28(2) of the Charter, and expressed the hope that these meetings would make an important contribution to the strengthening of international security.[51] Secretary-General Thant also considered that the practice instituted in 1970 'should be continued', but he added

> Such meetings should be more than mere formal occasions and should provide the members of the Council with an opportunity to carry out effectively their responsibilities for the maintenance of international peace and security. In my opinion, these periodic meetings should enable this body to take stock of the international situation and review the achievements made in the implementation of previous decisions. The Council could also take advantage of such meetings, held privately, if need be, to assess potential threats to the peace in areas of instability, make recommendations to the Governments concerned and thus fulfil its role in the prevention of international crises. In cases when, by means of a general consensus or as a result of the position of certain Governments, an important question is withheld from public discussion at the United Nations, I believe that the situation could usefully benefit from consideration by the Council in the course of its periodic meetings.[52]

Secretary-General Waldheim stated that the 1970 meeting 'was generally considered to be another step to enhance the authority of the Security Council'. Austria, Finland, Greece, and Sweden were in favour of holding further periodic meetings; Belgium, France, and Iran were also in favour, provided there were adequate preparation; Netherlands suggested setting target dates for such meetings at the beginning of each year, and Tunisia wanted the General Assembly to set a time-table of six periodic meetings every year.[53]

The lesson of the 1970 experience is not that the United Nations fails to provide a suitable framework for summit diplomacy. It is, first, that the need for summit diplomacy cannot easily be predicted; second, that the participation should be determined by the issues at stake rather than comprise five States designated in a Charter completed in 1945 and ten States elected by the General Assembly to fit a geographical pattern; and third, that summit diplomacy cannot succeed without adequate preparation.

5. PRIVATE (CLOSED) MEETINGS

I have referred in the first chapter (pages 10–11 and 16) to the sense of outrage felt by some medium and smaller countries when they discovered that the Security Council might sometimes meet in private. Diplomats were still under the spell of Woodrow Wilson's 'open covenants of peace, openly arrived at', whereas in fact many of the most crucial and lasting covenants of peace have to be arrived at privately. As Paul-Henri Spaak put it:

> Those who are involved [in open diplomacy] are forced to pay more attention to the repercussions of their actions in the outside world than to the goal they are seeking to achieve. They are bent on asserting themselves rather than trying to convince others of the rightness of their cause. They give far more thought to public opinion at home than to the problems which call for a solution.[54]

There are, to be sure, diplomatic activities which ought to be conducted in the full light of day. 'Nobody, however distinguished,' according to Lord Robert Cecil, 'works any worse for knowing that his proceedings will come up later for public discussion before the world.'[55] Certain functions of criticism and debate are suitably undertaken in public: but negotiation is usually best conducted in private.[56]

The Security Council normally meets in public (Rule 48), but there is one matter which, according to the Rules of Procedure, must be conducted in private (discussion and decision of any recommendation to the General Assembly regarding the appointment of the Secretary-General, Rule 48); and, as a matter of custom, the Council meets in private to discuss the draft Annual Report prepared by the Secretariat. The Council may decide that, for a private meeting, the record shall be made in a single copy only, to be kept by the Secretary-General (Rule 51). Any UN Member which has taken part in a private meeting has the right to consult the single copy of the record in the Secretary-General's office. Authorized representatives of UN Members which have not taken part in the meeting may, if the Council agrees, be granted similar access at any time (Rule 56). The Council issues a *communiqué* through the Secretary-General after each private meeting (Rule 55), and this is published in the official records in place of a verbatim record.

The first volume of the *Repertoire* of the Security Council covering the period 1946–51 stated that, at a private meeting to recommend a person for appointment as Secretary-General, the Council voted 'in such a manner as to ascertain whether any permanent member had cast a negative vote'.[57] This sentence has not appeared in later volumes of the *Repertoire*. The *communiqué* issued after the private meeting on 12 October 1950 says nothing about voting, but Trygve Lie reported in his memoirs that the Soviet Union vetoed a Yugoslav proposal that he be reappointed.[58] The *communiqué* of the private Council meeting held on 13 March 1953 states that a Canadian proposal to appoint Lester B. Pearson as Secretary-General was vetoed, without naming the member voting negatively; but Lie reports that it was the Soviet Union.[59]

In 1961 and 1966, there was general agreement to recommend the appointment of U Thant as Secretary-General. The only reference to voting in the three *communiqués* issued in December 1971, when Kurt Waldheim was recommended for appointment, is that 'having received a number of nominations for the post of Secretary-General, the Council voted by secret ballots on those nominations. As a result of the balloting, the Security Council proceeded to adopt unanimously the following resolution . . .', which recommended the appointment of Kurt Waldheim.[60] If there were vetoes in December 1971 over the appointment of the next Secretary-General, the details have not been made public.

The Council has increasingly been meeting privately and informally preparatory to meeting in public. When the Council meets in private, members tend to be more critical of past failures by UN organs than when the Council meets in public—

at least, so I am told. Sometimes it is not entirely clear to all the members whether the Council is engaged in informal consultations or is holding a closed meeting. On 27 October 1973, the Council was summoned to meet at 10.30 a.m. to consider the situation in the Middle East. Members duly gathered and engaged in informal discussion until 7.45 p.m. One member later described this as 'an informal, closed meeting' (India), another as an 'informal consultative meeting' (Soviet Union), a third as 'our informal discussion' (Sudan), the President (Australia) as 'informal consultations', while a fifth member told me afterwards that, in his opinion, it had been a formal but closed meeting.[61]

An even stranger occasion was the meeting held on 15 December 1973, also to consider the Middle East. The President (China) stated the previous day that it would be 'a formal closed meeting'. He began the proceedings by saying that, as a result of consultations, he understood that there was general agreement not to invoke Rule 51, which provides that, for a private meeting, the record shall be kept in a single copy alone. Accordingly, the verbatim record would be circulated in all the working languages as an unrestricted document, which is the normal procedure set out in Rule 49 for ordinary open meetings. Nevertheless, as the meeting was 'private', a *communiqué* would be issued, as required by Rule 55. As a result of these confusing decisions, a full verbatim record is available for what was supposedly a private meeting, a resolution was adopted, and a *communiqué* was issued at its conclusion.[62]

One can only speculate as to the circumstances on this occasion. The non-permanent members undoubtedly wanted to have a meeting of the Council to consider the relationship between the United Nations and the conference on the Middle East due to open shortly in Geneva. The United States and the Soviet Union, the co-sponsors of the conference, would have preferred not to have had a Security Council discussion of this delicate matter, but in the end the pressure became irresistible. Could it be that the meeting was private (closed) so as to avoid having one or more of the parties to the Middle East conflict make strident pronouncements just before they were about to embark on peace negotiations? And could it be that a verbatim record was made public in the ordinary way because at least one member of the Council was more interested in getting views on the record than in adopting a bland resolution or issuing a *communiqué*? In the event, a resolution was adopted by the votes of the ten non-permanent members, the two super-powers, France, and the United Kingdom abstaining, and China not participating in the vote. It would seem, from the verbatim record, that the non-permanent members were those who were most eager to adopt a resolution, and that France was the member most eager to get a point of view on the record.

Three private meetings were held for more conventional reasons to consider the Suez Canal problem in October 1956.[63]

6. THE AGENDA

It is necessary to start this section with four definitions.

The *Provisional Agenda* is the document drawn up by the Secretary-General, and approved by the President of the Council, which is placed before each meeting of the Council; it contains 'the list of matters suggested for the consideration of the Council at a specific meeting' (Rule 7).[64]

The first item of the Provisional Agenda is the adoption of the *Agenda* (Rule 9), which is the list of matters which the Council decides should be discussed at a particular meeting.

All items adopted on the agenda and not disposed of or expressly deleted are contained in the *Summary Statement of matters of which the Security Council is seized* (hereafter referred to as the 'Summary Statement'), which the Secretary-General is required to communicate each week to the representatives on the Security Council (Rule 11). One representative defined the expression 'matters of which the Security Council is seized' as meaning 'matters which have been on the agenda of previous meetings and have not been finally disposed of . . .', and the Chairman of the Committee of Experts agreed with this interpretation.[65] The matters of which the Council was seized on 1 March 1974 are listed in Appendix 3, pages 351 to 359; matters of which the Council was no longer seized on 1 March 1974 are listed in Appendix 4, pages 360 to 364.

Under Article 12(2) of the Charter, the Secretary-General is required to notify the General Assembly each year of any *matters relative to the maintenance of international peace and security which are being dealt with by the Security Council.* The purpose of

Article 12 was to prevent two of the principal organs of the United Nations from acting simultaneously on the same matter. In 1946 and 1947, the consent of the Council for the notification was given at meetings of the Council; beginning in 1948, consent has been obtained through the circulation by the Secretary-General of a draft notification.[67] I examine this question in more detail on pages 226–7.

Certain recurring matters, such as recommendations regarding the appointment of the Secretary-General and the election of judges of the International Court of Justice (Appendix 4, items 1 and 2(a)), are placed on the agenda and the Summary Statement only when decisions are needed. The question of applications for UN Membership has been on the Summary Statement for twenty-five years, and five applications for Membership were still outstanding on 1 March 1974 (Democratic Republic of Viet-Nam, applied 22 November 1948; Republic of Korea, 19 January 1949; Democratic People's Republic of Korea, 9 February 1949; Republic of Viet-Nam, 17 December 1950; People's Republic of Bangladesh, 8 August 1972).

Rule 11 regarding the Summary Statement came into force on 9 April 1946, by which time five matters had been disposed of by the Council (Appendix 4, items 1, 2(a), 3, 13, and 14). Less than a week was to elapse before the Council was faced with the question how items in the weekly Summary Statement were to be deleted.

The issue arose when the Soviet Union addressed to the President of the Council a letter in which 'the Government of the USSR insists [*sic*] that the Iranian question should be removed from the agenda of the Security Council'.[68] The complaint of Iran, dated 19 January 1946, had been the first matter brought to the attention of the Security Council. Iran alleged that Soviet officials and armed forces were interfering in the internal affairs of Azerbaijan in Iran, causing a situation which might lead to international friction.[69] The matter was considered at three meetings of the Council at the end of January 1946, and the Council adopted a resolution noting the readiness of the parties to seek a solution by negotiation and asking that the Council should be kept informed of the progress of any negotiation. On 4 April, the Council adopted another resolution, 'to defer further proceedings on the Iranian appeal until 6 May, at which time [the parties] are requested to report to the Council whether the withdrawal of all USSR troops from the whole of Iran has been completed . . .'[70] Two days later, the Soviet Union addressed a letter to the President of the Council claiming that the Council's second resolution had been 'incorrect and illegal' and asking for the removal of the Iranian question from the agenda. On 9 April, Iran countered by asking that the Iranian complaint should remain on the Council's agenda; but six days later, Iran informed the Council that agreement with the Soviet Union had been reached and that 'the Iranian Government . . . withdraws its complaint'.[71]

When the Council met the next day, there were two documents before it. One was a draft resolution submitted by France, which would have asked the Secretary-General 'to collect the necessary information in order to complete the Security Council's report to the Assembly . . . on [the complaint of Iran] now withdrawn . . .'[72] The other was a memorandum from Secretary-General Lie on the legal aspects of the question of retaining Iran's complaint on the agenda.[73] Lie later summarized his view as follows:

> The Soviet Union had clearly put itself in a vulnerable position by violating the Tripartite Treaty [of 1942]; it had now given assurance that this violation would be promptly repaired, and Iran had expressed its satisfaction and withdrawn its complaint; in these circumstances I saw no point in keeping the question on the agenda. The United Nations, I felt, should aim to settle disputes, not to inflame them.[74]

Lie and Abraham Feller, his legal counsel, drew up a memorandum which Lie decided to present to the President of the Council (China). The President, however, took the view that this was a matter for the Council rather than the Secretary-General and did not accept the memorandum; but he did have it read to the Council when it met on 16 April.[75]

Lie's view was essentially a political one, although the memorandum was expressed in legal terms. With the advantage of hindsight, one must conclude that this was not one of Lie's happier efforts.

Lie argued that the Council was acting under Chapter VI of the Charter, under which three courses were open to it:

1. to call on the parties to settle their dispute by peaceful means (Article 33);
2. to undertake an investigation (Article 34);
3. to recommend procedures or terms of settlement (Articles 36–8).

The Council, Lie stated, had not decided on an investigation under Article 34. 'Now that Iran has withdrawn its complaint, the Council can take no action under Articles 33, 36, 37, or 38, since the necessary conditions . . . (namely a dispute . . .) do not exist.' In this situation, 'it may well be that there is no way in which [the Council] can remain seized of the matter'. Lie referred in passing to the argument that the matter 'is no longer a matter solely between the original parties, but one in which the Council collectively has an interest . . .' This, he thought, 'may well be true', but that did not alter the fact that the Council could act only under the precise terms of the Charter.

On the proposal of the President of the Council, the Secretary-General's memorandum was referred to the Committee of Experts.[76] The Committee duly met the next day and agreed 'in principle that when a matter has been submitted to the Security Council by a party, it cannot be withdrawn from the [Summary Statement] without a decision by the Security Council'. But there agreement ended; and the Committee had no option but to report to its parent body (which had the same membership as itself) that it had not been able to formulate a common opinion.

Three members (France, Poland, and the Soviet Union) had reached the same conclusion as the Secretary-General, though on the basis of different reasoning. They considered that the crucial question was whether the Iranian item was a *dispute* or a *situation*. A *dispute*, they held, was a subjective matter, 'a conflict between two or more States, which exists only by virtue of the opposition between the interested parties'. If the parties to a *dispute* reach agreement, the threat to peace disappears; and if they ask the Security Council to drop the dispute, the Council 'is bound to do so, after having noted that their agreement has put an end to the dispute'.* On the basis of this conclusion, the Iranian complaint should be deleted from the Summary Statement. In the view of the three members, however, a *situation*, unlike a dispute, has 'a clearly objective character', and the Council may remain seized of it even if the State which first brought the matter to the attention of the Council should wish to withdraw it.

The other eight members of the Council (Australia, Brazil, China, Egypt, Mexico, Netherlands, the United Kingdom, and the United States) thought that it would be a mistake to regard the problem from a purely legalistic point of view. These members considered ('with variations') that the memorandum of Secretary-General Lie 'had put the problem on too narrow a basis, since it referred only to a dispute and since it treated such a dispute merely as a lawsuit between two parties'. Such a definition implied an 'inexact understanding' of the functions and competence of the Council. Even after the parties to a dispute have reached agreement, 'circumstances may continue to exist . . . which might still leave room for fears regarding the maintenance of peace and which might justify the question's being retained among the matters entrusted to its care'. In particular, the Council might find it necessary to remain seized of a matter 'until the whole or part of the agreement has been executed, or even longer'.[78]

The Council considered the report of its Committee of Experts on 23 April. The Soviet representative reminded the Council that his Government 'insists that the Iranian question should be removed from the agenda . . .' France reintroduced her earlier proposal requesting the Secretary-General to collect the necessary information, but this was rejected by 8 votes to 3. The Soviet representative denounced this vote as 'contradictory to the United Nations charter' and stated that his delegation 'cannot in future take part in discussions of the Iranian question by the Security Council'.[79]

On 8 May, in the absence of the Soviet representative, the Council asked Iran to submit a report by 20 May on the with-

* The International Court of Justice, in its advisory opinion on Namibia in 1971, held that, for a matter to be a 'dispute' under Article 27(3) of the Charter, there must have been a 'prior determination by the Security Council that a dispute exists . . .'[77]

drawal of Soviet forces.[80] On 21 May, Iran reported that it did not have sufficient first-hand information as to the true state of affairs in Azerbaijan, but the next day Iran informed the Council that Soviet troops had in fact withdrawn some two weeks earlier.[81] On 22 May, again in the absence of the Soviet representative, the Council decided to adjourn the discussion 'until a date in the near future, the Council to be called at the request of any member'.[82] No meeting has in fact been called, and after twenty-eight years, the Council, still remains seized of the Iranian complaint (Appendix 3, item 1).

This *brouhaha* has not been repeated, and the practice now is that matters may be removed from the Summary Statement in one of three ways: by adopting resolutions or taking decisions which dispose of the matter (Appendix 4A); by the rejection of all proposals submitted (Appendix 4B); or by explicit decisions to delete, or the rejection of proposals to retain (Appendix 4C). In three cases, decisions to delete were taken by the adoption of resolutions in express terms, in order that the matter could be taken up by the General Assembly (Appendix 4C, items 19, 21, and 23). One item was deleted following the rejection of a proposal to retain the matter on the Summary Statement (Appendix 4C, item 20). One item was deleted at a meeting of the Security Council at the request of the State making the complaint (Appendix 4C, item 24).[83] Three items were deleted following informal consultations, two at the request of the complaining State (Appendix 4C, items 25 and 26) and the Indonesian question at the request of Indonesia itself (Appendix 4C, item 22).[84]

Over the years, there has been a trend towards vague and general formulations in the titles of items placed on the agenda. After all, as Dr. Pechota has pointed out, purposeful ambiguity has its uses. In the early years, items were generally given titles which indicated their substance: the Palestine question, the Czechoslovak question, the Indonesian question (Appendix 3, items 11 and 13, Appendix 4C, item 22). In 1948, however, the item on the situation in Berlin was entitled 'Identic notifications dated 29 September 1948 from the Governments of the French Republic, the United Kingdom, and the United

States of America to the Secretary-General' (Appendix 3, item 16). The majority of items are now identified by reference to the letter or telegram requesting the Security Council to take up the matter—a practice which has been criticized in the General Assembly.

If the title indicates the substance of the matter, it is usual for the Council to seek a reasonably objective form of words. In 1950, after the outbreak of the Korean war, the Provisional Agenda of the Council had as its second item 'Aggression upon the Republic of Korea'. On the proposal of the President (India), the words 'Complaint of . . .' were inserted.[86] Similarly, in 1952, when the Soviet Union alleged that the United States had resorted to bacteriological warfare in Korea, the Provisional Agenda of one meeting had as its second item 'Appeal to States to accede to and ratify the Geneva Protocol of 1925 for the prohibition of the use of bacterial weapons'. Even this formulation was thought to be objectionable, and the United States proposed, and the Council agreed, to insert 'Question of an . . .'[87] On a few occasions, the titles of items have, with the Council's approval, been changed in minor respects after the initial decision to include the item.[88]

The Council has taken what is usually described as a liberal attitude towards requests to place matters on the agenda. At one of the earliest meetings of the Council, the United States representative put the matter like this:

> The position of my Government has, consistently, since the organization of this body, been that the Council cannot [*sic*] deny to a member of the United Nations who states that a condition exists which is likely to threaten international peace and security, the opportunity to present its case . . .
>
> My Government thinks, without prejudice to the merits of the [Ukrainian] complaint [against Greece] or even to the good faith behind the complaint, that the Council should place a minimum of technical requirements in the way of consideration of situations brought to its attention . . .
>
> In my opinion, the Council will be derelict in its duty if it does not examine the complaint and all that may be said and brought to substantiate the complaint, with the most rigid objectivity.[89]

Other members of the Council have expressed similar views.[90]

Procedure can, of course, be used as a diplomatic instrument. A State may, for political reasons, wish to prevent the Council from taking up a matter which it finds embarrassing. There are a number of respectable arguments which can be used in favour of rejecting a proposed item, but the argument which does not now carry much weight in the Council is that the matter is outside the Council's competence. It has become the general view that the Council is not in a position to decide the question of competence until it has placed the matter on its agenda and heard the parties.[91] Here are some typical expressions of that view.

The Council will not prejudice its competence by including the communications addressed to it . . . Once the agenda has been adopted, the members of the Council will have ample opportunity to examine the questions relating to competence . . .—Belgium.[92]

It may . . . be thought that, in order to discuss its competency in the matter, the Council must first of all have decided to place the item on the agenda. The French delegation has always considered [that] procedure to be the more logical, and the more consistent with the good ordering of the work of the Council.—France.[93]

I should like to make it clear that the adoption of this item on the agenda does not in any way prejudice either the competence of the Security Council in the matter or any of the merits of the case.—Poland (President).[94]

The adoption of the agenda does not decide or affect in any way the question of the Security Council's competence . . .—United Kingdom (President).[95]

The agenda could be adopted without in any way prejudging either the competence of the Security Council or any of the merits of the case.—United States.[96]

The General Assembly has a Rule of Procedure to the effect that any motion calling for a decision on the competence to adopt a proposal shall be put to the vote before a vote is taken on the proposal.[97] The Security Council has no such rule in express terms, but it would be only common sense to follow the practice of the Assembly.

Differences of opinion regarding the agenda have to be resolved by voting, but motions regarding the agenda are procedural and thus outside the scope of the veto of the permanent members. In addition to proposals to vary the wording of items, which are usually adopted without a vote, the Council has voted on motions to include an item in, or delete an item from, the agenda; to include an item in the

TABLE 4

Frequency of votes regarding the agenda, 1946–1968

Year	*No. of meetings held*	*No. of new items submitted*	*No. of meetings at which votes were taken regarding the agenda*
1946	88	33	3
7	137	20	5
8	171	9	10
9	62	8	3
1950	72	10	8
1	39	6	1
2	42	4	6
3	43	4	1
4	32	5	4
5	23	3	2
6	50	7	7
7	49	0	3
8	36	7	1
9	5	2	1
1960	71	11	1
1	68	8	2
2	38	2	1
3	59	7	0
4	104	8	1
5	81	1	0
6	70	3	2
7	46	9	0
8	76	5	1
	Total 1,462	172	63

agenda but to postpone consideration; to add an item not included in the Provisional Agenda; to confirm or change the order of items; to combine two or more items; and to adopt or reject the Provisional Agenda as a whole. But as will be seen from Table 4, the frequency of voting on the agenda has declined. In the period 1946–57, the proportion of meetings at which such votes were necessary averaged about 6½ per cent, but during the period 1958–68 the proportion had declined to about 1½ per cent.

There is one aspect of the agenda which is sometimes the occasion of political manoeuvring. Let me illustrate. Item 72 of the Summary Statement is 'The situation in the Middle East'. If one side in the Middle East conflict requests a Council meeting, item 2 of the Provisional Agenda will be headed 'The situation in the Middle East', and underneath will be listed the letter or letters requesting the meeting. Thus, item 2 of the Provisional Agenda on 18 July 1972 was as follows,

2. The situation in the Middle East
   (a) Letter dated 5 July 1972 from the Permanent Representative of the Syrian Arab Republic to the United Nations addressed to the President of the Security Council (S/10730)
   (b) Letter dated 5 July 1972 from the Chargé d'affaires, *a.i.*, of the Permanent Mission of Lebanon to the United Nations addressed to the President of the Security Council (S/10731)[98]

These letters from Syria and Lebanon were in virtually identical terms and recalled part of a previous Council resolution calling for 'appropriate steps' which would lead to 'the release in the shortest possible time of all Syrian and Lebanese military and security personnel abducted by Israeli armed forces . . .'[99]

But there was a further item listed in the Provisional Agenda. As soon as Israel learned that a Council meeting was to be held to consider the complaints of Syria and Lebanon, she submitted her own letter requesting an urgent meeting of the Council 'to consider the *mutual* release of all prisoners of war . . .' (my italics). The third item of the Provisional Agenda thus read:

3. The situation in the Middle East
   Letter dated 17 July 1972 from the Permanent Representative of Israel to the United Nations addressed to the President of the Security Council (S/10739)[100]

When the Council met, several representatives pointed out that they had not been consulted by the President prior to the meeting about item 3 (China, France, Guinea, India, Japan, Somalia, Soviet Union, Sudan, Yugoslavia). The U.S. representative, having 'gone quickly through' the Rules of Procedure, claimed that there was no requirement for prior consultation.

The President of the Council (Argentina) then explained the course of events.

On 5 July, the representatives of Syria and Lebanon handed him the two letters requesting a meeting, but after discussion it was agreed to work for implementation of the Council's resolution without an immediate meeting. On 17 July, the representatives of Syria and Lebanon again met the President and expressed the view that it was now necessary to set a date for a meeting of the Council. The President, in response, suggested 3.30 p.m. the following afternoon 'so as to allow a 24-hour period to give both sides time for thought'. After the representatives of Israel had been informed that the meeting would be held, he stated his intention of submitting his own letter requesting a meeting of the Council. That letter, dated 17 July, reached the President at about noon on 18 July. The President said that, in accordance with 'unchanging practice', he had included Israel's letter in the Provisional Agenda. He also said, somewhat less adroitly, that those who complained of lack of consultation were mistaken. 'The President of the Security Council at the beginning of this meeting consulted all members . . . on the adoption of the agenda.'

He then proposed that the Council should vote on whether or not item 3 should be deleted. After a few more interventions, the Council voted by eight votes to none, with seven abstentions, in favour of deleting the item. Eight votes were one short of the number needed to take a decision. The Council thus found itself in an awkward situation.[101]

The correct procedure, of course, is to put to the vote *the adoption* of the agenda (which is how item 1 of the Provisional Agenda is worded) and not *the rejection* of the agenda or of any particular item. Usually, if the President proposes that the Council should vote on the *rejection* of an item, an alert member of the Council intervenes in time to prevent the Council from wittingly or unwittingly using faulty procedure.[102]

The situation on 18 July 1972, however, was that a simple majority of the members of the Council favoured the rejection of item 3, but this majority was less than the nine votes needed to take a decision. After further procedural debate, during the course of which the Japanese representative made a sensible but unsuccessful attempt to secure a twenty-minute adjournment for informal consultation, the Council approved item 2 of the Provisional Agenda on the understanding that item 3 would be dealt with at a separate meeting.[103] The Council had spent more than two hours deciding what business it should deal with.

Strictly, the Council should discuss only the adoption of the agenda or items in the agenda which the Council itself has approved. Occasionally, however, the Council has found itself listening to speeches concerned neither with the adoption of the agenda nor with items that have been approved. The Council met on 16 June 1969 'for the sole purpose of hearing . . . the views of [the President of Colombia] on certain aspects of the maintenance of international peace and security'.[104] When the Council met in Panama City in March 1972, it had a full discussion on racial discrimination without having approved an agenda. It so happened that, during the period of the Council's meetings in Panama, there occurred the annual International Day for the Elimination of Racial Discrimination (21 March). The Council met and heard statements from the Chairman of the UN Special Committee on Apartheid, Secretary-General Waldheim, the Council's President (Panama), and representatives of the Soviet Union and Kenya. It then adopted its agenda (peace and security in Latin America), bade farewell to a senior official in the Secretariat whose term of service had been completed, and at once adjourned. When questioned by the United States about the character of the meeting, the President stated that it had been 'planned and organized in agreement with the Secretary-General and the Chairman of the Special Committee on Apartheid'.[105]

In one respect, the Rules of Procedure are not strictly applied in connection with the agenda. Rule 10 reads

> Any item of the agenda of a meeting of the Security Council, consideration of which has not been completed at that meeting, shall, unless the Security Council otherwise decides, automatically be included in the agenda of the next meeting.

In presenting this Rule to the Council in draft form, the Chairman of the Committee of Experts explained that the term 'agenda' had been used advisedly. 'This rule means that the continued consideration of such business as is left over from one meeting shall constitute part of the agenda of the succeeding meeting.' The Committee of Experts thought that it should be left to the Secretary-General to indicate which items on the Provisional Agenda were new matters and which items had been held over from previous meetings.[106] The *Repertoire* of practice of the Security Council comments laconically, however, that 'in practice . . . the provisional agenda has not contained all items of unfinished business'.[107]

The fact that Rule 10 is not strictly applied has been raised in meetings of the Council from time to time. On one such occasion, the initiative for not applying Rule 10 had come from the Secretary-General, [108] but more usually the responsibility has been assumed by the President for the month, whether acting in the interest of orderly procedure or from more starkly political motives.[109] On more than one occasion, paradoxically, a President has been *blamed* for applying Rule 10 to the letter.[110] On one famous occasion on which Rule 10 was cited, the President (United States) voted against the adoption of the agenda which, in accordance with Rule 7, he had himself approved.[111] This was not as absurd as it may seem at first sight: the question proposed for inclusion in the agenda was the Guatemalan complaint in June 1954.

It may be doubted whether Rule 10 serves much useful purpose. The Council is free to take whatever decisions it wishes regarding the agenda, regardless of the precise contents of the Provisional Agenda.

7. REJECTION OF ITEMS

The Council has been reluctant to reject proposals for including new matters in its agenda. During the first twenty-seven years of its work, the Council decided not to admit eleven items (Table 5), but a reasonably full debate took place before the proposed items were rejected; indeed, in one case the debate extended over six meetings (Table 5, item 5).

Four arguments have been used, separately or in combination, why proposed items should not be admitted to the agenda. First, that the proposal was lacking in clarity or that more information was needed before a decision could be taken. This was the view taken by the majority regarding the Soviet proposal in 1946 requesting information on armed forces stationed on non-enemy territories, and also the Arab item in 1957 on Oman (Table 5, items 1 and 8).[112]

Secondly, it was argued by France that the proposed item on the Tunisian question should not be admitted in 1952 because no dispute or threat to peace existed (Table 5, item 4).[113]

A more usual argument, essentially political, is that consideration by the Security Council will have a harmful effect on the situation or dispute, that it will interfere with measures undertaken or contemplated outside the Security Council, or that the timing is inopportune. A variant of this argument has been used in almost every case listed in Table 5.[114]

Finally, States can invoke Article 2(7) of the Charter and claim that inscription of the proposed item would represent intervention in essentially domestic affairs.[115] This argument, which was successfully deployed in connection with item 11 of Table 5, is not often conclusive when used on its own, as the general view of the Council has been that to include an item in the agenda does not, of itself, constitute intervention.

It has sometimes been argued that a particular matter is being submitted only for propaganda purposes.[116] This argument must always be treated with some reserve. Indeed, David Gilmour has found that the most striking fact about debates in the Security Council on the inscription of items is 'the fact that the arguments used vary according to whose affairs are being brought to the attention of the Security Council'.[117]

Everyone knows that to explain one's own point of view is simply to give the facts, but that when one's adversary does the same, it is propaganda. Most States have at one time or another used the United Nations as a forum for propaganda. This may be a distressing business for those who have to listen; but who would deny that this is preferable to more violent means of struggle? UN deliberative organs serve a necessary function as international safety valves, allowing the escape of hot air without blowing up the whole machine.

The third column of Table 4 (p. 50) shows the number of new items included in the agenda. A. Leroy Bennett, having examined the number of substantive political issues considered by the Security Council and the General Assembly between

TABLE 5

Matters submitted to the Security Council which were not admitted to its agenda, 1946–1973

	Short title	*Submitted by*	*Date*	*Document ref.*	*Meeting(s) at which considered*
1	Information on Allied Forces on non-enemy territory	Soviet Union	29 Aug. 1946	S/144	57, 71–2
2	Relations of Members of the United Nations with Spain	General Assembly res. 114(II)	25 June 1948	S/622	327
3	The Greek question	Soviet Union	29 Aug. 1950	S/1735 and Corr. 1, S/1737	493
4	The Tunisian question	11 Afro-Asian States	31 Mar. 1952	S/2751	574–6
5	The question of Morocco	15 Afro-Asian States	21 Aug. 1953	S/3085	619–24
6	The situation in Algeria	13 Afro-Asian States	13 June 1956	S/3609, S/3589 and Add. 1	729–30
7	Non-compliance ... with the decision of the ... General Assembly of 2 November 1956 ... [to halt aggression against Egypt]	Soviet Union	5 Nov. 1956	S/3736	755
8	The situation in Oman	11 Arab States	13 Aug. 1957	S/3865 and Add. 1	783–4
9	Security Council Resolution 169 (S/5002) regarding the Congo question	Soviet Union	25 Jan. 1962	S/5064	989
10	Complaint of 22 February 1962 by Cuba	Cuba	22 Feb. 1962	S/5080	991
11	Question submitted by Ireland	Ireland	17 Aug. 1969	S/9394	1503

1946 and 1964, found that the number of such issues taken up by the Security Council each year averaged 'nearly eight for the first four years', falling to 'a yearly average of five' during the 1950s, and rising to 'nearly eight per year' during the early 1960s. 'Only during the first two years did the Security Council consider more political issues than the General Assembly.'[118]

8. INTERPRETATION AND TRANSLATION

In diplomatic jargon, 'interpretation' means the rendering into another language of an *oral* statement as it is being delivered (simultaneous) or immediately after its conclusion (consecutive); 'translation' refers to the process of rendering *written* documents into another language. The five languages of the Security Council are Chinese, English, French, Russian, and Spanish (Rule 41). All oral statements given in the Security Council are interpreted *simultaneously* into the four other languages by the highly skilled interpreters on the UN staff. Representatives who want to hear a speech in an official language other than the one being used by the speaker may use earphones by their seats and a dial to select the language of their choice (or, if they prefer, silence).

Formerly, the Security Council distinguished between *official* and *working* languages. The five *official* languages were those mentioned above, but only English and French were *working* languages. That meant that all speeches were interpreted both *simultaneously* into the four other official languages and *consecutively* at the conclusion of each statement into one or both *working* languages.

On 24 January 1969 the Council decided that the work of the United Nations would be enriched and the objectives of the Charter attained by the addition of Russian and Spanish among the *working* languages.[119] The Rules of Procedure were amended accordingly. On 17 January 1974, the Council decided that Chinese should be a *working* as well as an *official* language;[120] the distinction between *official* and *working* languages thus disappeared.

Originally, all statements made in the Council were similarly interpreted, but in January 1948 the Council gave up the *consecutive* interpretation of statements by non-members of the

Council. Occasionally the right to *consecutive* interpretation of statements by Council members was waived, but always on the express understanding that this did not constitute a precedent. The combination of *simultaneous* and *consecutive* interpretation was not followed in other UN organs, however, and during the course of 1972, *consecutive* interpretation was dropped by general consent, so that the Council is now satisfied with *simultaneous* interpretation into the four other languages. If a representative makes a speech in a language other than one of the five languages of the Security Council, 'he shall himself provide for interpretation into one of those languages' (Rule 44), but I recall no case of resort to this Rule. Permanent sound recordings of the proceedings of Council meetings are maintained.

It is interesting how fashions have changed about simultaneous interpretation. Fifty years ago, the difficulty of providing diplomats with simultaneous interpretation was regarded as a great boon.

> It is difficult if not impossible [wrote H. A. L. Fisher] to tune an assembly up to a high pitch of excitement if, no matter how fiery and provocative the declamation, the impassive neutrality of the translator is invariably intruded between provocation and reply. Translation therefore tends to keep down the temperature, and in an Assembly dedicated to the promotion of international peace, this adventitious circumstance, so inconvenient, so tedious, so wasteful of time, may not be without its advantages.[121]

There have, indeed, been occasions when the time taken for consecutive interpretation in the Security Council was used for quiet diplomacy, but it was more often the case that consecutive interpretation introduced an annoying element of delay into the proceedings of the Council.

In the early days, there was considerable resistance to the idea of simultaneous interpretation for the United Nations. A committee on the procedure and organization of the General Assembly pointed out in 1947 that, while simultaneous interpretation would contribute greatly to saving time, its use in all circumstances 'is not without serious disadvantages'. The first disadvantage was the sheer technical difficulty of interpretation when the word order of the original language differs from that of the language into which it is to be interpreted. 'In following word for word in a simultaneous interpretation, the interpreter is unable . . . to follow the general line of argument and set it forth clearly for those who are listening.' Secondly, the interpreter will not know in advance what documents will be quoted and is therefore unable to have at hand the official texts cited. Thirdly, the speaker 'does not hear the interpretation and is unable to control its accuracy or correct the errors of the interpreter'. In the case of *consecutive* interpretation, this difficulty did not arise. Indeed, I recall an occasion in the Security Council when the Soviet Ambassador, the late Arkady Sobolev (who presumably was without instructions from Moscow), interrupted the consecutive interpreter who had said in English 'the Soviet Government considers . . .' with the words 'No, the Soviet *delegation* considers . . .' The U.S. representative was no doubt choosing his words carefully when speaking on the request to consider the Tunisian complaint against France in 1962 (Table 5, no. 4): '*I am instructed* to submit to the Council the following views of my Government on this subject.'[122]

Finally, according to the 1947 committee, simultaneous interpretation creates a 'physical and psychological barrier' between the speaker and his colleagues. Representatives 'miss the opportunity of familiarizing themselves with the habits of thought and the languages spoken by the other representatives'. The 1947 committee concluded that simultaneous interpretation 'can be used with advantage' for ordinary debate, 'but that it is not suitable when detailed negotiations or the reconciliation of various drafts are necessary'.[123]

The difficulties envisaged by the 1947 committee have not, in fact, materialized to any serious extent.

One might expect a representative to use whichever of the five languages comes most easily to him, but one gifted and highly articulate diplomat, the late Víctor Andrés Belaúnde of Peru, permitted his mood to determine his choice of language. When he wished to be precise, he used French; when he wished to under-state, he used English; when he wished to exaggerate, he used Spanish.

Most of the work of the Secretariat is conducted in English and, to a lesser extent, French. The mother tongue of professional and higher-level staff in posts subject to geographical distribution was as follows on 30 April 1967:

Chinese	2·9
English	29·7
French	9·1
Russian	6·3
Spanish	9·7
Other (98 languages)	42·3

Of the senior staff in 1967 whose mother tongue was neither English nor French, 'the overwhelming majority work in English'.[124] An attempt has been made since 1967 to achieve a better language balance in recruiting new staff.[125]

9. DOCUMENTS AND RECORDS

To those who are not familiar with the documentation of the Security Council, the matter is bound to seem esoteric and perhaps unnecessarily complicated; but there are, in fact, three main groups of printed documents to which the practitioner or scholar may want to refer. First, there are the verbatim records of meetings of the Council, the 'Hansard' of the Council, which are issued in separate fascicles, one for each meeting, and which libraries usually bind in annual volumes. Each meeting is numbered, from no. 1 held on 17 January 1946 to no. 1,764 held on 28 February 1974; the record of each meeting is now divided into numbered paragraphs.

Second, there are letters and reports issued in the S/– series, of which 11,229 had been issued up to 1 March 1974; some of these also carry an A/– number if they are for circulation also to Members of the General Assembly. All of these S/– documents which are of long-term interest are now printed in numerical order in quarterly Supplements to the official records of the Council or, in the case of certain reports, such as those of *ad hoc* subsidiary bodies, in Special Supplements.

Third, there are the resolutions and decisions of the Council, those resolutions in express terms being numbered consecutively from resolution 1 dated 25 January 1946 to resolution 345 dated 17 January 1974. These are now printed annually as a volume of the official records: they are classified by subject matter at the front of each volume and listed chronologically at the back.

One other annual publication which may be useful to the novice is the report of the Council to the General Assembly, which summarizes the Council's activities. It is now always issued as Supplement no. 2 of the official records of the annual regular session of the General Assembly, the report for mid-1972 to mid-1973 being issued for the 28th regular session of the Assembly held in the autumn of 1973.

Since 1964, the Dag Hammarskjold Library of the United Nations has issued an annual Index to the proceedings of the Security Council, but this is probably of most value to those who are already familiar with the Security Council's system of documentation. *The United Nations Documentation Information System* (ST/LIB/33), published by the United Nations in 1974, provides information about the UN documents in microform. *United Nations Documentation* (ST/LIB/34), also published in 1974, is intended primarily for those who maintain collections of UN documents.

There is inevitably a delay in the publication of UN documents, and the system by which the documents of the Security Council are issued provisionally in mimeographed form is described in the following pages.

Virtually all documents of the Security Council are first issued in mimeographed form with the symbol S/–, followed by the document number. Document S/1, issued on 26 January 1946, was a letter from Iran to the President of the Security Council complaining about Soviet interference in the internal affairs of Iran.[126] Document S/10000, issued on 25 November 1970, was a letter from Yugoslavia condemning aggression against Guinea by 'foreign mercenary forces'.[127] Beginning in 1972, certain substantial documents of the Council have been printed by offset from typescript (litho.) Mimeographed documents and resolutions of the Council are issued in the five languages (Rule 46) and, except for a very small number which are ephemeral in character, are later printed in quarterly Supplements to the Official Records of the Security Council; resolutions of the Council (along with other decisions) are published in annual volumes. If the Security Council so decides, documents of the Council shall be published in a language other than one of the five languages of the Council (Rule 47).

A provisional verbatim record of each public meeting of the Council is issued in mimeographed form in the series S/PV.–, followed by the number of the meeting. The Rules of Procedure provide that provisional records shall be drawn up in the languages of the Council (Rule 45) and made available to representatives who have participated in a Council meeting by 10 a.m. of the first working day following the meeting (Rule 49), and that representatives shall inform the Secretary-General of 'any corrections they wish to have made' within two working days of receipt of the provisional record (Rule 50). Corrections which have been requested are approved, unless the President is of the opinion that they are sufficiently important to be submitted to the members of the Security Council. In that event, members must submit any comments they wish to make within two working days. In the absence of such objection, the record is corrected as requested (Rule 52).

To fulfil the requirements of Rules 50 and 52 regarding corrections, the provisional record bears a notice which, in the English language version, reads as follows:

> This record contains the original text of speeches delivered in English and interpretations of speeches in other languages. The final text will be distributed as soon as possible.
>
> Corrections should be submitted to original speeches only. They should be sent *in quadruplicate within three working days* to the Chief of the Official Records Editing Section, Office of Conference Services, Room LX–2332, and incorporated in a copy of the record.
>
> AS THIS RECORD WAS DISTRIBUTED ON . . ., THE TIME-LIMIT FOR CORRECTIONS WILL BE . . .
>
> The cooperation of delegations in strictly observing this time-limit would be greatly appreciated.

Corrections should be limited to actual errors and omissions. When a request is submitted for the deletion or addition of a passage, a check is made against the sound recording of the relevant speech. Only in cases of serious errors or omissions affecting the substance of the discussion is a mimeographed corrigendum, addendum, or revised text prepared and distributed, and then only as an exceptional measure.[128]

Normally, the application of the Rules regarding corrections causes no public difficulty. The only cases I recall of the verbatim record being seriously challenged occurred in 1950 and 1952. The provisional record of the Council meeting held on 16 November 1950 did not contain the text of a statement from the People's Republic of China, which had been read in full to the Council by its secretary. When the Council met the next day, the Soviet Union drew attention to the omission. The President (Yugoslavia) intervened at once to say that the matter would be rectified when the definitive official record was published.[129] On the second occasion, there was some misunderstanding as to whether or not the President had closed the meeting and therefore as to whether certain remarks should or should not form part of the record. Things were put right at the next meeting when a representative read from the sound recording the matter omitted from the provisional record of the previous meeting.[130]

After necessary corrections have been made to the provisional verbatim record, it is supposed to be 'signed by the President' (Rule 53) and 'published . . . as soon as possible' (Rule 54) in the series Security Council Official Records (SCOR),——year,——meeting (date) in the five languages of the Council (Rule 45); but the requirement that the President shall sign the record fell into disuse at an early stage.

In a few cases, written or photographic material referred to or circulated round the table at Council meetings has been incorporated into the Official Records or Supplements.[131] In 1971, a proposal was submitted by Sierra Leone that a film on Namibia (South West Africa) should form part of the Official Records of the Security Council, but the general view of the permanent members of the Council was that this would constitute a dangerous precedent. The French representative was reluctant to convert the Council into 'a kind of cinema club . . .' The U.S. representative admitted that he loved to watch movies, but was worried about establishing a precedent, and the British representative was afraid that, if films were shown on every matter before the Council, 'we may find ourselves with rather a lot of work'. To the Soviet representative, it was 'a rather clear, simple problem' and his answer was equally clear and simple: 'A film cannot become a document of the Security Council . . .' The President of the Council (Nicaragua) suggested that to create the precedent requested by Sierra

Leone 'would open up a Pandora's box'. He suggested, and Sierra Leone and other Council members agreed, that 'the film be placed in the files of the Secretariat and available to anyone who wished to see it . . .'[132]

The Council normally meets in public, but it can decide to meet in private, at the close of which it issues a *communiqué* through the Secretary-General. The Council may decide that, for a private meeting, a single copy of the verbatim record shall be made and kept by the Secretary-General. In that event, corrections may be submitted within a period of ten days (Rule 51). UN Members which have taken part in a private meeting 'shall at all times have the right to consult the record of that meeting in the office of the Secretary-General'. Other Members may have access to the record of a private meeting only if the Security Council so authorizes (Rule 56).

Most resolutions of the Security Council were, until 1965, issued in the S/– series and included in the Official Records or Supplements. Beginning in 1965, resolutions have been issued in mimeographed form under the symbol S/RES/–; previous resolutions were assigned numbers 1 to 199. The resolutions are printed in annual volumes as *Resolutions and Decisions of the Security Council* in the five languages.

The provisional agenda for each meeting of the Security Council is issued in mimeographed form in the series S/Agenda/–, followed by the number of the meeting.

The Council's annual report, which is a factual account of the work of the Council, is printed as a Supplement to the Official Records of the General Assembly.

Documents of subsidiary organs of the Security Council have been issued under the following symbols:

S/AC.4/–	United Nations Commission of Investigation concerning Greek Frontier Incidents, 1947
S/AC.7/–	Conference of the General Assembly and Security Council Committees on Procedure for the Admission of New Members, 1947
S/AC.8/–	Sub-Committee on the Greek Question, 1947
S/AC.10/–	United Nations Commission for Indonesia, 1947–51
S/AC.12/–	United Nations Commission for India and Pakistan, 1948–50

S/AC.13/–	Sub-Committee [on Laos] established under resolution 132 (S/4216) of 7 September 1959
S/AC.14/–	Expert Committee on South Africa established by resolution 191 (S/5773) of 18 June 1964
S/AC.15/–	Committee established in pursuance of resolution 253 (S/8601) [concerning the question of Southern Rhodesia], 29 May 1968
S/AC.16/–	Committee of Experts [on Mini-States] established at the meeting on 29 August 1969
S/AC.17/–	*Ad Hoc* Sub-Committee [on Namibia] established by resolution 276 (S/9620/Rev.1), 30 January 1970
S/AC.18/–	*Ad Hoc* Sub-Committee [on Namibia] re-established by resolution 293 (S/9892), 29 July 1970
S/AC.19/–	Committee on Council Meetings away from Headquarters (Article 28(3) of the Charter), 11 January 1972
S/C.1/–	Committee of Experts on the Rules of Procedure, 1947–
S/C.2/–	Committee on the Admission of New Members, 1947–
S/C.3/–	Commission for Conventional Armaments, 1947–50
S/CNM/–	Committee on the Admission of New Members, 1946
S/PROCEDURE/–	Committee of Experts on the Rules of Procedure, 1946–7
S/SCS/–	Sub-Committee of the Security Council on the Spanish Question, 1946

The Provisional Rules of Procedure of the Security Council bear the symbol S/96/Rev.6.

The Secretary-General is supposed to submit to the Council each year a list of records and documents which have been considered confidential, and the Council should decide which of these shall be made public and which shall remain confidential (Rule 57), but this Rule is not, in fact, applied.

10. COMMUNICATIONS

The public exchange of written communications within the framework of the Security Council has to some extent taken the place of debate, and the Rules regarding the circulation of such communications provide endless opportunities for UN gamesmanship. When the procedure for circulating communications from non-governmental sources was approved in 1946, there seemed to be general agreement that such communications should be circulated only if they deal with matters with which the Security Council is seized; that frivolous communications should be ignored; and that the Secretariat, in circulating a list of communications received, should have discretion to indicate the subject matter of each communication.[133] A list of all communications received from private individuals and non-governmental bodies is therefore circulated to members of the Council, and any member may obtain from the Secretariat a copy of any communication on the list (Appendix to the Rules of Procedure). Minor variations of this procedure occur if a member of the Council requests the circulation of a communication from a non-governmental body[134] (or, indeed, from an entity claiming to be a State or States, a regional organization, or an agency for collective self-defence). If a member of the Council transmits a communication and requests that it be circulated to members of the Council or all UN Member States, both the letter of transmittal and the communication are circulated.

The Secretary-General is required to bring to the Council's attention 'for the consideration of the Security Council in accordance with the provisions of the Charter' all communications from 'States [whether Members of the United Nations or not], organs of the United Nations, or the Secretary-General . . .' (Rule 6). If a State which is not a member of the Council asks to participate in the discussion of some matter, and the Council decides to postpone consideration of the request or to reject it (nowadays a rare proceeding), the Council may invite the State concerned to submit its views in writing for circulation to the Council.[135] The Secretary-General has occasionally circulated documents with a prefatory note to the effect that he is not able to determine whether he is required by the Rules of Procedure to circulate the communication, or that the communication is circulated for the convenience of members and the Secretary-General's action is not necessarily an application of Rule 6.[136]

The Secretary-General has also circulated to the Council

communications from the Organization of American States and its organs and from the Organization of African Unity, arising from the Charter obligation to keep the Security Council fully informed of activities for the maintenance of international peace and security undertaken or in contemplation under regional arrangements or by regional agencies (Article 54). On three occasions in the period 1946–8, communications concerning aspects of the Trieste question were circulated to the Council at the request of the Council of [four] Foreign Ministers.[137]

Only two communications have been circulated expressly to meet the Charter obligation to report immediately to the Council on measures taken in the exercise of the right of individual or collective self-defence after an armed attack has occurred (Article 51). The first was on 13 February 1958, when Tunisia reported on measures taken after France had attacked Sakiet-Sidi-Youssef;[138] the second was on 9 May 1972, when the United States reported that, because of North-Vietnamese aggression and intransigence, her ports were being mined.[139]

States have often claimed to be acting in self-defence—India and Pakistan in Kashmir, Israel and the Arab States in the Middle East, the United States in the Gulf of Tonkin, the Soviet Union in Czechoslovakia. But it is surprising how rarely States have cited Article 51 to explain the measures they have taken. Egypt cited Article 51 in 1951 to justify restricting shipping through the Suez Canal and in 1967 after the outbreak of the June war;[140] Lebanon in 1958 after asking the United States for help in stopping Egyptian interference in her internal affairs;[141] Israel on the day the Six Day War broke out in 1967, on the ground that there had been an Egyptian attack, as well as in August 1973, to justify the forcible diversion of an Arab passenger aircraft to a military air base in Israel in the mistaken belief that the plane was carrying an important Palestinian leader.[142]

One indirect reference to Article 51 took place in 1962, when Cuba complained that her exclusion from the Organization of American States was contrary to Article 53 of the UN Charter (Regional Arrangements). France suggested that Article 53 did not apply. The O.A.S. action was 'essentially a matter of collective protection which is justified under Article 51 . . .'[143]

—although nobody claimed that Cuba had engaged in 'an armed attack'.

Neither the Charter nor the Rules of Procedure expressly grant to the Secretary-General discretion regarding the circulation of communications. Secretary-General Hammarskjold stated on one occasion that the only information he had withheld from the Council in the Congo case was 'some information which I have not found it in order to put to the Council, following normal diplomatic rules as regards interests of various Member nations . . . Papers which would never be circulated . . . because of their character, or because of their origin, should not be circulated in this case . . ., unless explicitly requested by members.'[144] On another occasion, after the Soviet Union had refused to have dealings with Hammarskjold, the Soviet representative complained to the President of the Council that 'the United Nations Secretariat' was failing to implement Security Council decisions, and asked for the circulation of a letter from Mr. Antoine Gizenga, who was described in the Soviet letter as 'the Head of the Government of the Republic of the Congo', but who had described himself as 'Deputy Prime Minister'. Hammarskjold complied with the Soviet request without demur.[145] Later the same year, shortly after the death of Hammarskjold, the Secretariat was apparently reticent about circulating two communications from Mr. Moïse Tshombé, because Katanga was not a State but part of the Congo. When the matter was raised in the Security Council, however, U Thant readily agreed to circulate the communications.[146]

What is the Secretary-General to do if he is asked to circulate a document containing disrespectful, offensive, or insulting language? On 11 March 1963, for example, the Revolutionary Government of Cuba asked for the circulation of a document some 6,000 words in length. The strong language used in the document was not qualitatively unprecedented in the annals of United Nations invective; it was, rather, the *quantity* of abusive language which gave the document its distinctive character. A few extracts from the document follow.[147]

. . . lack of respect for the sovereignty of my country, the continual violations of our air space and territorial waters, the organization of a web of espionage and piracy throughout the Caribbean, the infiltration of saboteurs into our territory, and the atmosphere of hysteria which the United States is fostering . . .

. . . a den of spies, saboteurs and counter-revolutionaries and a hotbed of provocation, subversion and aggression.

. . . irresponsible, hypocritical and cynical statements full of rancour and provocations.

. . . stronghold of intervention, subversion, conspiracy and aggression . . .

Venezuela addressed four letters to the President of the Security Council, and Costa Rica and Paraguay one each, insisting that UN documents intended for circulation 'should be consistent with the importance and dignity of the highest international organization'.[148] The President (Brazil) could only reply that the language used in communications 'is the responsibility of the Government from which the communication emanates'. The President of the Council had no power 'to modify the language of a communication'.[149]

But the real opportunity for UN gamesmanship for more than five years concerned the circulation of communications from the German Democratic Republic—a matter which had also arisen in other UN organs. The matter was first raised in the context of the Security Council in 1967, in a note verbale from the Soviet Union to the Secretary-General. The gist of the Soviet complaint was that communications from the Federal Republic of Germany were circulated by the Secretariat as a matter of course, while communications from the German Democratic Republic were circulated only following a specific request by a member of the Council. As an example of the Secretariat's allegedly discriminatory practice, the Soviet Union cited what had happened about communications received from governments concerning the implementation of the Council's resolutions imposing sanctions against the illegal regime in Rhodesia. Not only had the Secretariat declined 'without any grounds whatsoever' to circulate a communication from the German Democratic Republic until requested to do so by Bulgaria, but the Secretariat had resorted to 'gross distortion' of the State's official name by referring to the State as 'Eastern Germany'. Moreover, at the time of the Bulgarian request, according to the Soviet Union, Bulgaria had been

President of the Council.* The practice of the Secretariat, argued the Soviet Union, was 'devoid of any legal foundation' and 'narrowly pro-Western and unobjective'.[150]

The fact that Secretary-General Thant did not reply until seven weeks later suggests that the matter was sufficiently complicated to necessitate consultations with some of the other States most concerned. The reply, when it appeared, was in two parts. First, on the specific matter of sanctions against the Rhodesian regime, the Security Council had called upon 'States Members of the United Nations or of the specialized agencies' to report to the Secretary-General. Under that formula, the Secretariat had acted properly in circulating the communication from the Federal Republic of Germany. Similarly, the Secretariat had followed the practice of the Council in circulating the communication from the German Democratic Republic as soon as requested to do so by a Council member.

On the wider question of the circulation of documents, the Secretary-General said it was beyond his competence to determine the status of areas in dispute. He could only continue the existing practice until he received from the deliberative organ concerned an explicit directive to the contrary.[151]

There the matter might have rested, but the Soviet Union soon returned to the attack. It was precisely the practice of the Council which the Soviet Union was challenging; the practice had, moreover, evolved without any express decision of a UN organ. The Soviet Union trusted that the Secretary-General would take steps to discontinue the Secretariat's 'abnormal practice'.[152]

The same problem arose periodically after 1967—in connection with a request from the German Democratic Republic to take part in the debate on the occupation of Czechoslovakia in 1968 (a request which was rejected by the Council);[153] in connection with a decision of the Council calling on 'all States' to refrain from dealing with 'the Government of South Africa purporting to act on behalf of the Territory of Namibia' (South West Africa), when a communication from the German

* This was slightly stretching a point; the Bulgarian request was dated 27 February 1967, while Bulgaria's presidency had been for the month of March.

Democratic Republic was circulated at the direction of the President for the month (Soviet Union), leading in due course to a protest by Britain, France, and the United States;[154] in connection with a proposal to amend the Statute of the International Court of Justice to permit the seat of the Court to be established at a place other than The Hague;[155] in connection with aggression by Portugal against Senegal and Guinea, when the communication was circulated at the direction of the President (Zambia), which led to restatements of the Western and East European positions;[156] in connection with the supply of arms to South Africa, when the communication was circulated at the direction of the President (Poland), which again led to restatements of the Western and East European positions;[157] in connection with a communication supporting the Security Council's resolution on Namibia adopted in pursuance of the advisory opinion of the International Court of Justice, which was circulated at the direction of the President of the Council (Poland);[158] on the occasion of the Security Council meetings in Addis Ababa, circulated at the request of the President of the Council (Somalia), and following a retaliatory raid by Israel against Lebanon, and on the occasion of the International Day for Action to Combat Racism and Racial Discrimination, both communications circulated at the request of the President for the month (the Soviet Union), to which the three Western powers submitted a comprehensive protest, leading in due course to a Soviet defence of the circulation of the documents;[159] about sanctions against the illegal regime in Rhodesia, circulated at the request of the President (Yugoslavia);[160] and about Portuguese aggression against Senegal, circulated at the request of the President (Guinea).[161]

The Western case throughout was simply that only the Federal Republic of Germany was entitled to speak on behalf of Germany in international affairs. The German Democratic Republic was, as the U.S. representative vividly put it in 1968, 'nothing more than a proxy for the Government of the Soviet Union'.[162] The East European case was that there were in Germany two separate States, a thesis which won increasing acceptance as Chancellor Brandt successfully pursued his *Ostpolitik*. By the end of 1972, the German Democratic Republic had been admitted to the UN Economic Commission for

Europe, and on 19 September 1973 both German States were admitted to UN Membership.

But even if the problem of circulating communications from the German Democratic Republic has vanished, Rule 6 will continue to provide a basis for UN gamesmanship. Indeed, in March 1970, during the presidency of Colombia, Israel requested the circulation of a speech by Abba Eban about the plight of Soviet Jewry, to which the Soviet Union protested, followed by a defence on the part of Israel and a second Soviet protest.[163] The United States took advantage of its presidency during February 1971 to circulate a note verbale from the Permanent Observer of the Republic of Viet-nam (South);[164] and a letter from the Chargé d'affaires of Bangladesh in Washington to the President of the Council for August 1972 (Belgium) was circulated by the latter.[165] The game is endless, and any number can play.

The general problem of circulating communications eventually caused Secretary-General Waldheim to ask for the guidance of the General Assembly. Israel had requested the Secretary-General to circulate an appeal from 239 Jews in the Soviet Union, asking to be allowed 'to reunite with our people in Israel'. The Soviet Union complained that this was 'a typical slanderous letter' circulated with 'the assistance of pro-Israeli members of the staff . . .' Secretary-General Waldheim then explained the practice which the Secretariat had followed for many years 'in the absence of guidelines on the part of the General Assembly'. Israel then complained that 'certain Member States' were using UN organs and facilities 'as mere instruments of their self-centred policies and propaganda'. Waldheim circulated the communication 'on the basis of long-standing practice', and announced his intention of asking the General Assembly to review the current practice regarding the circulation of communications from Member States and to provide him with guidance.[166] But the General Assembly was not able in 1973 to give Waldheim the guidance for which he had asked and merely took note of a memorandum setting out the existing practice.

CHAPTER 3

THE PEOPLE

> The Venetian ambassador to Rome was spending the night with the Duke of Tuscany, who complained that Venice had sent to his court as ambassador a man who possessed neither judgment nor knowledge nor even an attractive personality. 'I am not surprised,' said the Venetian ambassador, 'we have many fools in Venice.' 'We also have fools,' replied the Duke, 'but we take care not to export them.'

I. SECRETARY-GENERAL

THE responsibilities of the Secretary-General are derived from four main sources: the express and implied provisions of the Charter, the Rules of Procedure of the Security Council (whether the responsibilities are obligatory or discretionary), decisions of the Security Council and other UN organs, and those responsibilities which, by custom and usage, are generally recognized as attaching to the Office of Secretary-General.

The Charter describes the Secretary-General as 'the chief administrative officer' of the United Nations and states that he shall appoint such staff as the Organization may require, under regulations established by the General Assembly. As Secretary-General, he 'shall act in that capacity in all meetings . . . of the Security Council' and other deliberative organs, and shall 'perform such other functions as are entrusted to him by the organs.' As noted in Chapter 2 (pp. 42–3), the Secretary-General is required by the Charter, 'with the consent of the Security Council', to notify the General Assembly at each session of any matters relative to the maintenance of international peace and security which are being dealt with by the Security Council, and also to notify the Assembly (or UN Members, if the Assembly is not in session) immediately the Security Council ceases to deal with such matters. The Secretary-General and the staff shall neither seek nor receive instructions from any government or other authority external to the United Nations, and shall refrain from any action which might reflect on their position as international officials responsible only to the Organization. UN Members, for their part, undertake to respect the exclusively international responsibilities of the Secretary-General and staff, and agree 'not to seek to influence them' in the discharge of their responsibilities (Articles 12(2), 97, 98, 100, and 101(1)).

If that were all that the Charter had to say about the duties of the Secretary-General, there would be no need for much further comment. But Article 99 of the Charter confers on the Secretary-General a right which, although at first sight it may seem only procedural in character, in practice enables the Secretary-General to undertake a wide range of political and diplomatic activities. This famous Article 99 simply declares that the Secretary-General may bring to the attention of the Security Council 'any matter which in his opinion may threaten the maintenance of international peace and security'. If the Secretary-General brings a matter to the attention of the Council under Article 99, the President '*shall* call a meeting . . .' (Rule 3, my italics).

The right to call a meeting under Article 99 has only rarely been expressly invoked. The Security Council met when war broke out in Korea in 1950, and its agenda contained both a U.S. communication and a cablegram from the UN Commission on Korea. Secretary-General Lie later claimed that he had invoked Article 99 on that occasion, although his *arrière-pensée* in this regard was rather flimsily based.[1]

At the time of the Suez invasion in 1956, Secretary-General Hammarskjold told the Security Council that he would have invoked Article 99 had not the United States already taken the initiative.[2] When the invasion of Hungary took place four days later, Hammarskjold asked that it be recorded that the observations he had made when the Council met to consider Suez 'obviously apply also to the present situation'.[3] In the case of the appeal from Laos for a UN force in 1959, Hammarskjold made it clear that he was *not* invoking Article 99, as to have done so would have involved a judgment as to the facts for which he did not have a sufficient basis.[4] When the Congo crisis arose in 1960, however, Hammarskjold considered that there was an actual or potential threat to peace, and he therefore resorted to Article 99.[5]

Secretary-General Thant never expressly resorted to Article 99. He might have done so, but did not, after President Nasser had withdrawn his consent for the continued presence of the UN Emergency Force in 1967. He was invited by Haiti to invoke Article 99 in 1968 after Haiti had complained of 'armed aggression' by the Dominican Republic, but Haiti later asked for the Security Council to be convened in the ordinary way.[6]

The nearest U Thant came to using his powers to tell the Security Council that world peace was threatened came in the summer of 1971, when there was tension between India and Pakistan, which later in the year erupted into war and led to the birth of Bangladesh. But instead of resorting to Article 99, Thant addressed a letter to the President of the Security Council on 20 July, stating his 'reluctant conclusion' that the international community should no longer watch the deterioration of the situation. He was taking the 'unusual step' of reporting to the President of the Security Council 'on a question which has not been inscribed on the Council's agenda'. He stated that he was not in a position to suggest precise courses of action; 'it is for the members of the Council themselves to decide whether . . . consideration should take place formally or informally, in public or in private . . .' His purpose in writing was to provide 'a basis and an opportunity for such discussions to take place and to express my grave concern . . .' Two months later, he stated at a press conference that the situation 'in East Pakistan *vis-à-vis* the adjoining Indian States constitutes a threat to international peace and security'. He referred to his letter of 20 July and expressed his regret that the Security Council had failed to act.[7]

No doubt there were informal consultations in private, but the Security Council did not meet to consider the matter until war had broken out, and then it was rendered impotent by the veto.

The situation in the summer of 1971 was the kind of situation which the drafters of the Charter had had in mind when they decided to include Article 99. When a member of the Council is prepared to call for a meeting of the Council, there is no need to rely on the rights of the Secretary-General under Article 99: but when all members of the Council are inhibited from taking an initiative because of their relationship to one or other of the parties, it is in such situations that Article 99 attains its full importance.[8] There are, however, obvious limitations to the utility of Article 99. 'Nothing could be more divisive and useless', said U Thant in September 1971, 'than for the Secretary-General to bring a situation publicly to the Security Council when there is no practical possibility of the Council agreeing on effective or useful action.'[9]

While Article 99 has only rarely been expressly invoked, it has nonetheless provided successive Secretaries-General with a convenient hold-all to conduct such activities as they have deemed appropriate to their office, even (or perhaps especially) in the absence of the explicit authority of a policy-making body. Under the implicit responsibilities of Article 99, the Secretaries-General have appointed staff, authorized research, made visits, and engaged in diplomatic consultations. If challenged as to his right to undertake action of this kind, a Secretary-General can reply: 'How can I have an authoritative opinion about threats to world peace unless I have my finger on the pulse of world politics? I cannot accomplish this by sitting in an office on the 38th floor at UN Headquarters and simply waiting for the information to flow in. I must have effective means to gather information from the most reliable courses, and to sift and assess the information which reaches me, in order to judge for myself when international peace and security is threatened. I must do this without encroaching on the prerogatives of UN Members or of non-Member States, but the responsibilities under Article 99 are mine alone: I may neither seek nor receive instructions from others.'

Secretary-General Lie made this clear when the Security Council was considering the Ukrainian complaint against Greece in 1946. Lie intervened in the discussion 'to make clear my own position as Secretary-General and the rights of this office under the Charter'.

> . . . I hope the Council will understand that the Secretary-General must reserve his right to make such enquiries or investigations as he

may think necessary, in order to determine whether or not he should consider bringing any aspect of this matter to the attention of the Council under the provisions of the Charter.[10]

Secretary-General Hammarskjold was equally explicit. Addressing a meeting of a committee of the General Assembly in 1960, Hammarskjold asked how the Secretary-General could draw the attention of the Security Council to threats to peace and security if all he had to rely on were 'reports in the Press or from particular Governments'.

[The Secretary-General] had to find out for himself, and that could mean that he had to go himself . . . To deny the Secretary-General the right to such personal fact-finding was, in fact to erase Article 99 from the Charter.

The Secretary-General could not forget 'the responsibilities and needs which flowed from Article 99'.[11]

After Hammarskjold had accepted the invitation of President Bourguiba to visit Tunisia in 1961, he told the Security Council that it was 'obvious' that he could not discharge his responsibilities 'flowing from' Article 99 unless he could, in case of need, make visits in such a way as to be in a position 'to form a personal opinion about the relevant facts' of a situation which might threaten international peace and security.[12] U Thant made a similar point in 1971.[13] No member of the Council challenged the interpretation of the duties of the Secretary-General stated by Lie in 1946, or Hammarskjold in 1960 and 1961, or Thant in 1971.

I come next to those Rules of Procedure which expressly impose obligatory duties, or confer discretionary rights, on the Secretary-General. The obligatory duties, those functions which the Secretary-General 'shall' perform, are as follows:

1. He gives to representatives on the Security Council notices of meetings of the Council and its subsidiary organs (Rule 25);
2. He draws up the Provisional Agenda for each meeting of the Council for the approval of the President (Rule 7) and communicates it to representatives on the Council (Rule 8);
3. He provides the Council with the staff which it requires (Rule 24);

4. He examines and reports on the credentials of representatives (Rule 15);
5. He prepares documents required by the Council (Rule 26);
6. He brings to the attention of representatives communications concerning any matter for the consideration of the Council in accordance with the Charter (Rule 6);
7. If the Council decides that, for a private (closed) meeting, the record shall be kept in a single copy only, this record is kept by the Secretary-General (Rule 51);
8. Each week he communicates to representatives a Summary Statement of matters of which the Council is seized and the stage reached in their consideration (Rule 11);
9. Each year, he should submit to the Council a list of the records and documents which up to that time have been considered confidential (Rule 57), although this requirement is in practice disregarded;
10. He places before representatives on the Council each application for UN Membership (Rule 59).

The third item in the list of the Secretary-General's duties (the provision of staff) has not given rise to as much difficulty as one might have expected. In 1948, Secretary-General Lie decided solely on his own authority to accede to the request of Count Folke Bernadotte, the UN Mediator in the Middle East, to supply fifty armed guards to exercise control functions in connection with the Palestine truce. The Soviet Union considered Lie's action to be 'incorrect and without legal basis', but a senior official of the Secretariat explained that, before acting on Bernadotte's request, Lie had obtained the advice of the UN Legal Department. The Legal Department had advised that the Secretary-General was empowered to meet the request not only under the terms of a resolution of the General Assembly, which had asked the Secretary-General to 'provide the mediator with the necessary staff to assist in carrying out the functions assigned to [him]', but also in fulfilment of his duties as the chief administrative officer of the United Nations.[14]

In 1958, at the time of the Lebanon crisis, Secretary-General Hammarskjold told the Security Council that he intended to 'use all opportunities offered to the Secretary-General, within the limits set by the Charter and towards developing the United Nations effort', by strengthening and enlarging the already existing Observation Group in the Lebanon, even though proposals more or less to that effect had already been vetoed.[15]

At the time of the difficulties in the Dominican Republic in 1965, the Council invited Secretary-General Thant to send a representative to the troubled area for the purpose of reporting to the Council. U Thant informed the Council at another meeting later the same day of the action he was taking, and on a subsequent occasion he assured the Council that the UN staff in the Dominican Republic would be enlarged if that were necessary.[16]

In 1973, Secretary-General Waldheim arranged for Major-General Ensio Siilasvuo to be appointed Commander of the UN Emergency Force in the Middle East by an exchange of letters with the President of the Security Council.[17]

From these and other cases, it would seem that the usual basis for the appointment of special staff is to be found in Articles 97, 98, and 101(1) and (2) of the Charter, Rule 24 of the Rules of Procedure, and specific decisions of the Security Council. There have, nevertheless, been a number of appointments by the Secretary-General the legal basis for which was more ambiguous. In an address delivered in London in 1970, Secretary-General Thant said that some situations are so serious that the Secretary-General may decide that his duty requires him to act without the authority of a deliberative organ and sometimes even without a specific request from the parties. U Thant then gave a number of examples from his own term of office and that of Dag Hammarskjold. In some of the cases mentioned by U Thant, the action taken was the offer of the Secretary-General's good offices, and this may not have required the appointment of special staff. In some of the other cases cited by U Thant, it is difficult to assert categorically that the matters fell within the competence of the Security Council. But U Thant mentioned five cases which involved the appointment of special staff in connection with matters of which the Security Council had been seized.[18]

Special Representative of the Secretary-General in Amman, 1958;[19]

Special Consultant to the Secretary-General for co-ordination of UN Activities in Laos, 1959;[20]

Special Representative of the Secretary-General in the Middle East concerning Humanitarian Questions, 1967;[21]
Personal Representative of the Secretary-General in Jerusalem, 1967;[22]
Personal Representative of the Secretary-General in Bahrain, 1970.[23]

The discretionary rights of the Secretary-General, the functions which under the Rules of Procedure he 'may' perform, are three. He may

1. Authorize a deputy to act in his place at Council meetings (Rule 21);
2. Make oral or written statements to the Council concerning any question under consideration by it (Rule 22);
3. Propose that the Council should meet at a place other than Headquarters (Rule 5).

The Secretary-General is the recipient of credentials (Rules 13–15), of corrections which representatives wish to have made in the verbatim record (Rule 50), and of applications for UN Membership (Rule 58). He 'may be appointed . . . as rapporteur for a specified question' (Rule 23). The *communiqué* of a private meeting of the Council is issued through him (Rule 55), and representatives who have taken part in a private meeting for which only a single copy of the record was made may consult the record in the Secretary-General's office (Rule 56). As noted earlier, the President of the Council is required to call a meeting if the Secretary-General brings a matter to the attention of the Council under Article 99 (Rule 3), and Rule 28, taken verbatim from Article 98 of the Charter, requires the Secretary-General to 'act in that capacity in all meetings of the Security Council'.

There are several places in the Rules of Procedure and the Appendix where reference is made not to the Secretary-General but to the Secretariat. Chapter V (Rules 21–6) is headed 'Secretariat', and Rule 24 provides that the staff required by the Security Council 'shall form part of the Secretariat'. Rule 39 allows the Council to 'invite members of the Secretariat or other persons . . . to supply it with information or to give other assistance . . .' The Appendix to the Rules deals with the procedure for dealing with those communications from private individuals and non-governmental bodies which relate to matters of which the Council is seized. Paragraph B of the Appendix provides that the Secretariat 'shall', on request, give to any representative on the Council a copy of any such communication.

The Secretary-General may ask to make an oral statement in a meeting of the Council by virtue of his responsibilities under the Charter and the Rules of Procedure. A remarkable change in practice in this regard is illustrated in Table 6. The Secretary-General is now an active participant in discussions of the Council, not simply a passive listener. Moreover, the oral interventions of the Secretary-General are not necessarily limited to formal matters, such as expressions of condolence on the death of a distinguished Head of State or the transmission of information from UN field missions. Secretary-General Hammarskjold, in particular, increasingly participated in the discussion in the Council as one expression of his concept of the independent and non-partisan Office of Secretary-General and even as the conscience of the Organization, and he responded in blunt terms to Soviet attacks on his conduct of the UN operation in the Congo.

TABLE 6

No. of substantive oral statements made by the Secretary-General, 1946–70

Period	*No. of meetings*	*No. of substantive oral statements*
1946–50	530	2
1951–5	179	3
1956–60	211	29
1961–5	350	24
1966–70	294	31

The final group of duties entrusted to the Secretary-General are those contained in decisions of the Security Council. Such decisions may or may not specify the Articles of the Charter under which they are taken, but they all represent applications of Article 98, which empowers the Security Council to entrust the Secretary-General with 'functions'.

The number of such resolutions has been growing as the concept of the Office of Secretary-General has developed. In the first ten years of the work of the Security Council, 110 resolutions were adopted, of which only three expressly entrusted functions to the Secretary-General (see Table 7). In the ten-year period 1961–70, the Council adopted 131 resolutions, of which no fewer than 47 expressly entrusted functions to the Secretary-General. The proportion of such resolutions had risen from 2·2 per cent in 1946–50 to 38·9 per cent twenty years later. There is no reason to expect any significant diminution in the period 1971–5, but there has been a tendency in recent years to involve the President of the Security Council as well as the Secretary-General in following up the Council's decisions, and some people have seen in this a deliberate attempt to curtail the authority of the Secretary-General.

TABLE 7

No. of resolutions of the Security Council expressly entrusting functions to the Secretary-General, 1946–70

Period	*No. of resolutions adopted by the Security Council*	*No. of resolutions expressly entrusting functions to the Secretary-General*	*Percentage of Security Council resolutions which entrusted functions to the Secretary-General*
1946–50	89	2	2.2
1951–5	21	1	4·8
1956–60	50	6	12·0
1961–5	59	19	32·2
1966–70	72	28	38·9

Simply to give the figures in Table 7 without further explanation would be to give a misleading impression, however. Many resolutions adopted by the Security Council nowadays simply request the Secretary-General to inform the Council about the implementation of the resolution. This, it could be argued, is a normal responsibility of the Secretary-General, as the chief administrative officer of the Organization, which he would be expected to discharge whether or not the resolution contained a specific request to that effect. Confirmation of such an interpretation is to be found in the numerous reports submitted to the Council by Secretary-General Lie in the period 1946–53, when the requirement to report or take other action was specified by the Council on only three occasions.

This is true, but it is nevertheless a fact that the Council's resolution 113(S/3575) of 4 April 1956 on the Middle East initiated a new era, with a new concept of the role of the

Secretary-General. Previous resolutions had asked Secretary-General Lie 'to act as convenor of the Committee'; 'to advise the Security Council of all reports and petitions received from or relating to strategic areas under trusteeship, and to send copies thereof . . . to the Trusteeship Council . . .'; and 'to provide the United Nations representative for India and Pakistan with such services and facilities as may be necessary . . .' (Table 8, the first three resolutions). These were functions which the Secretary-General would be expected to perform in the normal way.

Resolution 113 of 4 April 1956 was, however, a new departure. On 20 March 1956, the United States had asked for an early meeting of the Council to consider the question of compliance with the Middle East General Armistice Agreements and three unanimous resolutions of the Council. The U.S. letter was circulated the following day, together with a U.S. draft resolution which *inter alia* asked Secretary-General Hammarskjold 'to arrange with the parties for the adoption of any measures which . . . he considers would reduce tensions along the Armistice Demarcation Lines . . .', and to 'report to the Council . . . on the implementation given to this resolution in order to assist the Council in considering what further action may be required'.[24] Six meetings of the Council were held, and all members welcomed the U.S. proposal so long as it was acceptable to the parties. The Soviet delegation considered it appropriate for the Council to invite the Secretary-General to investigate the extent to which the Armistice Agreements and relevant Council resolutions were being carried out, and to explore the possibility of measures to reduce tensions along the Armistice Demarcation Lines.[25] Some minor Soviet amendments were put to the vote and rejected, and the U.S. draft was then adopted unanimously.[26]

This resolution did not entrust the Secretary-General with a precisely defined task. It established a goal consonant with the Charter and previous resolutions of the Council, but allowed Hammarskjold pretty well unlimited discretion as to how the goal was to be realized.

Hammarskjold had earlier warned of the dangers of premature action without the requisite backing. 'It is not a good idea for the Secretary-General to jump up on the stage and try

TABLE 8

Resolutions of the Security Council expressly entrusting functions to the Secretary-General, 1946–73

Date	*Res. no.*	*Doc. no.*	*Appendix 4, item no.*
8 Oct. 1947	35	S/574	26
			Appendix 3, item no.
7 Mar. 1949	70	S/1280	9
30 Mar. 1951	91	S/2017/Rev. 1	12
4 Apr. 1956	113	S/3575	11
4 June	114	S/3605	11
1 Apr. 1960	134	S/4300	39
14 July	143	S/4387	42
22 July	145	S/4405	42
9 Aug.	146	S/4426	42
24 Nov. 1961	169	S/5002	42
11 June 1963	179	S/5331	54
31 July	180	S/5380	55
4 Dec.	182	S/5471	56
4 Mar. 1964	186	S/5575	58
13 Mar.	187	S/5603	58
9 Apr.	188	S/5650	60
9 June	190	S/5761	56
18 June	191	S/5773	56
25 Sept.	194	S/5987	58
30 Dec.	199	S/6129	66
14 May 1965	203	S/6355	68
19 May	204	S/6366/Rev. 1	52
22 May	205	S/6937	68
4 Sept.	209	S/6657	12
6 Sept.	210	S/6662	12
20 Sept.	211	S/6694	12
5 Nov.	215	S/6876	12
23 Nov.	218	S/6953/Rev. 1, as amended	55
14 Oct. 1966	226	S/7539	71
25 Nov.	228	S/7598	11
16 Dec.	232	S/7621/Rev. 1, as amended	57
6 June 1967	233	S/7935	72
7 June	234	S/7940	72
9 June	235	S/7960	72
11 June	236	—	72
14 June	237	S/7969/Rev. 3	72
10 July	239	S/8047	71
15 Nov.	241	—	71
22 Nov.	242	S/8247	72
22 Dec.	244	S/8289	58
25 Jan. 1968	245	—	73
14 Mar.	246	—	73
24 Mar.	248	—	72

TABLE 8—*continued*

Date	*Res. no.*	*Doc. no.*	*Appendix 3, item no.*
27 Apr.	250	S/8563	72
21 May	252	S/8590/Rev. 2	72
29 May	253	S/8601	57
27 Sept.	259	S/8825/Rev. 2	72
20 Mar. 1969	264	S/9100	73
3 July	267	S/9311	72
12 Aug.	269	S/9384	73
15 Sept.	271	S/9445, as amended	72
30 Jan. 1970	276	S/9620/Rev. 1	73
18 Mar.	277	S/9709, as amended	57
23 July	282	S/9882/Rev. 2	56
29 July	283	S/9891	73
29 July	284	S/9892	73
15 July 1971	294	S/10266	52
25 Sept.	298	S/10337 and S/10338/Add. 1	72
20 Oct.	301	S/10372/Rev. 1	73
24 Nov.	302	S/10395, as amended	52
21 Dec.	307	S/10465	84
4 Feb. 1972	309	S/10376/Rev. 2	87
4 Feb.	310	S/10608/Rev. 1	87
4 Feb.	312	S/10607/Rev. 1	87
28 Feb.	314	S/10541/Rev. 1 and Corr. 1, as amended	57
21 July	317	S/10742	72
28 July	318	S/10747	57
1 Aug.	319	S/10750, as amended	73
22 Nov.	322	S/10838/Rev. 1	55
6 Dec.	323	S/10846, as amended	73
10 Mar. 1973	329	S/10899/Rev. 1	78
20 Apr.	331	S/19108	72
23 Oct.	339	S/11039	72
25 Oct.	340	S/11046/Rev. 1	72
11 Dec.	342	S/11152/Rev. 1	58
15 Dec.	344	S/11156	72

to assume a role unless and until he is called for.' After the Council's decision, however, he was careful to insist that it neither detracted from nor added to the authority of the Secretary-General under the Charter. And the next day he explained:

. . . I felt that I should not hesitate to assume the responsibilities which the Council wished to put on the office of Secretary-General.

Of course, I would not take that stand unless I felt that something . . . useful could be done.[27]

Two days later, there were seven Arab guerrilla attacks on the road between Tel Aviv and Beersheba. General Burns, Chief of Staff of the Truce Supervision Organization, considered that a large-scale guerrilla outbreak had begun. The next day, Sunday, Hammarskjold was in Rome en route to the Middle East and he copied into his diary some words from Meister Eckhart:

> There is a contingent and non-essential will: and there is, providential and creative, an habitual will. God has never given Himself, and never will, to a will alien to His own: where He finds His will, He gives Himself.[28]

Early in May, in pursuance of the Council's request, Hammarskjold issued a three-page letter and a thirty-six-page report with ten pages of documentation. No effort to secure compliance with the Armistice regime, he wrote, would be fruitful or lasting unless it was firmly anchored in a reaffirmation of the cease-fire. Each violation of the cease-fire, however minor, had triggered off a chain of actions and reactions. Infringement of one article of the Armistice Agreements did not justify retaliatory infringement of the cease-fire itself. A tendency had developed to regard the UN truce observers merely as impartial investigators of the facts *after* the receipt of complaints. But the observers should also be able to operate in such a way as to *deter* violations, and for this they needed freedom of movement. The parties had agreed to this extension of the functions of UN observers as well as to certain local arrangements, such as the marking of demarcation lines and international frontiers by the erection of physical obstacles.

All the parties had given unconditional assurances of their intention to observe the cease-fire, restricted only by the right to act in self-defence as recognized in Article 51 of the Charter. In the event of non-compliance by one party, leading another party to invoke Article 51, 'the Security Council alone can decide whether this is the case or not'. Self-defence, wrote Hammarskjold, is 'under the sole jurisdiction of the Security Council . . .' It may be remarked that this was to give a strict interpretation to the provisions of Article 51.

Hammarskjold dealt at some length with what he called 'the time sequence between various steps in the direction of full compliance . . .' He stated that he had discussed this with the parties, and he reported on this in his distinctive style, which was to become increasingly convoluted.

This problem cannot be solved by any explicit agreements with any two parties because it is essentially a question of co-ordinated unilateral moves inspired by greater confidence in the possibility of a peaceful development, each of them provoked by and, maybe, provoking similar unilateral moves on the other side. In these circumstances I find it impossible to put on record any specific results of the discussions . . . Once the cease-fire has proved effective, and as the stands of all sides have been clarified, the road should be open for the achievement of full implementation by related unilateral moves.

He reported that he had devoted all his attention to his mandate and had left aside those other fundamental issues that so deeply influenced the situation in the Middle East. When questions outside his mandate had arisen, such as Israel's complaint of Egyptian interference with Israel's shipping through the Suez Canal or the Arab complaint that Israel was planning to divert the Jordan River, he had appealed for full respect for the cease-fire and the Armistice regime, as well as for past decisions of the Security Council. Compliance with previous agreements 'represents a stage which has to be passed through in order to make progress possible on the main issues . . .' A solution should not be imposed from outside. Co-operation should be fostered and encouraged which 'facilitates for the Governments concerned the taking unilaterally of steps to increase confidence and to demonstrate their wish for peaceful conditions'.[29]

On 4 June the Council commended the Secretary-General and the parties, and asked the Secretary-General 'to continue his good offices . . .'[30]

The broad mandate given to Hammarskjold in 1956 was the first of a series asking the Secretary-General to use his discretion in seeking the fulfilment of the purposes and principles of the Charter and previous decisions of the Council. So far has this practice been carried that almost any resolution of the Council which asks for action, whether the resolution be of a binding nature or not, includes as a matter of course a request to the Secretary-General to report on implementation.

To make such a request is usually superfluous: the Secretary-General would report in the normal course of events. It would be preferable to include a specific request addressed to the Secretary-General only if there were something out of the ordinary in the Security Council's wishes—a desire to have a report by a specific date (such as resolution 310 on Namibia, calling for a report by 31 July 1972) or a request that the Secretary-General should consult a specified person before acting (such as resolutions 294, 295, 298, and 302, all adopted during 1971, which called for joint action by the Secretary-General and the President of the Security Council), or a resolution expressly conferring unusual discretionary powers on the Secretary-General (such as resolution 169 on the Congo, adopted in 1961, which authorized Secretary-General Thant 'to take vigorous action, including the use of the requisite measure of force, if necessary, for the immediate apprehension, detention pending legal action and/or deportation of all foreign military and para-military personnel and political advisers . . . and mercenaries . . .').

The evolution in the United Nations by which broad responsibilities were conferred on the Secretary-General, by implication under Article 98 of the Charter, was not universally welcomed. The Soviet Union has always conceived of the Secretary-General as being only the chief of administration in the Secretariat, under the strict control of policy-making organs and the Security Council in particular. It was on this issue that the Soviet bloc broke with Lie and Hammarskjold. The clash between a dynamic concept of the role of the Secretary-General, of which Hammarskjold was a charismatic exponent, and the more passive and restricted role favoured by the Soviet Union, found expression in the differences of view about the control of UN peace-keeping. To some extent the sharpest divergencies have mellowed since the October war in the Middle East. The Soviet Union has supplied personnel for the UN Truce Supervision Organization, and a Polish contingent of 800 men is serving in the UN Emergency Force. The Security Council has evolved practical modalities for handling peace-keeping, but the Soviet Union has not abandoned its concept of the Secretary-General as an administrator.

The Secretary-General has implied powers arising from

Article 33(1), which lists means which may be used to achieve the peaceful settlement of disputes. Among the means are 'other peaceful means of their own choice', and, as noted above, States are free to request the Secretary-General to use his good offices with a view to seeking a solution.[31] He may also initiate humanitarian activities as a means of probing the opportunities for peace-making, as did Thant in connection with the Nigerian civil war and Waldheim in connection with the war on the South Asia sub-continent which led to the emergence of Bangladesh.[32]

The Secretary-General also exercises considerable indirect influence by reason of the fact that he supplies documentation for UN organs and, through the person of the Legal Counsel, issues legal opinions, some of which are reprinted in the *Juridical Yearbook*.

The totality of the functions of the Secretary-General under the Charter, under the Rules of Procedure, and under decisions of the deliberative organs, has given rise to the concept of the Office of the Secretary-General—not his material office on the 38th floor of the Secretariat building at UN Headquarters, but the sum of the multifarious responsibilities attaching to the position of Secretary-General. All four Secretaries-General have used this concept as a basis for attitudes and actions which have been within the competence of the United Nations; but it was Hammarskjold in particular who developed a distinctive style for the Secretary-General.

> By his style and demeanour, more than by any single thing he actually did, Hammarskjold projected the sense that the United Nations was extremely important.[33]

Indeed, the displeasure of the Soviet Union with Lie and Hammarskjold probably arose as much from the general attitudes of the two men as from particular actions. The 1960–1 *troika* proposal for a three-man board at the head of the UN Secretariat, rather than a single Secretary-General, would have had the effect of stripping the office of a certain mystique and would have turned the Secretary-General into what U Thant was later to call 'a glorified clerk'. When the question of Thant's reappointment arose in 1966, he made no secret of the fact that he had experienced 'increasing restrictions' on what he considered to be 'legitimate prerogatives of the Secretary-General'.[34] Indeed, it was widely believed that Thant had reluctantly agreed to a second term only after he had received assurances, perhaps muted, that the members of the Security Council would accord full respect to the office of Secretary-General as it had evolved during the previous twenty years. This, at any rate, would help to explain Thant's insistence on including in his statement of acceptance the words

> He notes with particular appreciation that, for its part, the Security Council respects his position in bringing to the notice of the Organization basic issues confronting it, and disturbing developments in many parts of the world.[35]

It would be tedious to iterate in detail here the difficulties which developed between both Lie and Hammarskjold and the Soviet Bloc in the latter part of their periods in office, but it should be noted that U Thant also encountered difficulties with Member States, even though relationships never erupted into open conflict. Indeed, Thant's problems were as much with the United States as with the Soviet Union, arising in the main from his attitude to U.S. military involvement in South-East Asia, and in particular his remark at a press conference early in 1965, before the major escalation of the war: 'I am sure that the great American people, if only they know the true facts and the background to the development in South Viet-Nam, will agree with me that further bloodshed is unnecessary . . .'[36]

Nevertheless, the Soviet Union was constantly wary to see that U Thant did not interpret his powers too freely. Not surprisingly, the Soviet Union insisted that the dispatch of UN observers to the Yemen in 1963 was not simply a matter to be settled by the parties and the Secretary-General, even although no UN funds were needed; express authorization by the Security Council was also required.[37] During the war between India and Pakistan in 1965, the Soviet Union twice asserted that U Thant's actions in strengthening UN observation procedures were 'at variance with the Charter.'[38] When U Thant appointed a Special Representative to help eliminate tension between Cambodia and Thailand in 1966, the Soviet Union made a point of emphasizing that decisions regarding international peace and security 'are taken by the Security Council.'[39] In 1969, when U Thant designated a personal representative to help resolve differences between Equatorial Guinea and Spain, he informed the President of the Council for the month (Hungary) of the action he was taking. The President thereupon sent a communication to all members of the Council 'to inform [them of] the content of our consultation . . .' Thant at once informed the President that there had been no consultation 'in any sense.' 'It was not my purpose . . . to establish any precedent of prior consultation.' The Soviet Union then addressed a letter to Thant reiterating its view that only the Security Council can decide on matters relating to international peace and security. The Soviet Union insisted that this was a 'position of principle . . .'[40]

U Thant found himself at loggerheads with other Member States. On 9 April 1966, the Security Council adopted a resolution calling upon Portugal not to permit oil for Rhodesia to be landed at Beira in Mozambique.[41] Portugal submitted a long letter to the Secretary-General expressing 'certain reservations' about the Council's decision.

First, no facts had been established as a basis for the Council's decision, much less proved. As the resolution dealt with possible future events, Portugal considered that it could only be a recommendation 'for general guidance' and not mandatory. Secondly, two permanent members had abstained on the vote so that in Portugal's view the strict requirements of Article 27(3) of the Charter had not been fulfilled. Portugal acknowledged that the jurisprudence of the Council had been to regard the abstention of a permanent member as not equivalent to a veto, but that doctrine had been advanced to deal with matters not involving Chapter VII of the Charter and when the Council had had only eleven members. With a Council of fifteen, all the permanent members could abstain on a proposal and yet the resolution could still be adopted. Was it really the case that the Security Council could decide to use force under Chapter VII even with all five permanent members abstaining? Thirdly, the Council's resolution constituted a clear denial of the freedom of the seas, and Portugal believed that 'the Security Council cannot legislate against international law . . .' Finally, Britain had always claimed that Rhodesia was within the exclusive jurisdiction of the United Kingdom; by what means, asked Portugal, had the matter been brought within the international jurisdiction of the Security Council? The letter concluded by asking the Secretary-General 'as a matter of urgency' for the comments of the UN Office of Legal Affairs.[42]

Three of the four matters in the Portuguese letter were no doubt useful debating points; only the second, about 'voluntary' abstentions in the enlarged Council, raised a new issue of interest and importance. The practice of not regarding a voluntary abstention by a permanent member as a veto was in apparent contradiction with the Charter, but had evolved in the early years when the Council had eleven members, when no decision could be reached without at least one permanent member casting an affirmative vote. With the Council enlarged to fifteen members, a decision could be taken without any of the permanent members voting affirmatively—as, indeed, happened in December 1973 on a resolution relating to the Middle East peace conference. But the practice of the Council had not changed after 1965, and the International Court of Justice was in 1971 to give its imprimatur to the Council's consistent and uniform practice which had 'continued unchanged' after the amendment to the Charter had entered into force in 1965.[43]

Be that as it may, it was almost two months before the Secretary-General replied to the Portuguese letter, and then it was to inform Portugal of his regretful conclusion that it was not appropriate for the Secretariat to respond in substance to a request regarding the validity and interpretations of decisions of principal organs. The Office of Legal Affairs could give legal advice, but only at the request of a UN organ. In the case under consideration, 'only the Security Council is in a position to give an authoritative interpretation . . .'[44]

Shortly afterwards, South Africa gave Portugal (and the illegal regime in Rhodesia) a verbal helping hand by reserving its own position regarding the validity of the Security Council's resolution.[45]

Portugal's next communication was addressed to the President of the Security Council rather than the Secretary-General. It began by asking formally that the Security Council should submit to the Secretary-General the Portuguese reservations, and that the Council should invite the views of the Secretary-

General 'through the Office of Legal Affairs'. But in the four-month interval since the Council's resolution on Rhodesia, some legal eagles in the Portuguese Foreign Ministry had evidently done some further study, and Portugal was able to submit a couple of new matters for consideration.

According to Portugal's letter, when the Security Council took its decision in April, it had dealt with the matter of Rhodesia in the light of Chapter VII of the Charter and had decided ('although the resolution approved is not explicit on this point') that it was acting under Article 42, which authorizes the use of military force under defined circumstances. Article 42, taken in conjunction with Article 43, undoubtedly authorizes the Security Council to take forcible measures, but nowhere does the Charter empower the Council to hand over its responsibilities to a Member State. The Council's decision to entrust the execution of certain measures to British naval forces 'without the relinquishment . . . of their national status' appeared to Portugal to be a violation of the Charter. The question might well arise in the future: 'To what authority can recourse be had by the victim or victims of such enforcement measures as the United Kingdom Command may decide to apply or institute?' In such an event, the Security Council might even refuse to give the aggrieved party a hearing. 'The Portuguese Government therefore asks whether it is the understanding of the Security Council that the Charter authorizes national forces involved in a dispute* to take enforcement action against third parties who have no means of recourse to or legal defence before independent bodies.'

The Portuguese letter concluded by referring to Article 50 of the Charter, which provides that a State which finds itself confronted with special economic problems arising from carrying out preventive or enforcement measures authorized by the Security Council 'shall have the right to consult the Security Council with regard to a solution of those problems'. Grave damage was being done to the economy of the province of Mozambique; Portugal wished to inquire 'whether the application of Article 50 of the Charter is contemplated . . .'

* Was not Portugal's acknowledgment of the existence of a dispute a partial answer to her earlier query as to how and why the Rhodesian question had become a matter of international concern?

After the adoption by the Council of a more extensive mandatory resolution on Rhodesia in December 1966, Portugal reiterated its queries and coolly added a note to the effect that, as a result of the Security Council's sanctions policy, the financial and economic losses in Mozambique had amounted to $17 million up to the end of 1967.[46]

In 1973, Portugal resumed its contest, this time with Secretary-General Waldheim. Portugal complained that the activities of the UN Office of Public Information were 'one-sided and partisan' when dealing with 'Portuguese Overseas Provinces.'[47] South Africa added its voice by complaining that UN publications were biased.[48]

These exchanges did not amount to an open break between the Secretary-General and Portugal, and Thant and Waldheim were able to act (or, when necessary, refrain from action) with the knowledge that they had the support of virtually all UN Members, while Portugal (and South Africa) were causing widespread indignation by permitting if not encouraging violations of the supposedly mandatory sanctions resolutions of the Security Council. Moreover, while Portugal could defy the sanctions policy, she had nothing to gain from making the issue the occasion of an open breach with the person of the Secretary-General.

A different situation prevailed in the period 1967–8, when a deadlock developed regarding investigations of human rights in the Middle East.[49] On 14 June 1967, the Security Council had adopted by unanimous vote a resolution calling upon Israel to ensure the safety, welfare, and security of the inhabitants of areas where military operations had taken place and to facilitate the return of those inhabitants who had fled; recommending that 'the Governments concerned' should scrupulously respect the humanitarian principles in the Geneva (Red Cross) Conventions of 1949; and asking the Secretary-General 'to follow the effective implementation of this resolution . . .' Resolutions in similar terms were adopted by the General Assembly and the Commission on Human Rights.[50]

On 6 July 1967, Secretary-General Thant appointed Nils-Göran Gussing as his Special Representative to obtain the first-hand information which he required under the resolutions of the Security Council and the General Assembly. An interim report based in part on information supplied by Mr. Gussing was issued on 18 August and a final report on 2 October 1967.[51] Between 26 February and 30 July 1968, there took place a lengthy exchange of communications between Secretary-General Thant and the governments of Israel and the neighbouring Arab States about a further humanitarian mission. The essence of the correspondence, which occupies some thirty pages of mostly small-type text in the Official Records of the Security Council, was quite simple. Israel was not prepared to allow further first-hand UN observation of Arabs under the administration of Israel, even for humanitarian purposes, unless there could at the same time be first-hand UN observation of Jews in all the Arab States in the area of conflict, also for humanitarian purposes. A brief legal analysis prepared by the UN Secretariat gave some support to Israel's position by indicating that, under a strictly legal interpretation, the resolution of the Security Council dealt only with territories occupied by Israel since June 1967; the resolution of the Council and other relevant resolutions 'do not apply to minorities in the territories of even those States most directly concerned'. The Gussing Mission, 'on a broad and humanitarian interpretation, which admittedly was tenuous', had earlier made inquiries about Jewish minorities in Syria and Egypt. 'There is no legal basis on which this precedent could be extended to Iraq and Lebanon or any other Arab State . . .'

Syria, Jordan, and Egypt stated that they were ready to receive and co-operate with a new humanitarian mission, but they rejected as *ultra vires* Israel's attempt to extend the scope of the mission. Israel refused to budge, and Secretary-General Thant reported his 'inescapable' conclusion that there was no basis on which the mission could proceed. This was regrettable, he wrote, since the obstacles to the dispatch of the mission 'could be easily surmounted . . .' It was, in Thant's view, most unfortunate that considerations involving the well-being of a great many people could not be given sufficient priority to override the obstacles which had been encountered.[52]

It was widely assumed at the time that Thant was exasperated with Israel for her obstinacy in the matter. That may indeed have been the case, but the published documents do not identify the party which was creating obstacles or refusing to consider the well-being of a great many people. It could be that the expression 'a great many people' was deliberately chosen to suggest that the victims of the deadlock were the Arabs in the territories occupied by Israel, and that, if Thant had been referring to the much less sizeable Jewish minorities in the Arab States, he would have chosen different words.

But at the time the correspondence was taking place, it was becoming evident that Israel did not intend any early withdrawal from territories occupied in 1967. As Israel's relative isolation in the UN context was becoming more apparent, Thant was perhaps sharing in a general irritation with Israel's obduracy, which was to become increasingly evident in the deliberative organs of the United Nations between 1967 and 1973.

Secretary-General Waldheim was not to be free of difficulties. The Soviet Union alleged that there had been bias in a press release of the Office of Public Information, and that 'a typical slanderous letter' from Israel had been circulated as a UN document, with 'the assistance of pro-Israeli members of the staff . . .' Waldheim denied the Soviet charges of intentional misrepresentation or bias, but reported his intention of convening the Consultative Panel on Public Information at an early date.[53]

2. PRESIDENT

The Charter allows the Security Council freedom to decide on the method of selecting its President (Article 30). The first draft of the rules of procedure provided for the rotation of the presidency in *French* alphabetical order, as had been the practice in the Council of the League of Nations.[54] The Executive Committee of the Preparatory Commission changed this so that the presidency would rotate on a monthly basis in the *English* alphabetical order of the names of the Council's members. The French delegation, not surprisingly, had reservations about this proposal, giving as the reason the fact that it would result in three of the permanent members of the Council serving in succession. France suggested that this difficulty could be avoided if the French alphabetical order were used; alternatively, the order might be determined by drawing lots.[55] The recommendation of the Executive Committee was, however, approved by the Preparatory Commission and later by the Council itself (Rule 18).[56]

The Executive Committee of the Preparatory Commission suggested that, at the Council's first meeting, the representative of the first member of the Council in the English alphabetical order should act as temporary chairman.[57] Accordingly, when the Council met for the first time on 17 January 1946, Norman Makin of Australia acted as temporary chairman. After a provisional rule regarding the presidency had been approved, Australia assumed the presidential chair, holding office until 16 February.[58]

After eleven months, all members of the Council had served a one-month term as President. Australia then suggested, and the Council agreed (the United States and the Soviet Union abstaining) to extend the term of office of the United States from 17 December until 31 December 1946, so that thereafter the term of office would correspond to a calendar month. This was done because the General Assembly had decided that the term of non-permanent members of the Council should begin on 1 January. If the change had not been made, a situation would have arisen in which a State might cease being a member of the Council during the term of its presidency.[59]

The presidency attaches to a Member State and not to the individual representative accredited to the Council.[60] The draft rules submitted by the Preparatory Commission contained no procedure for the temporary replacement of the President in case of absence or illness, and in practice no difficulty has arisen on this score.

The Rules of Procedure allow the President the discretion to cede the presidential chair to the member next in English alphabetical order whenever he 'deems that for the proper fulfilment of the responsibilities of the presidency he should not preside over the Council during consideration of a particular question with which the member he represents is directly connected . . .' (Rule 20).

Cases where Rule 20 has been raised are given in Table 9. Of the cases in group A, the only one calling for comment is the second: it was India which first drew attention to Rule 20, not the President himself (Nationalist China). On a number of other occasions it was suggested that the representative of

Nationalist China could not suitably act as President, but proposals to suspend Rule 18 or to change the presidency were not adopted.[61]

In the first of the two cases listed in Table 9B, the Council had already held a six-hour meeting under the presidency of the United States during which the Soviet representative had displayed some annoyance at the way the proceedings were being

TABLE 9

Cession of the presidency under Rule 20, 1946–1968

A. *Cases where the presidency was ceded for one or more meetings*

Date	*SCOR meeting and page or paragraph no.*	*Matter under consideration*	*Member ceding the presidency*
4 Oct. 1948	361, 1–2	The situation in Berlin	United States
10 Jan. 1950 12 Jan.	459, 8 460, 1–2	Representation of China	Nationalist China
1 Mar. 1951	533, 2	The India–Pakistan question	India
21 Jan. 1954	655, 37	The Palestine question	Lebanon
29 May 1968	1428, 2–4	The situation in Southern Rhodesia	United Kingdom

B. *Cases where the presidency was not ceded*

			Member declining to cede the presidency
29 Apr. 1958	814, 2–15	'Urgent measures to put an end to flights by United States military aircraft with atomic and hydrogen bombs in the direction of the frontiers of the Soviet Union'	United States
7 Dec. 1960	912, 3–122	The Congo question	Soviet Union

conducted. At the next meeting, the Soviet Union asked if the President intended to cede the chair, adding that his question was 'prompted by the fact that at the last meeting of the Council it was sometimes difficult to tell where the statements of the United States representative ended and those of the President of the Council began'. Several members said that the United States had conducted the previous meeting with complete propriety.* The United States representative, Henry Cabot Lodge, a former Senator (see pp. 127–8), suggested

* France, no doubt recalling the length of the meeting, pointed out that forced labour was within the competence of the Economic and Social Council rather than of the Security Council.

that the spirit of Rule 20 was to be found in the practice of those national parliamentary bodies in which a member disqualifies himself if the matter being considered involves his personal interests. As the Soviet complaint did not involve the selfish national interests of the United States, 'the present occupant of the Chair does not consider that he should vacate it'. The Soviet representative accepted the President's decision, but pointed out that Rule 20 contains 'not a single word . . . about the selfish national interest of any State.'[62]

In the second case listed in Table 9B, the Soviet Union had requested the meeting in a strong statement which attacked Secretary-General Hammarskjold, the UN operation in the Congo, and the United States. When the meeting convened under the presidency of the Soviet Union, the United States suggested that the Soviet representative was 'likely to be too prejudiced to fulfil properly [the] responsibilities as President in this case'. There followed a three-hour procedural debate in which several different questions became inextricably entangled: whether or not the President should cede the chair under Rule 20; whether discussion of the applicability of Rule 20 should precede or follow the adoption of the agenda; whether or not it was appropriate for the Council to list in the agenda a document which was described by France and other members as violent and extremist in tone; and how the agenda should be worded. An amended agenda was finally approved, after which the Soviet representative reminded the Council that France had presided during discussion of the Suez invasion in 1956. If he were to cede the presidency, it would devolve on the United Kingdom: 'could any member of the Security Council assert that the United Kingdom representative is less an interested party in the discussion of the question of the Congo than the Soviet representative—or than any other representative in this chamber?' He concluded by stating firmly that he had no intention of ceding the presidency. The representative of France intervened to say that France had had 'sincere doubts' about presiding during the 1956 Suez debates, but 'nobody had raised any objection or expressed any doubt'. It only remained for the Council to set the time for the next meeting.[63]

The comment of the United States about Soviet handling of the presidency in April 1958 draws attention to the important fact that the President performs a dual role. He is both the representative of a Member State and the presiding officer of the Council; indeed, he also represents the Council in its capacity as an organ of the United Nations, although always 'under the authority of the Security Council' (Rule 19). But the dual role of the President means that, whenever he speaks at Council meetings, he speaks as President, unless he expressly prefaces his remarks with words to the effect that he is speaking as the representative of Afghanistan, say, or Zambia.

Considering all the circumstances, it is surprising that this practice so rarely leads to difficulty—although the United States was once driven to remark:

> I believe that Mr Malik's reply was perhaps, at least in part, given as the representative of the USSR rather than as President, but I rather suspect that the President of the Security Council would agree with the representative of the USSR . . .[64]

The President represents the Council in its capacity as an organ of the United Nations, and the procedure for the devolution of the presidential chair in particular circumstances does not affect the representative capacity of the President (Rules 19 and 20). The Executive Committee of the Preparatory Commission stated that the provision that the President should represent the Council in its corporate capacity was 'intended to give him the requisite authority to nominate committees and to conclude agreements on behalf of the Council'.[65] In practice, the part of Rule 19 which declares that the President 'shall represent [the Security Council] in its capacity as an organ of the United Nations' has provided a basis for the President to appeal to the parties in situations of tension or conflict to exercise restraint. It has also enabled the President to submit draft resolutions or decisions, or to make oral statements of consensus or summaries.[66]

If the President of the Council, advised by the Council's Secretary, is not adequate to the task, difficulties are almost certain to ensue. The President, to quote Dr. Prandler, needs 'preparedness, authority and tactical sense'.[67] His duties are stated as follows in the Rules of Procedure:

1. He shall call a meeting of the Council, in circumstances which are set out in section 1 of Chapter 2 of this book (Rules 1–3);

2. He shall approve the provisional agenda for each meeting, which is drawn up by the Secretary-General (the President continues to discharge this duty even when he has ceded the presidency under Rule 20) (Rules 7 and 20);
3. He shall preside over meetings of the Council (Rule 19);
4. He shall call upon representatives in the order in which they signify their desire to speak (Rule 27);
5. He shall immediately state his ruling if a representative raises a point of order, and if the ruling is challenged, he shall submit the matter to the Council for immediate decision (Rule 30);
6. If two or more amendments to a motion or draft resolution are proposed, he shall rule on the order in which they are to be voted upon (Rule 36);*
7. The Rules note that he shall sign the verbatim record of a meeting of the Council once it has been corrected in accordance with the procedure laid down in Rules 49–51, after which it shall become the official record of the Secutity Council (Rule 53), though the practice of signing the record was discontinued after the first few meetings;
8. He shall, unless the Security Council decides otherwise, refer each application for UN Membership to a committee upon which each member of the Security Council is represented (Rule 59).

The Rules of Procedure specify four matters on which the President acts to some extent on his own discretion:

1. He calls ordinary meetings of the Council 'at any time he deems necessary . . .' (Rule 1);
2. He cedes the presidency whenever he deems that he should not preside during the consideration of a particular question with which the member he represents is directly connected (Rule 20);
3. He 'may accord precedence [in debate] to any rapporteur appointed by the Security Council' (Rule 29);
4. If the President is of the opinion that corrections submitted to the verbatim records are sufficiently important to be referred to representatives on the Council, this is done before the verbatim records are approved (Rule 52).

There are other procedural functions which the President performs even though these are not specified in the Rules of Procedure. The President declares the opening and closing of

* The application of this Rule is reviewed on pp. 192–5.

each meeting, puts the question, announces decisions, and in general is responsible for the maintenance of order and the observance of the Rules of Procedure. Sometimes, when consideration of a matter has been completed, the President declares that the Council remains seized of the item.[68] The President has no specific authority to call a speaker to order if his remarks are irrelevant, but it is open to any representative to raise such a matter as a point of order, and the President is then required to give a ruling. If consideration of a matter is not completed during a meeting, it is often left to the President to consult other members of the Council with a view to fixing the next meeting at a time convenient to the Council as a whole.

Under the terms of a resolution of the Security Council adopted in 1950, which was itself based on a recommendation of the General Assembly of the previous year, the Council decided that 'should an appropriate occasion arise', it would 'base its action upon the principles' contained in the recommendation of the General Assembly. This recommendation, which empowers the President to undertake conciliation, read as follows:

After a situation or dispute has been brought to the attention of representatives on the Security Council in accordance with rule 6 of the provisional rules of procedure of the Security Council [which provides that the Secretary-General shall immediately bring to the attention of representatives certain communications concerning matters for the consideration of the Council] and not later than immediately after the opening statements on behalf of the parties concerned,

(a) The parties shall be invited to meet with the President of the Security Council;

(b) They shall attempt to agree upon a representative on the Security Council to act as rapporteur or conciliator for the case. The representative so agreed upon may be the President or any other representative of the Council who will thereupon be appointed by the President to undertake the function of rapporteur or conciliator. The President shall inform the Security Council whether a rapporteur or conciliator has been appointed;

(c) If a rapporteur or conciliator is appointed, it would be desirable for the Security Council to abstain from further action on the case for a reasonable interval during which actual efforts at conciliation are in progress;

(d) The rapporteur or conciliator so agreed upon and appointed shall attempt to conciliate the situation or dispute, and shall in due course report to the Security Council.[69]

Other tasks have from time to time been laid on the President by decision of the Council: to obtain information; [70] to designate members of a subsidiary organ; [71] to confer with the Secretary-General; [73] to appeal to the parties to a conflict to exercise restraint or respect decisions of the Council; [73] to meet with the parties with a view to easing the tension; [74] to undertake informal consultations; [75] or to follow the implementation of resolutions or decisions of the Council.[76]

On three occasions in 1948, the President felt able to take a diplomatic initiative without consulting the Council in a formal meeting. In January 1948, the President (Belgium) sent identical communications to the Governments of India and Pakistan in connection with the situation in Jammu and Kashmir, appealing to the two States 'to refrain from any step incompatible with the Charter and liable to result in an aggravation of the situation . . .'[77]

On 1 April 1948, the Council adopted a resolution calling on the Jewish Agency for Palestine and the Arab Higher Committee 'to make representatives available to the Security Council for the purpose of arranging a truce . . .' When the Council met two weeks later, the President (Colombia) addressed the Council as follows:

> . . . the President was instructed to discuss the possible terms of the truce with the accredited representatives of the two parties. I met with them on two occasions, as I have already informed the Security Council at our informal meetings.

The President, in his capacity as representative of Colombia, then introduced a draft resolution pointing out that his proposal was 'the result of the conversations with other members of the Security Council . . .' After amendment, the draft resolution was adopted.[78]

In connection with the Berlin question in 1948, after the Soviet veto of a six-power proposal, the President of the Council (Argentina), 'in the exercise of his powers', established a Technical Committee on Berlin Currency and Trade from experts nominated by neutral members of the Council. The President for the following month (Belgium) extended the life of the Committee (Table 26(c), footnote on p. 283).[79]

These three instances of diplomatic initiative by the President date from 1948. Shortly after this, the role of the Council began to diminish as new functions were assumed by the General Assembly or entrusted to the Secretary-General. By 1959, the Council had so little business that it met only five times during the year (the average number of meetings a year since 1946 has been 63) and adopted only one resolution—and the legality of the proceedings in that one case was challenged by one of the permanent members.[80] Since its enlargement in 1966, however, the Council has gradually resumed its role as an important principal organ; but in present circumstances, the President would be likely to seek the Council's authority before taking any formal initiative along the lines taken by the Presidents in 1948.

Probably the most substantial mandate conferred on the Council's President occurred in 1957 in connection with the India-Pakistan question. A four-power draft resolution was introduced which would have asked the President of the Council, Ambassador Gunnar Jarring of Sweden, to visit India and Pakistan to examine with the two Governments proposals likely to contribute towards the settlement of their dispute. The Soviet Union sought to amend the proposal so as to eliminate from it parts unacceptable to India (including, in particular, references to a proposal made by Pakistan 'for the use of a temporary United Nations force' in connection with demilitarization). The proposed amendment was rejected, and the Soviet Union therefore vetoed the main proposal.[81] A new draft resolution was then introduced which omitted the parts unacceptable to India, and this was approved (the Soviet Union abstaining). Ambassador Jarring, in accepting the mission entrusted to him, made it clear that his acceptance was based on the express understanding that the parties were willing to co-operate with him. The result of the mission would largely depend upon the extent of the co-operation he would receive.

In the event, the extent of co-operation from the parties was insufficient, and Jarring reported to the Council in writing that although 'both parties are still desirous of finding a solution . . .', he was unable to suggest 'any concrete proposals which . . . are likely to contribute towards a settlement . . .'[82]

Five months were to elapse before the Council resumed its consideration of the India–Pakistan question. The debate was then characterized by marathon speeches by representatives of the two parties, but members of the Council vied with each other in showering praise on Mr. Jarring—'. . . debt of gratitude . . . cogent and perceptive analysis' (Australia); '. . . deep appreciation for his excellent performance of a very difficult mission . . .' (Nationalist China); '. . . skilful handling of the difficult mission . . .' (Cuba); '. . . warm tribute . . . unanimous in their congratulations and their praise . . .' (France); '. . . congratulate Mr. Jarring on the efficient way in which he has executed the mission . . .' (Iraq); '. . . wise and conscientious manner . . . tactful and objective . . . consummate skill . . .' (Philippines); '. . . deep appreciation for the able and conscientious way . . .' (United Kingdom); '. . . delicate and important task . . . appreciation . . . for the outstanding manner . . .' (United States).[83]

It was partly because Ambassador Jarring had shown such outstanding skill over the India–Pakistan question in 1957 that ten years later he was asked to 'promote agreement' over the even more intractable problems of the Middle East—a task which Jarring again discharged with courage and integrity.

3. PERMANENT MEMBERS

The Security Council has five permanent members: 'The Republic of China, France, the Union of Soviet Socialist Republics, The United Kingdom of Great Britain and Northern Ireland, and the United States of America . . .' (Article 23(1)). These five States have continuous membership of both the Security Council and the Military Staff Committee (Article 47(2)), and also the right to veto substantive decisions of the Council and amendments to the Charter (Articles 27(3) and 108). Pending the entry into force of agreements for making armed forces available to the Security Council (Article 43), the Five 'shall consult with one another and . . . with other Members . . . with a view to such joint action . . . as may be necessary for . . . maintaining international peace and security' (Article 106).

The major powers among the victorious allies intended to have a predominant role in maintaining international peace and security in the post-war future, and attempts by the medium and smaller countries at San Francisco to curb the primacy of the great powers were of little avail. The Security Council was accorded 'primary responsibility' for maintaining peace, and all UN Members (whether members of the Council or not) were to 'agree to accept and carry out' the Council's decisions (Articles 24(1), 25, and 49). The Council was to be organized so as to function on a continuous basis (Article 28(1)), and the five major victors were to have permanent seats.

The delegations of the five permanent members have thus been able to acquire cumulative experience of the working of the Council. T. F. Tsiang represented Nationalist China on the Council for fifteen years, a longer period than the term of office of any Secretary-General. Yakov Malik was Soviet representative for five of the worst years of the Cold War, and returned in 1968 as the era of détente and peaceful coexistence was beginning to unfold. Liu Chieh served for nine years, Henry Cabot Lodge for nearly eight, Arman Bérard for seven (two terms), and Warren Austin, Arkady Sobolev, Sir Pierson Dixon, and Lord Caradon for six years each.

Moreover, the possibility of exercising the veto on substantive proposals has meant that the permanent members are likely to be consulted during the process of drafting resolutions, except on those occasions when a veto is actually desired by the sponsors of a proposal in order to put the vetoing State in a bad light or so that the sponsors can claim credit for putting forward a militant but impractical proposal. The fact that permanent members are often consulted informally before proposals are submitted gives them the opportunity of suggesting changes, backed by the threat of withholding support from or actually vetoing unacceptable texts.

The attempt of the medium and smaller States at San Francisco to curb the powers of the five permanent members was ostensibly based on the fear that the Five would unite in order to impose their will on the rest. The Five tried to reassure the others that this possibility did not contain the dangers that had been alleged. In their famous statement on the veto, for example, the Five pointed out that they would not be able to act 'by themselves', since 'any decisions of the Council would have to include the concurring votes of at least two [now four] of the non-permanent members.' Any five (now seven) non-permanent members which found themselves in agreement could prevent the Council from taking a decision and therefore could exercise a veto. But of course, claimed the Five blandly, neither the permanent nor the non-permanent members would use their veto power wilfully to obstruct the operation of the Council.[84]

The truth seems to have been that some of those who were most vocal at San Francisco feared great power unity even more than they feared great power discord. At the Commonwealth Prime Ministers' Conference in 1971, President Nyerere of Tanzania quoted a Swahili proverb to the effect that, when two elephants fight, it is the grass that suffers. Prime Minister Lee Kuan Yew of Singapore capped this by pointing out that, when elephants make love, the grass suffers equally.

If the Charter were to be drafted *de novo* it is doubtful whether the present Five would now be given permanent membership and the right of veto—although it does happen that they are all nuclear-weapon powers. I consider on pages 169–71 some of the proposals that have been made to change the permanent membership of the Security Council.

In spite of the fears expressed at San Francisco, the Five have never formed a united group. Sometimes the General Assembly has addressed appeals to the Five to seek agreement on limiting the exercise of the veto,[85] and the General Assembly has on several occasions expressed the view that the permanent members have a special responsibility for contributing to the financing of peace and security operations.[86]

Those readers who are more interested in procedure than personalities may want to skip the next section and turn to section 5, on p. 133. The men who have represented the permanent members are listed on page 110, and cross-references to this Table occur elsewhere in the text.

4. . . . AND THE MEN WHO HAVE REPRESENTED THEM

Yes, they have all been men The Charter states optimistically that the United Nations shall place no restriction on the eligibility of men and women to participate 'in any capacity and under conditions of equality' in its work (Article 8), but it was not until 1972 that a member of the Security Council was represented by a woman. The honour fell to Africa, the country was

Guinea, a non-permanent member of the Council, and the representative was Mrs. Jeanne Martin Cissé. Mrs. Cissé exercised her responsibilities in the Council with consummate skill.

The individuals who have represented the Council's members have represented States, and the policies they have implemented have been the policies of governments. At a time when the United States and Britain were pursuing different policies in the UN Atomic Energy Commission, an American official reported to Washington as follows:

> I said that any government which wished to could, of course, lean heavily on the fiction that their representatives were speaking only for themselves, but that this should be recognised to be, in reality, a fiction.[87]

The best ambassadors undoubtedly find opportunities of influencing policy. They may not necessarily write their own briefs, but the effective ones are those who can ensure that the instructions they receive from their capitals can be followed without violation of conscience, and who are able to present unpalatable policies in a way which will arouse least opposition. Some representatives on the Security Council have sometimes found it hard to conceal how disagreeable has been the task of representing obnoxious policies, but this is exceptional. Most representatives most of the time have given the impression of enjoying the diplomacy of the Security Council.

The representatives of the permanent members are not necessarily more influential than those who represent non-permanent members. Indeed, there have been times when representatives of non-permanent members have played a decisive role, or when one of their representatives has won high esteem because of his personal qualities. It will not, I hope, seem invidious if I list some of those who have represented non-permanent members and who gained special respect from their colleagues for their contribution to the effective working of the Council.

Chief Simeon Adebo, Nigeria
Víctor Andrés Belaúnde,* Peru
Frederick Boland,* Ireland
Sir Claude Corea, Ceylon

Nasrollah Entezam,* Iran
Mahmoud Fawzi, Egypt
George Ignatieff, Canada
Max Jacobson, Finland
Gunnar Jarring, Sweden
Sir Muhammad Zafrulla Khan,* Pakistan
Bohdan Lewandowski, Poland
Dr. Charles Malik,* Lebanon
Sir Leslie Munro,* New Zealand
Dr. Djura Nincic, Yugoslavia
Radhakrishna Ramani, Malaysia
Sir Benegal Rau, India
Dr. Carlos Ortiz de Rozas, Argentina
General Carlos Romulo,* Philippines
Mongi Slim,* Tunisia
Hans R. Tabor, Denmark
Dr. Francisco Urrutia, Colombia

* Served also as President of the General Assembly.

But on the whole those who have represented the permanent members have had more influence, partly because they wield the threat of the veto, and partly because their period of service on the Security Council is not limited to two-year terms. Those who represented the permanent members between 1946 and 1973 are listed in Table 10.

Scholars have long debated whether individuals make history or history makes individuals. This is not the place to discuss that question, but I nevertheless believe that a series of brief profiles of the forty-one men who represented the permanent members of the Security Council between 17 January 1946 and 1 March 1974 conveys something of the quality of person who finds public diplomacy congenial and suggests the atmosphere in which the Council has worked.

CHINA

1. *Quo Tai-chi* (1946–7), China's first representative, had spent a lifetime of service in the politics of the Kuomintang. In 1932 he became Chinese Minister in London and in 1935 was elevated to the rank of Ambassador. He was for a brief period Minister of Foreign Affairs in the wartime Chinese Government in Chungking, and in 1942 he became a member of the Supreme

Table 10

Permanent Representatives of the permanent members of the Security Council, 1946–73

Republic of China

1. Quo Tai-chi (1946–7)
2. T'ingfu F. Tsiang (1947–61)
3. Liu Chieh (1962–71)

(*People's Republic of China*)

4. Huang Hua (1971–

France

5. Alexandre Parodi (1946–9)
6. Jean Chauvel (1949–52)
7. Henri Hoppenot (1952–5)
8. Hervé Alphand (1955)
9. Bernard Cornut-Gentille (1956)
10. Guillaume Georges-Picot (1957–9)
11. Armand Bérard 1959–62)
12. Roger Séydoux (1963–7)

— Armand Bérard (1967–70)

13. Jacques Kosciusko-Morizet (1970–2)
14. Louis de Guiringaud (1972–

Soviet Union

15. Andrei A. Gromyko (1946–8)
16. Yakov A. Malik (1948–52)
17. Valerian A. Zorin (1952–3)
18. Andrei Y. Vyshinsky (1953–4)
19. Arkady A. Sobolev (1954–60)
20. Vasily V. Kuznetsov (1960)

— Valerian A. Zorin (1960–2)

21. Nikolai T. Federenko (1963–7)

— Yakov A. Malik (1968–

United Kingdom

22. Sir Alexander Cadogan (1946–50)
23. Sir Gladwyn Jebb (1950–4)
24. Sir Pierson Dixon (1954–60)
25. Sir Patrick Dean (1960–4)
26. Lord Caradon (1964–70)
27. Sir Colin Crowe (1970–3)
28. Sir Donald Maitland (1973–

United States

29. Edward R. Stettinius, Jr. (1946)
30. Herschel V. Johnson (1946–7)
31. Philip C. Jessup (1948)
32. Warren R. Austin (1948–52)
33. Henry Cabot Lodge, Jr. (1953–60)
34. James J. Wadsworth (1960)
35. Adlai E. Stevenson (1961–5)
36. Arthur J. Goldberg (1965–6)
37. George W. Ball (1968)
38. James R. Wiggins (1968)
39. Charles W. Yost (1969–71)
40. George Bush (1971–3)
41. John Scali (1973–

National Defence Council. Sir Alexander Cadogan described Quo as 'courteous and dignified', 'a gentleman',[88] but he was a tough presiding officer.

2. *T'ingfu F. Tsiang* (1947–61) went to Moscow as Chinese Ambassador in 1936, and later served as Director of the Political Department of the Executive Yuan.* In 1961, after his service

* The Executive Yuan was one of the five major branches of the Chinese Government.

in New York, he was appointed Nationalist China's Ambassador in Washington.

From 1950, Tsiang had the impossible task of claiming to represent China when in reality he spoke only for the rump Nationalist regime which had sought refuge in Taiwan. Secretary-General Lie usually found Tsiang a placid person of 'considerable mental resources', and Sir Gladwyn Jebb (later to become Lord Gladwyn) commented that Tsiang was 'able and likeable, and thus made a direct appeal to many Americans . . .'[89] He was, a colleague recalls, 'a man with a very good mind and a realistic approach . . .'[90] He was an excellent presiding officer, skilled in reconciling differing views. He conducted himself with dignity and restraint, resisting the temptation to use his artificial position irresponsibly.

3. *Liu Chieh* (1962–71) came to the United Nations with a thirty-year background of diplomacy. After representing China on various League of Nations organs, he served successively in English-speaking countries—as Counsellor in London, Minister in Washington, and Ambassador in Ottawa. Liu claimed that it was he who at San Francisco invented the term 'non-self-governing territories', but that Lord Cranborne (later Lord Salisbury) objected because it 'contained too many hyphens and was unpronounceable . . .'[91] Liu was a man of personal charm, but quiet and sometimes even melancholic. He inevitably played a minor role, but sensibly and with moderation.

4. *Huang Hua* (1971–) was the first permanent representative of the People's Republic of China. He had participated in the Korean armistice talks as well as in the Geneva and Bandung Conferences (1954 and 1955), and had served as Ambassador to Ghana, Egypt, and Canada. He was the only Chinese Ambassador to stay at his post during the Cultural Revolution.

He is a man of considerable intelligence and capable of objectivity. 'He had the sense to keep his head down until he knew the form,' wrote one observer; and a Security Council veteran has written: 'His conduct of business as the presiding officer of the Council [in September 1972] was regarded by most diplomats at the UN as competent and fair.'[92] He soon mastered the technique of riling Soviet Ambassador Malik.[93]

FRANCE

The ten diplomats who represented France between 1946 and 1973 were all men of distinction, skill, and experience, but a close observer of UN affairs has written: 'I cannot recall that any of them have had any out-of-the-ordinary influence on the working of the Security Council.' [94]

5. *Alexandre Parodi* (1946–9) had served bravely in the French Resistance. He was a man of wide experience and considerable intellectual stature, a scrupulous though perhaps over-cautious diplomat. One of his colleagues on the Security Council used to say that the only point of speaking in debate was that Parodi could be convinced by rational argument.

6. *Jean Chauvel* (1949–52) began his diplomatic career in Peking in 1924 and eventually rose to be Secretary-General of the Ministry of Foreign Affairs. Trygve Lie admired Chauvel's 'clear and reliable thinking and his good juridical judgment', and Gladwyn Jebb wrote that he was 'full of good sense and always at hand with the right formula . . .' He was very much a traditionalist, however, much more at home in private diplomacy than in the cut-and-thrust of public Security Council debate. A diplomat who worked with him comments that he was 'very hard to . . . understand either in English or French'. Gladwyn Jebb wrote of Chauvel that he was 'greatly superior to myself . . . in ability and in diplomatic experience'; but when it came to the televising of Security Council debates on Korea, Jebb thought that Chauvel was at a considerable disadvantage because he spoke in French, was in no way an orator, and was slightly contemptuous of televised diplomacy. It would never have occurred to Chauvel, wrote Gladwyn Jebb, to concentrate on making an impression on the American public. [95]

7. *Henri Hoppenot* (1952–5) had been a member of the French diplomatic service since 1914, having served successively in Switzerland, Brazil, Persia, Chile, Germany, Syria, China, and Uruguay. He had been the Delegate of the French Provisional Government in Washington during the Second World War and later Ambassador to Switzerland. He was a man of exceptional ability and high principles, one of the very few representatives with sufficient confidence and skill to act wisely and confidently when he was without instructions.

8. *Hervé Alphand* (1955) served only briefly at the United Nations, having previously had mainly European experience—Director-General of the Ministry of Foreign Affairs, Deputy on the North Atlantic Council, Ambassador to the Organization for European Economic Co-operation, and Permanent Representative on the NATO Council. He had considerable charm and worked well with Secretary-General Hammarskjold. He was a great mimic and was much in demand for entertaining dinner guests.

9. *Bernard Cornut-Gentille* (1956) had the misfortune to be representing France, and President of the Security Council, at the time of the Suez fiasco. On 30 October 1956, he collapsed from a heart attack brought on by nervous exhaustion. He later served as Ambassador to Argentina, but in 1959 he returned to French domestic politics, first as a Minister in the central government and later for almost a decade as Mayor of Cannes.

10. *Guillaume Georges-Picot* (1957–9) was a career diplomat who served in a top UN Secretariat post in the early days. 'I made no happier appointment,' wrote Lie. Georges-Picot was somewhat shy, but Brian Urquhart describes him as 'a man of great intelligence and integrity'.[96]

11. *Armand Bérard* (1959–62 and 1967–70) must have enjoyed the United Nations, as he served two terms as France's representative. It cannot have been easy to represent the France of de Gaulle at the United Nations: France wanted all the prerogatives of a great power (if not more), but her UN policy was at that time narrow and constricted.

Bérard had a fine war record. He seemed to take pleasure in his impressive appearance, and did not always realize how intimidating and ascetic he appeared to those with less experience. He was meticulous in following his rather unimaginative instructions. He spoke clearly in debate, was completely straightforward and honest, but tended to be unyielding in negotiation.

12. *Roger Séydoux* (1963–6) was a very different kind of person—gentle, respected, popular even, always ready to negotiate, skilled in the search for compromise. His instructions were often on the negative side, but he was able to carry them out in such a way as to cause France's friends a minimum of embarrassment. He had considerable North African experience and was well

liked by diplomats from Arab and other Third World countries. He had also served in Moscow and knew better than most how to work with Soviet representatives. He was highly cultured and spoke elegantly in debate.

13. *Jacques Kosciusko-Morizet* (1970–2) had started in the academic world, had later turned to politics, and finally to diplomacy. He had spent six years as France's representative on the Trusteeship Council and five years as Ambassador to Zaire (Congo, Leopoldville–Kinshasa). One colleague describes him as 'uniformly courteous, intelligent and helpful'.[97] He was a skilled operator, and as an old Gaullist he had his own lines to the Elysée. He was proud of his knowledge of the Francophone States, but was apt to play his cards rather close to his chest.

14. *Louis de Guiringaud* (1972–) is a career diplomat, having served in Germany, as consul-general in San Francisco, as No. 2 in the French permanent mission at the United Nations, and as Ambassador to Ghana and Japan. He took over the presidency of the Security Council for the last two days of October 1956 after the collapse of Cornut-Gentille. He is a tough, skilled, and intelligent diplomat, even if he sometimes gives a dull impression.

SOVIET UNION

15. *Andrei A. Gromyko* (1946–8), now Soviet Foreign Minister, was his country's first representative at the United Nations. His rather grim-looking exterior can be misleading, for he undoubtedly has pleasing qualities and a sense of humour. Dean Acheson refers twice in his memoirs to Gromyko's 'sardonic humour', Adlai Stevenson found him 'cordial and agreeable' (1945), and Gladwyn Jebb describes him as 'perhaps not entirely humourless'. Herschel Johnson evidently got on well with Gromyko. He described him as 'friendly and apparently frank . . . very good humoured' (1946), 'friendly . . . and apparently reasonable' (1947). Lie, apropos an occasion in 1948, comments: 'His melancholy features lit up with sympathy'.[98]

Gromyko is a professional to the marrow, though at the time of his UN assignment he was evidently kept on a tight rein. Sir Alexander Cadogan noted in his diary (1944) that Gromyko was 'obviously terrified of departing a hair's breadth from his instructions'; and a year later, '. . . it's hopeless trying to negotiate with Gromyko: he doesn't dare to change a comma without reference back to Moscow'. But in other respects Cadogan found him 'a very nice and sensible fellow', and Gladwyn Jebb writes that 'the formidable Andrei Gromyko was imperturbable . . . scrupulous, . . . and formidably exact'. Gromyko never gets ruffled, not in public anyway; he is a serious and astute diplomat to do business with.[99]

16. *Yakov A. Malik* (1948–52 and 1968–) shares with Bérard and Zorin the distinction of having served two terms as permanent representative to the United Nations. He is a veteran, tough, thoroughly versed in UN procedure, and capable of making an indefensible case sound almost plausible. Gladwyn Jebb, recalling the Korea debates of 1950, sums him up as follows:

> He was (and is) a large, well-mannered bureaucrat with a pleasant voice and an easy smile. While hardly ever deviating from the party line, however absurd, he never indulged in crude abuse, . . . nor did he ever lose his temper—or indeed his head. He was therefore a formidable opponent. He could no doubt have been more formidable if he had had a better case . . . He was in fact . . . a little wooden, and thus inflexible, but he did his best and you could not help respecting him . . . [A] very good-looking and quite likeable fellow.[100]

James Wadsworth found him 'most personable and pleasant when not engaged in debate'. Malik told Wadsworth in 1954: 'You will never know how it hurt me personally to cast all those vetoes [38] a few years ago. It affected me so strongly each time that I felt sick. I am sure my heart trouble stems directly from this.'[101] Trygve Lie evidently found Malik difficult and wrote that his 'sabotage and splendid disregard of all rules and regulations' in August 1950 'bordered on the grotesque'; and others have described him as a bully, 'left over from the Cold War'. 'He is not bothered by lack of consistency and will use any argument that comes to hand, even if he has said the reverse the day before.'[102]

Gladwyn Jebb's comment that Malik never lost his temper or indulged in crude abuse might have to be slightly modified now in the light of developments since China took her seat in the

Security Council. Chinese diplomats have achieved something that eluded Western diplomats—to make Ambassador Malik appear rather annoyed in public.

17. *Valerian A. Zorin* (1952–3 and 1960–2) joined the Soviet Foreign Ministry in 1941. He was Ambassador in Prague prior to the 1948 coup and Ambassador in Bonn from 1955–60. He is often thought of as someone whose appearance at a trouble-spot denotes a tougher Soviet line. Those who have done business with him have found him an awkward colleague—unpleasant, unscrupulous, unreliable, rude, with a bullying attitude towards smaller countries. Francis Plimpton describes him as a 'heavy, tough Communist hatchet man, with a face like a battle-ax . . .' and Lester Pearson wrote in his diary that Zorin was 'a smooth and slippery customer . . . tough'.[103]

18. *Andrei Y. Vyshinsky* (1953–4) came to the United Nations with the unpleasant reputation of having been chief prosecutor in the pre-war Stalinist trials. Trygve Lie described him as an 'expert in dialectical fencing', Dean Acheson as 'a natural blackguard', Sir Alexander Cadogan as 'a great villain', Sir Gladwyn Jebb as 'horrible . . . odious', and James Wadsworth as 'sarcastic, ruthless'. His speeches, recalled Paul-Henri Spaak, 'bristled with accusations, imprecations, and often with oaths'; they were peppered with Marxist epigrams like 'law is the instrument of politics.'

Had Vyshinsky any redeeming qualities? 'I fail to see any . . .', writes someone who saw a good deal of him in 1953; but 'he could make a hostile UN audience . . . laugh at his sallies'. Cadogan called him 'quite a pleasant companion', Acheson found him 'cultivated and amusing', and Robert Murphy recalls that, even after the most bitter debate, 'he would discuss the most controversial issue good-humouredly in the delegates' private lounge'. Wadsworth writes that he was 'a man of humour, with a deep love of family'. But he never succeeded in transcending his obnoxious past.[104]

19. *Arkady A. Sobolev* (1954—60) could not have been more different. He served in the early years as an Assistant Secretary-General in the UN Secretariat, and Lie thought him 'a man of high ability . . . among the most intelligent people in the Secretariat'. Gladwyn Jebb, who first met Sobolev in 1944, found him 'most pleasant . . . then at the beginning of his

subsequently brilliant career', and Cadogan wrote in 1945 that Sobolev was 'the only man in the [Soviet] Delegation who was at all reasonable', adding (unpresciently), 'I expect he will have his head cut off.' The American found him so helpful at the San Francisco Conference that, when he unexpectedly returned to Moscow, Edward Stettinius wondered whether he had been 'unable to get along with Ambassador Gromyko because of his cooperation with the United States . . .' Brian Urquhart describes him as 'able and respected.' He was 'resourceful, his mind was subtle, his approach pragmatic.' Only Henry Cabot Lodge has written somewhat disparagingly of Sobolev, describing him as 'a cool and affable descendant of czarist civil servants'.[105]

My own recollections of Sobolev are of a man of innate decency, intelligent, straightforward in his dealings, genuinely doing his best, within the limits under which he operated, to achieve the ideals for which the United Nations is supposed to stand.

20. *Vasily V. Kutznetsov* (1960) served for a short time as Sobolev's successor. Kuznetsov, like Sobolev, had started life as an engineer, and had later been active in trade union affairs and in economic planning. In 1953, he went to Peking as Soviet Ambassador, and in 1955 returned to Moscow as Deputy Foreign Minister.

Kuznetsov has the reputation of being trustworthy and conciliatory, and Lord Caradon once welcomed him to the Security Council with the following impromptu verses:

> When prospects are dark and hopes are dim,
> We know that we must send for him;
> When storms and tempests fill the sky,
> 'Bring on Kuznetsov', is the cry.
>
> He comes like a dove from the Communist ark,
> And light appears where all was dark;
> His coming quickly turns the tide,
> The propaganda floods subside.
>
> And now that he has changed the weather,
> Lion and lamb can vote together.
> God bless the Russian delegation.
> I waive consecutive translation.[106]

21. *Nikolai T. Federenko* (1963–7), an oriental specialist, was outwardly smooth, sophisticated, and genial. He dressed stylishly and smoked interesting-shaped pipes. One of his favourite tricks was to offer Havana cigars to American diplomats. He was a good mixer and might have passed as a professor from a minor but progressive American university.

Western representatives describe him as a cynical and sometimes rather dangerous man, shifting quickly from extreme amiability to the most insulting sarcasm. A Third World diplomat has applied to Federenko some words used by Lord Palmerston of Count Orlov in 1856.

> He is civil and courteous externally, but his inward mind is deeply impregnated with Russian insolence, arrogance, and pride. He will do his best to bully without appearing to do so.[107]

Some people received the impression that he would have liked to be helpful in the pursuit of détente, but it is doubtful whether he carried much weight with his own government, and consequently his manoeuvrability was circumscribed.

UNITED KINGDOM

British representatives, writes one observer, have been 'at their best during behind-the-scenes consultations and negotiations'.[108]

22. *Sir Alexander Cadogan* (1946–50) was a diplomat of the old school, having previously served as Permanent Under-Secretary at the Foreign Office. His manner was urbane and unflappable, and his integrity shone through. His diaries for this period, not yet published, may show him to have been more cynical and intolerant than he appeared on the surface. Traditionalist though Cadogan was, Lie always believed that he was 'personally a staunch supporter of the United Nations . . .' One of his colleagues has written: 'Cadogan . . . provided me and other delegates with a sound education in fundamentals of multilateral diplomacy . . . He was never pompous with me although I was much younger . . . I found him an interesting and pleasant colleague.'[109] The editor of his diaries writes that Cadogan

> thought it a mistake to indulge in biting language too often. The

moment and the ground must be carefully chosen . . . At the Council, Cadogan's restraint and brevity contrasted with others' more flamboyant manners . . . His speeches were . . . delivered in his dry, deliberate manner, with scarcely a glance at the script, or sometimes without a text, but with everything well-shaped and rounded . . . Cadogan held a unique position at the UN, derived from a blend of receptivity, debating skill, unmatched experience, knowledge of procedure and obvious desire to make the organization work . . . Those who asked Cadogan's help received courteous attention and excellent advice, delivered modestly, almost diffidently, in his matter-of-fact fashion . . .[110]

23. *Sir Gladwyn Jebb* (1950–4) was totally unlike Cadogan. He had done a first-rate job as Executive Secretary of the UN Preparatory Commission (1945–6), but it had left him tired and discouraged. Bevin suggested his name as the first Secretary-General, though he did so a bit half-heartedly.[111]

When Jebb arrived in New York in 1950 for the Korea debates, he found himself in his element at once. Where Cadogan had been quiet and dry, Jebb was rumbustious and flamboyant. To his own surprise, Jebb found himself enjoying the drama of UN debate, and in his memoirs he prints as an appendix extracts from six of his speeches from that time. He recalls that his 'Hooper rating', by which television personalities were judged, placed him 'Number Three in America, immediately below Bob Hope and just in front of the wrestlers.' Dean Acheson notes that the only person who outshone Jebb as a television star was Iranian Prime Minister Mossadeq. It was not simply that Jebb was eloquent: he could also be witty. One colleague recalls that he was 'a man with an interesting mind and at home with ideas', and Lord Gore-Booth pays tribute to Jebb's imagination, energy, and *panache*.[112]

People were, and are, ambivalent about Jebb. Cadogan, writing in 1938, calls him 'excellent' on one page and, shortly after, a 'bloody fool' but 'very clever'.[113] He was immensely able over large issues, but tended to be slapdash over details. He could appear arrogant and contemptuous at one moment, and kindly and sympathic the next. One person who knew him well describes him as 'a classic British eccentric'.[114]

After retiring from the diplomatic service in 1960, Jebb was raised to the peerage as Lord Gladwyn and in 1964 he joined the Liberal Party, becoming Deputy Leader in the House of Lords in 1967; but the main cause to which he devoted his astonishing energies was that of West European unity.

24. *Sir Pierson Dixon* (1954–60), by contract, had no ambitions to become a television star. He was quiet, somewhat reserved, detached, conscientious, meticulous about detail. 'He knows too much about his subject,' wrote Cadogan, '[and] has made it incomprehensible to others.' Ernest Bevin and Anthony Eden, both of whom he served as Principal Private Secretary, held him in high regard. Eden recalls that Dixon had 'a remarkable sense of diplomacy'. The suppleness of his methods reminded Eden of the renaissance period. 'Though a scholar of repute, there is nothing academic about the thrust of his mind.'[115]

Bob Dixon's tragedy was to have had to represent Britain during the Suez adventure in 1956. Henry Cabot Lodge recalls seeing Dixon at the Metropolitan Opera in New York on the day hostilities began: 'his natural ruddy face turned white.' I watched him throughout the debates in the Security Council and I recall in particular how he blenched at the meeting on 31 October as a colleague thrust into his hand a piece of paper which presumably informed him that British aircraft were bombing Egypt. He told Lodge that 'if the bombardment of Port Said continued, he personally would resign'.[116] The whole affair, wrote Dixon in his diary a year later, was 'a miscalculation and a mistake'.

> We intervened by virtue of no clear and defensible principle, but, what was worse, gave a reason which was generally considered at best a lame excuse, at worst a conspiracy . . . I recall the sick-at-the-stomach feeling with which I defended our case . . . It came of the conviction that the operation was misconceived and probably would fail. The effort of concealing these feelings and putting a plausible and confident case was the severest moral and physical strain I have ever experienced.

Relations between Dixon and Dag Hammarskjold were strained by Suez and were never completely cordial again. Perhaps Dixon's weakness was his inability to weigh up other people.[117]

25. *Sir Patrick Dean* (1960–4) arrived at the UN as African criticism of Britain was beginning to mount. The Security

Council was trying to sort out the Congo question and particularly the attempted secession of Katanga. Britain was not in the dock in the sense that she had been over Suez, but it was becoming increasingly difficult to defend Britain's African policy in the UN forum. The Security Council was to have to deal with the problem of Kuwait (1961), the Cuban Missile Crisis (1962), civil war in the Yemen (1963), and the troubles in Cyprus (beginning in 1964).

Dean enjoyed his time at the United Nations. He had practised at the bar and also served as Assistant Legal Adviser at the Foreign Office. He was, therefore, naturally interested in the legal problems which came to the Security Council. Someone who knew him well writes: 'Sir Patrick Dean . . . enjoyed playing the UN "game" of resolutions and procedural points.' Another colleague comments: 'He was a master of the half sentence and the unfinished phrase, and concealed his acute appreciation of tactics under the bluff manner of the simple Englishman to perfection.' To some people he seemed diffident if not shy, but he was intelligent and astute. He was liked and respected, and implemented with aplomb and sensitivity a policy which was not very popular in UN circles. Whatever success the United Kingdom had during Dean's time, according to one observer, was 'due to the fact that the British delegation really knew and understood the Charter and the rules and had, therefore, as sound a foundation as possible on which to back . . . arguments on policy'. Harold Macmillan found him 'wise and resolute'.[118]

26. *Lord Caradon* (1964–70) was the first British representative not to have been a career diplomat. It was Labour Party policy in 1964 (as it was in the election of February 1974) to be represented at the United Nations by a political appointee. Sir Hugh Foot had had a distinguished career in the British colonial service, having started in Palestine in 1929, been Chief Secretary in Nigeria, and Governor of Jamaica and then Cyprus. Harold Macmillan writes: 'In all my dealings with him from the first time I met him until the end of the story I was to find him not merely resourceful but loyal.' In February 1959, Macmillan sent Foot a short letter, saying 'I shall always admire your strength of purpose and loyal support . . .', to which Foot sent a characteristic reply: 'Thank you, Sir, for as

kind a message as ever was sent from a Cavalier to a Roundhead.' In 1961, he went to the United Nations as Britain's chief representative on colonial matters, but he had resigned in 1962 because he had disagreed with the policy of the Macmillan Government over Rhodesia.[119] When the Labour Government took office in 1964, Sir Hugh Foot was raised to the peerage as Lord Caradon and appointed Minister of State in the Foreign Office and Britain's representative at the United Nations.

Caradon comes from a well-known West-country family with staunch radical traditions, but the left Foot has not always known what the right Foot has been doing. He brought to his job prodigious energy, considerable powers of oratory, the experience of more than thirty years in Britain's dependencies, an unswerving belief in the United Nations, and a deep personal commitment to racial equality and the right of colonial peoples to self-government. As a Minister rather than a career diplomat, he was not simply the instrument for implementing policy decided in London; he also had a share in the devising of policy. Moreover, he had once resigned on a point of political principle, and who could be sure that he would not do so again? Some Third World diplomats who had known Foot before 1964 hoped and expected that he would pursue a personal rather than a governmental policy at the United Nations. Some of them commented sadly after 1964 that they had preferred Sir Hugh Foot to Lord Caradon, but this was to misunderstand the nature of the British system of government and the principle of collective Ministerial responsibility. Caradon was no doubt sometimes as frustrated as were his Third World friends about the policy he had to represent; indeed, someone who knows him very well has summed up his situation between 1964 and 1970 as 'keen but confined'.[120]

His two favourite concepts were agreement and action. He worked tirelessly for the unanimous Security Council resolution on the Middle East in 1967. A sentence from one of his speeches earlier in 1967 is characteristic of the man.

The idea came from the representative of the Soviet Union, the enthusiasm from the representative of the United Kingdom and the precision from the representative of France.[121]

Caradon is a man of immense courtesy. He never had a meal at our house without sending a handwritten and thoughtful letter of thanks to my wife. He enjoys the company of young people and gives the impression that he would much rather join them in a protest march than make a speech in the House of Lords. Exiled political leaders from Southern Africa have commented how accessible Caradon always is, and he clearly finds it difficult to say no to a well-considered request for help.

Caradon's enthusiasm for the UN idea sometimes led him to be too uncritical in the face of human weakness. His admiration for Secretary-General Thant may have blinded him to some of Thant's deficiencies during the final phase of Thant's second term of office (1966–71). His professional colleagues in the Foreign Office sometimes complained that he was more committed to the strengthening of the United Nations than to the promotion and protection of British interests. He was supported and respected by a strong team in the British Mission to the United Nations, but he personally preferred the man or woman of large ideas to the perfectionist who niggled about what to him were mere technical details.

27. *Sir Colin Crowe* (1970–3), a career diplomat, was appointed to the United Nations after the 1970 election. It cannot have been easy following Lord Caradon. Britain was returning to the traditional practice of regarding the UN representative as a professional rather than a political appointment. The Conservative Party had created the impression during the election campaign that the main thrust of its foreign and defence policy would differ from that of the Labour Party—a more sympathetic attitude to South African requests for arms, a new attempt to settle the Rhodesian problem, a continuing military presence in Malaysia and Singapore, a review of the plan to reduce commitments in the Gulf, a staunch commitment to the unity of Western Europe rather than to world institutions, and so on. If Britain under a Labour Government had been under attack for its policies in Southern Africa, how much stronger would be the attack with the changed emphasis of the Conservative Government.

Crowe's diplomatic career had been remarkably varied. He had served in China (Peking, 1936–8, 1950–3; Shanghai,

1939–40), the Middle East (Tel Aviv, 1949–50; Cairo, 1959–61; Jedda, 1963–4), North America (Washington, 1940–5; United Nations, New York, 1961–3; Ottawa, 1968–70), and had also had experience of the Organization for European Economic Co-operation (1948–9) and the Imperial Defence College (1957–9). He had, moreover, served as Dean's deputy for two years.

Sir Colin Crowe is a gentle man of very great charm. Despite his varied experience, he is genuinely modest, tolerant, a good listener, always to be trusted, cool in a crisis. But beneath the quiet exterior is an inner man of steely strength, patient but persistent, adamant in matters of principle.

28. *Sir Donald Maitland* (1973–) joined the Foreign Office in 1947 after six years in the army. In addition to experience in the Middle East, Maitland served as Private Secretary to the Minister of State (1954–6), Head of the Foreign Office News Department (1965–7), Private Secretary to the Secretary of State (1967–9), Ambassador to Libya (1969–70), and Chief Press Secretary to the Prime Minister (1970–3).

Maitland was well qualified to handle the difficult Middle East questions arising from the Arab–Israel war of October 1973. He appreciated the potentialities of the United Nations, but without succumbing to any false utopianism. His previous experience with the news media was put to good account, and his occasional press conferences were well reported. He soon acquired a sound understanding of the potentialities, as well as the weaknesses, of the United Nations. He worked hard himself and expected his subordinates to do so too.

UNITED STATES

The thirteen U.S. representatives have had singularly varied backgrounds, although only two were career diplomats. One representative had been a businessman, another an academic, two were from the newspaper world, and several were lawyers. But the vocation which supplied the largest number of representatives was politics.

29. *Edward R. Stettinius, Jr.* (1946) was a handsome businessman who was never entirely at home in the perplexing world of diplomacy. Lester Pearson described him as 'a little bewildered by it all . . . a combination of a Rotary President and a Bible

Class leader'; Cadogan, who could be very sharp in the privacy of his diary, wrote that Stettinius looked like 'a dignified and more monumental Charlie Chaplin'; while Dean Acheson noted sardonically that Stettinius had 'gone far with comparatively modest equipment'.[122]

But Stettinius was well liked in UN circles. Secretary-General Lie commended his 'moderating influence', Gladwyn Jebb writes that, though he was naive and inadequately informed, he was 'the epitome of enthusiasm, honesty and drive', while Cordell Hull thought that he made 'a splendid showing', and Acheson noted 'his gift for public relations'.[123]

30. *Herschel V. Johnson* (1946–7) had served in the U.S. foreign service since 1920, with postings to Bern, Sofia, Tegucigalpa, Mexico City, London, and Stockholm, as well as two periods in the State Department in Washington. He had a heart attack in 1948, but was able to spend the next five years as U.S. Ambassador to Brazil. He was a career diplomat of the old school, well suited to the style of his British colleague, Sir Alexander Cadogan. He was more determined than were some of his U.S. colleagues to maintain a pragmatic working relationship with the Soviet Union.

31. *Philip C. Jessup* (1948), Acting Permanent Representative for a brief period, is one of the most distinguished of the forty-one men who have represented the permanent members of the Security Council. He joined the faculty of Columbia University in 1925 and in 1943 he accepted an assignment with the State Department. He was at the conference which established the UN Relief and Rehabilitation Administration in 1943, was Technical Secretary-General at the Bretton Woods Conference in 1944, and assistant to the U.S. delegation at the San Francisco Conference in 1945. In 1949 President Truman appointed him as Ambassador at Large. From 1961 to 1970, he was a judge of the International Court of Justice, author of a memorable dissenting opinion in the Court's *South West Africa Judgment* of 1966.[124] He has had a distinguished and influential career as a legal innovator and is one of the really great international lawyers of his generation. 'His writings are milestones in new approaches to the international sector of law . . .'[125] President Truman, in a masterly under-statement, described

Jessup as 'one of the leading authorities on international law' who gained respect for 'the statesmanlike manner' in which he handled the Berlin question in 1948–9.[126]

Lie wrote of Judge Jessup: 'He is an extraordinarily likeable person, with a sweetness of character not always found in men of his exceptional intelligence.' Someone has written: 'To see Phil Jessup at work has convinced me that personal goodness is by no means incompatible with the hurly-burly of politics and diplomacy.'[127] By believing the best of his fellow men, Jessup evoked the best in them.

32. *Warren R. Austin* (1948–52), a leading Republican Senator, was appointed by President Truman to assure the bipartisan nature of U.S. policy at the United Nations. President Truman regarded Austin as 'one of the most effective . . . leaders' of the Senate. 'He was not one to talk much for the headlines, but behind the scenes he knew how to make his influence felt and to bring factions to agree. I [Truman] have always considered myself very fortunate that I could find a man of his high qualifications for appointment to the ticklish U.N. job.'[128] Truman enhanced Austin's position 'by informally ranking [him] practically as a member of the . . . cabinet'.[129]

One colleague who knew Austin well has described him as 'rugged as Vermont granite', while another considered that he represented 'the spirit of old New England'.[130]

Austin won immense respect from his colleagues. Adlai Stevenson admired his genuine modesty, while both Lie and Mike Pearson recalled his dignity and upright character, and Robert Murphy wrote that he was 'by nature a peace-maker [who] disliked public controversy as much as he disliked personal publicity'. Gladwyn Jebb respected his shrewdness and honesty, but (in a comment which reveals as much about Jebb as it does about Austin) noted

> Nobody could say that he was particularly brilliant in controversy . . . It was pretty clear that he was a little old-fashioned both in his oratory and his outlook and probably therefore not entirely suitable to represent the USA in what was to develop into a sort of triangular diplomatic boxing match.[131]

The building near the United Nations erected by the Carnegie Endowment for International Peace contained an auditorium dedicated to Austin, with the following plaque:

> The righteous zeal of informed public opinion
> is the life blood of our cause.
> Warren R. Austin

Austin attained immortality in UN circles by appealing to Jews and Moslems in a critical Middle East debate: 'Come, come, my friends! Let us sit down together and resolve our differences like good Christians.'[132]

33. *Henry Cabot Lodge, Jr.* (1953–60), also a Republican Senator from New England, was a very different kettle of fish. President Eisenhower considered that Lodge's qualifications for the UN appointment 'seemed almost unique'. He later appointed Lodge to Cabinet rank 'with a seniority just below that of Secretary of State'.[133]

Lodge was 'youthful-looking and handsome, with a speaking voice well suited to television . . . one of the best-known personalities in American public life'. He had served in the Senate, and Eisenhower considered that this experience would stand him in good stead at the United Nations.[134] Lodge was never able wholly to divest himself of his politician's way of thinking and acting. He would address the Security Council as though it were a public meeting, graciously acknowledging applause from the galleries. He 'decided that every Russian attack should be countered sharply [by] immediately challenging Soviet misrepresentation', but someone who saw him at work has written that he was 'more interested in the rhetoric of the Cold War than in the negotiating situation of the UN'. He was proud of the fact that the United States had not 'lost a vote' on an important issue since his appointment to the United Nations. He combined 'aristocratic scorn with political aggressiveness'.[135] He may not have been vain or arrogant, but he would sometimes give that impression.

He was, however, a competent and hard-working representative, fluent in French, who soon learned his way around the UN system and eventually managed to get on reasonably good terms with Secretary-General Hammarskjold. He also carried more weight in Washington than have most other U.S. representatives. From the point of view of the State Department, looking after Lodge was 'a full-time job in itself'. Lodge claimed virtual autonomy for the U.S. Mission and would tolerate no poaching. The U.S. Mission to the United Nations became 'a second Foreign Office . . .' Once, when Secretary of State Dulles approved some instructions to him, Lodge expostulated: 'Instructions? . . . I am a member of the President's Cabinet and accept instructions only from him [Eisenhower] . . . I *take note* of the Department's *opinions*.'[136]

Gladwyn Jebb describes him as 'a first-class operator in the Security Council where he sometimes gave the impression of being, as it were, a power in his own right'. When he left the United Nations 'his aggressive manner had changed very much, and he was respected and liked by many of his colleagues'.[137]

Lodge, while presiding in the Security Council, had the misfortune to ask the Soviet representative, 'For what purpose does the gentleman wish to be recognized?' to which he received the sharp retort, 'I am not a "gentleman", I am the representative of the Soviet Union . . .'[138]

34. *James J. Wadsworth* (1960) was Lodge's deputy and, for a brief period, his successor. He was a solid man in every sense of the word. He had served for ten years in the New York State Assembly and had worked with the Marshall Plan from 1948 to 1950. He was an amiable and competent man, able to crack jokes at the bar of the delegates' lounge with diplomatic adversaries, conciliatory in tense situations. He was an ideal deputy to Lodge, holding the U.S. team together and ensuring that Lodge was well briefed and loyally supported. Eisenhower described him as 'an experienced negotiator, a man of patience and with a sense of humour . . .', but Lodge himself only recalls that Wadsworth was 'one of the most naturally musical men I have ever known'.[139]

35. *Adlai Stevenson* (1961–5) was both an attractive and a tragic figure. His learning, wit, and charm were legendary, but everyone thought of him as the man who might have been President. He had had intermittent experience of the United Nations going back to 1945: at the San Francisco conference, he recalled later, 'my job was to act as spokesman for the United States Delegation and sub rosa to conduct an underground news leakage office for the US press. It was all a little ridiculous . . .' He was considered for a top post in the UN

Secretariat and also as a possible successor to Stettinius in 1946.[140]

But his interests were very much wider than international affairs. He wished to make a success of the assignment with which President Kennedy had entrusted him, but he could not refrain from enjoying and contributing to the cultural and intellectual life of New York City. He accepted too many obligations outside the United Nations and therefore had to keep going at an inhuman pace. He disliked diplomatic receptions and sometimes had to be prodded into going by his staff. He 'had the grace of making everything look easy and the habit of disparaging his own success'.[141]

His tragedy was that he was often kept in ignorance and occasionally deceived by his colleagues in Washington. Kennedy intended that Stevenson should be kept fully informed: 'The integrity and credibility of Adlai Stevenson constitute one of our great national assets.' But over the Bay of Pigs (1961) and the Gulf of Tonkin Incident (1964), for instance, Stevenson was supplied by Washington with half-truths, even untruths, which he in good faith imparted. He sometimes found it difficult to conceal the disgust he felt for causes he had to defend and information he had to purvey. He told Pierre Salinger that the Bay of Pigs episode was the most humiliating of his years of government service. 'Stevenson felt that he had been made a fool of and that his integrity had been seriously damaged.' 'I did not tell the whole truth,' Stevenson later told a friend; 'I did not know the whole truth.'[142]

Stevenson had expected to be appointed Kennedy's Secretary of State, but Kennedy thought he might be too indecisive. The two men respected each other. Kennedy admired Stevenson's gifts and his capacity for original thought, but was not blind to his idiosyncrasies. Stevenson was never wholly at ease with the President, seeming at times 'stiff, even . . . solemn and pedantic'.[143]

Stevenson, though in no sense naive, was an idealist. His vision was of 'an ordered rational world society'. When international diplomacy becomes cynical, the idealist stands out.

But Stevenson depended very much on the support of a skilled team. Harold Macmillan once commented to Dean

Acheson that Stevenson was 'a good staff officer but without the stuff of command'.[144] The catholicity of his interests caused some people to think of him as a dilettante. Trygve Lie respected Stevenson's 'superior abilities', and Gladwyn Jebb regarded him as 'a great servant of the United Nations'. He was much respected by Third World diplomats, probably because of his previous record. He was, however, beginning to lose heart by the time he went to the United Nations, and one of his friends considers that he should have 'resigned rather than died of a broken heart'.[145]

Stevenson's fire blazed briefly during the debate on the Cuban missile crisis in 1962. Zorin had made an abrasive speech in which he had accused the United States of faking the evidence ('. . . there is no such evidence . . . except fake evidence . . .'); whereupon Stevenson turned on Zorin and asked him point blank: 'Do you, Ambassador Zorin, deny that the USSR has placed and is placing . . . missiles and sites in Cuba? Yes or no? Do not wait for the interpretation. Yes or no?' Zorin retorted sharply that he was not in an American court of law and had no wish to answer a question put in the manner of a prosecuting counsel. 'You are in the courtroom of world opinion . . .', interjected Stevenson. Zorin intervened later to say that the Soviet Union had no need to deploy weapons in Cuba; Stevenson's question had been merely rhetorical. Stevenson responded with a plea to stop sparring.

We know the facts, Mr Zorin, and so do you . . . Our job, Mr Zorin, is to save the peace. If you are ready to try, we are.[146]

Arthur Goldberg (1965–8), appointed to the United Nations by President Johnson, had had a highly varied experience. He had worked as a lawyer from 1929 to 1961, specializing in labour union matters. He served President Kennedy as Secretary of Labour and was then appointed to the U.S. Supreme Court. President Johnson considered Goldberg to be 'a skilled arbiter and a fair-minded man' who 'yearned for more freedom and activity' than was appropriate for a Supreme Court Justice. At the United Nations, according to Johnson, he proved 'an extremely able and effective representative . . .'[147] He was an able negotiator in private, but his public speeches, delivered in a flat monotone, and without wit or sparkle, were unbelievably dull. Goldberg seemed to lack a sense of humour and perhaps took himself too seriously, but he put his long experience of labour bargaining to good effect. He presided over the Security Council in September 1965, almost immediately after taking up his UN appointment, and the prompt termination of the India–Pakistan war was due in part to his skill. He is believed to have been the author of a compromise formula on Rhodesia in 1965 which was accepted because nobody was quite sure what it meant—that the Rhodesian situation was grave 'and that *its continuance in time* constitutes a threat to international peace and security'.[148] He worked hard for an agreed resolution on the Middle East in October and November 1967.

Goldberg had more freedom from State Department control than Stevenson had had, although not as much as Lodge. Speeches were usually initiated in New York and submitted to Washington for approval, and on one occasion Goldberg wrote a set of formal instructions which he asked Washington to transmit to him. He was 'permitted to plan his own tactics with little or no consultation either at White House or Secretary of State level'.[149]

It was hard for a member of the Jewish faith to represent the United States in 1967. Goldberg did his best to be impartial about the Middle East, at any rate at that time, but he was the target of persistent pressure from American Jewish organizations. When taunted by the Syrian representative with being 'the representative of Israel' rather than of the United States, his knuckles whitened under the desk as he gripped hard to hide how deeply he had been hurt.[150] His instincts were liberal and humane. He had hoped for great things from the United Nations, but he left as a rather sad and disillusioned figure.

37. *George W. Ball* (1968) had been in law practice in Illinois and was a member of Adlai Stevenson's circle of friends. He went to Washington soon after Pearl Harbor, undertaking a variety of government assignments. He had 'enormous intelligence, personal charm, and international legal training'. He showed himself to be hard-headed, original, and articulate during his three months at the United Nations, but he was not

on the job long enough to prove his real worth. His main focus of interest was West European–North American relationships, and he sometimes seemed rather impatient with, if not contemptuous of, the United Nations. 'What makes Ball's appointment so intriguing [one observer has written] is that he was at odds with major aspects of American policy during his service as a high policy-making official.'[151]

38. *James R. Wiggins* (1968) went to the United Nations at the age of sixty-five, after forty-six years of experience in journalism. He was well liked, and his commonsense did much to compensate for his lack of diplomatic experience.

39 *Charles W. Yost* (1969–71) was a career diplomat of phenomenally wide experience, having served in Egypt, Poland, Thailand, Czechoslovakia, Austria, Greece, Laos, France, Syria, and Morocco, as well as two spells in Washington. He had been present at the San Francisco Conference, had been a member of the U.S. delegation to the UN General Assembly in 1946, and had served as deputy to Stevenson and Goldberg President Nixon brought him out of retirement, and he served a two-year stint at the United Nations with distinction.

Yost represents everything that is finest in the American diplomatic traditions. He was 'a superb Foreign Service officer, quiet, reflective and tough'.[152] He combines scholarship with practical experience, and is a man of unusual independence, integrity, and idealism. He continues to be active in American public life, and writes sensibly about the United Nations from the standpoint of one who has known its defects but values its potentialities.

40 *George Bush* (1971–3) had served for four years in the U.S. House of Representatives before being appointed to the United Nations. In spite of the unpopularity of U.S. policy in South East Asia at the time, Bush gained much personal esteem because of his consistently courteous and friendly attitude. When his appointment was first announced, it was regarded by some as almost an insult to the United Nations, but his personal qualities soon shone through, and there was genuine regret when he left. 'He knew everyone in the UN . . . by their names, and he was a man of transparent honesty.'[153] I received the impression that he put his heart and soul into the job, and enjoyed doing it.

41. *John Scali* (1973–) had been a reporter for twenty years when he was appointed to the United Nations. During the Cuban Missile Crisis, he had conveyed an important message from a Soviet official to the U.S. Government. Salinger notes that Scali was 'held in great respect in our own [U.S.] State Department'; he was 'not only a great reporter but a great American', noted for enterprise and integrity. And Salinger adds that he was 'the meanest man who ever sat down at a poker table'.[154]

A man may be skilled as a journalist and renowned as a poker-player, but out of his depth in diplomacy. Scali was never quite at home at the United Nations, and many representatives found him an awkward colleague during the complex Middle East diplomacy of 1973.

5. NON-PERMANENT MEMBERS

Those who drafted the Charter seem to have been obsessed with negative concepts—non-self-governing territories, non-procedural decisions, non-intervention * in essentially domestic matters, non-governmental organizations, non-strategic trust territories, non-permanent members of the Security Council. This is, indeed, a common feature of texts drafted by collective bodies. Someone prepares a first draft, such as: 'All pigs are equal'. Some visionary proposes that the wording be amended to read: 'All *animals* are equal'. This is too much for a traditionalist, who wishes to reinstate the original text and add a new sentence: 'Non-pigs are almost as equal as pigs'.

All members of the United Nations are declared to be sovereign and equal (Article 2(1)). This, according to the Charter, is one of the principles according to which 'the Organization and its Members' shall act. But in reality all Members are not equal. The permanent members of the Security Council possess veto rights specified in the Charter. Other UN Members do not possess such rights; they have the right of *access* to the Security Council, a right which is virtually unfettered, and the right to declare themselves candidates for one of the elective seats on the Council, a right which is now governed formally by a decision of the General Assembly on the

* Lord Palmerston did not permit his ambassadors to use the word *intervention* in their dispatches, on the ground that it was a foreign word.

distribution of elective seats,[155] and informally by the system of regional or ideological groups, blocs, and caucuses.

The non-permanent members of the Security Council are elected by the General Assembly for terms of two years. Retiring members are not eligible for immediate re-election (Article 23(2)). The election of non-permanent members is one of the 'important' questions for which a two-thirds majority of the Members of the General Assembly present and voting is required (Article 18(2) of the Charter and Rule 85 of the General Assembly's Rules of Procedure). It is stated in the General Assembly's Rules of Procedure that all elections shall be held by secret ballot and that there shall be no nominations (Rule 94). The ballot is undoubtedly secret, but aspirants for elective seats on the Council have always been candid about their availability.

The Charter states that in the election of non-permanent members, due regard shall be specially paid

> . . . in the first instance to the contribution of Members of the United Nations to the maintenance of international peace and security and to the other purposes of the Organization, and also to equitable geographical distribution (Article 23(1)).

The British delegation at the Dumbarton Oaks Conference suggested on the insistence of Canada that the Charter should specify that, in the election of non-permanent members of the Security Council, due regard should be paid to the *military* contributions of States to the maintenance of international peace and security. Both the United States and the Soviet Union had reservations about the proposal in this form, and the British delegate therefore agreed to the omission of 'military'.[156] The idea of linking the election of non-permanent members of the Council to contributions to peace and security was revived at San Francisco. Britain suggested adding 'equitable geographical distribution' as another criterion, and the reference to 'the other purposes of the Organization' was inserted because of the difficulties the League of Nations had experienced in collecting financial contributions.[157]

During the first session of the General Assembly, all six elective seats had to be filled.[158] On the first vallot, *five* States received more than the required majority: Brazil, Egypt,

Mexico, Netherlands, and Poland; Australia and Canada were runners-up. Canada withdrew after the third ballot, and Australia was accordingly elected.[159] The pattern of election at the first session was thus as follows:

Latin America	2
Middle East	1
Eastern Europe	1
Western Europe	1
Commonwealth	1

This was not fortuitous; the pattern was based on an informal understanding between the Council's permanent members. The precise content of the agreement has not, to my knowledge, been published although several U.S. officials were under the impression that there had been a moral commitment to the Soviet Union to ensure 'the continuous presence of two East European countries . . .';[160] but those official spokesmen who have referred to the agreement, and those scholars who have written about it, have tended to use inconsistent language. One of the most thorough studies, by L. C. Green, refers to the following descriptions which people have used for the groups initially represented on the Council:[161]

Latin America, South America
Middle East, Arab States
Eastern Europe, 'the Slav countries'
Western Europe
Commonwealth, 'South Pacific or Commonwealth', 'Pacific or Asia'

The Soviet Union has always maintained that the permanent members reached a gentlemen's agreement in 1946 on the distribution of the elective seats. The Five, in the Soviet view,

> . . . undertook to support the election to the Council of candidates nominated by the countries of the five main regions of the world. In accordance with that plan it was agreed that in the election of non-permanent members support would be given to two countries from the Latin-American region . . . while one seat would be allotted to the British Commonwealth, one to the Middle East, one to Western Europe, and one to Eastern Europe.[162]

The Soviet Union has maintained that the General Assembly should, as a matter of course, endorse the choices already made informally and privately by regional or other groups.

The United States, for its part, has claimed that the 1946 agreement was intended to apply to the first election only; that the only factors to be taken into account in connection with subsequent elections are those specified in Article 23(1) of the Charter; that the States of the Soviet bloc failed to contribute to the maintenance of international peace and security; that the Charter refers to equitable geographical *distribution* and not *representation*, and that this principle was maintained, at any rate until 1962, by the election for the East European seat of such States as Greece, Turkey, and Yugoslavia.

Some States which were not parties to the 1946 understanding have not felt bound by it. The Indian representative stated this explicitly during the second session of the General Assembly (1947), after reluctantly withdrawing from the contest to permit the election of the Ukraine.[163]

We have been told that the allocation of seats on the Council is based in some arrangement privately arrived at among some of the Powers. But the distribution of Council seats by secret diplomacy to which the members of the General Assembly are not a party cannot, I am sure, find any support in this august body.

Without in any way desiring to offend any of the Powers concerned, the delegation of India must challenge this arrangement.

Our withdrawal should not be taken to mean, nor does it imply, that we accept the so-called agreement between certain Powers for the distribution of seats.[164]

The Charter requirement that a two-thirds majority of the members present and voting is required for the election of non-permanent members of the Security Council means that, if a seat is contested, balloting can be a tedious and lengthy process. Indeed, a determined minority of one-third of the Members plus one has the possibility of compelling the General Assembly to engage in inconclusive ballots for an indefinite period and, in case of extreme intransigence, might render the Security Council ineffective.

During the second session of the Assembly (1947), there were eleven inconclusive ballots for one of the seats before, as noted above, India withdrew in favour of the Ukrainian SSR. There were thirteen inconclusive ballots during the fifth session (1950) before Lebanon withdrew in favour of Turkey. It was not until the nineteenth ballot during the sixth session (1951) that Greece received a two-thirds majority.

During the tenth session (1955), with three seats to fill, no less than thirty-six ballots were necessary. On the first ballot, thirty-nine votes were needed for election, and Cuba and Australia obtained the required majority; Poland and the Philippines had thirty-four and thirty-three votes respectively. After four ballots, Poland withdrew in the hope that Yugoslavia might be acceptable as a compromise candidate. Twenty-five further inconclusive ballots were held, with Yugoslavia varying between twenty-five and thirty-three votes; on all these ballots, except the nineteenth, the Philippines was in the lead, but was always at least seven votes short of the required majority.

After the twenty-ninth inconclusive ballot had taken place, the President of the Assembly drew the attention of hungry and weary delegates to the serious situation.

If no agreement is reached, I for my part am ready to assist the Assembly [the verb was nicely chosen] in reaching a decision by calling a meeting which would not rise until the vacant seat has been filled . . .[165]

The session of the Assembly was due to close on 10 December, but two days before this the closing date was changed to 16 December. The admission of sixteen new members on 14 December introduced a new element into the situation. For the next five ballots, which were held on the morning of 16 December, the required two-thirds majority fluctuated between forty-four and forty-six votes. On the thirty-second ballot, the Philippines obtained forty votes, its highest, but still six short of two-thirds.

At 9 o'clock on the evening of 16 December (the revised date for the closing of the session), after all other business had been disposed of, the General Assembly returned to the election. Thirty-four ballots had been held without the third vacancy on the Council being filled. The President announced that there had been consultations with a number of delegations, including the two rivals for the seat, with the object of finding an acceptable solution.

It was felt that this purpose would be achieved if lots were drawn in the President's office between the two candidates I have already mentioned to decide which should withdraw from the present elections. After completing the first year of the term, the other candidate would offer its resignation from the Security Council. The agreement is that the vacant seat would then be filled for the remainder of the term by the election of the other candidate at the eleventh [1956] session.

The spirit of this compromise solution, for which I do not hesitate to assume a moral responsibility that will certainly be shared by the other representatives, must ensure that the agreement will be faithfully observed.

In accordance with the procedure I have outlined, lots were drawn in the President's office; as a result the Philippines has withdrawn its candidature at this time in favour of Yugoslavia.

I am sure that the Assembly, in approving this procedure, will recognize that it does not set a precedent and will further agree that, in view of the unusual circumstances, the arrangement should be accepted and carried out.[166]

Following the President's statement, several representatives expressed reservations about the procedure which had been outlined. A few stated flatly that it was illegal; others announced that they had no instructions in connection with such an unexpected development; others expressly said that they could not at that time commit their governments regarding the future, and in particular as to how they would vote in 1956 if Yugoslavia should resign the seat after one year. After an inconclusive debate, the Philippines suggested that a further ballot be held. This time Yugoslavia received thirty-four votes and the Philippines nineteen (forty votes required for election). The President thereupon declared that he released the two parties from the agreement. The Assembly, having at 10.30 p.m. rejected a motion to suspend the meeting and resume it one hour later, decided to extend the session until 20 December.[167]

On the morning of 20 December, the Assembly returned to the question, and on the thirty-sixth ballot Yugoslavia received forty-three votes, five more than the required majority. The three-month session closed, as is the custom, with one minute of silent prayer or meditation.

Having served on the Council during 1956, Yugoslavia informed the Secretary-General that she would not be in a position to serve in 1957.[168] A by-election to fill the vacancy was therefore held in accordance with Rule 141 of the Assembly's Rules of Procedure, and the Philippines was elected on the first ballot, obtaining one vote more than the required majority. Following the election, the Soviet representative stated that there has been a flagrant violation of the rights of the Eastern European Members. He referred to the informal agreement of 1946 and said that the decision just reached illustrated the fact that the United Nations was dwindling in importance.[169]

A similar situation developed during the fourteenth session of the Assembly in 1959. The terms of office of Canada, Japan, and Panama were due to expire at the end of the year. After a certain amount of preliminary manoeuvring, it was agreed informally that Ceylon and Ecuador should succeed Canada and Panama respectively, and they were duly elected on the first ballot. Poland and Turkey were candidates for the third vacancy.

Poland's candidature was announced in July, though, for some months before that, Polish diplomats in New York and elsewhere had been preparing the ground. At one time it seemed likely that Greece would be Poland's rival for the seat, but at the last moment Greece withdrew and Turkey was substituted. It was the view of Turkey's supporters that the seat for which she was a candidate should, if possible, be filled by an Eastern European country. One difficulty was that Turkey had, for a time in 1959, been a candidate for one of the Vice-Presidencies of the General Assembly intended for 'Western European and other States', but at the last moment had switched her candidature to one of the Afro-Asian vacancies. By contesting an East European vacancy on the Security Council, Turkey was in effect claiming to belong to three different regions at once. Moreover, the announcement of Turkey's candidature was not made until after the session had begun, by which time some States had already made commitments to Poland.

Fifty-two ballots were needed to resolve the question. The two-thirds majority required for election varied between fifty and fifty-four votes, which meant that a State with at least twenty-eight supporters in every ballot could prevent any other State from being elected. In the event, Poland's vote never fell

TABLE 11

Non-permanent members of the security Council, 1946–74

	Latin America	*Africa and Asia*	*Eastern Europe*	*Western Europe*	*Older Commonwealth States*
1946	Brazil Mexico	Egypt	Poland	Netherlands	Australia
1947	Brazil Colombia	Syria	Poland	Belgium	Australia
1948	Argentina Colombia	Syria	Ukrainian SSR	Belgium	Canada
1949	Argentina Cuba	Egypt	Ukrainian SSR	Norway	Canada
1950	Cuba Ecuador	Egypt India	Yugoslavia	Norway	
1951	Brazil Ecuador	India	Yugoslavia	Netherlands Turkey	
1952	Brazil Chile	Pakistan		Greece Netherlands Turkey	
1953	Chile Colombia	Lebanon Pakistan		Denmark Greece	
1954	Brazil Colombia	Lebanon		Denmark Turkey	New Zealand
1955	Brazil Peru	Iran		Belgium Turkey	New Zealand
1956	Cuba Peru	Iran	Yugoslavia (resigned)	Belgium	Australia
1957	Colombia Cuba	Iraq Philippines		Sweden	Australia
1958	Colombia Panama	Iraq Japan		Sweden	Canada
1959	Argentina Panama	Japan Tunisia		Italy	Canada
1960	Argentina Ecuador	Tunisia Ceylon (Sri Lanka)	Poland (resigned)	Italy	
1961	Chile Ecuador	Ceylon (Sri Lanka) Liberia (resigned) United Arab Republic (Egypt)		Turkey	
1962	Chile Venezuela	Ghana United Arab Republic (Egypt)	Romania (resigned)	Ireland	
1963	Brazil Venezuela	Ghana Morocco Philippines		Norway	
1964	Bolivia Brazil	Ivory Coast Morocco	Czecho-slovakia (resigned)	Norway	

TABLE 11—*continued*

	Latin America	*Africa and Asia*	*Eastern Europe*	*Western Europe*	*Older Commonwealth States*
1965	Bolivia Uruguay	Ivory Coast Jordan Malaysia		Netherlands	

	Latin America	*Africa and Asia*	*Eastern Europe*	*Western European and other States*
1966	Argentina Uruguay	Japan Jordan Mali Nigeria Uganda	Bulgaria	Netherlands New Zealand
1967	Argentina Brazil	Ethiopia India Japan Mali Nigeria	Bulgaria	Canada Denmark
1968	Brazil Paraguay	Algeria Ethiopia India Pakistan Senegal	Hungary	Canada Denmark
1969	Colombia Paraguay	Algeria Nepal Pakistan Senegal Zambia	Hungary	Finland Spain
1970	Colombia Nicaragua	Burundi Nepal Sierra Leone Syria Zambia	Poland	Finland Spain
1971	Argentina Nicaragua	Burundi Japan Sierra Leone Somalia Syria	Poland	Belgium Italy
1972	Argentina Panama	Guinea India Japan Somalia Sudan	Yugoslavia	Belgium Italy
1973	Panama Peru	Guinea India Indonesia Kenya Sudan	Yugoslavia	Australia Austria
1974	Costa Rica Peru	Cameroon Indonesia Iraq Kenya Mauritania	Byelorussian SSR	Australia Austria

below thirty-six, and—until the last ballot—Turkey's vote never fell below thirty-three.

Balloting began on 12 October. Thirty-one ballots were held during that month, twelve more during November, and six more on 1 December. The Assembly was due to close on 5 December, though the session was later extended. Turkey let it be known in mid-November that she would consider 'splitting the term' with Poland, and discussions about this took place during the last few days of the session. At the night meeting at the end of the session, 12/13 December, the General Assembly was able to endorse an agreement which had been negotiated in private. The President stated that consultations had taken place between the two candidates and their supporters, as a result of which it had been agreed that Poland was the only candidate but would resign after one year. Turkey would then be the only candidate for the vacancy thus created. 'In the vote, it is understood that the Members of the Assembly will confirm that agreement.'[170] At 2.30 a.m. the Assembly proceeded to the election by secret ballot. Poland obtained seventy-one votes, thus being elected on the fifty-second ballot. Three diehards maintained their support for Turkey; Greece and Yemen obtained one vote each; four members abstained, and two (understandably) were absent.

The decision to split the 1956–7 term between Yugoslavia and the Philippines had been reluctantly accepted by the General Assembly as an exceptional measure and on the understanding, as the President put it, 'that it does not set a precedent'. The adoption of the same expedient in 1959 soon came to be regarded as a normal arrangement. In 1960, after thirteen inconclusive ballots, it was announced that Liberia and Ireland would split the 1961–2 term. The following year, after nine inconclusive ballots, Romania and the Philippines agreed to split the 1962–3 term, and the 1964–5 term was split between Czechoslovakia and Malaysia.

As will be explained in Chapter 5 (pp. 232–4), the election of Malaysia to serve during 1965 was the occasion for Indonesia's temporary withdrawal from the United Nations.

There had been two distinct but related difficulties over the distribution of elective seats. From 1950 onwards, there was disagreement over the seat originally earmarked for Eastern

Europe. This difficulty was aggravated by the growth in the total UN Membership, especially in 1955 and 1960, so that it was increasingly difficult to achieve 'equitable geographical distribution' with only six seats to be filled by General Assembly election. To make matters worse, the requirement of a two-thirds majority for election meant that a determined minority of UN Members (one-third plus one) could, theoretically, prevent a vacancy on the Council from being filled and thus

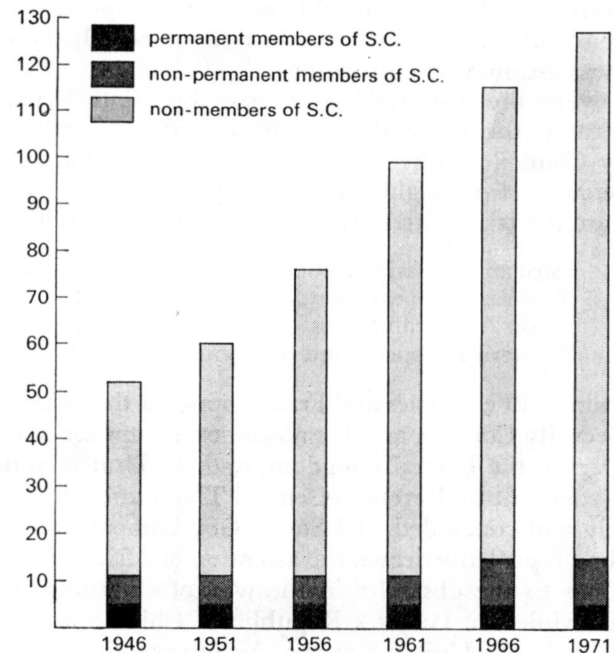

Chart 1. UN Membership, 1946–71 (1 January)

make it impossible for the Council to function, 'continuously' or otherwise.

The obvious solution, to enlarge the Council, presented two problems. The first was a straightforward matter of mechanics: the larger the Council, the easier it would be to achieve 'equitable geographical distribution'; but beyond a certain point, bigness would constitute an obstacle to effective working. In due course, it became apparent that an increase from 11 to 15 would provide the optimum size—enough to ensure equitable distribution, but not so much that size *per se* would add materially to the difficulties already faced by the Council.

The other difficulty was that enlargement could be achieved only by amending the Charter, a matter subject to veto by any of the permanent members, and the Soviet Union had taken the position that no Charter amendments were acceptable until the question of Chinese representation had been rectified. For the Soviet Union to have persisted with this position might have been logical, but it would have been imprudent, for it would have alienated Third World opinion which the Soviet Union was assiduously cultivating.

In 1963, on the initiative of a group of forty-four African and Asian States, the General Assembly decided to enlarge the Security Council to fifteen members (and the Economic and Social Council from eighteen to twenty-seven members), and to allocate the ten elective seats on the Council as follows:[171]

African and Asian States	5
Eastern European States	1
Latin American States	2
Western European and other States	2

The Communist countries and France opposed the enlargement of the Security Council, and the abstainers comprised Portugal, South Africa, the United Kingdom, and the United States.

In a letter sent to Secretary-General Thant after the General Assembly had concluded, the Soviet Government pointed out that it had repeatedly drawn the attention of African and Asian delegations to the obstacles in the way of enlarging the two Councils while the People's Republic of China was deprived of its rights in the United Nations. As an exceptional measure, the Soviet Government would have agreed to enlargement of the Councils 'provided the Government of the People's Republic of China explicitly declared its consent . . .' On 8 December 1963, however, the Chinese Government had informed the Soviet Government that it approved of solving the problem not by enlarging the Councils but 'by means of a just distribution of the seats now available'.[172]

In spite of Chinese opposition to enlargement, Secretary-General Thant was able to report on 27 September 1965 that sufficient ratifications had been received, including those of the permanent members of the Security Council, for the Charter amendments to have entered into force,[173] and elections for the enlarged Council were held during the course of the 1965 session of the General Assembly.

6. OTHER PARTICIPANTS

If the Security Council is to fulfil its primary responsibility for maintaining international peace and security, non-members of the Council must have access to it; and this right of access is laid down in the Charter and the Rules of Procedure—though in a somewhat complicated manner.

1. UN Members which are not members of the Security Council
   (a) '*shall be invited* to participate, without vote, in the discussion' relating to a dispute *to which it is a party* (Article 32, my italics);
   (b) '*may be invited*, as the result of *a decision of the Security Council*, to participate, without vote . . .' in the discussion of 'any situation which might lead to international friction or give rise to a dispute' or 'any dispute' which the Member has brought to the attention of the Council (Article 35(1) and Rule 37, my italics);
   (c) '*may* participate, without vote, in the discussion of any question brought before the Security Council *whenever the latter* considers that *the interests of that Member are specially affected*' (Article 31 and Rule 37, my italics);
   (d) when a Member not represented on the Council is called upon to provide armed forces which the Council has decided to use, the Member *shall be invited* to participate, *if it so desires, in the decisions* (not simply in the discussions) concerning the employment of contingents of that Member's armed forces (Article 44, my italics). It has never been necessary to resort to this provision.
2. A non-Member of the United Nations may bring to the attention of the Council (or, indeed, the General Assembly) '*any dispute to which it is a party* if it accepts in advance, for the purposes of the dispute, the obligations of pacific settlement provided in the . . . Charter' (Article 35(2)). Such a non-Member '*shall be invited* to participate, without vote, in the discussion [in the Security Council] relating to the dispute. The Security Council shall lay down such conditions as it deems just' for the participation of non-Members of the United Nations (Article 32, my italics). Representatives of non-UN

Members which are not parties to a dispute could presumably be invited to participate under Rule 39 if the Council considered them competent to supply information or give other assistance.

3. Members of the Secretariat whom the Council considers competent for the purpose may be invited by the Council to supply it with information or to give other assistance in examining matters within the Council's competence (Rule 39).
4. 'Other persons' may be similarly invited by the Council to supply information or give other assistance (Rule 39).

Requests to participate have been steadily increasing, and no fewer than thirty-two UN Members which were not members of the Security Council took part in the debates on the Congo question in the period 1960–4, when the Council itself had only eleven members; and, on one occasion, four African foreign ministers participated 'on behalf of all African States . . .'[174] Often there are not enough seats around the Council table for all who have been invited to participate. In that event, representatives are called to the table in order to address the Council and then return to reserved seats alongside the table.[175]

TABLE 12

Requests by UN Members to participate, without vote, granted by the Security Council, 1946–65

	No. of requests granted	*No. of meetings of Security Council*	*No. of UN Members (mid-point of period)*
1946–50	43	530	60
1951–5	22	179	76
1956–60	70	211	99
1961–5	181	350	118

Table 12 gives the number of requests to participate which were granted in five-year periods. *The Repertoire of Practice* states that 'material relevant to participation . . . cannot . . . be satisfactorily arranged within a classification derived directly from [the] texts', since on many occasions the Council has extended invitations 'in circumstances the correspondence of which to those envisaged in [the] texts has been the subject of no definite pronouncement by the Council.'[176] This is merely

Secretariat-style for saying that the Council has issued invitations without much regard to the requirements of the Charter and Rules of Procedure. Certainly there have been many cases in which the basis on which the invitation was granted was by no means clear.

Requests by UN Members to participate in the discussion are rarely rejected. The only cases of rejection of requests from UN Members have been that of the Philippines to participate in the discussion of the second phase of the Indonesian question (7 August 1947), a decision which was soon reversed; 11 Members in connection with Tunisia (14 April 1952); and 13 Members in connection with Morocco (3 September 1953). Other proposals which have been rejected were by Belgium that East Indonesia and Borneo be invited to participate in the discussion of the second phase of the Indonesian question (14 August and 22 August 1947), a proposal by Pakistan that Sheikh Abdullah be invited to participate in the debate on the India–Pakistan question (12 May 1964), and a request from a representative of the illegal regime in Rhodesia in connection with the situation in Southern Rhodesia (18 May 1966). In a few cases, Members which have asked to participate in the discussion have been invited to submit their views in writing.

Proposals regarding the participation of non-Members of the United Nations (Category 2) are listed in Table 13. In the cases in which requests to participate were rejected, the issue was not simply whether the non-Member was or was not a party to a dispute or whether its representative was or was not competent to supply the Council with information, but whether an invitation to participate in the proceedings of the Security Council would confer unwarranted legitimacy on the applicant.

There are two express limitations to the participation of non-members of the Council. First, the Charter states that the participation of non-members is 'without vote' (Articles 31 and 32). Second, UN Members may submit proposals and draft resolutions, but these will be put to a vote 'only at the request of a representative on the Security Council' (Rule 38).

The normal practice of the Council is to hear first the Member State or States submitting the matter, and then any other States directly concerned; this is sometimes followed by statements of reply. The Council then proceeds to a general debate. When a representative is invited to participate, he may do so until that particular phase of the discussion of the matter is completed. If, after one phase is completed, the Council later resumes discussion of the same item, a new invitation is sought. Sometimes requests to participate are received after the initial phase of the Council's consideration of a question, and such requests are not denied solely because of the lateness in applying. In the case of States not Members of the United Nations, the usual practice about speaking first

TABLE 13

Invitations to Non-Members of the United Nations to Participate in the Discussion in the Security Council, 1946–73

A. *Requests granted*

Date	*Item*	*Invitation to*
9 Sept. 1946	Ukrainian complaint against Greece	Albania
10 Dec. 1946	Greek Frontier Incidents	Albania
10 Dec. 1946	Greek Frontier Incidents	Bulgaria
16 Dec. 1946	Greek Frontier Incidents	Albania
16 Dec. 1946	Greek Frontier Incidents	Bulgaria
20 Jan. 1947	Corfu Channel Incidents	Albania
12 Aug. 1947	Indonesian question	Indonesia
7 July 1948	Palestine question	Israel*
16 Sept. 1948	Hyderabad question	Hyderabad
25 June 1950	Complaint of aggression upon the Republic of Korea	Republic of Korea (South)
29 Sept. 1950	Complaint of armed invasion of Taiwan (Formosa)	People's Republic of China
16 Oct. 1950	Palestine question	Jordan
8 Nov. 1950	Complaint of aggression upon the Republic of Korea	People's Republic of China
29 Oct. 1953	Palestine question	Jordan
4 May 1954	Palestine question	Jordan
31 Jan. 1955	Hostilities in the area of certain islands off the coast of China	People's Republic of China
5 July 1961	Question relating to Kuwait	Kuwait
7 May 1963	Admission of new Members	Kuwait
19 May 1964	Complaint concerning acts of aggression against Cambodia	Republic of Viet-Nam (South)
7 Aug. 1964	Incidents in the Gulf of Tonkin	Democratic Republic of Viet-Nam (North)
		Republic of Viet-Nam (South)

* At the 253rd meeting of the Security Council, a representative of the Jewish Agency for Palestine was invited to participate; at the 330th meeting on 7 July 1948, he was for the first time referred to as the representative of the State of Israel.

TABLE 13—*continued*

B. *Requests rejected*

Date	*Item*	*Invitation to*
25 June 1950	Complaint of aggression upon the Republic of Korea	People's Republic of Korea (North)
27 June 1950	Complaint of aggression upon the Republic of Korea	People's Republic of Korea (North)
29 Aug. 1950	Complaint of armed invasion of Taiwan (Formosa)	People's Republic of China
1 Sept. 1950	Complaint of aggression upon the Republic of Korea	People's Republic of Korea (North) and Republic of Korea (South)
6 Sept. 1950	Complaint of aggression upon the Republic of Korea	People's Republic of China
11 Sept. 1950	Complaint of bombing of China	People's Republic of China
28 Sept. 1950	Complaint of armed invasion of Taiwan (Formosa)	People's Republic of China
8 Nov. 1950	Complaint of aggression upon the Republic of Korea	People's Republic of China
1 July 1952	Alleged bacterial warfare	People's Republic of China and People's Republic of Korea (North)
24 Aug. 1968	Situation in Southern Rhodesia	German Democratic Republic

cannot always be followed. If a State invited to participate has to send a special delegation to New York, or wherever the Council may be meeting, the Council may be unwilling to suspend all consideration of the matter pending its arrival.[177]

On a number of occasions, proposals have been made that representatives of States not members of the Council should be invited to take part in the discussion regarding the adoption of the Agenda, but the Council has rejected such proposals, or allowed non-members to comment on the Agenda only after the vote on it has been taken. Only rare exceptions to this practice have occurred, and the circumstances were unusual. On 6 January 1948, the Council began discussing the situation in Jammu and Kashmir; discussion on the item continued at four further meetings. On 22 January, however, in the Provisional Agenda for the meeting, the item was entitled 'India–Pakistan question'. The President explained that this change had been made on his own responsibility 'in consequence of a letter . . . addressed to me by the Pakistan Minister for Foreign Affairs'. He suggested that the Council should make an exception to its usual practice and allow the Indian representative to speak. A long discussion ensued, in which India took part, and in the end the Council adopted the Provisional Agenda with the item in its amended form.[178]

Another example was on 20 August 1969. Ireland had requested an urgent meeting to consider 'the situation in the six counties of Northern Ireland'. Britain asked the Council to reject the Provisional Agenda on the ground that the matter was one of domestic jurisdiction and therefore beyond the Council's competence. By pre-arrangement, and without any objection from the United Kingdom, Ireland's Foreign Minister was invited to address the Council. The British representative replied in conciliatory terms. Zambia then proposed that, without taking a decision on the Provisional Agenda, the Council should adjourn, and the motion was adopted unanimously. The honour of all concerned was satisfied.[179]

It is the orthodox view that an invited representative does not have the right to raise points of order or take part in procedural discussions.[180] When the issue first arose in 1947, the President (Syria) stated: 'I am sorry but the raising of points of order is limited to members of the Council.'[181] On a very few occasions, however, invited representatives have succeeded in overcoming the obstacles.[182] Once an interruption occurs, even if improperly, it is difficult to proceed with the discussion until the President has disposed of the question which has been raised.

Invited representatives are not entitled to vote, but have been permitted to make statements about a resolution either before or after its adoption.[183] Invited representatives have also been allowed to make statements on the question of postponing discussion and fixing the date of the next meeting.

Cases have occurred in which a UN Member which is not a member of the Council has been invited to participate but has declined to do so, or has withdrawn immediately after making a statement.[184]

Rule 39 permits the Council to invite members of the Secretariat or other persons whom it considers competent for the purpose to supply it with information or to give other assistance. This rule has been used to secure the participation of the presiding officers of UN organs dealing with matters within the Council's competence (Military Staff Committee, Committee of Experts, Committee on the Admission of New Members, Commission of Investigation concerning Greek Frontier Incidents, Committee of Good Offices on the Indonesian question, Palestine Commission, the Commission for India and Pakistan, the President of the General Assembly, the Assembly's committee on decolonization, the Special Committee on Apartheid, and the Council for Namibia), as well as individuals having responsibilities within the Council's sphere of responsibility (Mediator and Acting Mediator for Palestine, Chief of Staff of the UN Truce Supervision Organization in

TABLE 14

Invitations to Persons to Participate in the Discussion in the Security Council, 1946–73

Date	*Item*	*Person invited*
24 Feb. 1948	Palestine question	Representative of the Jewish Agency for Palestine
24 Feb. 1948	Palestine question	Representative of the Arab Higher Committee
15 Apr. 1948	Palestine question	Representative of the Arab Higher Committee
22 Mar. 1948	Czechoslovak question	Mr. Jan Papanek
28 Sept. 1948	Hyderabad question	The Nawab Moin Nawaz Jung
27 Feb. 1964	Cyprus question	Mr. Rauf Denktash
13 May 1965	Situation in the Dominican Republic	Mr. Rubén Brache Mr. Guaroa Velázquez
20 Dec. 1967	Cyprus question	Mr. Osman Örek
3 May 1968	Palestine question	Mr. Rouhi El-Khatib
27 Sept. 1971	Situation in Namibia	H.E. Mr. Moktar Ould Daddah
30 Sept. 1971	Situation in Namibia	Mr. Sam Nujoma
2 Dec. 1971	Situation in Southern Rhodesia	Mr. Joshua Nkomo*
2 Dec. 1971	Situation in Southern Rhodesia	The Rev. Ndabaningi Sithole*
28 Jan. 1972	Questions relating to Africa	Emperor Haile Selassie I H.E. Mr. Moktar Ould Daddah
1 Feb. 1972	Questions relating to Africa	Mr. Mohammed Fouad El-Bidewi
1 Feb. 1972	Questions relating to Africa	Mr. Amilcar Cabral
1 Feb. 1972	Questions relating to Africa	Mr. M. Luvualo
1 Feb. 1972	Questions relating to Africa	Mr. M. Dos Santos

* As Mr. Nkomo was in detention and Mr. Sithole was serving a prison sentence in Rhodesia, neither was able to appear before the Council.

TABLE 14—*continued*

Date	*Item*	*Person invited*
1 Feb. 1972	Questions relating to Africa	Mr. Peter Mueshihange
1 Feb. 1972	Questions relating to Africa	Mr. M. K. H. Hamadziripi
1 Feb. 1972	Questions relating to Africa	Mr. Portlako Leballo
1 Feb. 1972	Questions relating to Africa	Mr. Alfred Nzo
1 Feb. 1972	Questions relating to Africa	Mr. George Silundika
1 Feb. 1972	Questions relating to Africa	Mr. Abdul Minty
1 Feb. 1972	Questions relating to Africa	The Rev. Canon Burgess Carr
1 Feb. 1972	Questions relating to Africa	Mr. Johnny Eduardo
16 Feb. 1972	Situation in Southern Rhodesia	Bishop Abel Muzorewa
28 Sept. 1972	Situation in Southern Rhodesia	Mr. Eshmael Mlambo
16 Nov. 1972	Territories under Portuguese Administration	Mr. Marcelino Dos Santos
16 Nov. 1972	Territories under Portuguese Administration	Mr. Gil Fernandes
17 Nov. 1972	Territories under Portuguese Administration	Mr. Manuel Jorge
1 Dec. 1972	Situation in Namibia	Mr. Peter Mueshihange
15 Mar. 1973	Peace and Security in Latin America	Mr. Héctor Gros Espiell
19 Mar. 1973	Peace and Security in Latin America	H.E. Mr. Mamadou Diarra
19 Mar. 1973	Peace and Security in Latin America	H.E. Mr. Talib El-Shebib
14 Aug. 1973	Situation in the Middle East	H.E. Mr. Talib El-Shebib *
11 Dec. 1973	Situation in Namibia	Mr. Mishake Muyongo

* The Council's decision to invite Mr. El-Shebib is unaccountably omitted from the *Resolutions and Decisions of the Security Council 1973*.

Palestine, Representative for India and Pakistan, as well as a former President of the Council, General A. G. L. McNaughten of Canada, who had been asked to consult with India and Pakistan about some of the issues between the two countries).

More controversial have been requests to participate from individuals claiming to represent substantial bodies of opinion, such as the Jewish Agency for Palestine before the creation of the State of Israel, the Arab Higher Committee, spokesmen for the Turkish-speaking community in Cyprus, and representatives of African liberation movements (see Table 14). Regional organizations are supposed to keep the Security Council fully informed of activities undertaken or contemplated for the maintenance of international peace and security (Article 54), but this requirement has not been consistently observed.

7. PERMANENT MISSIONS*[185]

The Charter makes no specific provision for permanent diplomatic missions of Member States. They were established, in the first instance, by members of the three Councils provided for in the Charter (Security, Economic and Social, Trusteeship) and, as UN organs meeting between sessions of the General Assembly proliferated, were found to be necessary by almost all UN Members. In 1948, the General Assembly gave its blessing to the idea of permanent missions because they 'assist in the realization of the purposes and principles of the United Nations and, in particular, [help] to keep the necessary liaison between Member States and the Secretariat . . .'[186] Specific provisions regarding the status of permanent representatives are contained in the Convention on the Privileges and Immunities of the United Nations, the Headquarters Agreement with the United States, and the Vienna Convention on Diplomatic Relations.[187] While the establishment of permanent missions at UN Headquarters is not obligatory, most Members have found it convenient to do so. At the time of the last report of Secretary-General Waldheim in 1973, only two Members (Gambia and the Maldives) had not established permanent missions.[188] The Maldives had a permanent mission from the time of its admission to the United Nations in 1965 until 1969. Gambia, also admitted in 1965, has never maintained a permanent mission at UN Headquarters.

The normal diplomatic practice of obtaining prior agreement that a diplomatic agent is acceptable to the State to which he or she is accredited is not followed at the United Nations. In 1949, Secretary-General Lie suggested a standard form of credentials, but there is no question of the Secretary-General granting or withholding recognition. The head of a permanent mission presents his credentials to the Secretary-General on assuming his post, but there is nothing like the traditional ceremonial which is used at the Court of St. James's and in some other capitals.

* The word *mission* sometimes causes confusion in UN circles. *Diplomatic missions* accredited to the United Nations are distinct from *Visiting Missions* set up by the Trusteeship Council (Article 87). Needless to say, members of these two kinds of mission are never called 'missionaries'.

Secretary-General Hammarskjold greatly valued the system of permanent representation.

Over the years, the diplomatic representatives accredited to the United Nations have developed a cooperation and built mutual contacts in dealing with problems they have in common, which in reality makes them members of a kind of continuous diplomatic conference, in which they are informally following and able to discuss, on a personal basis, all political questions which are important for the work of the Organization. These continuous informal deliberations do not lend themselves to publicity, and they receive none. But it would be a grave mistake to conclude from this that they are unimportant. On the contrary, the flexible and confidential forms in which these discussions can be pursued have given them a particular value as a complement to other diplomatic contacts and to all the various conferences and public exchanges . . . which constitute the normal operating procedures in a more traditional diplomacy.

The permanent delegations, wrote Hammarskjold, are 'pioneers in the development of international cooperation . . .' The system of permanent representation 'may well come to be regarded as the most important "common law" development which has taken place so far within the constitutional framework of the Charter.'[189]

8. GROUPS

If the development of permanent missions can be thought of as pioneering, even more so can the evolution of a rudimentary party system at the United Nations. The groups, to paraphrase Edmund Burke, are bodies of UN Members, united 'for promoting by their joint endeavours' certain regional or ideological interests, sometimes upon 'some particular principle in which they are all agreed'.

The system of blocs, groups, and caucuses *in the General Assembly* has by now been much studied by scholars: it hardly needs saying that they system also operates in the Security Council, although in a somewhat different manner. The emergence of groups was a natural corollary of the fact that like-minded Members tended to desire the same outcome at the conclusion of a UN debate, and it was therefore prudent to concert tactics in advance. The twenty Latin American

Republics started this practice at the San Francisco Conference.

In the early days, it soon became apparent that the East East European Members (after 1948, including Czechoslovakia, but not Yugoslavia) pursued a common line, with the Soviet Union playing a dominant role. Opposed to the Soviet bloc on many issues was a less cohesive body of Members under U.S. leadership, comprising Northern, Western, and Southern Europe, Latin America, and the older Commonwealth States. Ten States from Africa, the Middle East, and Asia were relatively uncommitted. By 1950, an Arab-Asian Group had come into existence, and after the Bandung Conference of 1955 this was transformed into an Afro-Asian Group. It was this Group which benefited from the new admissions in and after 1955, and by 1970 it had for many purposes separated into an Asian Group and an African Group, with an Arab Group comprising both Asian and African States.

Three developments have served to crystallize the group system. First, the so-called Gentlemen's Agreement of 1946 about the distribution of elective seats on the Security Council was based more on ideas of ideological or regional solidarity than on 'contribution . . . to the maintenance of international peace and security and . . . the other purposes of the Organization' (Article 23(1)). Second, the General Assembly decided in 1963 on geographical patterns for the non-permanent membership of the Security Council (and for the Economic and Social Council), and for the distribution of chairmanships and vice-presidencies in the General Assembly.[190] Third, in July 1971, the UN *Journal* began publishing monthly information regarding the current chairmanship of regional groups.[191]

On the basis of the elections by the General Assembly since formal geographical patterns came into effect as well as the information contained in the *Journal*, it is possible to discover the membership of the regional groups, although the information must be interpreted with care. Some Members (Albania, Cuba, Israel, South Africa, United States) apparently do not meet consistently with any regional group at the present time. Some Members change groups for no apparent reason: Turkey, for example, was chairman of 'Western European and other States' in March 1972 and November 1973, but was chairman of the Asian Group in December 1972. For certain purposes, Japan has more affinity with 'Western European and other States' than with the Asian regional group.

Non-membership and dual membership confuse the picture, but the membership of the regional groups (including inactive members) appeared to be as follows on 1 January 1974:

Group		Total
African States (excluding South Africa), of which 8 are members of Arab League		41
Asian States, of which 12 are members of Arab League		34
East European States (including Byelorussian and Ukrainian SSRs)	10	11
Albania	1	
Latin America: 17 Spanish-speaking, 1 Portuguese-speaking (Brazil), 1 French-speaking (Haiti), 5 former British colonies in the Carribean	24	25
Cuba	1	
Western European and other:		
Western Europe	18	21
Older Commonwealth	3	
Israel, South Africa, United States		3
		135

The Commonwealth, with members in all regions except Eastern Europe, has twenty-nine members* and meets occasionally as a group.

Within the regions or overlapping them are various sub-groups: the Nordic States, members of the European Economic Community, the Francophone States in Africa, and the so-called 'Group of 77' developing countries (numbering ninety-six, comprising all African UN Members except South Africa, all Middle East and Asian Members except China, Israel, Japan, and Mongolia, all Latin American and Caribbean Members except Bahamas, and Yugoslavia).

The most overt manifestations of the group system in the Security Council takes the form of communications or speeches made on behalf of a regional group—'in conformity with the instructions of the Organization of African Unity', 'as Chairman of the African Group for the month';[192] 'as Chairman of the Arab Group'; 'on behalf of the Arab Group';[193] 'The African-Asian Group Members of the United Nations . . .',[194] 'as Chairman of the Latin American Group';[195] 'in accordance

* Nauru, Tonga, and Western Samoa are Commonwealth members which have not applied for UN Membership. Bangladesh has applied for UN Membership, but the application was vetoed by China on 25 August 1972.

with the mandate given to me by the representatives of Non-Aligned Countries . . .'[196]

These overt manifestations are, of course, only the tip of the iceberg. The groups represent forums for a great deal of private multilateral diplomacy. Because the United Nations has become a somewhat unwieldy body, the group system facilitates its working in some respects, and the groups are undoubtedly valued by representatives with only minimal instructions from their capitals.

The case against the groups is much like that often made against the party system at the national level: that the practice of caucusing before discussion and debate tends to make debate meaningless and diplomacy impossible, since members of groups may have already made commitments to their partners from which they cannot later disengage. Adlai Stevenson took a strong line in 1946 against full United States participation in the Latin American or any other regional group.[197]

9. CREDENTIALS

The draft rules of procedure recommended by the Preparatory Commission contained no provisions for the examination of credentials in the Security Council. The Committee of Experts, in a report dated 5 February 1946, proposed rules to the effect that each member of the Council should be represented at meetings by an accredited representative; that the credentials of representatives should be examined by the President and two other members of the Council, who would report their findings to the Council for approval;* that, pending the approval of the credentials of representatives, they should be seated provisionally with the same rights as other representatives; and that any representative to whose credentials there had been objection should have the same rights as other representatives until the matter had been decided.[198]

In a revised draft submitted later in 1946, there were a number of additions and changes. Credentials were to be submitted to the Secretary-General 'not less than twenty-four hours' before a representative took his seat; a Prime Minister or Minister of Foreign Affairs of a member of the Council

* This was similar to the procedure adopted by the Economic and Social Council.

should be entitled to sit on the Council without submitting credentials; a UN Member not a member of the Council, if invited to participate in the Council's deliberations, should submit credentials in the same manner as for members of the Council; and credentials should be examined by the Secretary-General rather than by the President and two other members of the Council: nothing was said about the person authorized to issue credentials. The changes were approved by the Council, except that 'Head of Government' was substituted for 'Prime Minister'.[199]

A further change in the Rules of Procedure relating to credentials was made in 1950, arising out of discussion of the question of Chinese representation. India suggested that the Rules should state that credentials should be issued either by the Head of the State or of the Government, or by the Minister for Foreign Affairs. The Committee of Experts, and later the Council, approved the proposal.[200] This change was to acquire special significance a decade later when the President of the Congo (Leopoldville), Joseph Kasavubu, and the former Prime Minister, Patrice Lumumba, designated different people to represent the Congo in the Security Council. The Council escaped from this predicament by not inviting *either* to participate in its proceedings (14 September 1960).

In the early years, the practice was to include in the Provisional Agenda the report of the Secretary-General regarding his examination of credentials and, after the adoption of the Agenda, to approve the credentials if there had been no objection. Since 1948, reports of the Secretary-General on credentials have not been included in the Provisional Agenda but are circulated to members of the Council. The reports are regarded as having been approved unless there is a specific request that they be considered.

In practice, credentials are submitted and reported on by the Secretary-General only when changes are made in the representation of members of the Council and when non-permanent members are newly elected.[201] In the case of non-members of the Council, the strict requirements of the Rules of Procedure have not always been enforced.[202]

Apart from the question of the representation of China, which is reviewed on pp. 160–167, difficulties regarding credentials have not been frequent. They have arisen either following sudden and fundamental changes of government after which the status of the diplomatic staff in New York was for a time uncertain (as in the case of Hungary in November 1956[203] and Iraq in July 1958[204]) or where competing authorities in a country have purported to issue credentials in respect of different people (as in the case of the Congo, Leopoldville-Kinshasa, now Zaire, in September 1960[205] and the Dominican Republic in May 1965[206]). In such cases, the main issue was not the validity of the credentials but the legitimacy of the issuing authority. While these situations provide opportunities for members of the Council to make political points in the guise of discussing credentials, the Council has been content to evade the issue until the picture has become clear. Secretary-General Thant has expressed the view that the 'clearest' of these cases was in connection with the representation of Iraq. In that instance, the President interpreted rule 17 as indicating that the representative of Iraq, who had been occupying the seat of Iraq, should continue to sit in that seat with the same rights as other representatives, until the Council arrived at another conclusion. Following the submission of a further report on the credentials of the representative of Iraq by the Secretary-General on 6 August 1958 and the receipt of a letter from the previous representative dated 5 August, a new representative of Iraq was seated at the 838th meeting of the Council on 7 August 1958.[207] In other words, a decision on disputed credentials after a change of government is deferred until it has become clear that a particular government has established its authority.

At the first meeting of the Council held in 1968, Algeria asked whether Rule 15* meant that the Council should give 'tacit' approval to the Secretary-General's report on credentials, or whether it was 'necessary for these reports to be approved explicitly'. The President (Pakistan) stated what had been the Council's practice. This, however, did not clear up the point raised by Algeria. If objection had been raised to the credentials of one or several representatives, said Algeria, 'it becomes

* Rule 15 reads in part: 'The credentials of representatives on the Security Council . . . shall be examined by the Secretary-General who shall submit a report to the Security Council *for approval*' (my italics).

necessary . . . for the report to be approved explicitly'. France and the Soviet Union supported the Algerian interpretation, and the President disposed of the matter by suggesting that the Secretary-General should present to the Council 'some information in regard to the recent practice . . .'[208] This was duly done, and the information provided by the Secretary-General was that 'in the absence of any request that [the reports of the Secretary-General] be considered by the Council, [they] have been approved without objection'.[209]

10. REPRESENTATION OF CHINA[210]

This was never a question of credentials but, in the words of Secretary-General Thant, 'would appear instead to have concerned the question of the proper authority to submit such credentials'.[211] The Central People's Government of the People's Republic of China had been established in Peking on 1 October 1949. On 18 November 1949, Foreign Minister Chou En-lai sent statements to the President of the General Assembly and to Secretary-General Lie stating that the delegation appointed by the Nationalist Government had no authority to speak for the Chinese people.[212] The General Assembly was in session at the time but the credentials of the Chinese representatives had already been approved, and no action was taken.[213]

After the conclusion of the session, the Soviet Union raised the question of Chinese representation at a meeting of the Security Council held on 29 December 1949 to consider the Kashmir question. The Soviet representative said he supported the Chinese communication and that the Soviet Government would not regard 'the Kuomintang representative . . . as being empowered to represent the Chinese people . . .' He did not, however, submit a formal proposal of his own. The representative of Nationalist China declared that he represented the legitimate government of China. The President (Canada) pointed out that the matter was not on the Council's Provisional Agenda and suggested that the Council, having heard the statements, should pass to other business. The Soviet representative raised no objection, and the Council proceeded with its work.[214]

On 8 January 1950, Chou En-lai sent another note to

Secretary-General Lie as well as one to the members of the Security Council, protesting at the Council's failure 'to expel the illegitimate representative of the Chinese Kuomintang reactionary clique'. The next meeting of the Council was held on 10 January 1950, with the representative of Nationalist China in the chair. As soon as the meeting opened, the Soviet representative repeated his opposition to the presence in the Council of a representative of Nationalist China, and formally proposed that his credentials be not recognized and that he be excluded from the Council. The Nationalist Chinese President stated that the Soviet proposal would be printed and distributed, whereupon the Soviet representative objected to a ruling from 'a person who does not represent anyone . . .' The President put his ruling to the vote, and it was upheld by eight votes to two (Soviet Union and Yugoslavia), India abstaining. The Soviet representative then declared that he could not participate in the work of the Council 'or take part in this meeting . . . until the Kuomintang representative has been excluded . . .', whereupon he left the Council chamber.[215]

When the Council met two days later, the Soviet representative was in his place, and the first item was the Soviet proposal from the previous meeting. On this occasion Nationalist China ceded the presidency to Cuba. After a debate extending over two meetings, the Soviet draft resolution was rejected by six votes to three, with two abstentions. The Soviet representative then declared that he could not sit in the Council 'until the representative of the Kuomintang group . . . has been removed' and that he would not 'recognize as legal any decision of the Security Council adopted with the participation of the representative of the Kuomintang group'. The Soviet representative then left the chamber,[216] and did not return until the following August, when it was his turn to preside. It was in the absence of the Soviet Union that the Council authorized UN military action to support South Korea.

On 19/20 January 1950, Chou En-lai sent a further communication to Secretary-General Lie and members of the Security Council announcing that Chang Wen-t'ien* had been

* Also known by his *nom de plume* as Chang Lo-fu or simply Lo Fu. Chinese Ambassador to the Soviet Union, 1951–5; Vice Minister for Foreign Affairs, 1954–9; Acting Foreign Minister during the absence abroad of Chou En-lai,

appointed 'Chairman of the delegation of the People's Republic of China to attend the meetings and to participate in the work of the United Nations . . .'[217] Secretary-General Lie has summarized his views at the time as follows.

. . . I did not feel that approval or disapproval of a régime was in question: it was a matter of recognizing the facts of international life . . . It was *China*, not Chiang Kai-shek, that belonged to the United Nations . . . How could Chiang Kai-shek speak for China . . .?[218]

Lie entered into informal conversations, first with four of the permanent members of the Security Council, then with the non-permanent members, and finally with the representative of Nationalist China. Sir Alexander Cadogan of the United Kingdom surprised Lie by suggesting that the Soviet attitude might be based on 'a calculated policy of discouraging rather than encouraging recognition of the new Chinese government by either the United States or France. China, he pointed out, could thereby be kept more effectively in isolation from the West . . .' Dr. T. F. Tsiang, the representative of Nationalist China, was 'highly excited during most of the conversation', which was 'unlike his normal placid self . . .' (see pp. 110–11). He stated several times that the Peking government 'would never survive the two to three months famine period'.[219]

Lie had asked Abraham Feller and Ivan Kerno, legal experts in the Secretariat, to prepare a memorandum on the legal aspects of UN representation, and had given copies of the memorandum to members of the Security Council on a confidential basis. The press got wind of this, so on 8 March, Lie sent a copy to the President of the Security Council for publication.[220]

It was stated in the legal memorandum that the primary difficulty was that the question of the representation of China had been linked to the question of recognition by Member States. This linkage was unfortunate from the practical standpoint, because it made representation dependent entirely on a numerical count of the number of Members in a particular organ which recognized one government or another. It was also wrong from the standpoint of legal theory, since recog-

April 1955 and November 1956 to February 1957; not active in public life since September 1959.

nition of a State is a unilateral act which is decided by each State in accordance with its own free appreciation of the situation. The practice in organs of the United Nations had, until the Chinese question arose, been consistently to distinguish between representation and recognition. 'The United Nations is not an association limited to like-minded States and governments of similar ideological persuasion . . . It must of necessity include States of varying and even conflicting ideologies.' The Chinese case was unique not because it involved a revolutionary change of government but because it was the first in which two rival governments existed. Where a revolutionary government presented itself as representing a State, in rivalry to another government, the question should be which of the two governments was in a position to employ the resources and direct the people of the State in fulfilment of the obligations of Membership. This meant an inquiry as to whether the new government exercised effective authority within the territory of the State and was habitually obeyed by the bulk of the population.[221]

The representative of Nationalist China immediately protested at Secretary-General Lie's action.

> Your memorandum is . . . an attack on the cause of freedom throughout the world . . . If it is too much to expect you to use your influence against Communism, it is certainly not too much to expect you to remain at least neutral . . . In the present instance you have supplied argument against my delegation and in favour of the Soviet Union delegation. You have destroyed public confidence in the impartiality of the Secretariat.[222]

Thereafter, the Chinese Nationalists treated Secretary-General Lie with considerable reserve and abstained in both the Security Council and the General Assembly later in the year when the extension of Lie's term of office was put to the vote.

During the course of the Security Council meetings in January 1950, India had suggested that the Council's Rules of Procedure were defective in not stating who may issue credentials. As already noted, India proposed an amendment to provide that credentials should be issued either by the Head of the State or the Government concerned or by its Minister for Foreign Affairs. India also proposed that a decision to change the representation of a State in the Council should not be made until all Member States had had the opportunity of expressing their views on the matter. These proposals were referred to the Committee of Experts, which approved the first concerning the issuance of credentials. As to the second, there was general agreement in the Committee that it would be desirable to establish some uniform procedure which could be adopted by all organs of the United Nations, but the majority were of the opinion that this was a matter for the General Assembly. The Committee considered, therefore, that the Council should not, for the moment, take a decision on the second proposed amendment. These recommendations of the Committee were approved by the Council.[223]

In August it was the turn of the Soviet representative to preside over meetings of the Security Council. The Council met on the first day of the month, and the Soviet President at once ruled that 'the representative of the Kuomintang group' did not represent China and therefore could not take part in meetings of the Council. This decision having been challenged, it was put to the vote and overruled by eight votes to three. For two days thereafter, the Council considered a Soviet proposal to include in the agenda an item entitled 'Recognition of the representative of the Central People's Government of the People's Republic of China as the representative of China', and eventually decided by five votes to five with one abstention to reject the Soviet proposal.[224]

The question of Chinese representation was raised by the Soviet Union on four subsequent occasions: 10 November 1951, 31 January 1955, 8 September 1955, and 24 May 1967. On the second of these occasions, the Council adopted a United States proposal 'not to consider any proposals to exclude the representative of the Government of the Republic of China, or to seat representatives of the Central People's Government of the People's Republic of China'.[225] The matter was also raised by Somalia on 9 February 1971, but the Council took no action on the statements in favour of seating the People's Republic of China.[226]

The question of Chinese representation was finally resolved later in 1971 in the General Assembly. The matter had first been raised in the General Assembly by Cuba in 1950, but the Assembly had adopted an inconclusive resolution. From 1951 to 1953, the Assembly decided to postpone consideration of proposals on Chinese representation, and from 1954 to 1960 decided 'not to consider' such proposals. From 1961 to 1970, the Assembly considered proposals to seat the People's Republic of China, on seven occasions (1961 and 1965–70) voting also that any proposal to change the representation of China would be 'important', within the meaning of Article 18 of the Charter, thus requiring a two-thirds majority. In 1966, 1967, and 1968, the Assembly rejected proposals to set up committees to study the question. Finally, at a marathon meeting lasting from 5 p.m. to 11.25 p.m. on 25 October 1971, during the course of which a Swedish diplomat allegedly made a rude remark about Saudi Arabian Ambassador Baroody and a Tanzanian diplomat expressed his glee by dancing in one of the aisles, the

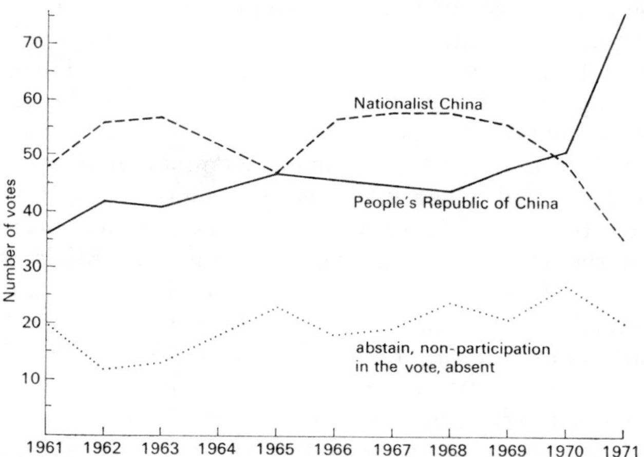

Chart 2. General Assembly voting on the Representation of China, 1961–71

Assembly voted by 76 votes to 35, with twenty States abstaining or absent, 'to restore all its rights to the People's Republic of China . . . and to expel forthwith the representatives of Chiang Kai-shek from the place which they unlawfully occupy . . .'[227] The Chinese delegation formally took its seat in the Assembly three weeks later and, after some embarrassed speeches of welcome, a statement was made by China's Deputy Minister of Foreign Affairs, Ch'iao Kuan-hua.[228]

It was almost exactly twenty-one years since a representative of the People's Republic, Wu Hsiu-ch'üan,* had taken part in the proceedings of the Security Council, during discussion of complaints of aggression upon the Republic of Korea and of armed invasion of Taiwan.[229] Few people remembered, however, that, on the urging of the United States, the Chinese delegation at San Francisco had not been exclusively Kuomintang but had included Communist and other political elements. Among those who signed the UN Charter was Tung Pi-wu, at the present time (1 March 1974) Acting President of the Chinese People's Republic.

On 26 October 1971, Secretary-General Thant circulated to members of the Security Council the text of the resolution which the General Assembly had adopted the previous night. It is, of course, required by the Charter that the Security Council shall be so organized as to be able to function continuously and for this purpose its members are to be represented at all times at the seat of the Organization (Article 28(1)). There was, presumably, a hiatus of about a week when the Council was unable to function, but on 2 November U Thant informed the Council that the Chinese People's Republic had appointed Huang Hua and Chen Chu as representative and deputy representative respectively. On 19 November, the Secretary-General reported to the Council that the credentials of Mr. Huang and Mr. Chen were, in his opinion, in order, and when the Council met two days later, members of the Council were unanimous in expressing their welcome to the Chinese.[230] †

During the twenty-two-year period when China's UN seat was occupied by a representative of the rump Kuomintang government which had taken refuge on Taiwan, the situation had become increasingly absurd. Security Council diplomacy on matters relating to China was more and more unreal. When it was China's month to preside, the normal arrangements for informal consultations under the auspices of the President could not be relied on, and members of the Council would solemnly thank the representative of Nationalist China the following month for his consideration in not calling any meet-

* Vice Minister for Foreign Affairs, 1951–5; Ambassador to Yugoslavia, 1955–58; severely criticized in 1967 for ideological deviations.

† The Soviet representative was, however, careful to call Mr. Huang of China 'colleague', while Mr. Kulaga of Poland was addressed as 'comrade'.

ings. Occasionally a discordant note was introduced into the proceedings of the Council when the Soviet representative would address the representative of Nationalist China as plain 'Mr. Liu'.[231] The change of representation in 1971 injected the bitter Sino-Soviet dispute into the proceedings of the Council and caused other difficulties; but the Security Council is supposed to mirror the real world, and the change was long overdue.

11. PROPOSALS FOR MORE PERMANENT MEMBERS

From the time that the enlarged Security Council of fifteen members began work in 1966, suggestions have been made that there should be an increase in the number of *permanent* members. The present five permanent members happen also to be nuclear-weapon States, and M. Michel Debré has made the surprising suggestion that, if France were to abandon her *force de frappe*, she would lose her permanent seat on the Security Council.[232] Be that as it may, there have been major changes in the world power situation since 1945. It is sometimes said that, if the Council is to reflect the realities of power, other States should have permanent membership as well as the present five or instead of some of them. Among the countries which have been mentioned in this connection are Brazil,[233] Ethiopia,[234] the Federal Republic of Germany,[235] India,[236] Italy,[237] Nigeria,[238] and Zaire (Congo, Leopoldville–Kinshasa).[239] The names of Argentina and Egypt have also been mentioned in corridor gossip. But the most persistent aspirant for permanent membership has been Japan, which has undertaken a discreet diplomatic campaign which has had a marked effect on the literature.[240]

There are two distinct aspects of the question, and these should be kept separate. First, are there any States, in addition to the Five, whose contribution to the purposes of the United Nations is consistently such that their full participation in the work of the Security Council is always needed? The Charter was deliberately drafted so as to prevent continuous membership (except of the Five) by making a retiring State ineligible for immediate re-election (Article 23(3)). *Almost* continuous membership could be achieved, however, if a regional group were willing to support a particular candidate after its year of ineligibility, thus securing membership for two years out of three;[241] but fully continuous membership would necessitate a revision of the Charter.[241]

The second aspect concerns the veto, or rule of unanimity. Are there any States, in addition to the Five, whose interests are consistently such that they should have the right to prevent the Council from reaching substantive decisions or the Members from amending the Charter, by casting a negative vote? If the answer is 'yes', then, again, revision of the Charter would be needed.

It is sometimes suggested that two of the present Five (namely, Britain and France) might be willing to 'share' permanent membership, thus making a permanent seat available for another region; or that the European Economic Community might have one, or perhaps two, permanent seats in place of Britain and France; and even more ingenious ideas have been mooted.[242]

The most considered case for enlarging the Council and changing the permanent membership has been made by Arthur Lall, a former Indian ambassador to the United Nations. Lall draws attention to 'the profound shifts in power [since 1945], as well as the emergence of new structures of power'; but this is not the heart of his argument. Indeed, he challenges what he calls the 'facile view' that military and economic power determines the capacity to make decisions in international affairs.[243]

Lall's central thesis is that the Council as at present constituted is increasingly incapable of discharging its Charter functions. This 'crass apathy and undeniable negligence' he ascribes to the 'structure of the Council' and in particular to the narrow interests and attitudes of 'the Inner Circle' of permanent members. In some situations of crisis, he points out, the Council has even failed 'to convene timely meetings', and he mentions in particular the Middle East, Cyprus, India–Pakistan, and Korea.[244]

Lall does not indicate when the Council should have met to deal with Cyprus but failed to do so. In the case of Korea, he suggests that 'earlier meetings', that is to say, before the invasion of South Korea, 'might have helped to prevent the outbreak of hostilities'—a suggestion which is hard to substantiate or refute. With regard to India–Pakistan, the Council responded promptly in 1965 but, as Lall notes, failed lamentably in 1971.

Lall is perhaps unfair to the permanent members over the period leading up to the Middle East war of 1967. Canada had proposed at the meeting held on 24 May that 'we should consult immediately following this meeting, with the hope that members of the Council might attain unanimity on this matter as soon as possible'. It was not a permanent member but India which made no secret of its unwillingness to take part in *any* informal consultations with regard to the draft resolution submitted by Canada and Denmark, a position which evoked support in varying degrees and for differing reasons (or none at all) from Bulgaria, Ethiopia, Mali, Nigeria, and the Soviet Union. Egypt was opposed to convening the Council again, and Nationalist China was President for the month, a circumstance which undoubtedly complicated the consultative process.[245]

All this is largely by the way, however. Lall's point is that the Five 'are incapable . . . of interesting themselves fully in disruptive and peace-endangering situations . . .' and that, conversely, other States are 'deprived, mainly because of lack of status and authority, from playing a significant and effective role . . .' He believes that the answer lies in 'a wider diffusion of decision-making power in the Security Council', to be achieved by making the Council more 'representative' of the various regions than it is at present.[246]

It will be seen that Lall does not expressly call for an increase in the number of veto States. He addresses himself primarily to the question which States are best qualified to contribute to the maintenance of peace and security, and he comes down in favour of a Council enlarged to nineteen members and composed of eight permanent and eleven non-permanent members, as overleaf.[247]

This would leave China, the Soviet Union, and the United States as permanent members as at present; give one permanent seat to the EEC countries in place of Britain and France; and confer permanent membership on India, Japan, Brazil or a rotating seat for Latin America, and a rotating seat for the Middle East and Africa.

This would be consistent with a number of other proposals for enlargement made by Italy and Mexico, for example, but

	Permanent member(s)	*Non-permanent member(s)*	*Total*
North America and non-Spanish-speaking Caribbean	United States	1	2
Latin America	Brazil or 'composite [i.e., rotating] seat'	1	2
Western Europe	EEC	2	3
East Europe	Soviet Union	1	2
Middle East and Africa	'composite seat'	2	3
South and Southeast Asia	India	1	2
East Asia	China	1	2
Pacific	Japan	1	2
'floating' seat	—	1	1
	8	11	19

would not wholly satisfy the proposal of the Yemen for two Arab seats, 'one representing the Arab States in Asia and the other representing the Arab States in Africa'.[248]

It is notable that most of those who advocate an increase in permanent membership, whether as official spokesmen or on a personal basis, make a careful detour around the veto problem. It is, clearly, difficult to argue that to increase the number of veto powers would improve the efficacy of the United Nations. It is impossible to escape the fact that the primary purpose of the veto is not to foster co-operation but to prevent action. Arthur Lall is too experienced a participant in and observer of the United Nations at work to evade the issue, and he argues that the veto is not as big a problem as most people think, since 'really damaging vetoes have been few'.[249] As he quotes from one of my own books to reinforce this conclusion, I can hardly dissent from it, even though I would want to qualify it in some important respects.

I do not find Lall's central thesis convincing. That the Security Council has often failed to achieve the high purposes entrusted to it in the Charter is a matter of public record. That one or other of the permanent members, because of its great power or special interests, has been able to prevent the Council from acting in the common interest is undeniable. But the striking thing about the permanent members is not their similarities but their differences. Any explanation which treats the permanent members as States with similar interests and policies, and therefore as equally blameworthy for past failures, seems to me implausible.

When the Council was increased from eleven members to fifteen, the role of the five permanent members was diluted. A further enlargement would lead to a greater dilution. If to add to the number of non-permanent members is thought to be a desirable goal, this can be pursued on its merits. Its purpose would be frustrated if the number of permanent members were also increased.

If it is thought that the Council would be more effective if certain States had continuous membership, that also could be pursued on its merits. For such a policy to be convincing, it would be necessary to demonstrate that the States to be added have characteristics which would ensure that the Council operated more effectively if they were always present. It is difficult to draw this conclusion, or the reverse, from an examination of the performance of the Council during the years when the States suggested for addition were present as non-permanent members. The successes and failures seem to have been due to other and more complex factors.

A third goal might be to increase the number of States with the right of veto, but I have encountered no serious arguments which demonstrate that this would increase the Council's effectiveness.

The case for increasing the number of permanent members probably has its origin in one or both of two factors: a belief that the present system is 'unfair' in giving the veto privilege to five States, and five only; or in the ambitions of the aspirants to play a more active role in world politics.

These are respectable and laudable arguments, but they are not likely, on their own, to persuade the States which now have the right to veto amendments to the Charter that it would be in their interests to add to their number.

If there is no immediate possibility of enlargement, as at present seems to be the case, it should be possible to pay greater attention in the election of non-permanent members to the contribution which States have made to the maintenance of peace and security and other UN purposes, without violating the principle of equitable geographical distribution. This has, indeed, been urged by the U.S. Commission on the twenty-fifth anniversary of the UN and by a panel of the U.S. United Nations Association, as well as by several Member States.[250]

CHAPTER 4

DIPLOMACY, DEBATE, DECISIONS

> Thus the great secret of negotiation is to bring out prominently the common advantage to both parties of any proposal . . . Make each proposition which you put forward appear as a statement of the interests of those with whom you are negotiating.

DEBATE and decisions are the visible parts of diplomacy. Debate can serve several purposes: to get certain facts or points of view on the record, to satisfy public opinion at home, to please friends or annoy adversaries, sometimes even to influence the outcome. But debate is only a part, and often only a minor part, of the process by which the Security Council tries to achieve its purposes. Public debate on controversial questions may be useful, but usually only if it is accompanied by private discussion and negotiation.

Debate is thus part of the diplomatic process, and I have called this Chapter 'Diplomacy, Debate, Decisions' in order to emphasize the fact that debate is rarely an end in itself. Indeed, occasions occur when debate is unnecessary or even harmful. When the Security Council decided by consensus in April 1972 to increase the number of UN observers on the Lebanese side of the frontier between Lebanon and Israel, 'a formal meeting of the Security Council was not considered necessary . . .' The President, Sir Colin Crowe of the United Kingdom (see pp. 123–4), consulted members of the Council informally and evidently discovered that public debate would reveal differences which would hamper agreement. Indeed, the President issued a note expressing China's reservations, although the reservations were evidently not substantial enough to lead to a Chinese veto.[1]

Diplomacy is governed by custom and etiquette, but debate

takes place in accordance with both written and unwritten procedures. I intend in a later volume to examine aspects of the diplomacy of the Security Council. Here I am concerned with debate and decisions, and in particular with the rules which are contained in Chapter VI of the Rules of Procedure entitled 'Conduct of Business'.

The Charter states that the Council shall adopt its own rules of procedure (Article 30), but the present Rules are only provisional. The President, declares Rule 19 tautologically, shall preside over the meetings of the Council. The President declares the opening and closing of each meeting, calls upon speakers, puts questions, announces decisions, and maintains order.

1. ORDER OF SPEAKERS

The order of speakers is governed by two Rules. Rule 27 states that the President *shall* call upon representatives in the order in which they signify their desire to speak. For this purpose, the secretary of the Council, sitting on the President's left during meetings, maintains a list of speakers. But Rule 27 is qualified by Rule 29, which designates certain people who *may* be accorded precedence: any rapporteur appointed by the Council, the chairman of a commission or committee for the purpose of explaining its report, or the rapporteur appointed by a commission or committee to present its report.

As a result of presidential rulings which have been confirmed or which have not been challenged or overruled, one can reach the following conclusions about the practice of the Council:

1. The word *representative* used in Rule 27 applies not only to members of the Council, but also to UN Members which are not members of the Council, and to States which are not members of the United Nations but which have been invited to participate without vote under Rules 37–9.[2]
2. Representatives who wish to inscribe their names on the list of speakers should inform the secretary of the Council rather than the President. To keep two separate lists, as has sometimes been done, makes for confusion.[3]
3. Speakers may place their names on the list of speakers even before the agenda is adopted.[4]
4. A representative whose name is on the list of speakers cannot normally yield his place to another representative; to suspend

Rule 27 and change the order of speakers requires an express decision of the Council.[5] Very occasionally, the normal practice is relaxed. In October 1973, for example, the President (Australia), 'with the consent of the representative of Indonesia' who was next on the speaker's list, himself suspended Rule 27 to allow representatives to express condolences regarding those diplomats and UN officials and their families who had been killed during an air attack on Damascus.[6]

5. A Member of the United Nations which calls for a meeting of the Security Council may speak first. In November 1950, for example, the United States called for a meeting of the Council to discuss the Korean question. Soviet Ambassador Malik (see pp. 115–116) objected to the adoption of the agenda, but found himself in a minority of one when the matter was put to the vote. He then proposed that China be invited to participate, adding that the Soviet delegation 'insists' that his proposal be considered before the Council discussed the substance of the Korean question. The President (Yugoslavia) then stated that

> it is the established practice in the Security Council—a practice confirmed by a series of precedents—that the delegation requesting a meeting of the Council should be called upon to speak first . . .[7]

6. In the case of non-UN Members, the precedents are inconclusive. When the Hyderabad question was considered in 1948, the representative of Hyderabad spoke first.[8] In November 1950, however, a meeting of the Council was called by the Soviet Union, 'which took into account the request of the delegation of the People's Republic of China . . .' The practice of the Council, said Soviet Ambassador Malik, was that, when a State placed an item on the Council's agenda, its representative should be the first to outline his position. 'First the accuser [said Malik], and then the accused . . .' The matter was not that simple, however, as the United States had already placed its name at the head of the speakers' list. After a lengthy discussion, the President (Yugoslavia) put the Soviet proposal to the vote, and it was rejected.[9]
7. Parties to a situation or dispute, whether or not Council members, almost always speak immediately after the Member which called for the meeting. There have, it is true, been a few occasions when this practice was not followed. At one meeting, called jointly by the United Kingdom and Cyprus to discuss

the Cyprus question, the United Kingdom spoke first.[10] When the Council met on 9 November 1967 at the request of Egypt to consider the Middle East question, the speakers' list was headed by Egypt, with Israel seventh on the list. Ambassador Goldberg (see pp. 130–31) proposed that Israel should be allowed to speak second. After some discussion, the U.S. proposal was put to the vote but failed to obtain the affirmative vote of nine members.[11] The circumstances in these two cases were to some extent unusual, and they may be regarded as exceptions to established custom.

8. Subject to paragraphs 5 and 7 above, members of the Council usually speak before non-members;[12] very often, the President speaks last in his capacity as his country's representative.[13]

The order of speakers, unless changed by express decision of the Council, is thus usually as follows:

Member requesting the meeting
Other parties to the question, situation, or dispute
Members of the Council
President of the Council, in his capacity as representative.
Non-members of the Council.

Sometimes a speaker will address a question to another speaker and demand an immediate answer, as Stevenson did to Zorin (see pp. 116 and 128–30) during the Cuban missile crisis.[14] In nine cases out of ten, this amounts to a proposal to change the order of speakers, and a President would be fully within his rights in refusing such a request or insisting that it be put to the vote.[15] Similarly, representatives who have asked to exercise the right of reply must wait their turn, unless the President obtains the agreement of the Council to vary the order of speakers.[16]

Express requests to change the order of speakers, especially those which are politically motivated (and which of them are not?), are likely to be rejected if put to the vote,[17] although changes which have been informally agreed among the representatives usually cause no difficulty.[18]

2. INTERRUPTING THE SPEAKER

The purpose of the Rules of Procedure is to enable the work of the Council to proceed smoothly and within predictable limits. It is, nevertheless, necessary to have an emergency procedure for interrupting the debate if a breach of the Rules or other abnormal development occurs. Any procedure which permits a representative other than the President to interrupt a speaker is open to abuse, and many so-called points of order are nothing of the kind: they are matters of substance in disguise.

Nowhere in the Rules of Procedure is a point of order defined, and this lacuna provides endless scope for confusion (or, indeed, deliberate obfuscation). The point of order is believed to have been a British invention, and is defined as follows in the standard work on British parliamentary procedure:*

> Although it is the duty of the President to interfere in the first instance for the preservation of order when, in his judgment, the occasion demands his interference, it is also the right of any member of the Council who conceives that a breach of order has been committed, if the President refrains from interfering (either because he does not consider it necessary to do so, or because he does not perceive that a breach of order has been committed), to rise in his place, interrupting any representative who may be speaking, and direct the attention of the Chair to the matter, provided he does so the moment the alleged breach of order occurs.[19]

A committee on rationalizing the procedures of the UN General Assembly defined a point of order as follows (1971):

> A point of order is basically an intervention directed to the presiding officer, requesting him to make use of some power inherent in his office or specifically given him under the rules of procedure. It may, for example, relate to the manner in which the debate is conducted, to the maintenance of order, to the observance of the rules of procedure or to the way in which presiding officers exercise the powers conferred upon them by the rules.[20] Under a point of order, a representative may request the presiding officer to apply a certain rule of procedure or he may question the way in which the [presiding] officer applies the rule. Thus, within the scope of the rules of procedure, representatives are enabled to direct the attention of the presiding officer to violations or misapplications of the rules by other representatives or by the presiding officer himself . . .
>
> Points of order . . . involve questions necessitating a ruling by the

* I have adapted the quotation to the terminology of the Security Council by changing 'Speaker' to 'President', and 'Member' to 'member of the Council' on the first occasion and 'representative' on the second.

presiding officer, subject to possible appeal. They are therefore distinct from procedural motions provided for in [Rule 33], which can be decided only by a vote and on which more than one motion may be entertained at the same time, rule [33] laying down the precedence of such motions. They are also distinct from requests for information or clarification, or from remarks relating to the material arrangements (seating, interpretation system, temperature of the room), documents, translations etc., which—while they may have to be dealt with by the presiding officer—do not require rulings from him . . .[21]

The only proper way by which a representative other than the President may interrupt another representative while he is speaking is by raising a point of order. If a representative raises a point of order, the President shall immediately state his ruling. If the ruling is challenged, the President shall submit the matter to the Council for immediate decision, and it shall stand unless overruled (Rule 30).

The method of raising and disposing of points of order is stated in Rule 30 of the Council's Rules of Procedure just cited, but one must take account also of the established practice of the Council. It is useful, in addition, to bear in mind Rules 73, 90, 115, and 130 of the General Assembly's Rules of Procedure and the 1971 report of the committee on rationalizing the procedures of the General Assembly. From these sources, the following conclusions emerge.

1. A point of order, being a matter to be decided by the President, should not deal with any matter outside the President's competence. In particular, a point of order should not concern the substance of the matter under discussion. The purely procedural nature of points of order calls for brevity.[22]

The only circumstances in which the President may refuse to entertain a point of order raised by a member of the Council is if an earlier point of order has not been resolved. As Mr. Lange of Poland put it when he was President of the Council in 1946,

. . . any representative can raise a point of order at any time, and it is a matter for his own judgment at what moment to do so.[23]

2. A point of order raised while voting is in progress should concern only the actual conduct of the voting.[24]

3. A point of order must be immediately decided by the President in accordance with the Rules of Procedure, taking precedence over any other matter, including procedural motions.[25] If the Rules of Procedure are correctly followed, no point of order on the same or a different subject may be entertained until the initial point of order and any challenge thereto have been disposed of.*[26]

4. It is for the President to rule on a point of order. Nevertheless, both the President and representatives may request information or clarification regarding a point of order. The President may, if he considers it necessary, request an expression of views from representatives before giving his ruling; but the President should terminate an exchange of views and give his ruling as soon as he is ready to announce it.[27] There is no provision in the Rules of Procedure for submitting a point of order for the decision of the Council—although Sir Pierson Dixon of the United Kingdom (see p. 120) was able to secure a vote on whether the Yugoslav proposal to convene the General Assembly in emergency special session over Suez in 1956 was in order or not.[28]

5. According to the English text of the Rules of Procedure, if a representative challenges the President's ruling, he shall 'submit his ruling to the Security Council for immediate decision and it shall stand unless overruled'; according to the French text, '*S'il y a contestation, le President en réfère au Conseil de Sécurité pour décision immédiate . . .*' In English, it is the ruling, in French the challenge (*contestation*), which is submitted for the Security Council's immediate decision. In Spanish and Chinese, the Rules of Procedure correspond to the French text; the Russian version is more like the English in that it declares that, if a ruling is challenged, the President shall submit his ruling to the Security Council's consideration for immediate decision.

The first volume of the *Repertoire* states that, beginning with the meeting of the Council held on 1 August 1950, 'all votes resulting from challenges to Presidential rulings have been entered in the Official Records as votes on proposals to overrule'.[29] What one may call the French practice is now usually followed.[30]

* A Committee of the General Assembly once managed to accumulate 84 unresolved points of order!

As one would expect, the French text is more logical than the English. Consider a ruling by the President which is supported by eight members of the Council and opposed by seven members. If the ruling is challenged, and, using the English text, the *ruling* is submitted to the Council and secures eight votes, it will be defeated, because nine votes are needed for an affirmative decision. If the French-Spanish-Chinese text is used, the *challenge* is submitted to the Council, secures seven votes, and therefore fails, so that the President's ruling stands. To be on the safe side, the President should always use the French, Spanish, or Chinese version—unless for some bizarre reason he should wish his own ruling to be defeated.

6. Any challenge to the President's ruling shall be decided by the Council immediately. A point of order or any challenge to a ruling thereon is not debatable.[31]

7. A representative may interrupt the speech of another representative to raise a point of order; but unless a grave breach of order is alleged to be occurring, a point of order should, if possible, be delayed until the end of a speech.[32]

8. In spite of a few breaches in the past, it is not proper for non-members of the Council to raise points of order.[33]

9. In no circumstances should a motion or proposal made by the President, or by any other representative, be converted into a 'ruling'. In October 1947, when Sir Alexander Cadogan of the United Kingdom (see p. 118–19) was President, he proposed that the Council should meet again in two days' time, but when this proposal was put to the vote, it was found to be unacceptable. When questioned by Soviet Ambassador Gromyko (see p. 114–15) about the procedural situation, Sir Alexander replied uncertainly: 'I might be held to have given a ruling, and the vote might have had the effect of reversing my ruling. I am not sure.' He then proceeded to 'rule' that the Council should meet the following week, twice repeating that this was the President's 'ruling'. Colonel Hodgson of Australia then intervened to say, 'The President can rule only when a point of order has been raised.'[34]

A similar confusion arose in 1948. The Council had been discussing a proposal that it should request information from the Committee of Good Offices in Indonesia. Towards the end of the meeting, the President (the Ukrainian SSR) tried to sum up the situation with the words, 'The President has made a ruling . . . that a telegram should be sent to the Committee of Good Offices . . .' This led the United Kingdom to complain about the 'extraordinary procedure' by which, if a procedural proposal were made, the President could apparently simply rule on it. 'There is a great deal of difference between a question of procedure and a point of order.'[35]

The practice just described has continued to trouble the Council.[36] A procedural motion may be submitted to and adopted by the Council with or without a vote; but a motion or proposal should never be disguised as a ruling.

3. MOTIONS, PROPOSALS, SUGGESTIONS

To avoid confusion later, we must start with attempted definitions of expressions used in the Rules of Procedure or in the customary language of the Security Council. The expressions to be defined are:

1. Motion (Rules 34–36), motion of order;
2. Proposal, draft resolution, proposed resolution (Rules 31–6, 38);
3. Substantive motion (Rule 31);
4. Original proposal (Rule 36);
5. Principal motion (Rules 32, 33);
6. Suggestion.

1. Procedural proposals were sometimes called *motions of order* by the Committee of Experts. The chairman reported that the Committee thought that the Rules of Procedure dealing with the conduct of business should contain some detailed provisions concerning 'points and motions of order . . .' It is safe to assume that motions of order were procedural motions, because it was while discussing them that the question of closure of debate was raised.[37] In the Rules of Procedure, the expression 'motions or order' is not used, but Rules 34–6 use the word *motion*. A motion, if approved, becomes a *decision*, the several meanings of which in UN parlance are discussed below.

2. *A proposal* (Rule 38), also called a *draft resolution* (Rules 32–6 and 38) or *proposed resolution* (Rule 31), is submitted in express terms and is usually concerned with substance rather than procedure. When a proposal is approved by the Council,

it becomes a decision or a resolution; a draft or proposed resolution, when approved, becomes a resolution.

3. When the relevant Rules were first considered by the Council, Australia suggested that *substantive motions* (Rule 31) are 'motions which deal with matters of substance in contrast with proposed resolutions which might deal with any question'—a definition which was not challenged.[38] If this interpretation is correct, a substantive motion is synonymous with what would now be called a substantive proposal or draft resolution, that is to say, a proposal or draft resolution or proposed resolution on a matter of substance.

4. The *original proposal* is a proposal to which amendments have been offered, and it is not put to the vote until all amendments and sub-amendments thereto have been disposed of (Rule 36).

5. When we come to *principal motions* (Rules 32 and 33), we encounter only obscurity. In reply to a question raised by the United Kingdom, the chairman of the Committee of Experts said that the term 'principal motions' covered 'both substantive motions *and amendments*'; the term had been used to enable 'a distinction to be made between principal motions and draft resolutions, on the one hand, and motions on points of order proper, on the other hand'. That, one might have thought, was reasonably clear. A principal motion, according to that interpretation, is a proposal or amendment on the substance of a matter, what in Rule 31 is called a substantive motion, while a plain motion concerns procedure. But an intervention a few minutes later by Australia, assuredly meant to be helpful, had the effect of causing utter confusion. In the opinion of the Australian representative, a principal motion was a motion or draft resolution 'moved originally *before any amendment is offered* . . .', in other words, 'the original proposal' as used in Rule 36 and defined in paragraph 4 above. The intention, thought the Australian representative, had been to distinguish between 'principal motions *in contrast to amendments* . . .'

Sir Alexander Cadogan, the British representative (see pp. 118–19), almost certainly with his tongue in his cheek, expressed his gratitude to the Australian representative.

> I confess that I had not understood the thing. I think I do now . . . This discussion will be on the record, and I think that will explain the apparent conflict of terminology in the future.[39]

All one can say with certainty is that a principal motion is either a substantive proposal (chairman of the Committee of Experts) or an original proposal (Australia).

6. A *suggestion* is less formal than a motion or a proposal. It is a trial balloon floated by a representative during the course of a meeting, sometimes without much premeditation, and not necessarily in very precise language. If the response to a suggestion is favourable, it may be converted into a formal motion or proposal. A suggestion *per se* is not put to the vote.

At a very early meeting of the Council, the President (Australia) asked whether a Soviet 'suggestion' had a seconder. Brazil said that, as a matter of courtesy, *any* proposal should be discussed: 'I do not think that a proposal by one member of the Council should be disposed of because there is no supporter.' As no opposing view was expressed, the President expressed the wishes of the Council 'that we should not seek a seconder to a resolution . . .'[40] The Council later adopted a Rule to the effect that it was unnecessary for a motion or draft resolution to be seconded before being put to the vote (Rule 34).

According to Rule 31, proposed resolutions, proposed amendments, and proposed substantive motions 'shall normally be placed before the representatives in writing'. The Council has, wisely, paid full regard to the adverb 'normally' in Rule 31 and has not insisted that *all* proposals and amendments be circulated in written form.[41] Occasionally there has been some minor bickering as to whether a particular proposal fell within one of the precise categories contained in Rule 31, but the skill of the President or the commonsense of representatives has made it possible for the Council to overcome such obstacles expeditiously.[42]

Rule 32 provides that principal motions and draft resolutions shall have precedence in the order of their submission. The Council may, if it so wishes, suspend this Rule by a procedural vote and afford priority to a particular draft resolution. Even when circumstances have been abnormal, the Council has tended to vote on draft resolutions in the order of their submission,[43] but on a few occasions the Council has voted to consider proposals in a different order.[44]

On one occasion, uncertainty arose as to whether a draft

resolution, submitted by a non-member and put to the vote in amended form at the request of a member in accordance with Rule 38, should have precedence over proposals submitted by members of the Council. On 22 December 1955, Syria, a non-member of the Council, had submitted a draft resolution. On 9 January 1956, the Soviet Union submitted an amended version of it and asked that the amended proposal be put to the vote. Other proposals were submitted later by other delegations, and in the end the Council voted to grant priority to one of these.[45]

4. 'PRECEDENCE MOTIONS' (RULE 33)

A Security Council debate may have clearly defined phases: the opening statements by the parties and other interested States, a general debate, a debate on proposals and amendments. Often the phases will not be sharply separated and the Council will move imperceptibly from one phase to the next.

For an ingenious representative, there is a whole range of filibustering techniques which can be used to prevent the Council from passing to the next phase or from coming to a decision. If armed conflict is taking place, the friends of the State or States which expect to win may want to prolong debate in the Security Council and prevent the early adoption of a resolution calling for a cease-fire. The friends of the losing side, on the contrary, will want to hurry the debate or even skip it, and proceed to a cease-fire call as soon as possible. These tendencies were evident at times during the Korean War between 1 August and 8 November 1950, for example, during the Suez fiasco at the end of October 1956, during the Six Day War in 1967, and during the October War in 1973, to cite only four examples.

Filibustering, as a form of deliberate obstruction, is a negative phenomenon. There can, on the other hand, be positive reasons for discontinuing debate: to obtain certain facts from impartial observers, to enable representatives to receive advice or instructions from their capitals, to explore informally the possibilities of agreement, and so on. For this reason, the Council has at its disposal a variety of techniques by which debate can be suspended or terminated, either to facilitate positive purposes or to frustrate negative ones. These techniques are listed in Rule 33:

1. Suspension of the meeting;
2. Adjournment of the meeting;
3. Adjournment of the meeting to a certain day or hour;
4. Reference of any matter to a committee, the Secretary-General, or a rapporteur;
5. Postponement of the discussion of a question to a certain day, or indefinitely;
6. Introduction of an amendment.

All the motions listed in Rule 33 'shall have precedence in the order named over all principal motions and draft resolutions relative to the subject before the meeting'. Rule 33 further stipulates that any motion for the suspension (1 above) or for the simple adjournment of a meeting (2 above) shall be decided without debate. All 'precedence motions', as they may be called, are beyond the scope of the veto. If a 'precedence motion' is moved by a non-member of the Council, it may be put to the vote only at the request of a Council member.[46]

How should a representative move a 'precedence motion' if the only means by which he may jump the queue of representative awaiting their turn to speak is by raising a point of order, which is by definition a matter subject to presidential ruling? Strictly speaking, the representative should ask for the floor on a point of order. When he has the floor, he should ask for the President's agreement to his moving a 'precedence motion', and this agreement should be granted automatically. The representative is then free to move one of the motions listed in Rule 33.* In practice, the stages of the correct procedure are nearly always conflated.[48]

The Committee of Experts considered whether provision should be made for the closure of debate (which was desired by the United States),[49] but in the end no recommendation to provide expressly in the Rules of Procedure for the closure was made.

Although there is no provision in the Rules for making a clear separation between the general debate of an item and the discussion of proposals, Presidents have generally followed, as

* The same procedure should be followed if a representative seeks information or clarification.[47]

one President (Poland) put it, 'a good and normal practice that the general debate should come to an end at some time, and then the concrete [draft] resolutions can be taken up'.[50]

a. *Suspension of meeting*

The first kind of motion listed under the first paragraph of Rule 33 is for the suspension of the meeting. This means that the meeting is stopped for an agreed period of time (which is almost always exceeded), often for informal consultations; when the Council resumes, it is still the same meeting so that it is not necessary to re-adopt the agenda or re-invite the participation of non-members.

The suspension of the meeting for consultation was not often resorted to in the early days. The first case of which I am aware was at the Council's eighth meeting on 5 February 1946. At the next meeting, held on 6 February 1946 to elect members of the International Court of Justice, there were six suspensions totalling more than six hours.[51] There was another suspension in 1946, which was called 'a recess', which lasted thirty-seven minutes.[52] I recall a meeting on the admission of new Members being suspended in 1952, a suspension in 1953 during consideration of the Palestine question, one in 1955 on the admission of new Members, and two suspensions during one meeting in 1957 on the Palestine question.[53] There was also a fifteen-minute suspension on 24 November 1961 following the Soviet veto of a U.S. amendment to a proposal of Egypt, Ceylon, and Liberia relating to the Congo. The suspension was moved by Adlai Stevenson, and the President, Soviet Ambassador Zorin (see p. 116), was most reluctant to put the motion to the vote.[54] A meeting of the Council held in August 1964 was distinguished by three suspensions—first, a suspension of thirty-five minutes so that the Ambassador of Cyprus could take a telephone call, then a suspension of ten minutes so that the Soviet Ambassador could do likewise, and finally a suspension which lasted more than two days, suggested by the President (Norway), during which the members of the Council were 'at the disposal of the President'.[55]

Since the triple suspension in 1964, the Council has been quite happy to agree to brief suspensions to enable informal consultations to take place or for similar purposes.[56] On one occasion, the Council, instead of suspending the meeting, adjourned 'for fifteen minutes' (which in the event was extended to thirty-five minutes), and then started a fresh meeting.[57] This was a suspension in everything but name.

b. *Adjournment of meeting*

There are two kinds of adjournment provided for in Rule 33, an adjournment *sine die* (in the second paragraph of the rule called 'the simple adjournment') or an adjournment to a certain day or hour. In deciding which form of adjournment to move, a representative will be guided by the fact that the simple adjournment 'shall be decided without debate', whereas adjournment to a named hour or day can be debated before being put to the vote (Rule 33).

The Council has only rarely resorted to the simple adjournment. The first occasion on which it did so, the Council immediately thereafter proceeded to fix the day and time of its next meeting![58] On another occasion (Table 15, Case 7), the Council decided upon the simple adjournment, whereupon the President (Denmark) said:

> The motion is adopted. The meeting will be adjourned until tomorrow. I take it that it should be tomorrow morning.[59]

On another occasion (Table 15, Case 4), immediately after the adoption of an agenda concerned with the Congo question, Governor Stevenson of the United States (see pp. 128–30) moved the simple adjournment, adding that the motion 'is not debatable, and I request that it be put immediately to the vote'. It took the President, Sir Patrick Dean of the United Kingdom (see pp. 120–21), an hour and a half before he managed to put the U.S. motion to the vote, because of bogus points of order raised by Soviet Ambassador Zorin (see p. 116).[60]

The cases of simple adjournment, with the date of the next meeting on the same item, are given in Table 15. It will be seen that Case 1 was a reasonable adjournment to enable China to respond to an invitation to participate in the discussion. In Case 2, the item got submerged by more serious and pressing Middle East questions following the Suez episode. In Cases 3, 6, and 7, meetings were convened quite soon after the adjournment. The Congo question (Case 4) was allowed to lapse by general consent, and was not discussed by the Security Council after January 1962. Benedetto Conforti considers that the decision in this case was 'illegal' because 'the dissenting minority was deprived even of the possibility of expressing its opinion on the adoption of the agenda'.[61]

The one curiosity in Table 15 is Case 5 on Kashmir. After

TABLE 15

Cases of simple adjournment under Rule 33, 1946–68

Case no.	*Date*	*Meeting and para. no.*	*Subject (short title)*	*Date of next meeting on same item*
1	31 Jan. 1955	690, 148–9*	Hostilities in the area of certain islands off the coast of China	14 Feb. 1955
2	29 Oct. 1956	747, 11 †	French complaint concerning military assistance tendered by the Egyptian Government to the rebels in Algeria	No meeting held
3	12 Sept. 1960	898, 8–14	The Congo question	14 Sept. 1960
4	30 Jan. 1962	989, 30–75	The Congo question	No meeting held
5	17 Feb. 1964	1093, 4–22	The India–Pakistan question	17 Mar. 1964
6	7 June 1967	1350,85–105	The situation in the Middle East	8 June 1967
7	13 June 1967	1358, 329–34	The situation in the Middle East	13 June 1967

* Meeting adjourned following an invitation to the People's Republic of China to participate in the debate.

† Meeting adjourned 'to give the Egyptian delegation time to make its preparations'.

debate extending over six meetings, Pakistan had on 17 February 1964 requested 'a few days' postponement . . .' Morocco had then proposed a simple adjournment, to which the Council had agreed. A fortnight later, on 4 March, Pakistan had requested the President to convene a meeting. On 8 March, India had objected to an early meeting. Faced with irreconcilable requests from Pakistan and India, the President (Nationalist China) convened the Council on 17 March so that it could consider how to resolve the matter. India and Pakistan participated fully in the procedural debate, and in the end the

Council adjourned for three more days, 'at which time [stated the President] the Council will proceed at once with a discussion, if necessary, to decide whether to resume consideration of this item.' The Council duly met on 20 March and decided to adjourn until 5 May, when it at last turned its attention to the substance of the problem.[62]

Once a motion for the simple adjournment has been adopted, no other motion is in order.[63]

Each motion to adjourn to a fixed time is a motion in its own right and not an amendment to a previous adjournment motion. On one occasion, disagreement had arisen in the Council between Soviet Ambassador Sobolev (see pp. 116–17) and U.S. Ambassador Lodge (see pp. 127–8) about the time of the next meeting, and both had made proposals. In an attempt to be helpful, Yugoslavia suggested a compromise, which the President (Peru) surprisingly treated as an amendment to one of the proposals. Both the Soviet and the U.S. motions were put to the vote and failed to secure sufficient affirmative votes. In the circumstances, the President wisely changed his mind and treated the Yugoslav suggestion as a formal proposal which should be adopted in the absence of alternatives, and the Council raised no objection.[64]

c. '*shall be decided without debate*'

Rule 33 states that motions for the suspension or simple adjournment of meetings shall be decided without debate. The sole exception to this rule is the general practice about points of order, namely, that these may be raised at any time, that the President shall rule immediately, and that if the President's ruling is challenged, the challenge (French-Spanish-Chinese text) shall be submitted to the Council for immediate decision (Rule 30).

A variety of circumstances have made it impossible to apply consistently the rule about deciding on the suspension or simple adjournment without debate: an ingenious or unscrupulous representative, a weak or inexperienced President, insistence on explaining a vote, the raising of a second point of order before the first one has been disposed of, discussion of whether a motion for adjournment or postponement phrased in an unusual way is for indefinite adjournment or postponement or to a certain day—all these are among the means by which representatives have managed to engage in debate contrary to the Rules of Procedure.[65]

Much trouble would be saved if representatives would use the precise language of Rule 33 rather than such expressions as 'take a recess' (a great favourite with American representatives, this),[66] 'defer consideration',[67] 'defer action',[68] 'postpone voting',[69] or 'postpone a decision'[70] which are not to be found in the Rules of Procedure and have no formally agreed and precise meanings. The consistent use of the language of Rule 33 would avoid the misfortune which overtook Soviet Ambassador Sobolev (see pp. 116–17) at the time of the Hungarian revolt in 1956. Sobolev moved the postponement of discussion for three or four days to enable the Council to obtain information. The President, Ambassador Cornut-Gentille of France (see p. 113), interpreted Sobolev as moving not postponement of the discussion but the simple adjournment of the meeting. He therefore ruled that no discussion was permissible and quickly put the motion to the vote.*[71]

d. *Reference to a committee, the Secretary-General, or a rapporteur*

Motions to refer any matter to one of the agencies cited in Rule 33 have rarely given rise to difficulty. It is true that in 1947 a proposal was made by Poland to submit Hungary's application for UN Membership to the Committee on Admission of New Members. Colombia, somewhat hesitantly, asked whether this motion should not have precedence under Rule 33. The President, Ambassador Quo of China (see pp. 109–10), who was at times brusque and indeed arbitrary, ruled that another proposal had priority 'because it was submitted even before the meeting began'.[72] Ambassador Quo must have forgotten that Rule 33 has precedence over Rule 32; in the absence of a decision to the contrary by the Council, the Polish motion should have been put to the vote first.

There is the possibility of confusion over the precise meaning of 'a rapporteur'. This has been interpreted to include any individual to whom the Council has entrusted responsibilities.

* In mitigation of Cornut-Gentille's venial mistake, it should be added that the coincidence of the Suez and Hungarian crises with his presidency of the Security Council had imposed a considerable strain on him. He collapsed two days later.

Thus, when in 1957 the Council wanted information on two incidents in the Middle East, the President (Cuba) stated:

. . . I considered, as I still do, that the representative of the Philippines proposed something for which provision is made in Rule 33 (point 4) . . . that is, that we ask a rapporteur—in this instance the Chief of Staff [of UNTSO] . . . to submit two reports.[73]

It should be noted that 'a committee' is not limited to a subsidiary organ of the Council. After the allegation that the United States had resorted to germ warfare in Korea, the Soviet Union proposed that the Council should appeal to States to ratify the Geneva Protocol of 1925, which bans the use in war of chemical and bacteriological weapons. The United States moved that, 'pursuant to rule 33, paragraph 4 . . . the Soviet Union draft resolution be referred to the Disarmament Commission . . .' which had been established by the General Assembly, not the Security Council. Soviet Ambassador Malik (see pp. 115–16) pointed out that the Disarmament Commission was 'not a commission or a committee set up by the Security Council. Consequently rule 33 . . . does not apply.' No representative supported the Soviet Union on this point. Nevertheless, Malik, who was presiding, insisted that the matter be put to the vote. This was duly done, but his position secured only one affirmative vote, with ten abstentions.[74]

e. *Postponement*

As motions to postpone discussion have so often led to confusion, it may be as well to look first at the precise wording of Rule 33, to see in particular what the differences are between postponement and adjournment. Rule 33 deals in one clause with postponement 'to a certain day' as well as postponement 'indefinitely', but postponement relates to 'discussion of the question', whereas adjournment relates to 'the meeting'.

If it is decided to resume consideration on a particular day, the distinction between adjournment and postponement is almost always a distinction without a difference. There is, however, a discernible difference between 'the simple adjournment' and postponement 'indefinitely': the former implies that the Council will resume consideration after an undetermined lapse of time, whereas indefinite postponement has no such implication.

The question of postponement first arose before the Council had adopted Rule 33. The Council had just begun its consideration of the complaints of Syria and Lebanon about the continued presence of British and French troops in their countries. The question had been raised whether the matter was a situation or a dispute, an issue which could have had a bearing on whether Britain and France would have had to abstain on any substantive proposal on the matter. China suggested that the Council should delay taking a decision on the question until the parties had been heard, a suggestion supported by Netherlands. 'This is a new body', said the Dutch Ambassador; 'We must work very guardedly in these matters.' The Council agreed to the Chinese proposal.[75]

Rule 33 was adopted on 16 May 1946, and the question of postponement next arose the following August, when the United States urged the Council to 'take no action' or 'postpone consideration' of the applications for UN Membership of Albania and Mongolia, so that he could avoid 'the painful necessity of casting a negative vote [veto] at this time'. Netherlands pointed out that a motion for postponement had precedence under Rule 33, and the President (Poland) agreed that this was 'logical'. Secretary-General Lie was asked for his opinion, but it is clear from his answer that he had misunderstood the question. The U.S. motion was then put to the vote and defeated, whereupon proposals to admit Albania and Mongolia were also defeated.[76] Most subsequent decisions to postpone were 'to a certain date',[77] but two cases of what were, in effect, indefinite postponements are worthy of note.

On 9 January 1947, at the suggestion of the President (Australia), the Council 'deferred until a later meeting' a letter transmitting the first report of the Atomic Energy Committee. The matter was taken up by the Council again on 13 February 1947.[78]

The other case is of greater interest. When the Council met on 31 January 1955 to consider the hostilities between China and the rump Kuomintang regime based on Taiwan, Soviet Ambassador Sobolev (see pp. 116–17) questioned the right of 'the bankrupt Chiang Kai-shek group' to represent China. U.S.

Ambassador Lodge (see pp. 127–8) then moved that the Council should decide 'not to consider' proposals to exclude the Chinese Nationalists or to seat representatives of the People's Republic of China—a proposal which Lodge had successfully moved during the previous session of the General Assembly. Lodge was supported by Sir Pierson Dixon of Britain and Ambassador Henri Hoppenot of France (see pp. 112 and 120) as well as by Turkey, and the U.S. motion was quickly adopted by ten votes to one.[79]

f. *Introduction of an Amendment*

I review in the next section the means by which the Council determines the order in which amendments shall be put to the vote, and it is only necessary to note here that the introduction of an amendment is the last form of 'precedence motion': that is to say, in the absence of a motion to suspend or adjourn the meeting, or to refer any matter to a committee, the Secretary-General, or a rapporteur, or to postpone discussion of a question, the introduction of an amendment has precedence over all motions and draft resolutions relative to the subject before the meeting (Rule 33).

5. AMENDMENTS

If two or more amendments to a motion or draft resolution are proposed, the President shall rule on the order in which they are to be voted upon. Ordinarily, the Security Council shall first vote on the amendment furthest removed in substance from the original proposal and then on the amendment next furthest removed until all amendments have been put to the vote, but when an amendment adds to or deletes from the text of a motion or draft resolution, that amendment shall be voted on first (Rule 36).

At first sight, this Rule raises almost as many questions as it answers. What is the relationship between the first and the second sentences? Is it intended that the procedures outlined in the second sentence should apply in *ordinary* circumstances and that the President should be required to rule only when the circumstances are *extraordinary*? Or does the second sentence represent guidance to the President as to how he should *ordinarily* rule? Is a Presidential ruling open to challenge, and if so, is it the ruling or the challenge which is put to the vote?

Why is the second part of the second sentence (beginning 'but when an amendment adds to . . .') placed at the end rather than at the beginning of the sentence?

Before these questions can be answered, some further explanation is needed about presidential rulings. The President is required by the Rules of Procedure to rule on points of order (Rule 30) and on the order in which amendments shall be put to the vote (Rule 36). I have suggested earlier that in no circumstances should a motion or proposal, whether submitted by the President or by another member of the Council, be converted into a 'ruling'. In an earlier book on the Security Council, I suggested that, in spite of one precedent to the contrary, the President should not attempt to settle whether a motion or proposal is procedural or substantive (and therefore whether or not it is subject to veto) by a 'ruling'. The permanent members of the Council clearly intended at San Francisco that the so-called preliminary question should be settled by a vote of the Council—in other words, that the preliminary question would be as much subject to veto as the main question, what is often called the double veto.[80]

Are there any circumstances, then, in which the President may be asked or required to make a ruling other than those arising from Rules 30 (points of order) and 36 (order of voting on amendments)?

The answer is unquestionably 'yes'. In enforcing the Rules of Procedure, or reminding members of the customary practice of the Council, or in dealing with issues of procedure not expressly covered by the Rules or by precedent, the President cannot avoid offering interpretations or expressing opinions. Sometimes one or more members of the Council will ask the President to go further and 'rule' on a question of procedure, or even insist that he do so.

No President can be compelled to give a ruling if he is adamant in his refusal to do so, as was Soviet Ambassador Malik (see pp. 115–16) at five successive meetings of the Council in 1950. Nationalist China had asked: 'Does the President consider it obligatory upon him to carry out the decision of the Security Council of 25 June [1950] by inviting the representative of the Republic of [South] Korea to take his place at the Council table?' This point of order, as it was termed by

Nationalist China, was repeated in identical or similar terms by six other representatives. Fourteen times the President refused to rule. The question raised by Nationalist China, said the President, was not a point of order but a proposal. In the President's view, the matter should not be the subject of a presidential ruling but should be discussed until the Council was ready to decide the matter.[81] Even if the question raised by Nationalist China was hardly a genuine point of order, the President's conduct was, in the circumstances, a scarcely concealed filibuster.

Usually, however, the President will prefer to interpret the Rules and practice of the Council for the guidance of representatives, or express an opinion, or give a ruling. In spite of the clear provision in the Rules of Procedure on the order in which motions and proposals shall be put to the vote ('. . . the order of their submission', Rule 32), the President may be asked whether a different order would not be more logical or more fair. The President rules on such a question by reference to the appropriate Rule of Procedure or precedent.[82] If he gives a ruling, it can be challenged, and the challenge can be put to the vote in accordance with the French-Spanish-Chinese text of Rule 30.[83] If, on the other hand, the President wishes to deal with a situation not covered by the Rules of Procedure, or for which the Council has no agreed practice, by offering a motion or proposal of his own rather than by giving a ruling, as was the wish of Ambassador Malik in connection with the participation of North Korea and China in the work of the Council in August 1950,[84] and if one or more members object to the President's motion or proposal, then it can be submitted to the Council for decision.

There have, to be sure, been occasions when it has not been entirely clear which course the President was adopting. How is one to understand a situation in which the President, when asked whether a particular text was a proposal or an amendment, replies: 'I have decided it is an amendment . . . but I do not want to impose my own personal opinion . . . I am now going to ask the Council whether it considers the majority proposal [of the drafting committee] to be an amendment'?[85] Perhaps it is best to regard occasions of this kind as aberrations from the norm rather than helpful precedents.

We can now return to the questions posed at the beginning, which fortunately can be answered relatively briefly. Rule 36 about the order of voting on amendments was approved on 16 May 1946. Six weeks later, the question arose as to its meaning, and Soviet Ambassador Gromyko (see pp. 114–15) asked if the Assistant Secretary-General in charge of Security Council affairs could elucidate the matter, which he did in the following terms.

If there are two or more amendments, the President shall rule [in French, *déterminera*] the order in which these amendments should be put to the vote. If there are disagreements with the ruling [*la décision*] of the President, the Council shall decide which amendment . . . shall be put to the vote first.[86]

As nobody challenged this interpretation, it can be assumed to have represented the view of the Council at the time. One can, then, answer the questions posed earlier as follows. First, both parts of the second sentence are intended to guide the President in making a ruling. Second, if a ruling is challenged, the challenge should be put to the vote. Third, regarding the two parts of the second sentence, there seems no reason why they should not be reversed.

If this interpretation is correct, one might paraphrase Rule 36 as follows.

If two or more amendments to a motion or proposal are submitted, the President shall rule on the order in which they are to be voted upon. If the ruling is challenged, the President shall submit the challenge to the Security Council for its decision.

In making his ruling, the President shall bear in mind that ordinarily when an amendment adds to or deletes from the text of a motion or proposal, that amendment shall be voted on first, and that in other cases, the Council shall first vote on the amendment furthest removed in substance from the original proposal, and then on the amendment next furthest removed, until all amendments have been put to the vote.

It is easy to conceive of situations in which it is by no means clear whether a particular text is an amendment or a separate proposal disguised as an amendment in order to gain a procedural advantage. On one early occasion, following the submission of a U.S. proposal, various alternative suggestions were made in the course of the debate. The questions then arose whether these suggestions represented amendments to the U.S. proposal and therefore should be put to the vote first, or were separate proposals to be voted on in the order of their submission in accordance with Rule 32. The debate on this question was somewhat confused, but the President (Poland) finally ruled that suggestions, if not accepted by the sponsor of the original proposal, had to be put in the form of amendments and be formally introduced if they were to take precedence over the original U.S. proposal. This was a sound ruling and was accepted by the Council.[87]

But consider a more complicated case in which it is proposed that the Council recommend to the General Assembly that a mixed bag of States be admitted into UN Membership. Imagine a further text which proposes to add a couple more States to the list. Is that a *bona fide* amendment, or a separate proposal?

This is not, as it happens, a hypothetical example: it is precisely what happened in December 1955. Brazil and New Zealand had proposed that the Council, having considered separately a list of eighteen applications for UN Membership in the order of their submission, should recommend the admission of all of them. Nationalist China submitted an amendment to add the Republic of [South] Korea and the Republic of [South] Viet-Nam.[88] It was taken for granted that the Soviet Union would accept the admission of both South *and* North Korea, and both South *and* North Viet-Nam, but that, if only the two Southern Republics were being proposed for admission, the Soviet veto would operate, as it had previously. How would Soviet Ambassador Sobolev (see pp. 116–17) play this, one asked oneself, and how would the President deal with whatever procedural tangle would inevitably arise?

Ambassador Sobolev began by describing the action of Nationalist China as deliberate obstruction (which was not very wide of the mark). The text was, in Sobolev's view, not an amendment but a completely new proposal.

The President (New Zealand) then stated how he intended to proceed. He would first put to the vote the first preambular paragraph of the original proposal, then the introductory words of the second preambular paragraph ('*Having considered . . .*'), then in separate votes the two countries named in the Nationalist Chinese text, then the eighteen countries named in the original proposal, and then the final operative paragraph. This, it seemed to me at the time, was to treat the text of Nationalist China as an amendment rather than a separate proposal, but not to apply to the full the last part of Rule 36, which declares that, when an amendment adds to the text of a draft resolution, the amendment shall be voted on first.

Sobolev, whose experience of the Security Council spanned a decade, was quick to react to the statement of the President's intentions. The procedure suggested by the President was, he said, 'incomprehensible and inexplicable'. The amendment added to the original proposal and should be put to the vote first, as indicated in Rule 36. But then Sobolev must have realized that he might be setting a trap for himself, for if the procedure he had just suggested were to be followed, he would be forced to veto South Korea and South Viet-Nam early in the proceedings, with the risk that this would wreck the 'package deal' on which informal agreement had been reached. If the Council were to encounter two vetoes before it reached the main business, the informal agreement might collapse and the Soviet Union would incur the odium. So Sobolev went quickly into reverse and, forgetting all about Rule 36, suggested that the 'normal and logical and . . . correct' procedure would be to vote first on the eighteen applicants named in the original proposal, and then on 'those new States' mentioned by Nationalist China. And as if to emphasize the confusion which threatened, Sobolev added plaintively: 'What is happening here? Could we not have an explanation?'

The procedural debate which ensued did nothing to dispel the confusion. The President asserted that he was following normal practice. Sobolev proposed that all the applications for Membership should be taken in the chronological order of their submission. The President reiterated his intention; Sobolev reiterated his new proposal; the President put the Soviet proposal to the vote; to nobody's surprise, it was defeated.

The Council then proceeded as the President had all along intended;[89] but who could be sure at the end of the day whether the text submitted by Nationalist China was an amendment or a separate proposal?

In the instance described, a reasonable case could be made for treating Nationalist China's text either as a proposal or as an amendment. Often it will be a matter of no great importance which way the decision goes. In the case just described, the Soviet Union vetoed South Korea and South Viet-Nam; Albania's application was approved; Mongolia came next and was vetoed by Nationalist China; of the remaining sixteen applicants, the Soviet Union vetoed all which had non-Communist governments: the package deal seemed in danger of collapse. Two days later, however, a smaller package deal went through, but two of the original eighteen, Japan and Mongolia, had their applications deferred.

The situation in 1955 was without precedent. Normally, each application for Membership comes before the Council as a separate proposal. In 1955, what was being sought was a 'package' of admissions. Some minor tinkering with previous practice was unavoidable, and attention was being focused on the 'package deal' aspect to such an extent that representatives had little time for the precise status of the text submitted by Nationalist China.

There had, indeed, been earlier cases in which representatives had tried to convert a proposal into an amendment, in order to have it put to the vote before a proposal submitted earlier by another representative. Quite properly, the Presidents had refused to countenance such manoeuvres.[90]

6. VOTING

When the debate on a particular phase of an item is concluded, there is no requirement on the Council to adopt a resolution. The debate itself may have served an adequate purpose, in which case further discussion can be postponed to a particular day or indefinitely; or the Council may wish to close the matter for the time being by the acceptance of a statement of consensus.* But often the Council will wish to dispose of the

* Chapter VII of my book *Voting in the Security Council* dealt briefly with Consensus in the Security Council. Since it went to press in 1968, the UN Institute for Training and Research has published *Consultation and Consensus in the Security Council* by F. Y. Chai (UNITAR, PS 4, 1971). Mr Chai uses more rigorous definitions of consensus than I used in my own book and, moreover, had a significantly larger number of cases on which to base his analysis. I gladly acknowledge that his monograph supersedes Chapter VII, 'Different Kinds of Consensus', in my

matter by taking a decision or adopting a resolution in express terms.

A proposal (or draft resolution) may be submitted by any member of the Council, and that member is known as the sponsor of the proposal; if more than one member, they are the co-sponsors. A Member of the United Nations which is not a Council member may also submit a proposal, but it is put to the vote only at the request of a Council member (Rule 38).

A procedural motion or draft resolution may be withdrawn at any time 'so long as no vote has been taken with respect to it'. If a procedural motion or draft resolution has more than

---

earlier book. Since my book went to press, the following decisions by consensus have been taken, several without a meeting of the Council:

	Date	*Item*	*Doc. no.*
1	4 Apr. 1968	Situation in the Middle East	1412th meeting, para. 122
2	8 Sept. 1968	Situation in the Middle East	1448th meeting, para. 73
3	30 Jan. 1970	Situation in Namibia	S/9632
4	10 Apr. 1970	Situation in Southern Rhodesia	S/9748
5	15 May 1970	Situation in Namibia	S/9803
6	12 June 1970	Periodic meetings (Article 28(2))	S/9824
7	30 Sept. 1970	Situation in Southern Rhodesia	S/9951
8	26 Aug. 1971	Complaint by Guinea	S/PV. 1576, pp. 3–5
9	30 Nov. 1971	Complaint by Guinea	S/PV. 1603, pp. 3–5
10	4 Feb. 1972	Meetings held in Addis Ababa	S/10535
11	29 Mar. 1972	Situation in Southern Rhodesia	S/19578
12	13 Apr. 1972	Situation in Southern Rhodesia	S/10597
13	19 Apr. 1972	Situation in the Middle East	S/10611
14	20 June 1972	Hijacking of Aircraft	S/10705
15	30 Oct. 1972	Situation in the Middle East	S/10818
16	31 Oct. 1972	Strengthening of international security	S/10822
17	21 Mar. 1973	Peace and Security in Latin America	S/PV. 1704, p. 112
18	30 Mar. 1973	Situation in the Middle East	S/10907
19	30 Apr. 1973	Situation in the Middle East	S/10922
20	14 June 1973	Situation in the Middle East	S/PV. 1726, pp. 137–40
21	2 Nov. 1973	Situation in the Middle East	S/PV. 1754, p. 6
22	12 Nov. 1973	Situation in the Middle East	S/11104
23	23 Nov. 1973	Situation in the Middle East	S/11127
24	19 Dec. 1973	Arrangements for the proposed Peace Conference on the Middle East	S/11162
25	28 Feb. 1974	Situation on frontier between Iraq and Iran	S/11229

India had 'considerable reservation' about the procedure followed in case 14. 'Any action or decision by the Council without a formal meeting . . . can have serious and far-reaching legal and other consequences.' India believed that the procedure should not constitute a precedent for the future.[91]

one sponsor ('has been seconded', as the Rules of Procedure put it) and the first sponsor decides to withdraw it, the other sponsor or sponsors may require that it be put to the vote with the same 'right of precedence as if the original sponsor had not withdrawn it' (Rule 35). What Rule 35 says about the withdrawal of a motion or draft resolution is generally taken to apply to an amendment or sub-amendment, although there is no provision to this effect in the Rules of Procedure. A distinction is made in practice between the decision of a sponsor not to press to a vote a motion, draft resolution, or amendment, and a decision formally to withdraw such a text.[92]

In one early case, a Council President (Ambassador Quo of China, see pp. 109–10) refused to allow the sponsor of an amendment to change it into a draft resolution, maintaining that the amendment, 'having been submitted to the Council, has become the property of the Council . . .'[93] This now seems rather a severe practice, but the idea that a proposal becomes 'the property' of the Council was reinforced by an incident which occurred in 1962. Cuba, not a member of the Council, had submitted a draft resolution, which was being put to the vote at the request of the Soviet Union. A separate vote was requested on one paragraph, which was then defeated. From the Cuban point of view, the deletion of this paragraph emasculated the proposal, so the Soviet Union, with Cuba's agreement, stated that Cuba 'does not insist on a vote on the remaining parts of the resolution'. The President (Venezuela) did not take the narrow view that the amended proposal was now the property of the Council, but he cited the first sentence of Rule 35, to the effect that a motion or draft resolution can at any time be withdrawn so long as no vote has been taken with respect to it. As a vote had already been taken on the third paragraph, he ruled that 'no one is entitled to withdraw the draft resolution'. The Soviet Union challenged the ruling, but it was upheld. The Council then rejected the amended Cuban proposal.

The Soviet Union objected strongly to the way the matter was handled. 'Against the will of the sponsor of the draft resolution and after certain provisions by which the sponsor sets great store have been rejected, an attempt is still being made to have the remaining part of the draft resolution put to the vote, in a form which is unacceptable to the sponsor.'[94] One has some sympathy with the Soviet point of view in this case. Even if the Rules of Procedure, strictly interpreted, were on the side of the President, commonsense was surely on the side of the Soviet Union and Cuba.

A motion or draft resolution almost always consists of several parts, which shall be put to the vote separately at the request of any representative, except when the original sponsor objects (Rule 32). Sponsors have freely exercised their right to object to parts of a draft resolution being voted on separately, usually on the ground that the text as a whole represented a delicate balance which would be upset by the deletion of certain parts.[95]

The question has sometimes arisen whether a proposal, having been put to the vote in parts and all parts having been approved, should then be put to the vote as a whole. Although there have been some exceptions,[96] members of the Council have usually considered that approval of the separate parts is insufficient and that the proposal as a whole should also be put to the vote.[97] Sir Alexander Cadogan of the United Kingdom (see pp. 118–19) expressed clearly the reasons for this course.

> There may be certain paragraphs of the resolution of which I entirely approve, but which I do not accept in the context in which they stand.
>
> Similarly, one may vote against a particular paragraph because one sees some objection to it, and yet, because of the context and because of the importance of getting the whole resolution, one may vote for the whole resolution.[98]

Curious as it may at first seem, it follows from Sir Alexander Cadogan's remarks that, even if all the parts of a draft resolution have been *rejected*, there might still be a case for putting the proposal as a whole to a vote. This has, indeed, happened on at least one occasion—perhaps unnecessarily, as all the parts had been vetoed, as was the fate of the proposal as a whole.[99]

In applying the Rules of Procedure about voting separately on parts of a proposal, the question has arisen who is 'the original mover' (Rule 32) in cases where the author of a proposal is not a member of the Council but where the proposal is being put to the vote at the request of a Council member (Rule 38). The question can be illustrated by reference to an incident in 1962. Cuba had called for the convening of the Council after the Organization of American States had suspended Cuba's membership at a meeting of Foreign Ministers held at Punta del Este in Uruguay. Cuba proposed, in particular, that the Security Council should ask the International Court of Justice for an advisory opinion on certain legal questions related to the Punta del Este decisions, and should also, as a provisional measure under Article 40 of the Charter, call for the suspension of the decisions. Ghana asked for a separate vote on one paragraph, and this required the consent of 'the original mover'. Egypt stated that this was the first occasion on which a non-member of the Council (Cuba) had submitted a proposal under Rule 38, and that it was being put to the vote at the request of the Soviet Union. 'There seems to be some doubt about who is the author of such a draft resolution.' After considerable discussion, the Council wisely agreed that out of courtesy to Cuba, and as an exception, not setting a precedent, Cuba should be asked whether she objected to having a separate vote on the paragraph in question—to which Cuba agreed in a statement precisely thirteen words in length.[100]

The Egyptian representative may have been factually correct in stating that the 1962 incident was the first time that a proposal submitted by a non-member was being put to the vote under Rule 38, but the situation was not completely unprecedented. The question had first arisen in 1946, but before the adoption of Rule 38. The Council was considering the situation in Indonesia at the request of the Ukrainian SSR, a non-member. During the course of the debate, the Ukrainian SSR submitted a draft resolution, and the President (Australia) immediately consulted the Council as to whether the Ukrainian SSR was entitled to submit a proposal. China, Egypt, France, Netherlands, Poland, and the Soviet Union favoured allowing the Ukrainian SSR to submit a proposal 'without prejudice and . . . not . . . a precedent'. U.S. Ambassador Stettinius (see pp. 124–5) at first expressed reservations, but later withdrew them. The Ukrainian proposal was duly put to the vote but was rejected.[101]

I have referred on pp. 196–8 to the difficulty of distinguishing between a proposal and an amendment when the Council is dealing with a 'package' of applications for UN Membership. The question of voting on proposals in parts has twice arisen in the same context. In 1947, the Soviet Union favoured the admission of five applicants, but the West insisted on having them considered individually, with the result that applications supported by the Soviet Union (Hungary, Romania, Bulgaria) failed to obtain sufficient affirmative votes, while applications supported by the West (Finland, Italy) encountered Soviet vetoes. To secure this result, the West asked the Council to hold 'a separate and final vote on each application . . .'[102]

In 1955 there was agreement in the Council on recommending the admission of sixteen applicants, but as Nationalist China had vetoed Mongolia, the Soviet Union retaliated by vetoing Japan. The Soviet Union then submitted a proposal recommending the admission of both Mongolia and Japan. France expressed the view that there should be two separate votes, to which the Soviet Union objected. The President (New Zealand), correctly interpreting the political situation in the Council, but disregarding the strict requirement of Rule 32, put the Soviet proposal to the vote as a whole, and it secured only one vote.[103]

7. DECISIONS

The word *decision* is used in several different senses in the parlance of the Security Council, and this naturally makes for confusion. There is, in the first place, the wording of Article 27 of the Charter: 'Decisions of the Security Council . . . shall be made by an affirmative vote of . . . members.' Article 27, presumably, uses the word in the same sense as in other Articles of the Charter which refer to decisions of the Security Council (Articles 25, 44, 48) or to the Council's power to decide (Articles 37(2), 39, 40, 41, 49). According to a report prepared by Secretary-General Lie in 1950,

> the term 'decisions of the Security Council' in Article 27 of the Charter refers to all types of action which the Security Council may take, whether it does so under Chapter V on procedure and organization, or under Chapter VI in relation to the pacific settlement of disputes, or whether it makes 'recommendations' or 'decisions' under Chapter VII.

These observations show that the term 'decisions' *in the Charter*

Articles relating to voting is used in a broad sense to cover all types of action by United Nations organs.[104]

In the *Repertoire* of Security Council practice, the word *decision* is defined as follows:

The term 'decision' has necessarily been used . . . as a technical term . . . and should be understood solely in this sense, and *not in the sense of its usage in the Charter.* These decisions include not only 'decisions' to which specific reference is made in the text of Articles of the Charter, but all significant steps decided upon by the Council, whether by vote or otherwise, in the course of consideration of a question [my italics].[105]

The annual publication, *Resolutions and Decisions of the Security Council* . . . uses 'decision' in a narrower sense. Proposals in express terms which have been approved by the Council are called 'resolutions'; 'decisions', whether relating to procedure or substance, are not in express terms and 'are usually taken without vote, but in cases where a vote has been recorded, it is given immediately after the decision'.[106] Among the matters on which such 'decisions' are usually taken are statements of consensus, invitations to participate in the Council's discussion of a question, 'Precedence Motions' as set out in Rule 33, and the election of members of the International Court of Justice.

Finally, there are some who use the word 'decision' as meaning those resolutions of the Council which are intended to be mandatory or binding, as opposed to mere recommendations (or, indeed, expressions of opinion). And, to confuse the picture still further, there are some who consider (mistakenly, as I think) that the Council can take mandatory or binding decisions only under Chapter VII of the Charter. I revert to this matter below.

I have tried in this book to use the word *decision* as in the *Repertoire*, that is to say, any type of action which the Security Council may take for which the Charter provides, together with all other significant steps decided on in the course of consideration of a question; but nowhere do I use the word *decision* without qualification in the strictly limited sense of a mandatory or binding resolution.

There have been differences of view regarding the Council's power to take decisions which are mandatory or binding, and it must be admitted that the Charter alone is an insufficient basis for resolving these differences. Nobody doubts the Council's right to recommend. It may make recommendations to the General Assembly under Articles 4–6 of Chapter II of the Charter about UN Membership, under Articles 93(2) and 94(2) of Chapter XIV about the International Court of Justice, under Article 97 of Chapter XV about the appointment of the Secretary-General, under Article 4(3) of the Statute of the International Court of Justice about the election of judges, and under Article 69 of the Statute about amendments to the Statute.

The Council may make recommendations regarding a system for the regulation of armaments under Article 26 of Chapter V of the Charter. Under Chapter VI (Pacific Settlement of Disputes), the Council may call upon the parties to a dispute to settle it by peaceful means (Article 33(2)), recommend appropriate procedures or methods of adjustment of a dispute or a situation of like nature (Article 36(1)), recommend such terms of settlement as it may consider appropriate if the Council deems it likely that the continuance of a dispute will endanger peace and security (Article 37(2)), or make other recommendations with a view to pacific settlement if all the parties so request (Article 38)).

Under Chapter VII (Action with respect to Threats to the Peace, Breaches of the Peace, and Acts of Aggression), the Council may call upon the parties to comply with such provisional measures as it deems necessary or desirable (Article 40), make recommendations to maintain or restore international peace and security (Article 39), or call upon Members to apply non-military enforcement measures (Article 41). Under Chapter VIII, the Council may encourage the development of pacific settlement of local disputes through regional arrangements or agencies (Article 52(3)). So much for recommendations.

It is also beyond question that the Council can take internal organizational and procedural decisions under Chapter V which bind the Council itself, and has the power under Chapters VII and VIII to take decisions which are binding on non-members. Indeed, the Council has in practice taken such decisions—even though it may have lacked the means to enforce them fully. Moreover, the International Court of Justice has advised that 'it is the Security Council which, exclusively, may order coercive action'.[107] Articles 39, 41, 42, and 53(1) empower the Council to decide on measures to maintain or restore peace, and Article 49 states that Members 'shall' join in affording mutual assistance in carrying out the measures decided upon by the Council. This obligation is reinforced by the general principle stated in Article 2(5), that Members shall give every assistance in any action the United Nations takes in accordance with the Charter; and by the more specific commitment of Article 25, by which UN Members agree to accept and carry out the Security Council's decisions in accordance with the Charter.

In practice, the Council may incorporate references to Articles 25 or 49 in its decisions, as it did in connexion with the Congo in 1960;[108] Rhodesia in 1966,[109] 1968,[110] 1970,[111] and 1972;[112] and Namibia (South West Africa) in 1969.[113] But the absence of a specific reference to Articles 25 or 49 does not necessarily mean that a resolution is not mandatory or binding: the Council's decision of 14 March 1968 regarding Namibia[114] 'might be considered as containing an implied reference to Article 49', as the *Repertoire* so delicately puts it.[115] And whether or not the Council cites Article 25 or 49, UN Members have by Article 24 conferred on it the primary responsibility for maintaining peace and security, irrespective of the specific powers laid down in other parts of the Charter, and the Council has from time to time cited Article 24 or used its language to emphasize its general responsibilities.[116]

The question remains whether the Security Council can take mandatory or binding decisions under Chapter VI. In its Advisory Opinion on Namibia (1971), the International Court of Justice noted that the reference in Article 24(2) of the Charter to specific powers of the Council 'does not exclude the existence of general powers to discharge the responsibilities conferred in [Article 24(1)]'. The Court rejected the view that Article 25 of the Charter applies only to enforcement measures adopted under Chapter VII.*

Article 25 is not confined to decisions in regard to enforcement

* The Court could properly have added a reference to enforcement action under Article 53(1) of Chapter VIII.

action but applies to 'the decisions of the Security Council' adopted in accordance with the Charter.

When the Council adopts a decision under Article 25 in accordance with the Charter, said the Court, it is for UN Members to comply with that decision, including those members of the Council which voted against it and those UN Members which are not members of the Council. Whether the powers under Article 25 have been exercised in any particular case is to be determined by reference to 'the terms of the resolution to be interpreted, the discussions leading to it, the Charter provisions invoked and, in general, all circumstances that might assist in determining the legal consequences of the resolution . . .' The Court advised that specified decisions of the Council on Namibia are 'binding on all States Members of the United Nations, which are thus under obligation to accept and carry them out'.[117]

This Advisory Opinion answers part of the question posed earlier: the Council can invoke Article 25 when taking decisions under Chapter VI. But can the Council take binding decisions under Chapter VI if Article 25 is not invoked? In particular, are decisions to investigate under Article 34 'binding' on UN Members, which are thus under obligation 'to accept and carry them out'?

This question was much debated in 1947, when Western powers wished to investigate charges of Communist subversion directed against Greece. The Western view then was unambiguous, and is illustrated by the following extracts from debates in the Council.

A decision to investigate . . . is surely more than a recommendation (Australia).[118]

Is . . . resolution [23(S/330/Corr.1), 18 April 1947, establishing a subsidiary group to investigate alleged border violations] applicable . . . as an injunction or as a simple recommendation? It would definitely seem to be an injunction. The terms of Article 34 show that it is a decision involving an obligation . . . This conclusion [that parties to the dispute were bound to comply with the resolution] is supported by Article 25 of the Charter . . . (Belgium).[119]
The argument to the effect that the Security Council, in acting under Chapter VI, must limit itself to adopting recommendations is entirely unfounded (Brazil).[120]

Article 34 authorizes the Security Council to make investigations, and the power of investigation imposes an obligation upon the States to collaborate with the Commission of Investigation (Brazil).[121]

It seems to me that, if they [Albania, Bulgaria, and Yugoslavia] refuse to co-operate when requested to do so . . ., they will put themselves in the grave position of a deliberate defiance of the United Nations, which, in the case of Yugoslavia, would be a refusal by a Member to carry out obligations; in the case of the other countries, it would be a refusal to abide by obligations [of pacific settlement] which they voluntarily assumed . . . (United States).[122]

The Communist States took the view that decisions under Chapter VI, including decisions to investigate, are recommendations only, and that Article 25 does not apply in the case of recommendations.

Under Chapter VI of the Charter, the Council is only called upon to make recommendations . . . (Bulgaria).[123]

The Security Council's decisions under Chapter VI cannot be considered as other than recommendations . . . It is clear that any decision taken on this question is a decision taken in conformity with Chapter VI . . . [and] will be in the nature of a recommendation and will have nothing in common with the decisions provided for in Article 25 . . . (Soviet Union).[124]

All decisions taken under Chapter VI, including decisions to conduct an investigation, are in the nature of recommendations . . . The steps which can be taken by the Council under Chapter VI are of a limited character . . . That is precisely the difference between Chapter VI and Chapter VII (Soviet Union).[125]

When the Palestine question came before the Council the following year, there had been a slight but perceptible shift of emphasis on the part of Western States. The question in 1948 was not whether to investigate, because everyone knew that Palestine was aflame with fighting: the question was whether the Council should seek to restore peace by acting under Chapter VI or under Chapter VII of the Charter. The United States submitted a proposal which included a determination that the situation in Palestine constituted a threat to and breach of the peace under Article 39 of Chapter VII. Argentina, Belgium, Canada, China, and the United Kingdom immediately expressed a preference for a Chapter VI resolution, since the Council had neither the will nor the power to impose a solution. But the interesting thing about the 1948 debate is that speakers took it for granted that a decision under Chapter VI would be in the nature of a recommendation while a decision under Chapter VII would be 'coercive', to use the jargon of the time.[126]

This interpretation was strengthened during the Kashmir debates in 1957. Krishna Menon of India repeatedly said that Chapter VI resolutions are only recommendations, and that India was bound only by those resolutions to which she had consented. If the Security Council wished to enforce its decisions, according to Menon, it must first make a determination under Article 39 of Chapter VII.[127]

Secretary-General Hammarskjold tried to stem the tide when dealing with the Congo in 1960 and 1961. In one of its early decisions, the Security Council had requested States to refrain from any action which might impede the restoration of law and order in the Congo, or the exercise by the Government of its authority, or which might undermine the country's territorial integrity and political independence.[128] Later, the Council called upon UN Members to carry out its Congo decisions 'in accordance with Articles 25 and 49 of the Charter'.[129] Hammarskjold pointed out on several occasions that the Council's decisions were 'binding', 'obligatory', and 'mandatory'.[130]

The reference to Article 49 in the second resolution cited by Hammarskjold provided a basis for claiming that the Council had acted under Chapter VII. On 21 February 1961, the Council reaffirmed previous decisions and authorized 'the use of force, if necessary, in the last resort'.[131] Hammarskjold thereafter regarded this resolution, 'like the early resolutions on the Congo . . . as a mandatory decision . . . in accordance with Article 25 . . .' and 'binding on all Member States'; and he repeatedly stressed the resolution's 'peremptory and unconditional nature' which demanded 'prompt and unconditional implementation'.[132]

Hammarskjold put the matter in a broader context in the Introduction to his last Annual Report. Article 25, he wrote, had the effect of making decisions of the Security Council mandatory, 'except, of course, when such decisions take the form of "recommendations" within the terms of Chapter VI or certain other articles of the Charter'. There had, however, been a tendency to regard the Council's decisions, even when taken under Chapter VII, as recommendations, binding only to the extent that the party concerned had freely committed itself to carry them out. Here was a clear dichotomy between the aims of the Charter and general political practice, he wrote. If the co-operation needed to make the Charter a living reality were not to be achieved, and if respect for the obligations of Article 25 were allowed to diminish, 'this would spell the end of the possibilities of the Organization to grow into what the Charter indicates as the clear intentions of the founders . . .'[133]

But in spite of Hammarskjold's stand, it was increasingly taken for granted that the Council could take decisions binding on others only under Chapter VII. It is true that the Arab countries and the States of the Soviet bloc tried from time to time to have the famous resolution 242 on the Middle East regarded as binding. A Soviet statement in 1968 maintained that resolution 242

> is not a recommendation or an opinion that Governments are free to follow or ignore. In joining the United Nations, every State has undertaken to fulfil unconditionally the decisions of the Security Council taken in accordance with the United Nations Charter.[134]

This was not the position which the Soviet Union had taken in the early post-war years. Moreover, the Western countries had also changed their minds, but in the opposite direction. Indeed, when the Council came to debate the 1971 Advisory Opinion of the International Court of Justice on Namibia, three West European States (Belgium, France, and the United Kingdom) stated that the Council could take binding decisions only under Chapter VII and after an express determination under Article 39,[135] while Italy simply said that it was for the Council to decide when its resolutions have a mandatory character.[136]

Yet, as Dr. Higgins has pointed out,

> Both the *travaux préparatoires* and the wording of the Charter lead one in the direction that the application of Article 25 is not limited to Chapter VII resolutions . . . In certain limited, and perhaps rare, cases a binding decision may be taken under Chapter VI . . .[137]

CHAPTER 5

RELATIONS WITH OTHER ORGANS

An ambassador's speeches should contain more sense than words . . . He should therefore at the outset think rather of what is in their minds than of immediately expressing what is in his own.

I. MILITARY STAFF COMMITTEE

EVERY other Thursday, the United Nations *Journal* announces that a meeting (closed) of the Military Staff Committee (MSC) will take place that morning in Conference Room 14; the 748th such meeting was held on 21 February 1974. We may be sure that what happens at a closed meeting of a UN organ is known only to the members of the organ and the very discreet officials designated to service it, but it is no secret that meetings of the MSC now last only a few minutes, and that the only business transacted is to approve the provisional agenda and to confirm that another meeting will be held after an interval of fourteen days. If the published records are to be believed, the MSC has done no substantive work since 1948.[1]

The functions of the MSC are laid down in the Charter as being to advise and assist the Security Council on all questions relating to the Council's military requirements for the maintenance of international peace and security; to advise and assist the Council on the employment and command of armed forces placed at its disposal, and to be 'responsible for the strategic direction' of such forces; to assist the Council with plans for the application of armed force; to assist the Council to establish limits regarding the strength and degree of readiness of, and plans for the combined action of, national air-force contingents to be made available for urgent international enforcement action; to advise and assist the Council on all questions relating to the regulation of armaments, and possible disarmament; and the MSC may, with the authorization of the Council and after consultation with appropriate regional agencies, to establish such regional sub-committees as may be needed (Articles 26, 45–7).

The MSC is composed of the five permanent members of the Council—or, to be precise, 'the Chiefs of Staff of the permanent members . . . or their representatives'. Any UN Member which is not a member of the MSC 'shall be invited . . . to be associated with it when the efficient discharge of the Committee's responsibilities requires the participation of that member in its work' (Article 47(2)).

The Preparatory Commission recommended that the provisional agenda for the first meeting of the Security Council should include an item 'Adoption of a directive to the Military Staff Committee to meet at a given place and date' and, further, that the directive should instruct the MSC 'as its first task, to draw up proposals for its organization (including the appropriate secretarial staff) and procedure, and to submit these proposals to the Security Council'. Accordingly, on 25 January 1946, the Council, after some mild banter initiated by Andrei Vyshinsky (see p. 116) about the fog in London ('political and otherwise', interjected Ernest Bevin) adopted its first resolution without a vote, instructing the MSC to begin its work in London on 1 February 1946. The Council also had on its agenda an item 'Discussion of the best means of arriving at the conclusion of the special agreements [for the provision of forces and facilities] referred to in the Charter, Article 43,' but consideration of this was deferred.[2]

The MSC was not, in fact, established until 4 February 1946, but it was quickly able to prepare a draft statute and draft rules of procedure. On 14 February, the MSC adjourned pending the move of the Security Council to New York, and the chairman transmitted to the President of the Council the two drafts.[3]

On 16 February, the Council took three decisions about the work of the MSC. First, it instructed the Committee of Experts to examine the MSC report (containing the draft statute and draft rules of procedure, together with a detailed commentary thereon prepared by the Secretariat). Second, it authorized the

MSC to operate provisionally along the lines of its own proposals for procedure, pending the approval by the Council of the two drafts. Third, it requested the MSC 'as its first task, to examine from the military point of view the provisions contained in Article 43 of the Charter (special agreements for making armed forces, assistance, and facilities available to the Security Council).[4]

The MSC resumed its work on 25 March 1946 at the Henry Hudson Hotel in New York, and a sub-committee was set up to advise on the basic principles which should govern the organization of United Nations forces; this sub-committee met for the first time on 28 March, and the five members agreed to submit in writing by 3 April 'a statement of the principles which shall govern the organization of United Nations forces . . .' The three Western members and China met the deadline, but the Soviet Union was silent.[5] In desperation, the four other members proposed that another sub-committee should be established, and on 5 June the MSC set up a sub-committee to study the question of preparing a draft form of special agreement between the United Nations and Member States concerning the provision of forces.

Meanwhile, the chairman of the MSC and Secretary-General Lie had engaged in a lengthy correspondence. It would seem that Lie considered that the MSC, in its draft statute and rules of procedure, had not given sufficient recognition to the important responsibilities and prerogatives of the Secretary-General under the Charter.[6] The difficulties were eventually ironed out, and the MSC issued revised texts on 1 August 1946.[7] But the MSC had not come to the end of its difficulties, for the Committee of Experts poured out a stream of requests for elucidation.[8] On 17 July 1947, however, the Committee of Experts issued its report on the two MSC drafts, which the Security Council had requested seventeen months earlier.[9]

On 13 February, 1947, the Security Council had adopted a resolution on disarmament (the Soviet Union abstaining), to give effect to two resolutions of the General Assembly. The decision of the Security Council included a request to the MSC to submit 'as soon as possible and as a matter of urgency' the recommendations which the Council had asked for a year earlier 'and, as a first step, to submit . . . not later than 30 April 1947, its recommendations with regard to the basic principles which should govern the organization of the United Nations armed force'. The Security Council, by the same decision, set up a Commission for Conventional Armaments and asked it, *inter alia*, to 'make such proposals as it may deem desirable concerning the studies which the Military Staff Committee . . . might be asked to undertake'.[10]

As a result of the renewed request of the Security Council, the MSC issued a report on 30 April 1947, consisting of forty-one draft articles, some with alternative texts reflecting disagreements within the Committee.[11] Twenty-five articles were approved by the Security Council on a provisional basis, most of them unanimously, although a few were adopted with abstentions. But on the remainder, which concerned the most important questions, agreement was impossible, and the debate simply petered out and was never resumed. Of the sixteen articles on which agreement had not been reached, the Soviet Union was on the minority side in fourteen cases, France in five, China and the United Kingdom in one each and the United States not at all. The United States was determined to show that the Soviet Union bore the responsibility for the failure to agree, but the British Foreign Office had urged the press to take the line that the MSC report repre sented progress, and not to stress the failure to reach full agreement.[12]

After the lapse of more than twenty-five years, the MSC report remains an interesting review of the practical problems of international enforcement. Inis Claude has written of 'the official mythology of the Western bloc' which ascribes to the Soviet Union sole responsibility for the failure of the United Nations to establish enforcement machinery. The negotiations which led to this failure, writes Claude, 'revealed a complex pattern of disagreements' which involved 'largely but by no means exclusively a Western–Soviet cleavage'. The Soviet Union 'suspected that the Western powers were intent upon rigging the United Nations enforcement mechanism so that it could be used to promote their own political and military purposes'. The Western powers, for their part, were 'attempting to forestall the possibility that Soviet ground forces might be brought into troubled areas under United Nations auspices . . .'[13]

The MSC report of 30 April 1947 was considered inconclusively during all or part of eleven meetings of the Council in June and July 1947. At one point, the Council decided by ten votes, with one abstention, to invite the representative of the chairman of the MSC to sit at the Council table to interpret the recommendations of the MSC, but in fact the interpretation of the MSC's recommendations was undertaken in writing.[14]

Meanwhile, the MSC on 16 May 1947 decided on a four-point programme of work and set up a sub-committee to examine informally the first item in the programme, namely, to establish a preliminary estimate of the over-all strength and composition of the armed forces to be made available to the Security Council. On 16 June 1947, the Security Council formally asked the MSC to continue its work concurrently with the Council's consideration of the MSC report.[15] The MSC sub-committee submitted progress reports on 30 June and 15 July 1947, and on 23 December 1947 the sub-committee returned to the MSC the task which had been entrusted to it. On 23 June 1948, the MSC completed consideration of the sub-committee's report without reaching agreement, and on 2 July the chairman of the MSC informed the President of the Security Council that the MSC was deadlocked.[16] The divergent views of the members of the MSC were expressed in two letters to the Security Council in August 1948.[17]

The MSC has continued to meet briefly every other week, although even these formal meetings were boycotted by the Soviet Union from 19 January to 26 October 1950, when its representatives were boycotting the Security Council because of the failure to expel Nationalist China.[18] Although the MSC has done no substantive work for more than twenty-five years, the Security Council still remains seized of the two items:

2. Special agreements under Article 43 and the organization of the armed forces to be made available to the Security Council.
4. Statute and rules of procedure of the Military Staff Committee.

Proposals to resuscitate the MSC have been made from time to time,[19] but so far without concrete result.

TABLE 16

Military Staff Committee: chronology, 1946–1948

		Doc. ref.
1946		
25 Jan.	Security Council (SC) directs MSC to draw up proposals for its organization and procedure.	2nd mtg., pp. 12–14; S.C. res. 1
4–14 Feb.	MSC meets in London.	
14 Feb.	MSC transmits to SC draft statute and draft rules of procedure.	S/10 (restricted)
16 Feb.	SC authorizes MSC to operate provisionally in accordance with its own proposals for procedure and directs it to examine Article 43 from the military point of view; sends draft statute and draft rules of procedure to Committee of Experts.	23rd mtg., p. 369
25 Mar.	MSC resumes work in New York and establishes sub-committee to consider basic principles which should govern the use of UN forces.	
9 Apr. to 24 July	Exchange of communications with Secretary-General	
5 June	MSC establishes sub-committee to consider standard form of agreement for the provision of military forces.	
1 Aug.	MSC issues revised statute and rules of procedure.	S/115 (restricted)
1947		
13 Feb.	SC asks MSC to hasten reply to its directive of 16 Feb. 1946 and, as a first step, to report on the basic principles which should govern the organization of UN armed force.	S/268/Rev. 1/Corr. 1
30 Apr.	MSC issues study of general principles governing the organization of UN armed force.	Special Supplement no. 1, S/336
16 May	MSC agrees on future programme of work and establishes sub-committee to discuss informally the over-all strength and composition of armed forces to be made available to the SC.	
4 June to 15 July	SC considers work of MSC.	138th mtg., pp. 952–62; 139th mtg., pp. 963–87; 140th mtg., pp. 989–1002; 141st mtg., pp. 1005–20; 142nd mtg.,

TABLE 16—*continued*

		Doc.ref.
1947 4 June to 15 July		pp. 1023–41; 143rd mtg. pp. 1053–64; 145th mtg., pp. 1066–91; 146th mtg., pp. 1094–113; 149th mtg., pp. 1157–79; 154th mtg., pp. 1266–76; 157th mtg., pp. 1294–312
16 June	SC asks MSC to continue work concurrently with SC.	141st mtg., pp. 1018–20
18–20 June	MSC clarifies Articles 5 and 6 of its report.	142nd mtg., pp. 1027, 1029–31, 1034–7; 143rd mtg., pp. 1053–4 (S/380) and 1061–2 [China, France, United Kingdom, and United States]
24 and 27 June	MSC clarifies Article 18 of its report.	145th mtg., pp. 1078, 1082–91; 148th mtg., p. 1158
25, 26, and 30 June	MSC provides estimate of over-all strength of armed forces needed by SC.	146th mtg., pp. 1104, 1107–13; Supplement no. 13, pp. 133–40, S/394
30 June	Sub-committee appointed 16 May transmits progress report to MSC.	
30 June and 7 July	MSC supplies provisional estimate of forces to be supplied by permanent members of SC.	149th mtg., pp. 1175, 1178–9; 154th mtg., p. 1267
15 July	Sub-committee appointed 16 May transmits further progress report to MSC.	
17 July	Committee of Experts reports on draft statute and rules of procedure.	S/421 (restricted)
23 Dec.	Sub-committee reports to MSC on strength and composition of armed forces needed by SC.	
1948 2 July	MSC informs SC that it is deadlocked.	S/879 (mimeo.)
6 Aug.	Views of four permanent members [China, France, United Kingdom, and United States] as to reasons for deadlock	MS/417 (mimeo.)
16 Aug.	Soviet views as to reasons for deadlock.	MS/420 (mimeo.)

2. GENERAL ASSEMBLY

The relationship between the Security Council and the General Assembly is intricate and fluid. The Council consists of a limited number of States (originally eleven, later fifteen), the Assembly of all UN Members. The Council has primary responsibility for a specific task, the maintenance of international peace and security, and Members have agreed that the Council acts on their behalf, while the Assembly has broad responsibilities and may discuss any matter within the scope of the UN Charter. Substantive decisions of the Council are susceptible to veto by any of the five permanent members, whereas the Assembly decides important questions by a two-thirds vote without any veto. The Council may take decisions regarding peace and security which are binding on all UN Members; the Assembly makes recommendations on such matters. The Council is so organized as to be able to function continuously, meeting when there is work to be done, whereas the Assembly convenes for a routine three-month session, usually in September. If the Council is the favoured organ of the major powers, the Assembly is the egalitarian forum of the medium and smaller countries.

To be sure, the Assembly has some influence on the Council. It elects the non-permanent members of the Council (Article 23(2)), and receives from the Council annual and special reports (Articles 15(1) and 24(3)). The Assembly may call the attention of the Council to situations which are likely to endanger international peace and security (Article 11(3)), thus paralleling the responsibilities of the Secretary-General under Article 99, and may also make recommendations to the Council with regard to the general principles of co-operation in the maintenance of international peace and security (Article 11(1)). If any question relating to the maintenance of international peace and security is brought before the Assembly by the Council, the Assembly may discuss it and may make recommendations, except that the Charter states that the Assembly may not make recommendations with regard to a dispute or situation if the Council is exercising the functions assigned to it in the Charter in respect of that dispute or situation (Articles 11(2) and 12(1)). Any question 'on which action is necessary' shall be referred by the Assembly to the Council, either before or after discussion (Article 11(2)).

The Secretary-General notifies the Assembly of matters relative to the maintenance of international peace which are being dealt with by the Council, and when the Council ceases to deal with such matters (Article 12(2). The Assembly meets in special sessions at the request of the Council (Article 20).

Significant power of the Council is derived from the fact that it addresses recommendations on specified matters to the Assembly, and in the absence of such recommendations, the Assembly is powerless to act.[29] The Council makes recommendations to the Assembly regarding the admission, suspension, or expulsion of Members (Articles 4(2), 5, and 6), the conditions under which a State which is not a UN Member may become a party to the Statute of the International Court of Justice (Article 93(2)), the appointment of the Secretary-General (Article 97), and the conditions under which a State which is a party to the Statute of the International Court of Justice but is not a Member of the United Nations may participate in electing members of the Court and in making amendments to the Statute (Articles 4(3) and 69 of the Statute). The Security Council and the General Assembly proceed independently of one another to elect members of the Court (Article 8 of the Statute, also Articles 10–12).

The Security Council is clearly the senior partner, and its recommendations carry incomparably more weight than those of the Assembly. The recommendations of the Council regarding Membership or the appointment of the Secretary-General are not very likely to be rejected by the Assembly, whereas the Council has had no hesitation in disregarding recommendations of the Assembly—regarding the veto, for example. In the early years (1946–9), an attempt was made to operate the United Nations along the lines envisaged by the founders, but the frequent use of the veto by the Soviet Union led to various attempts to accord a dominant position to the General Assembly.[21] The Assembly played a pre-eminent role from 1950 to 1955, but there then followed a period lasting until 1961 in which Secretary-General Hammarskjold was entrusted with or assumed major diplomatic and operational responsibilities. With the enlargement of the Security Council from eleven to fifteen members, which took effect on 1 January 1966, there took place 'a gradual return to Charter fundamentals', as Secretary-General Thant put it, and the Security Council in particular began 'to return to something like the original Charter concept.'[22] U Thant considered, nevertheless, that the General Assembly might regain a crucial role. In the Introduction to his final Annual Report, Thant wrote:

> The General Assembly . . . could become increasingly effective over the whole field of United Nations operations, including the maintenance of international peace and security, primary responsibility for which is vested in the Security Council . . . Any balanced and sober recommendations which it can adopt [added Thant optimistically] will surely not go unheeded even in the most powerful nations in the world.[23]

Unfortunately, powerful nations seem to find little difficulty in refusing to heed the General Assembly, even when its resolutions are sober and balanced.

In the U.S. drafts for an international organization, the body which later became the Security Council was called the Executive Committee,[24] suggesting that the Security Council—Executive Committee was to *execute* policy laid down by the Assembly. Indeed, there was a tendency at one time to think of the Security Council as a kind of UN cabinet and the Assembly as a kind of legislature. Such analogies can be highly misleading, and it is probably best to think of the Security Council as *sui generis*.

1. The Annual Report of the Security Council is drafted by the Secretariat and circulated on a confidential basis among Council members. Proposed amendments are discussed at closed meetings of the Council, and final approval is also given at closed meetings. When the draft has been approved, a *communiqué* is issued instead of a verbatim record, reading:

> At its . . . meeting held in private on . . ., the Security Council considered its draft report to the General Assembly covering the period from . . . to . . . The Security Council approved the report unanimously.

The report formerly covered the period 16 July to 15 July a year later, but, beginning in 1970, the period covered by the report 'was adjusted, with the consent of the Council, so that the closing date would coincide with that of the report of the Secretary-General . . .', namely, 15 June.[25]

The report consists of four parts together with Appendices. The first part deals with questions considered by the Council under its responsibility for the maintenance of international peace and security. The second part deals with 'other matters', such as UN Membership, the appointment of the Secretary-General, and questions relating to the International Court of Justice. Part 3, now only three lines in length, states blandly that the Military Staff Committee has functioned continuously under its draft rules of procedure and held twenty-six meetings 'without considering matters of substance.' Part 4 deals with matters brought to the attention of the Council but not discussed. The appendices list the members of the Council, give the names of accredited representatives and alternates, the President each month, meetings of the Council and subjects discussed, resolutions adopted, meetings of subsidiary organs, and representatives serving on the Military Staff Committee. In recent years, the report has contained fuller summaries of speeches by Soviet and other East European representatives than formerly. It has been taking longer than it did to reach agreement in the Council on the precise wording of the report, and this has meant that it becomes available to Members of the General Assembly rather late in the Assembly's annual session. Some consideration has been given to the possibility of having a more compact document, but it remains to be seen whether this will commend itself to a majority of members.

Before 1969, the General Assembly did not debate the substance of the Council's report but adopted a resolution taking note of it. In 1969, however, Malta submitted a proposal to the Assembly by which the Security Council would have been invited to 'intensify its efforts to elaborate permanent rules of procedure', to consider an improved format of its annual report 'and the timely submission thereof' in order to facilitate its consideration by the Assembly, and to 'de-seize itself of . . . matters . . . which it has not considered for at least a decade'.[26]

Malta explained to the Assembly the intentions behind its proposal but, 'in a spirit of conciliation . . . and to avoid any possibility of misunderstanding,' did not formally introduce it during the 1969 session. Zambia, as President of the Council for the month, was authorized by all the members of the Council to state 'politely but firmly' that the proposal of Malta did not have the support of members of the Council.[27]

Complaints and suggestions of Malta	*Comments of Zambia, on behalf of all members of the Council*
Many items of which Council seized are formulated too vaguely.	—
Council should delete items which have disappeared from the contemporary scene.	While logical to purge list of items, this would raise grave and controversial questions; preferable Council give main attention to current issues.
Council should adopt permanent rules, eliminating those which are in practice consistently ignored.	Council's procedures and working methods are designed to enable it to carry out its unique responsibilities; to adopt permanent rules for Council alone to decide; permanent rules not as urgent as other matters.
Military Staff Committee is reported as still meeting regularly, but its basic task unaccomplished after more than a generation.	—
Format of report is unsatisfactory compromise between brevity and length; its publication is unnecessarily delayed because each member scrutinizes that part which reflects its own views.	Report is in form which members of Council have found useful for their work; historians should not be denied valuable information which report contains; delay in publication due to translation into working languages.
Combine annual report of Council and list of items being dealt with as one item in Assembly's agenda.	—
Assembly is content with ritualistic ceremony of taking note of report of principal UN organ 'on very last day—sometimes the last hour—of a long session'.	—

The only other participant in the debate was Ghana, which proposed that the Assembly should note not only the report, but also 'the comments made thereon.' This was approved by fifty-two votes to twenty-nine, with thirty-six abstentions.[28]

In 1970, the Assembly reverted to the usual formula for approving the Council's report, but in 1971 the Assembly asked the Secretary-General to submit 'suggestions concerning ways and means of enhancing the effectiveness of the Security Council . . .'[29] The Soviet Union took the position that the Secretary-General was not competent to submit proposals on ways of enhancing the effectiveness of the Council, but Tunisia pointed out that the intention of the proposal was to elicit the views of Members and that this was fully in accord with Article 10 of the Charter. Japan, significantly, expressed the hope that suggestions for Charter revision would not be excluded. The proposal, which was sponsored by Belgium, Burundi, and Tunisia, was approved by seventy-six votes to ten, with twenty-four abstentions.[30]

A year later, Burundi and Tunisia were joined by Madagascar, Senegal, and Sudan in sponsoring another more-than-routine proposal. Tunisia expressed regret that the Council's report was being taken so late in the session (four days before it ended) and that so little time for debate was available. The Charter required the Assembly not merely to take note of the report but to discuss and criticize it, and if necessary to make recommendations. The report itself was 'brief, cautious, and edifying'. Tunisia believed that the Council would be revitalized if it met from time to time in Third World capitals.[31]

The Soviet Union reiterated its view that only the Council may determine how to increase its effectiveness, and what procedures and methods should govern its work. The Soviet representative then pointed to four methods which the Council had adopted to improve its operations: the dispatch of observers from the Council; the sending of missions to make on-the-spot investigations; fuller use of subsidiary organs; and the creation of new subsidiary bodies.[32]

The Assembly then decided by ninety-nine votes to none, with twenty-three abstentions (including the Soviet Union), to appeal to Members to express their views on ways and means of enhancing the Council's effectiveness and to consider the matter again in 1973. The Assembly then voted by 123 votes to none, with eight abstentions, to call upon Members 'to ensure the strict application of the decisions of the Security Council in accordance with Article 25 of the Charter . . .' One may perhaps deduce against whom this paragraph was directed from the fact that the eight abstainers included Malawi, Portugal, South Africa, the United Kingdom, and the United States.[33]

In 1973, an even longer resolution was proposed, sponsored this time by Austria, Indonesia, Peru, and Sudan. They referred to the growing concern about various aspects of the

Council's work. While care had to be taken to distinguish between the competences and prerogatives of the Council and the Assembly, the latter organ was entitled to make comments and pass resolutions arising from the Council's report. The report itself should contain 'a more substantial introduction' and should be available earlier in the session. For more than twenty years, consideration of the Council's report had been 'a mere formality, taking no more than five minutes, perhaps . . .' But 'institutional reforms without political will are inadequate'.[34]

The Soviet Union again took the position that the Security Council was competent to manage its own affairs. Any attempt by the General Assembly to impose procedures on the Council 'would be at variance with the Charter'. The Council had made a number of innovations, including the holding of one 'periodic' meeting, as well as meeting away from Headquarters.[35]

The General Assembly decided by 107 votes to none, with twelve abstentions, to take note of the report as well as of the views and suggestions of Member States. The resolution went on to state that the Assembly

> *Draws the attention* of the Security Council, when considering steps to enhance its effectiveness in accordance with the principles and provisions of the Charter of the United Nations, to the views and suggestions submitted by Member States in response to General Assembly resolutions 2864 (XXVI) of 20 December 1971 and 2991 (XXVII) of 15 December 1972, as contained in the annexes to the Secretary-General's reports submitted in accordance with these resolutions;
>
> *Requests* the Secretary-General to transmit to the Security Council any further views and suggestions which might be submitted by Member States in response to resolutions 2864 (XXVI) and 2991 (XXVII).[36]

2. Article 11(3) of the Charter empowers the Assembly to call the attention of the Council to situations which are likely to endanger international peace and security.* If the Assembly refers a matter to the Council, it need not expressly invoke Article 11(3).

* Article 99 confers on the Secretary-General the duty of bringing to the attention of the Council 'any matter which in his opinion may threaten the maintenance of international peace and security'.

Perhaps the most significant implied use of Article 11(3) was the Assembly's decision of 29 November 1947 on the Palestine question.[37] The Assembly directed three requests to the Council:

(a) to take the necessary measures for implementing the plan for the future government of Palestine;
(b) to consider whether the situation in Palestine constituted a threat to the peace
(c) to determine that any attempt to alter by force the settlement envisaged in the Assembly's decision would constitute a threat to the peace, breach of the peace, or act of aggression.

Under Article 11(1), the Assembly may make recommendations to the Security Council (or to UN Members, or to both) with regard to 'the general principles of co-operation in the maintenance of international peace and security, including the principles governing disarmament and the regulation of armaments . . .' An example of a recommendation with regard to the general principles of co-operation directed by the Assembly to the Council is to be found in part of a resolution of 28 April 1949 recommending the appointment of a rapporteur or conciliator when a situation or dispute is brought before the Council. The Security Council noted the Assembly's decision and decided to base its action upon the principles contained in it, should an appropriate occasion arise.[38] Recommendations of the Assembly bearing upon the principles governing disarmament and the regulation of armaments were addressed to the Council in the early years,[39] but are now addressed to the disarmament negotiating committee in Geneva.

Article 11(2), which has to be read in conjunction with Articles 10 and 12(1), empowers the Assembly to make recommendations to the Council (or to the State or States concerned, or to both) with regard to any questions relating to the maintenance of international peace and security. 'Any such question on which action is necessary shall be referred to the Security Council by the General Assembly either before or after discussion.' Article 10 empowers the Assembly to make recommendations to the Council (or to UN Members, or to both) on any questions or matters within the scope of the Charter or relating to the powers and functions of any organ provided for in the Charter.

On the face of it, Article 12(1) states a limitation on the Assembly's right to recommend, in that while the Council is 'exercising in respect of any dispute or situation the functions assigned to it in the . . . Charter', the Assembly shall not make any recommendation with regard to that dispute or situation unless the Council so requests. This raises questions about the meaning of such phrases as 'while the Security Council is exercising . . . the functions assigned to it . . .' and 'on which action is necessary', as well as the more general question of the relationship between the broad responsibilities of the Assembly and the 'primary' responsibility of the Council concerning the maintenance of international peace and security. Let us examine some of the Charter expressions.

'The Secretary-General, with the consent of the Security Council, shall notify the General Assembly at each session of any matters relative to the maintenance of international peace and security which are being dealt with by the Security Council and shall similarly notify the General Assembly . . . immediately the Security Council ceases to deal with such matters' (Article 12(2)).

The intention at San Francisco was to give a role concerning world peace to both the Council and the Assembly, though the Council's responsibility was to be 'primary', and the duties carried out under that responsibility were to be undertaken on behalf of all UN Members. Both the Council and the Assembly were given broad powers of discussion; both organs were given the right to make recommendations; but when it came to taking binding decisions in order to maintain or restore world peace, the task was laid squarely on the Council.

In order to avoid a situation in which both organs might act simultaneously on the same matter, the Secretary-General was to notify the Assembly of matters 'being dealt with' by the Council. This Notification is in practice based on the Summary Statement prepared by the Secretary-General under Rule 11 (see page 42 of Chapter 2 and page 78 of Chapter 3), but some items are excluded from the Notification as they are not considered to relate directly to the maintenance of international peace and security (the excluded items are numbers 3, 4, 8, 9, 10, 82, 86, and 90 of Appendix 3).

In 1946 and 1947, the consent of the Council required by Article 12(2) was given at formal meetings. Since 1947, the consent has been obtained through the circulation by the Secretary-General of a draft. Since 1951, the Notification has had two main categories: matters discussed by the Council since the previous Notification, and other matters of which the Council remains seized. The Notification also contains a note of any items which have been deleted from the list of matters of which the Council was seized during the period under review. Although Article 12(2) requires the Secretary-General to inform the General Assembly or UN Members 'immediately' the Council ceases to deal with a matter relating to peace and security, in practice this is done conveniently rather than hurriedly. The formal Notification for 1973, for example, was issued on 18 September. Six days later, Indonesia requested the deletion of the item 'The Indonesian question', of which the Council had been seized since 1947. Following informal consultations, the Council agreed to the deletion, but neither the General Assembly nor UN Members were formally notified. The matter came to light only when the first Summary Statement for 1974 was issued (7 January) (see Appendix 4C item 22).[40] It is open to the Secretary-General to bring the deletion to the attention of the General Assembly in the 1974 Notification. A similar procedure had been followed over the deletion of the Jordanian complaint against the United Arab Republic in 1964 and the Eichmann case in 1965 (see Appendix 4C, items 25 and 26).

'*The General Assembly may discuss any questions or matters . . .*' (*Article 10*). '*The General Assembly may discuss any questions . . .*' (*Article 11(2)*).

The Assembly clearly has very wide powers of discussion. When the Council was discussing China's complaint that the United States was preventing the liberation of Taiwan in September 1950, Nationalist China opposed discussion on the ground that much the same item was on the agenda of the General Assembly. The Soviet Union argued (quite correctly) that nothing in the Charter was designed to forbid *discussion* of the same question simultaneously in the Council and the Assembly. The United States admitted that the situation was complicated, promising nothing but confusion; but as to the procedure to be followed, the United States was willing to have the charges against it heard in either or both organs. The Council then twice rejected a paragraph in draft resolutions submitted by Ecuador which would have noted that a similar complaint was being considered by the Assembly.[41] It is a fair deduction from the language of the Charter, from opinions of the UN Legal Counsel,[42] and from practice by the Council and the Assembly, that the simultaneous *discussion* of the same matter by the Council and the Assembly is not forbidden, even if it may sometimes be imprudent.

'The General Assembly . . . may make recommendations with regard to [questions relating to the maintenance of international peace and security] . . . to the Security Council . . . While the Security Council is exercising in respect of any dispute or situation the function assigned to it under the . . . Charter, the General Assembly may not make any recommendation with regard to that dispute or situation unless the Security Council so requests' (Articles 11(2) and 12(1)).

We must first examine the words 'while the Security Council is exercising . . . the functions assigned to it . . .' If the Council deletes an item from the list of matters of which it is seized, or decides to defer consideration of a question, then the Council is not exercising the functions assigned to it. That was the course followed in connection with the Spanish question (1946),[43] Greek frontier incidents (1947),[44] complaint of invasion of Taiwan (1950),[45] and complaint of aggression upon the Republic of Korea (1951).[46] A similar situation arises if the Council expressly asks the Assembly to take up a matter, as was done in the case of the Palestine question (1948),[47] the Suez invasion (1956),[48] the question of Hungary (1956),[49] the questions of Lebanon and Jordan (1958),[50] and the situation in the Congo (1960).[51] But what is to be done if the Council neither deletes an item from the matters with which it is seized, nor defers consideration, nor expressly brings a matter to the attention of the Assembly?

A sensible interpretation of the Charter was expressed by Mexico as long ago as 1946:

If [an] item is kept on the agenda, and if the Security Council is to exercise the functions assigned to it, some kind of action will be necessary; but merely to keep something . . . on the agenda is not to take action, and therefore not to exercise a function.[52]

It seems to us that when the Security Council is not engaged in the study of a problem or in its solution, when it has not taken any interim measures . . ., but is merely leaving the matter on its agenda to show that it is keeping the . . . problem in mind or under its observation, then . . . it is not fitting to regard such procedure as constituting the continuous exercise of the Council's functions within the meaning of Article 12 . . .[53]

This commonsense interpretation of Article 12(1) has allowed the Assembly to make recommendations regarding such matters as Tunisia, South Africa, Angola and other Portuguese territories in Africa, Southern Rhodesia, and Namibia (South West Africa). Indeed, the UN Legal Counsel noted in 1964 that 'the General Assembly, beginning in 1960, adopted several resolutions clearly containing recommendations in cases of which the Security Council was then seized and . . . in none of these cases . . . did a member object to the recommendation on the ground of Article 12'. Nevertheless, continued the Legal Counsel, 'it would be difficult to maintain that it [Article 12] is legally no longer in effect'.[54] And in 1968, the Legal Counsel advised:

Article 10 of the United Nations Charter states that the General Assembly may discuss any question or any matters within the scope of the Charter or relating to the powers and functions of any organs provided for in the Charter, and, except as provided in Article 12, may make recommendations to the Members of the United Nations or to the Security Council. Article 12 provides that, while the Security Council is exercising in respect of any dispute or situation the functions assigned to it in the Charter, the General Assembly shall not make any recommendation with regard to that dispute or situation unless the Security Council so requests . . . However, the Assembly has interpreted the words 'is exercising' as meaning 'is exercising at this moment'; consequently, it has made recommendations on . . . matters which the Security Council was also considering.[55]

'Any . . . question [relating to the maintenance of international peace and security] on which action is necessary shall be referred to the Security Council by the General Assembly . . .' (*Article 11(2)*).

This expression inevitably led to a good deal of contention during the period when the Council, hindered by the threat or use of the veto, was eclipsed by the Assembly. The problem was epitomized in part of the 'Uniting for Peace' resolution of 1950.[56] Much that was in that resolution should have raised no difficulty: the Assembly is fully within its rights in establishing procedures for meeting at short notice, for example, or in recommending that the permanent members of the Security Council should discuss problems likely to threaten world peace. But it was the intention of the sponsors of the resolution, confirmed in practice since it was adopted, that if the Security Council should be unable to fulfil its primary responsibility for world peace, the Assembly should be entitled to *recommend* enforcement measures.

This is not the place to review the history of the complex interaction between the Council and the Assembly regarding the maintenance of peace and security. I have discussed on pp. 204–10 of Chapter 4 the circumstances in which, as I understand it, the Security Council can take binding decisions. My own understanding of the Charter and of UN practice since 1945 is that, while the responsibility of the Council is primary, it is not exclusive. The Assembly has a residual or secondary concern for world peace. If peace is imperilled, and if the Council should fail to act, the Assembly is entitled both to discuss the matter and to *recommend* enforcement measures 'to the Members . . . or to the Security Council or to both', as Article 10 has it, but not to *order* them.

From the beginning, the United Kingdom and the United States have regarded 'action' in Article 11(2) as meaning enforcement action. In 1962, the International Court of Justice advised that 'action' refers to 'coercive or enforcement action'; the word 'action' must mean 'such action as is solely within the province of the Security Council'.[57]

3. Under Article 20, the Council may convoke special sessions of the General Assembly. According to Rule 8 of the Assembly's Rules of Procedure, special sessions of the Assembly convoked

by the Council (or by UN Members) shall be convened within fifteen days, emergency special sessions within twenty-four hours. Table 17 lists sessions of the Assembly which have been called by the Council under Article 20.

TABLE 17

Sessions of the General Assembly called by the Security Council, 1946–73

Date	*S.C. res.*	*Subject*
1 Apr. 1948	44 (S/714, II)	Palestine question
31 Oct. 1956	119 (S/3721)	Complaint by Egypt against France and the United Kingdom (Suez)
4 Nov. 1956	120 (S/3733)	Situation in Hungary
7 Aug. 1958	129 (S/4083)	Complaints by Lebanon and Jordan
17 Sept. 1960	157 (S/4526)	Congo question

In addition, the Security Council by resolution 303 (S/10429) on 6 December 1971 referred the situation in the India/Pakistan Sub-continent to the 26th regular session of the General Assembly.

When the Security Council, by procedural vote, refers a matter to the General Assembly, it is implicitly admitting its failure to discharge its primary responsibility for world peace, and acknowledging that the Assembly should now exercise its secondary role. But the fact that a matter has been referred by the Council to the Assembly does not of itself eliminate the constitutional constraints under which the Assembly has to operate and, in particular, the fact that the Assembly cannot take binding decisions to maintain world peace.

4. Certain subsidiary organs established by the Assembly have played a part in the work of the Council, either because they have been placed by the Assembly in a special relation to the Council or because the Council has made use of the services of a subsidiary organ of the Assembly already established, as shown in Table 18.

5. The admission, suspension, or expulsion of Members is effected by 'the General Assembly upon the recommendation of the Security Council' (Articles 4(2), 5, and 6). The Assembly has always taken a liberal attitude to applications for Membership and has periodically chided the Council for failing to recommend the admission of applicants.[58]

Under Rule 60, the Council is to transmit to the Assembly

within specified time limits a record of its discussion of each application. If the Council does not recommend admission, or postpones consideration, it is to transmit also 'a special report'. In practice, a favourable recommendation is accompanied by any report of the Council's Committee on the Admission of New Members; in case of a failure to recommend admission, the Council's special report lists the applicants, how they were included in the agenda of the Council, an indication

TABLE 18

Subsidiary organs of the General Assembly which have played a part in the work of the Security Council, 1946–68

Date of creation	*G.A. res.*	*Date of termination*	*Subsidiary organ*
24 Jan. 1946	1(I)	11 Jan. 1952	Atomic Energy Commission
29 Nov. 1947	181A(II)	14 May 1948	Palestine Commission
14 May 1948	186(S–II)	11 Dec. 1948	Mediator in Palestine
11 Dec. 1948	194(III)	—	Conciliation Commission for Palestine
12 Dec. 1948	195 (III)	7 Oct. 1950	Commission on Korea
15 Apr. 1961	1601(XV)	11 Nov. 1961	Committee of Investigation on the death of Mr. Lumumba
20 Apr. 1961	1603(XV)	14 Nov. 1962	Sub-Committee on the Situation in Angola
27 Nov. 1961	1654(XVI)	—	Special Committee on decolonization
6 Nov. 1962	1761(XVII)	—	Special Committee on Apartheid
19 May 1967	2248(S–V)	—	Council for Namibia (South West Africa)

of the position of members of the Council, and the Council's decision on each application.

In no case has the Council discussed or recommended the suspension of any Member from the exercise of the rights and privileges of Membership after preventive or enforcement action has been taken against the Member, or the expulsion of any Member for persistently violating Charter principles. Withdrawal from the United Nations is not provided for in the Charter, but Indonesia decided to discontinue active participation in the work of the United Nations during 1965 and part of 1966, and in 1965 Pakistan warned the Security Council that if it failed to secure an equitable and honourable settlement in

Jammu and Kashmir, 'Pakistan will have to leave the United Nations.'[59]

Indonesia's withdrawal from active participation in the work of the United Nations was ostensibly caused by the election of Malaysia as a non-permanent member of the Security Council on 29 December 1964, to serve a one-year term in place of Czechoslovakia. President Sukarno had accused Malaysia of neo-colonialism, and Indonesia stated that it was taking the 'revolutionary' step of withdrawing because the fact that Malaysia ('this feeble and highly controversial new "State" ') had been elected to the Security Council was a violation of the Charter, and also in the hope that the act of withdrawal would become 'the catalyst to reform and retool the United Nations . . .'[60]

Secretary-General Thant held private consultations with members of the Security Council and 'heads of regional groups', and then circulated an informal aide-mémoire about 'some practical effects' of the Indonesian letter (e.g. removal of the Indonesian flag from outside the Headquarters building). Thant sent a letter to Indonesia expressing 'profound regret' at Indonesia's action and looking forward to a resumption of co-operation by Indonesia; Malaysia claimed that her own election to the Security Council was neither illegal nor improper nor in any other way questionable; the United Kingdom insisted that Indonesia's withdrawal was not justified and did not relieve her from honouring 'the fundamental principles embodied in Article 2 of the Charter relative to the maintenance of international peace and security'; while Italy pointed out that the Charter made no provision for withdrawal.[61] Czechoslovakia and the Soviet Union used the occasion to point out that splitting the two-year term for membership of the Security Council between Czechoslovakia and Malaysia had 'unlawfully' deprived Eastern Europe of the place in the Security Council 'which by right belongs to the socialist [*sic*] countries . . .'[62]

Sukarno lost effective power in Indonesia in 1965, and on 19 September 1966, Indonesia decided 'to resume full co-operation with the United Nations'. The Office of Legal Affairs in the UN Secretariat advised Thant that if UN Members were in general willing to interpret Indonesia's action as a cessation of co-operation rather than withdrawal from the United Nations, the Secretary-General could take the necessary administrative action for Indonesia to participate again in UN proceedings. Indonesia's Foreign Minister conferred with the Secretary-General and the President of the General Assembly on 22 September, and on 28 September the General Assembly agreed without objection to Indonesia's return to the fold.[63] In 1971, Indonesia's Foreign Minister, Adam Malik, was elected President of the General Assembly, and in 1973, the Indonesian question was removed from the list of matters of which the Security Council is seized.

6. The question of financing field operations which have been launched by the Security Council (see Table 26, part (d), p. 284) would require a book in itself if it were to receive thorough treatment. In my own book on the General Assembly, I have reviewed the difficulties over paying for the first Emergency Force in the Middle East and for the Congo operation.[64] Other peace-keeping operations have been paid for either by the parties, as in Yemen in 1963–4; or from the regular budget, as in the case of the Military Observer Group for India and Pakistan since 1948, the Truce Supervision Organization in the Middle East since 1949, and the India–Pakistan Observer Mission in 1965–6; or by voluntary contributions, as in Cyprus since 1964. When the Yemen Observation Mission was being discussed, the Soviet Union reiterated its view that the financial aspects were the responsibility of the Security Council, even though the parties themselves were meeting the expenses; the Soviet Union abstained when the Council voted to establish the Mission. When the Council established the Force in Cyprus, the Soviet Union expressly pointed out that the resolution 'imposes no financial obligations on Members of the United Nations who contribute no contingents to those forces'. When the Observer Mission for India and Pakistan was created, the Soviet Union again emphasized that 'only the Security Council' was competent to decide on financing.[65]

Thus when the Council came to re-establish a UN Emergency Force for the Middle East in 1973, it was clear that difficulties would be avoided only if the Security Council were to play a crucial role in decisions about financing. Ambassador Malik (see pp. 115–16) repeated the Soviet position of principle about the authority of the Security Council, and when it was suggested that the entire cost of the Force should be borne by the two super-powers, he remarked acidly that, on the contrary, the aggressor should pay. In spite of the fact that the authorizing resolution contained no reference to finance, the Soviet Union voted in favour 'by way of an exception and in this particular instance' out of respect for the non-aligned members of the Council and Egypt. China did not participate in this or several other votes on the Middle East.[66]

The question of finance seems to have been resolved at a series of informal meetings. Secretary-General Waldheim had suggested that the costs of the Force should be considered as 'expenses of the Organization' and should be borne by Members as apportioned by the General Assembly, and this proposal was approved by the Security Council. The Advisory Committee on Administrative and Budgetary Questions favoured creating a special account rather than providing for the expenses within the regular budget. The Committee thought that voluntary contributions in cash or in kind should be sought and that Governments providing contingents should be invited to waive all or part of any reimbursements due to them. On 11 December 1973, the General Assembly decided by 108 votes to 3 (Albania, Libya, and Syria), with one abstention (Portugal), and 23 absentees (including Bolivia, China, Democratic Yemen, Honduras, Iraq, Nigeria, Paraguay, Saudi Arabia, and Zambia) to apportion the first $30 million of expenses as follows:[67]

	%
5 permanent members of the Security Council	63·15
23 'economically developed' Members	34·78
82 'less developed' Members	2·02
25 'least developed' Members	·05
	100·00

3. ECONOMIC AND SOCIAL COUNCIL

Although Article 65 of the Charter provides that the Economic and Social Council (ECOSOC) may furnish the Security Council with information and shall assist the Security Council upon its request, there is little direct connection between the two bodies. Both organs may deal with self-determination and other aspects of human rights, ECOSOC being required by the Charter to promote these goals because they are necessary for peaceful and friendly relations, the Security Council being called on to deal with situations in which their denial leads to friction or endangers world peace. ECOSOC may also consider problems relating to refugees or war victims arising from matters which are within the competence of the Security Council.[68] In 1972, the President of the Economic and Social Council, after consulting the Vice-Presidents, sent a note verbale to the Secretary-General stressing the 'close connection and a positive interrelationship' between matters within the purview of the Security Council on the one hand and economic and social development on the other.[69] There has been some slight overlap between the two bodies in implementing the Security Council's policy of sanctions against the Rhodesian regime and the consequential need for assistance to Zambia. The Security Council strayed into the preserves of ECOSOC when it met in Panama City in March 1973 and adopted a resolution which dealt with 'permanent sovereignty over the natural resources of Latin American countries'.[70]

4. TRUSTEESHIP COUNCIL

There are two links between the Security Council and the Trusteeship Council, one relating to trust territories designated as strategic areas and the other arising from the fact that permanent members of the Security Council are also permanent members of the Trusteeship Council. The Security Council has also considered the fact that one territory formerly held under the mandate system of the League of Nations (South West Africa, now known as Namibia) has not been placed under UN trusteeship.

1. Article 77 of the Charter designates territories which 'may be placed' under trusteeship, and Article 82 provides that any trust territory may be designated 'a strategic area or areas'. The approval of the terms of the trusteeship agreements for strategic trust territories, as well as their alteration or amendment, is the responsibility of the Security Council, whereas for ordinary trust territories this responsibility is exercised by the General Assembly assisted by the Trusteeship Council. The Security

Council, rather than the General Assembly assisted by the Trusteeship Council, exercises 'all functions of the United Nations' relating to strategic trust territories. The Security Council 'shall' avail itself of the assistance of the Trusteeship Council relating to non-strategic matters in strategic trust territories (Article 83). In respect of all trust territories, the administering authority 'shall play its part in the maintenance of international peace and security' (Article 84).

Only one administering authority has designated a trust territory as a strategic area: the United States so designated the Pacific Islands,[71] formerly administered by Japan under League of Nations mandate and taken by the United States during and after the second world war (the Marshall, Mariana, and Caroline Islands). These islands and atolls have a combined area of some 700 square miles, with a population of 48,000 in 1947 and 114,600 in 1972.

In February 1947, the United States submitted to the Security Council a draft trusteeship agreement for the Pacific Islands. Canada, India, Netherlands, New Zealand, and the Philippines (members of the Far Eastern Commission which were not members of the Security Council) were invited to participate without vote in the Council's consideration of the draft, which after amendment was unanimously approved by the Council.[72] On 15 November 1947, the Security Council asked the Committee of Experts to advise on how the Council should exercise its functions regarding strategic trust territories.[73] A report of the Committee of Experts was considered by the Council in June 1948, and the Council decided to accept a proposal of the Trusteeship Council that the two bodies should confer. On 7 March 1949, the Security Council approved a proposal which had been submitted by the non-Communist members of the Committee of Experts, by which the Trusteeship Council was asked to exercise the supervisory functions specified in Articles 87 and 88 of the Charter relating to the political, economic, social, and educational advancement of the inhabitants of strategic trust territories, and to submit to the Security Council its reports and recommendations thereon. The Secretary-General was asked to advise the Security Council of all reports and petitions from or relating to strategic trust territories.[74]

The first report of the Trusteeship Council on the Pacific Islands was submitted to the Security Council on 22 July 1949, and annually thereafter. Since 1956, this has been issued as Special Supplement No. 1 to the official records of the Security Council. The United States has reported to the Security Council periodically, and has from time to time given notice of periods when access to parts of the trust territory has been restricted for security reasons. The Security Council has taken no action on the reports and notifications; item 9 of the list of items of which the Council is seized reads 'Reports on the Strategic Trust Territory of the Pacific Islands pursuant to the resolution of the Security Council of 7 March 1949.'

2. The question of the composition of the Trusteeship Council arose from two provisions of the Charter which eventually proved incompatible: that the Trusteeship Council should be equally divided between Members administering trust territories and Members which do not, and that all the five permanent members of the Security Council should also be permanent members of the Trusteeship Council (Article 86(1)(b) and (c)).[75] The first provision had been proposed at San Francisco by the United States, the second by the Soviet Union.[76] The balance of membership between administering and non-administering members was to be maintained by elections by the General Assembly.

It does not seem to have occurred to anyone at San Francisco that the objective of 'self-government or independence' might eventually be achieved for some territories and that this would complicate the problem of constituting the Trusteeship Council, but this possibility was raised by the United Kingdom later in 1945. If a State ceased to be an administering authority, commented the United Kingdom, it would lose its membership of the Trusteeship Council and, in order to maintain parity of membership, the result would be to displace one of the members elected by the General Assembly. If, however, the administering authority happened to be also a permanent member of the Security Council, the effect would be to displace *two* elected members.[77]

This rather surprising result can be illustrated by what happened in 1947. By the end of 1946, five States had submitted trusteeship agreements which had been approved by the

General Assembly, and two States had been elected by the General Assembly. The Trusteeship Council was therefore constituted as follows:

Administering members (*Article 86(1)(a)*)	*Non-administering members*
	permanent members of the Security Council (Article 86(1)(b))
Australia	China
Belgium	Soviet Union
France	United States
New Zealand	
United Kingdom	
	elected by the General Assembly (Article 86(1)(c))
	Iraq
	Mexico

When the Trusteeship Agreement for the Pacific Islands had been approved on 7 March 1949, the United States moved from the right-hand column to the left-hand column, increasing the number of administering members from five to six, and reducing the number of non-administering members from five to four. The General Assembly elected Costa Rica and the Philippines to maintain the parity required by the Charter. It would follow, in reverse, that when France, or the United Kingdom, or the United States ceased to administer trust territories, they would move from the left-hand to the right-hand column and displace *two* elected members each; and in like circumstances, Australia, Belgium, and New Zealand would lose their membership of the Trusteeship Council and displace *one* elected member each.*

In 1960, Italy and France ceased to be administering members; Italy left the Council, France moved to the right-hand column, and three elected members had to be displaced to maintain parity of five in each column. In 1962, Belgium ceased to be an administering authority, displacing another elected member. This left the Trusteeship Council as follows:

Administering members	*Non-administering members*
Australia	China
New Zealand	France
United Kingdom	Soviet Union
United States	1 elected member

* Italy became a member of the Trusteeship Council following her admission to UN Membership in 1955, and the General Assembly elected Burma to the Trusteeship Council in order to maintain parity.

Nauru, administered by Australia on behalf also of New Zealand and the United Kingdom, became independent in 1968. New Zealand ceased to be a member of the Trusteeship Council, displacing the remaining elected member, and the United Kingdom moved from the left-hand to the right-hand column. This left the Trusteeship Council composed of two administering members (Australia and the United States) and four non-administering members (China, France, the Soviet Union, and the United Kingdom). Parity had vanished without trace.

But it was constitutional parity which had disappeared, not political parity: the latter had gone five years earlier when France became a *non*-administering member of the Trusteeship Council, while continuing to administer overseas territories outside the UN trusteeship system. But the *principle* of parity in colonial matters had gone anyway, with the creation by the General Assembly in 1961 of a committee on decolonization composed on a basis of geographical distribution rather than parity between Members administering colonial territories and non-administering Members.

3. The only territory under League of Nations mandate which was not brought within the UN trusteeship system was South West Africa (Namibia). South Africa, the administering authority, informed the General Assembly in 1946 that a majority of the inhabitants of the territory desired its incorporation with South Africa. Thus began a conflict between South Africa and UN organs about the present and future status of the territory. Initially, the problem concerned the General Assembly and the International Court of Justice, but in 1968, the question of South Africa's 'continuing defiance . . . of the authority of the United Nations and its complete disregard for world opinion' was referred to the Security Council.[78]

Two years earlier, the General Assembly had decided to terminate South Africa's mandate over South West Africa.[79] but the States with the will to expel South Africa from the territory did not have the means to do so. In 1968, the Security Council condemned South Africa for refusing to comply with the General Assembly's decision, and later in the year censured South Africa for its defiance of the United Nations by disregarding the earlier resolution of condemnation.[80] The following year, the Security Council went a stage further by formally recognizing that the General Assembly had terminated the mandate of South Africa over the territory.[81] The Council has continued to concern itself with the matter,[82] and remains seized of the item 'The situation in Namibia'.

5. INTERNATIONAL COURT OF JUSTICE

I have described the procedure for nominating and electing members of the International Court of Justice in my *Voting in the Security Council.*[83] There remain five other functions which the Security Council performs, or may perform, in connection with the International Court of Justice, two of them by making recommendations to the General Assembly.

1. The Council lays down the conditions under which the Court shall be open to States which are not parties to the Statute (Article 35(2) of the Statute);
2. The Council makes recommendations to the General Assembly regarding the conditions under which each State which is not a Member of the United Nations may become a party to the Statute of the Court (Article 93(2));
3. The Council makes recommendations to the General Assembly regarding the conditions under which a party to the Statute which is not a Member of the United Nations may participate in electing the members of the Court and in making amendments to the Statute (Articles 4(3) and 69 of the Statute);
4. The Council may request the Court to give an advisory opinion on any legal question (Article 96(1));
5. The Council may recommend that the parties to a legal dispute should refer it to the International Court of Justice (implied in Article 33 and 36).

1. Under Article 35(2) of the Statute, the Security Council lays down the conditions under which the Court shall be open to States which are not parties to the Statute, although 'in no case shall such conditions place the parties in a position of inequality before the Court.' In 1946, the Security Council approved a proposal for this which had been drafted by the Committee of Experts and was analogous to the resolution of the Council of the League of Nations of 17 May 1922, with such modifications as were necessary to adapt the text to the UN Charter and the new Statute. The procedure was based on two principles: first, to give the freest possible access to the Court to

States not parties to the Statute; and second, not to place upon the parties to the Statute any new obligations, so that no party to the Statute could be forced to appear before the Court against its will and consent. The Council rejected a Polish proposal which would have excluded those non-parties to the Statute 'whose régimes have been installed with the help of the armed forces of countries which have fought against the United Nations [during the second world war], so long as these régimes are in power'.[84]

The sole requirements contained in the decision of the Security Council are that non-parties to the Statute desiring access to the Court shall deposit a declaration accepting the jurisdiction of the Court in accordance with the UN Charter and the Court's Statute and rules, and accepting also the obligation, which UN Members have assumed, to comply with the decisions of the Court in any cases to which they are parties (Article 94 of the Charter). The Security Council reserved the right to amend or rescind this resolution.[85] The decision of the Council did not need to deal with the financial obligations of non-parties, since Article 35(3) of the Statute declares that when a State which is not a UN Member is a party to a case, the Court itself shall fix the amount which that party is to contribute towards the expenses of the Court, except where that State is already bearing a share of the expenses of the Court (see next four paragraphs).

2. A State which is not a Member of the United Nations may not only be a party to a case before the Court; it may, if it wishes, become a party to the Statute of the Court on conditions to be determined 'in each case' by the General Assembly upon the recommendation of the Security Council (Article 93(2)). On 26 October 1946, Switzerland asked what were the conditions under which she could become a party to the Statute. The request was referred to the Committee of Experts,[86] which recommended that Switzerland might become a party after accepting, first, the provisions of the Statute; second, the obligation to comply with decisions of the Court in any case to which it is a party (Article 94(1)); and third, an undertaking to contribute to the expenses of the Court. The Committee of Experts pointed out that the second of the three conditions used precisely the same wording as in the Council's resolution setting

the conditions under which the Court should be open to non-parties to the Statute. The Committee expressed the opinion that

> the obligations of a Member of the United Nations under Article 94 [compliance with the decisions of the Court] include the complementary obligations arising under Articles 25 ['accept and carry out the decisions of the Security Council in accordance with the . . . Charter'] and 103 [obligations under the UN Charter prevail over obligations under any other international agreement] . . . in so far as the provisions of those Articles may relate to the provisions of Article 94 . . .

Thus the Committee was seeking to define the obligations of Article 94 in the same way for UN Members, non-Members which become parties to the Statute, and non-parties which have been given access to the Court.

With regard to the third condition regarding the expenses of the Court, the Committee of Experts noted that Article 35(3) of the Statute seems to contemplate a general contribution towards the expenses of the Court by parties to the Statute which are not UN Members, the assessment being within the competence of the General Assembly. The Committee also pointed out that the conditions for becoming a party to the Statute were to be determined 'in each case', and that the conditions recommended by the Committee as appropriate for Switzerland 'are not intended to constitute a precedent . . .' When Switzerland had become a party to the Statute, the Committee noted, it would be eligible to participate in electing members of the Court and in making amendments to the Statute, in accordance with Article 4(3) and 69 of the Statute (see below).[87] The recommendations of the Committee of Experts were duly approved by the Security Council.[88]

Liechtenstein, Japan, and San Marino later applied to become parties to the Statute and were informed that the same conditions would operate as in the case of Switzerland.[89]

Switzerland will contribute $342,000 to the expenses of the Court in 1974–6, about the same as Argentina; Leichtenstein and San Marino will each pay the minimum rate of $8,340.

3. While all Members of the United Nations are *ipso facto* parties to the Statute of the Court, all parties to the Statute are not necessarily Members of the United Nations. Switzerland,

though not a UN Member, became a party to the Statute of the Court on 28 July 1948, and it thereupon became necessary to lay down the general conditions under which parties to the Statute could participate in the election of members of the Court (Article 4(3) of the Statute) and in making amendments to the Statute (Article 69 of the Statute).[90] The Committee of Experts had made it clear in 1946 that, while applications to become parties to the Statute are determined on a case-by-case basis, the conditions under which parties may participate in elections and in amending the Statute were to be 'generally applicable'.[91]

Upon the proposal of Belgium, the Security Council laid down the following conditions under which a State which is a party to the Statute but not a UN Member may participate in the election of judges:[92]

(i) Such a State should be on an equal footing with UN Members in respect to the nomination of candidates;
(ii) Such a State should participate in the electon of members of the Court in the same manner as UN Members;
(iii) Such a State should be subject to the provisions of Article 19 of the Charter regarding withdrawal of the vote in the General Assembly when in arrears in the payment of its contribution equalling or exceeding the amount of its contribution for the preceding two full years.

This recommendation was approved by the Assembly ten days later.[93]

This was intended to be a once-and-for-all decision, although there would seem to be no reason why the conditions could not be varied by the same means as were used in making the original decision.

It has not yet been necessary to put to a vote any proposed amendment to the Statute.

4. Under Article 96(1) of the Charter, the Security Council may request the Court to give an advisory opinion 'on any legal question.' Proposals to seek the Court's advice were made from time to time,[94] but it was not until 1970 that the Security Council actually asked the Court to render an advisory opinion. By resolution 276 (S/9620/Rev.1) adopted on 30 January 1970, the Council had declared that the continued presence of the South African authorities in Namibia was

illegal and that all acts by the South African Government 'on behalf of or concerning Namibia' subsequent to the General Assembly's decision to terminate the mandate (27 October 1966) were 'illegal and invalid'. On the proposal of Finland, the Security Council then decided to ask the Court for its advice on 'the legal consequences for States of the continued presence of South Africa in Namibia, notwithstanding Security Council resolution 276 . . .' of 30 January 1970.[95] Three members of the Security Council abstained on the Finnish proposal. The Soviet Union and Poland wanted political action rather than a legal opinion. The United Kingdom, in which a new Conservative Government had only just taken office, was unable to support a proposal whose basis lay in earlier resolutions on which Britain had abstained.[96]

The Court's advisory opinion was in three parts. First, the continued presence of South Africa in Namibia being illegal, 'South Africa is under obligation to withdraw its administration from Namibia immediately and thus put an end to its occupation of the Territory.' Second, UN Members are under obligation 'to recognize' the illegality of South Africa's presence in Namibia and the invalidity of its acts on behalf of or concerning Namibia, and to refrain from any acts implying recognition of the legality of, or lending support or assistance to, such presence and administration. Third, it is incumbent on States which are not UN Members to assist in the action of the United Nations with regard to Namibia.[97]

The Council agreed with this Advisory Opinion.[98] Of the members of the Council which abstained when the request for an Advisory Opinion was addressed to the Court in 1970, Poland had ceased to be a member of the Council by the time it came to take a decision on the Court's Opinion, but the United Kingdom (and France) abstained on the vote agreeing with the Court. The United Kingdom, having had serious reservations about 'the legal effectiveness' and 'validity' of the General Assembly's decision to terminate South Africa's mandate over Namibia, had nevertheless considered the Court's Advisory Opinion with great respect, yet at the same time taking account of the fact that 'such an Opinion is in law not binding'. Britain was unable to accept the legal consequences deduced by the Court, or the Court's other conclusions.

But the British Government has not published a 'closely reasoned analysis of the legal conclusions which it has reached on this case', and it is not surprising that Rosalyn Higgins should find some of the points made by the United Kingdom in the Security Council 'open to debate'.[99]

The Soviet Union abstained on the request to the Court in 1970, but voted in favour of the resolution agreeing with the Court's advisory opinion in 1971.

5. Under Articles 36–8 of the Charter, the Security Council may make recommendations regarding the pacific settlement of disputes. Article 33(1) mentions 'judicial settlement' as one of the means open to the parties, and Article 36(3) states that legal disputes should 'as a general rule' be referred by the parties to the International Court of Justice. From time to time, members of the Security Council have suggested that a matter be referred to the Court,[100] but only in one case has the Security Council expressly recommended that a dispute should be referred to the International Court of Justice.

Two British naval vessels had been damaged by mines in the Corfu Channel on 22 October 1946, and forty-four sailors had been killed and forty-two injured. The United Kingdom held Albania responsible and requested an apology and compensation. As Albania's response was unsatisfactory, the United Kingdom took the matter to the Security Council. The Council appointed a sub-committee 'to examine all the available evidence', and the sub-committee reported that the relevance of some of the allegations depended on the interpretation of points of law. A British proposal to find that Albania had laid an unnotified minefield in the Corfu Strait was vetoed by the Soviet Union, whereupon Britain proposed that the Council should recommend that the parties should refer the dispute to the International Court of Justice. The second British proposal was approved by the Council, Poland and the Soviet Union abstaining and the United Kingdom, as a party to the dispute, not participating in the vote. The President of the Council pointed out that, although Albania was not a Member of the United Nations, it had accepted the obligations of Membership as contained in the Council's invitation to Albania to participate in the discussion of the case, and that consequently Albania was 'obliged to comply with the provisions of both the

Charter and of the Statute of the International Court of Justice'.[101]

In its judgment of 9 April 1949, the Court found that Albania was responsible under international law for the explosions which had occurred on 22 October 1946 in Albanian waters and for the consequent damage and loss of life, and was under a duty to pay compensation. The Court found that the United Kingdom had not violated Albanian sovereignty by sending ships through the Strait, but that the subsequent minesweeping operation by the United Kingdom was a violation of Albanian sovereignty. On 15 December 1949, the Court found that compensation of £843,947 was due to the United Kingdom. Although Article 94(1) of the Charter requires compliance with the Court's decision, Albania has not in fact paid the compensation.

If a party to a case fails to perform the obligations incumbent upon it under a judgment, Article 94(2) of the Charter permits the other party to have recourse to the Security Council. The Council, if it deems necessary, may 'make recommendations or decide upon measures to be taken to give effect to the [Court's] judgment'. It is not clear from the text of the Charter or the Statute whether the 'recommendations' and 'measures' referred to in Article 94(2) are those which have been conferred on the Council under earlier chapters of the Charter or whether Article 94(2) confers on the Council powers which it would not otherwise have.

The United Kingdom did not invoke Article 94(2) in the Corfu Channel case; but in the Anglo-Iranian Oil Company case in 1951, the United Kingdom implicitly invoked Article 94(2) of the Charter as well as Article 41(2) of the Statute of the Court, under which the parties and the Security Council are to be given notice of any provisional measures which ought to be taken to preserve the respective rights of either party, pending 'the final decision'.

On 20 March 1951, the Iranian Parliament had nationalized the oil industry. As a consequence of this action, the United Kingdom instituted proceedings against Iran in the International Court of Justice, requesting the Court to indicate interim measures of protection. This the Court did on 5 July 1951 by an order indicating measures which were to be reciprocally observed.[102] The United Kingdom maintained that by this order the Court had implicitly recognized the accuracy of the British contention that the actions of the Iranian authorities threatened to bring the production and refining of oil to a standstill, endangering life and property. Iran, however, declared that the Court lacked competence and that its order was invalid. Iran then ordered the expulsion of the remaining staff of the Anglo-Iranian Oil Company, whereupon the United Kingdom asked the Security Council to consider the matter 'as one of extreme urgency . . .'[103]

The debate on the British complaint has been described by Shabtai Rosenne as 'limpid . . . [giving] evidence of some general scepticism, probably due to the general *malaise*' which had beset the Security Council,[104] but this was not the fault of the spokesmen of the parties, both of whom commanded a certain flamboyance. Mohammed Mossadeq, Prime Minister of Iran, maintained that, under Article 41(2) of the Statute, only 'final' decisions of the Court and not provisional measures have binding force, and that in any case the Council was not competent to act in regard to matters within Iran's domestic jurisdiction. Sir Gladwyn Jebb (see pp. 119–20), for the United Kingdom, argued that a necessary consequence of the binding character of the final decision was that interim measures intended to preserve its efficacy should be equally binding, and that the fact that the Court had indicated interim measures showed that the case was 'at least *prima facie*, internationally justiciable and not therefore a pure matter of domestic jurisdiction'.[105]

It became clear during the debate on the British complaint that several members of the Council (Nationalist China, Ecuador, France, India, Yugoslavia) had doubts on legal aspects,[106] although there was general agreement that the parties should be encouraged to settle their differences directly.

In the absence of sufficient votes to take a decision, the Council approved a French motion to adjourn the debate until the Court had ruled on its own competence. On 22 July 1952, the Court declared that it lacked jurisdiction, the British judge (Sir Arnold McNair) concurring in the conclusion reached in the judgment. Nevertheless, the Security Council remains seized of the British complaint (Item 20 of the Summary Statement).

In the Fisheries cases between Britain and Iceland and the German Federal Republic and Iceland, the Court made Orders on 17 August 1972 indicating interim measures of protection to prevent an aggravation or extension of the disputes pending the Court's final decisions. In the Nuclear Tests cases between Australia and France and New Zealand and France, the Court similarly made Orders on 22 June 1973 indicating interim measures of protection. Iceland and France failed to comply with these Orders. Neither Britain nor the German Federal Republic in the Fisheries cases, and neither Australia nor New Zealand in the Nuclear Tests cases, complained to the Security Council that Iceland and France respectively had failed to comply with the provisional measures of protection indicated by the Court.

CHAPTER 6

SUBSIDIARY ORGANS

There is all the difference between the attempt to debauch the subjects of a sovereign prince in order to ensnare them into conspiracy against him, and the legitimate endeavour to use every opportunity for acquiring information. The latter practice has always been permissible, and indeed is a necessary part of diplomacy.

ARTICLE 29 of the Charter states the right of the Security Council to establish 'such subsidiary organs as it deems necessary for the performance of its functions'. A subsidiary organ can be one man or a committee or a peace-keeping force; it can be established either by the Security Council or by the President of the Council and/or the Secretary-General pursuant to a dedicision of the Council; it can conduct its operations at UN Headquarters or in the field; it can be given an *ad hoc* assignment or a continuing responsibility. The only Rule of Procedure govering the appointment of subsidiary organs is no. 28, which simply states that the Council may appoint a commission or committee or a rapporteur for a specified question.

I consider first a number of subsidiary organs which have dealt or still deal with questions of a recurring nature, and then other kinds of subsidiary organ.

1. COMMITTEE OF EXPERTS

The Committee of Experts consists of all the members of the Security Council. It has no formal terms of reference, but it was established at the first meeting of the Council to examine and report on the provisional rules of procedure drafted by the Preparatory Commission.[1] Its responsibilities have always been in the procedural and constitutional field, and it has been thought of primarily as a working body in which debate plays

TABLE 19

Tasks entrusted to the Committee of Experts and Reports of the Committee, 1946–53

Date			*Meeting and page or para. no.*	*Date(s) of report(s)*	*SCOR*
17 Jan. 1946 16 Feb. 1946	1	To consider the provisional rules of procedure recommended by the Preparatory Commission	1, p. 1111 23, p. 368	5 Feb., 13 and 31 May, 17 June 1946	1st year, 1st series, Supplement no. 2, pp. 1–8, 20–30, 39–40, 41–3, S/6, S/57, S/71, S/88
1 Feb. 1946	2	To indicate how communications from non-governmental bodies and persons should be dealt with	6, p. 72	5 Apr. 1946	31st meeting, p. 117, S/29
16 Feb. 1946	3	To examine the draft statute and draft rules of procedure submitted by the Military Staff Committee	23, p. 369	17 July 1947	S/421 (restricted)
16 Apr. 1946	4	To examine and report on a memorandum from the Secretary-General concerning the retention of the Iranian question on the agenda	33, p. 145	18 Apr. 1946	1st year, 1st series, Supplement no. 2, pp. 47–50, S/42
10 July 1946	5	To examine and report on the conditions under which the International Court of Justice should be open to States not parties to the Statute	50, pp. 7–8	24 Sept.	1st year, 2nd series, Supplement no. 6, pp. 153–6, S/169

30 Oct. 1946	6	To examine and report on the conditions on which Switzerland might become a party to the Statute of the International Court of Justice	78, pp. 486–7	12 Nov.	1st year, 2nd series, Supplement no. 8, pp. 159–61, S/191
29 Nov. 1946	7	To appoint a sub-committee to confer with a committee of the General Assembly with a view to preparing rules governing the admission of new Members	81, pp 504–5	25 Aug. 1947	2nd year, Supplement no. 19, pp. 157–65, S/520 and Add. 1.
27 Aug. 1947	8	To consider and report on the recommendations of the General Assembly of 13 Dec. 1946 (G.A. res.40(1)) regarding the voting procedure in the Security Council	197, pp. 2267–81	—	—
15 Nov. 1947 19 Dec. 1947	9	To report on the respective functions of the Security Council and the Trusteeship Council with regard to strategic trust territories	220, pp. 2756–63 224, pp. 2812–17	12 June 1948	3rd year, Supplement for June 1948, pp. 1–10, S/642
8 Apr. 1949	10	To report on the request of Leichtenstein to become a party to the Statute of the International Court of Justice	423, pp. 16–17	23 June 1949	4th year, Supplement for July 1949, pp. 2–3, S/1342
17 Jan 1950	11	To consider Indian draft amendments to the Provisional Rules of Procedure of the Security Council concerning representation and credentials	462, pp. 10–13	14 Feb. 1950	5th year, Supplement for, January to May 1950, pp. 16–18, S/1457 and Corr. 1
23 Nov. 1953	12	To study and report on the conditions on which Japan and San Marino might become parties to the Statute of the International Court of Justice	641, paras. 1–3	1 and 2 Dec. 1953	8th year, Supplement for October to December 1953, pp. 72–3, S/3146, S/3147

a less important role than in the Council itself. The tasks which have been entrusted to the Committee of Experts are set out in Table 19. Two proposals to refer matters to the Committee of Experts have been made in the Security Council but not pressed to a vote.[2]

It would seem that all but one of the reports of the Committee (Table 19, no. 3) have been issued in unrestricted form and that the Committee has reported on all the matters entrusted to it, except no. 8 in Table 19. On ten occasions, the chairman of the Committee of Experts was invited to sit at the Council table in order to introduce and interpret the Committee's report.[3] This was a somewhat curious procedure, as the membership of the Committee and the Council is identical.

The Committee of Experts last met on 1 December 1953.

2. COMMITTEE ON ADMISSION OF NEW MEMBERS

The work of the Committee on Admission of New Members has to be considered in two phases. During the first phase (1946–9), applications for Membership were, with four exceptions to be noted below, referred to the Committee as a matter of course and examined by the Committee with some care. After 1949, applications were dealt with by the Security Council without the help of a committee. Indonesia was admitted in 1950, and after the package deal of sixteen admissions in 1955, applications were accepted by the Security Council without much question until 1971, when the practice was resumed of referring all applications to the Committee.

The Committee on Admission of New Members was established on 17 May 1946. The draft rules of procedure prepared by the Preparatory Commission had provided that a State desiring to become a Member of the United Nations should submit to the Secretary-General an application, accompanied by a declaration of its readiness to accept the obligations contained in the Charter; that the application should be placed before the Security Council, which would decide whether the applicant was peace-loving, and able and willing to carry out the obligations of the Charter; and that, should the Security Council decide to recommend an applicant for admission, the recommendation would be placed before the General Assembly.[4] The Committee of Experts recommended two changes in this procedure. First, the Committee proposed that 'unless the Security Council decides otherwise, the application shall be referred by the President to a committee of the Security Council upon which each member of the . . . Council shall be represented . . . [and the] committee shall examine any application . . . and report its conclusions . . .' Secondly, the Committee of Experts 'thought it useful to lay down time limits . . .'[5]

Australia, at that time spearheading the campaign to increase the rights of the medium and smaller UN Members, was opposed to the proposal of the Committee of Experts that applications should go to the Security Council before going to the General Assembly. Australia held that the Security Council 'was not in any sense the executive committee of the Organization' but 'a body with defined powers . . .' The General Assembly was 'the only organ entitled to speak on this matter for all Members' and 'the only body which . . . can make the final and binding decision on the subject of admission'. Nor was the Security Council empowered to establish the route along which an application for Membership should travel. Indeed, the correct procedure was that each application should go first to the General Assembly, which would decide whether the application should be entertained, after which it should be remitted to the Security Council. Australia urged the Council to defer a decision pending consultation with the General Assembly.[6] Australia was in a minority of one, however, and the Council approved the procedure recommended by the Committee of Experts.[7]

Australia raised the matter again the following year and again proposed that the General Assembly should consider applications for Membership before remitting them to the Security Council. The proposal was submitted first to a joint meeting of a body appointed by the General Assembly and a sub-committee of the Committee of Experts, and then to the Council itself, but again without success. In 1950, the International Court of Justice made it clear in an Advisory Opinion that, irrespective of which UN organ considers an application first, the admission of a State 'cannot be effected by a decision of the General Assembly when the Security Council has made no recommendation for admission . . .'[8]

The Council's rules for dealing with applications for Membership were revised in 1947, as follows:[9]

1. Formerly an application had to be accompanied by a declaration of the applicant's readiness to accept the obligations contained in the Charter. This was changed to provide that each application should contain a declaration 'made in a formal instrument' that the applicant accepts the Charter obligations.
2. New provisions were inserted to require the Security Council to forward to the General Assembly with each positive recommendation 'a complete record of the discussion'.
3. In the event that the Security Council should not recommend an applicant for admission or should postpone consideration, the Council was required to submit to the Assembly 'a special report . . . with a complete record of the discussion'.

The Council's Rules of Procedure regarding the admission of new Members have never required that each application should necessarily be submitted to the Committee on Admission of New Members, but that this should be done 'unless the Security Council decides otherwise . . .' (Rule 59). During the period 1946–9, the Security Council referred to the Committee twenty-five applications or re-applications from twenty states (see Table 20, part A).[10] The President of the Council referred to the Committee applications from Austria, Bulgaria, Burma, Ceylon, Israel, Nepal, Romania, and Yemen: the Security Council itself decided to refer to the Committee applications from Afghanistan, Albania, Hungary, Iceland, Ireland, Italy, Jordan (Transjordan), Republic of [South] Korea, Mongolia, Portugal, Sweden, and Thailand (Siam). During the same period (1946–9), the Council considered the application of Finland without referring it to the Committee (although the proposal to admit Finland was vetoed by the Soviet Union);[11] after the partition of India, recommended the admission of Pakistan without first referring the application to the Committee;[12] decided not to refer to the Committee the application from the Democratic People's Republic of [North] Korea;[13] and took no action on the application of the Democratic Republic of [North] Viet-Nam.

It was intended that the Committee on Admission of New Members should obtain the information necessary to judge whether each applicant satisfied the requirements of Article

TABLE 20

Applications for UN Membership referred to the Committee on Admission of New Members, 1946–9 and 1971–3

A. 1946–9

Applicant	*Date of application*	*Referred to Committee: SCOR meeting and page or para. no.*	*Report of Committee SCOR*	*Date Security Council recommended admission*	*Date General Assembly decided on admission*
Afghanistan	2 July 1946	42, pp. 278–85	1st year, 2nd series, Supplement no. 4, p. 67, S/133	29 Aug. 1946	19 Nov. 1946
Albania	undated *	42, pp. 278–85	1st year, 2nd series, Supplement no. 4, pp. 56–64, S/133	14 Dec. 1955	14 Dec. 1955
		152, pp. 1229–31	2nd year, Special Supplement no. 3, pp. 4–8, S/479 and Corr. 1	14 Dec. 1955	14 Dec. 1955
Austria	2 July 1947	154, pp. 1260–6	2nd year, Special Supplement no. 3, S/479 and Corr. 1, p. 24	14 Dec. 1955	14 Dec. 1955
Bulgaria	26 July 1947	178, pp. 1826–8	2nd year, Special Supplement no. 3, S/479 and Corr. 1, pp. 25–6	14 Dec. 1955	14 Dec. 1955
Burma	27 Feb. 1948	261, p. 2	3rd year, Supplement for April 1948, pp. 1–3, S/706	10 Apr. 1948	19 Apr. 1948
Ceylon	25 May 1948	318, p. 2	3rd year, Supplement for August 1948, p. 78, S/859	14 Dec. 1955	14 Dec. 1955
Hungary	22 Apr. 1947	132, pp. 820–1	2nd year, Special Supplement no. 3, pp. 21–2, S/479 and Corr. 1	14 Dec. 1955	14 Dec. 1955
Iceland	2 Aug. 1946	51, pp. 14–16	1st year, 2nd series, Supplement no. 4, pp. 74–5, S/133	29 Aug. 1946	19 Nov. 1946
Ireland	2 Aug. 1946	51, pp. 14–16	1st year, 2nd series, Supplement no. 4, p. 72, S/133		

* application received by Secretariat on 25 Jan. 1946

		152, pp. 1229–31	2nd year, Special Supplement no. 3, pp. 15–16, S/479 and Corr. 1	14 Dec. 1955	14 Dec. 1955
Israel	29 Nov. 1948	383, pp. 7–25	3rd year, Supplement for December 1948, pp. 119–20, S/1110 and Corr. 1	4 Mar. 1949	11 May 1949
Italy	7 May 1947	137, pp. 945–6	2nd year, Special Supplement no. 3, pp. 22–4, S/479 and Corr. 1	14 Dec. 1955	14 Dec. 1955
Korea, Republic of	19 Jan. 1949	409, pp. 3–12	4th year, Supplement for April 1949, pp. 1–5, S/1281	—	—
Mongolia	24 June 1946	42, pp. 278–85	1st year, 2nd series, Supplement no. 4, pp. 64–7, S/133		
		152, pp. 1229–31	2nd year, Special Supplement no. 3, pp. 8–13, S/479 and Corr. 1	27 Oct. 1961	27 Oct. 1961
Nepal	13 Feb. 1949	423, p. 16	4th year, Supplement for September to December 1949, pp. 10–12, S/1382	14 Dec. 1955	14 Dec. 1955
Portugal	2 Aug. 1946	51, pp. 14–16	1st year, 2nd series, Supplement no. 4, pp. 72–4, S/133		
		152, pp. 1229–31	2nd year, Special Supplement no. 3, pp. 16–17, S/479 and Corr. 1	14 Dec. 1955	14 Dec. 1955
Romania	10 July 1947	161, pp. 1389–91	2nd year, Special Supplement no. 3, pp. 24–5, S/479 and Corr. 1	14 Dec. 1955	14 Dec. 1955
Siam (Thailand)	20 May 1946 †	51, pp. 14–16	1st year, 2nd series, Supplement no. 4, pp. 75–7, S/133	12 Dec. 1946	16 Dec. 1946
Sweden	9 Aug. 1946	51, pp. 14–16	1st year, 2nd series, Supplement no. 4, pp. 77–8, S/133	29 Aug. 1946	19 Nov. 1946
Transjordan (Jordan)	26 June 1946	42, pp. 278–85	1st year, 2nd series, Supplement no. 4, pp. 68–72, S/133		
		152, pp. 1229–31	2nd year, Special Supplement no. 3, pp 14–15, S/479 and Corr.1	14 Dec. 1955	14 Dec. 1955

† application received by Secretariat on 3 Aug. 1946

TABLE 20 (*continued*).

Applicant	*Date of appliation*	*Referred to Committee: SCOR meeting and page or para. no.*	*Report of Committee SCOR*	*Date Security Council recommended admission*	*Date General Assembly decided on admission*
Yemen	21 July 1947	168, pp. 1549–50	2nd year, Special Supplement no. 3, p. 25, S/479 and Corr. 1	18 Aug. 1947	30 Sept. 1947
B. 1971–3					
Bahamas	10 July 1973	1731, para. 6	S/10968	18 July 1973	18 Sept. 1973
Bahrain	15 Aug. 1971	1574, para. 2	26th year, Supplement for July to September 1971, p. 54, S/10294, paras. 3–4	18 Sept. 1971	21 Sept. 1971
Bangladesh, People's Republic of	8 Aug. 1972	PV.1658, p. 47	27th year, Supplement for July to September 1972, pp. 93–4, S/10773	—	—
Bhutan	22 Dec. 1970	1565, para. 126	26th year, Supplement for January to March 1971, p. 65, S/10109	10 Feb. 1971	21 Sept. 1971
German Democratic Republic	12 June 1973	1729, para. 1	28th year, Supplement for April to June 1973, pp. 77–8, S/10957	22 June 1973	18 Sept. 1973
Germany, Federal Republic of	13 June 1973				
Oman	24 May 1971	1574, para. 2	26th year, Supplement for June to August 1971, p. 54, S/10294, para. 2; Supplement for September to December 1971, p. 69, S/10345	30 Sept. 1971	7 Oct. 1971
Qatar	4 Sept. 1971	1577, para. 3	26th year, Supplement for September to December 1971, p. 63, S/10318	15 Sept. 1971	21 Sept. 1971
United Arab Emirates	2 Dec. 1971	1608, paras. 5–9	26th year, Supplement for September to December 1971, p. 96, S/10430	8 Dec. 1971	9 Dec. 1971

4(1) of the Charter, namely, whether the applicant was a State, peace-loving,* accepted the obligations of the Charter, was able to carry out the obligations, and was willing to do so.

In some cases, the Committee has had before it summaries of information prepared by the Secretariat concerning the applicant State. On occasion, the Committee has seen fit to draw up and communicate to the applicant for reply a questionnaire concerning various matters on which the Committee wished to be informed . . .[15]

In one case, the application of Israel, the Committee reported on 7 December 1948 that it was 'not . . . in possession of the requisite information to enable it to come to any decision'.[16] In another case, the application of Nepal, the Committee decided to transmit to the Government of Nepal the Secretariat working paper and the summary records of its own discussion of the application, with a request that the Government of Nepal provide 'additional information . . . particularly concerning its sovereignty and . . . independence'.[17]

During the late 1960s, a number of the major powers had become uneasy at the rather casual way some applications for Membership were being dealt with by the Security Council, and in 1970 France suggested the reactivation of the Council's Committee on the Admission of New Members. Informal consultations among Council members followed. On 10 October 1970, when Fiji's application for Membership was being considered, the Council decided to reinstate the former practice, but not to apply it in Fiji's case;[18] and on 9 February 1971, the Council referred Bhutan's application to the Committee on the Admission of New Members, the first such referral for more than two decades.[19]

The Committee met thirty-four times between 31 July 1946 and 22 August 1949, and five times in 1971, twice in 1972, and

* There was a certain irony in the fact that, to demonstrate its peace-loving nature and thus qualify for original Membership, a State had to declare war on the Axis powers. Franco Spain claimed in 1946 that it was an eminently pacific country 'since it has remained neutral in the last two European wars . . .' Colombia proposed in 1972 that the 'peace-loving' requirement should be dropped in order to 'open the doors of the Organization to all States . . .' willing to accept and fulfil the obligations of Membership.[14] UN wits allege that 'loving' has only carnal connotations in Spanish.

twice in 1973.* The Committee submitted seven reports to the Council in 1946–9 and eight in 1971–3. In the case of its first four reports (1946–8), the chairman of the Committee was invited to sit at the Council table to introduce and interpret the Committee's report.[21]

Of the twenty States whose applications for Membership were considered by the Committee during the period 1946–9, seven were recommended for admission by the Security Council during that period. As noted earlier, Pakistan was recommended for admission in 1947 without referring the application to the Committee. All but one of the applications in the period 1971–3 were recommended for admission. The only case in the second period on which there was any delay was the application of Oman. The Committee first delayed acting on the application on a technicality (Rule 60), and when the Committee's favourable recommendation was eventually considered by the Council, Democratic Yemen opposed admission on the ground that Oman was still a British colony.[22] The proposal to recommend admitting Oman was, nevertheless, unanimously approved by the Council on 30 September 1971, and the General Assembly decided on admission a week later—by 117 votes to one (Democratic Yemen), with twelve Members abstaining or absent.[23]

The only application which did not receive a favourable recommendation from the Committee during 1971–3 was that of Bangladesh, which applied for Membership on 8 August 1972. China opposed the admission of Bangladesh 'pending the full implementation of the relevant United Nations resolutions and a reasonable settlement of [other] issues . . .' Eleven members of the Committee favoured admission, and three expressed a wish to have the matter postponed. The Committee duly reported to that effect to the Security Council, and on 25 August 1972, a proposal by India, the Soviet Union, the United Kingdom, and Yugoslavia that Bangladesh be recommended

* UN *Journal* no. 445 (26 June 1968) announced that the Security Council's Committee on the Admission of New Members would meet on 27 June 1968. According to the annual reports of the Security Council, however, the Committee's thirty-fourth meeting was held on 22 August 1949 and its thirty-fifth meeting on 9 February 1971.[20] If a meeting did indeed take place on 27 June 1968, it must have been an informal one, and it is likely that discussion was directed to the question of mini-States, which had been drawn to the Council's attention the previous December.

for admission was vetoed by China. The General Assembly later went on record as considering Bangladesh 'eligible for Membership' and as desiring its admission 'at an early date'.[24]

When the Committee on Admission of New Members recommends admission, it now reports to the Security Council in a standard format, as follows:

1. At the . . . meeting, held on . . ., the Security Council had before it the application of . . . for admission to membership in the United Nations (S/ . . .) In accordance with rule 59 of the provisional rules of procedure, the President of the Security Council referred the application to the Committee on the Admission of New Members, requesting it to examine the application and report its conclusions.
2. At its . . . meeting, held on . . ., the Committee considered the application of . . . and unanimously decided to recommend to the Security Council that . . . be admitted to membership in the United Nations.
3. Accordingly, the Committee decided to recommend that the Security Council adopt the following draft resolution:

'*The Security Council*,

'*Having examined* the application of . . . for admission to membership in the United Nations (S/ . . .),

'*Recommends* to the General Assembly that . . . be admitted to membership in the United Nations.'

Chart 3. UN Membership, 1946–73

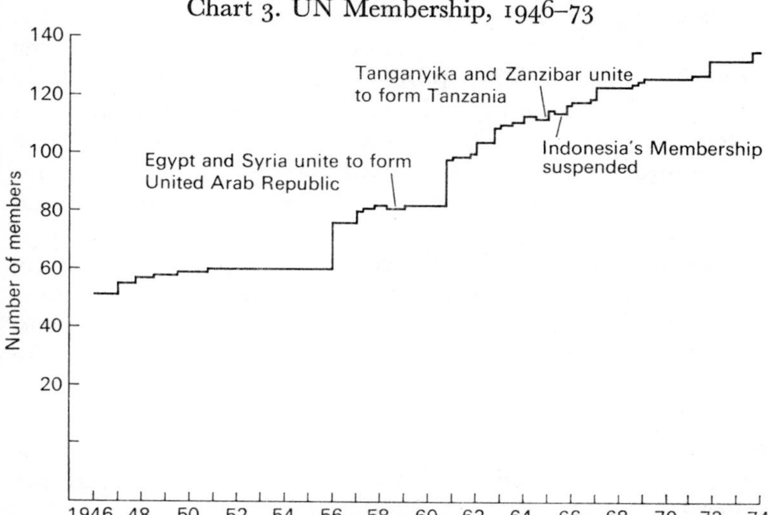

3. COMMITTEE OF EXPERTS ESTABLISHED AT ITS 1506TH MEETING [MINI-STATES]

The Security Council has in recent years paid some attention to the question of mini-States. As already noted, the criteria stated in Article 4 of the Charter for judging applicants for UN Membership are that they must (1) be States, (2) be 'peace-loving', (3) accept the obligations of the Charter, and (4) 'in the judgment of the Organization, are able and willing to carry out these obligations'. Largely as a result of decolonization, UN Membership increased from the fifty delegations which had been present at San Francisco to 123 in 1967 and 135 on 1 March 1974. It is well known that most of the new States are 'have not' countries, and that one consequence of this is a disparity between voting strength in the General Assembly and effective power. Moreover, a number of UN Members are quite small in size or have quite small populations, and therefore may find it difficult to provide the resources to meet all the obligations of UN Membership—Iceland (population 200,000) and Luxemburg (300,000) among the founder Members, and Gambia, Lesotho, Malta, and Zanzibar (300,000 each), Barbados (200,000), and the Maldive Islands (100,000) among the States admitted in 1963–6.

It is the twenty or so dependent territories with populations below 100,000 but which aspire to full Statehood which now constitute the mini-State problem. Secretary-General Thant drew attention to this in the Introduction to his Annual Report in 1967. Even the smallest colony had the right to determine its own future, he wrote, but UN Membership imposes onerous obligations. A distinction should therefore be made between the right to independence and the question of full UN Membership. He suggested that the competent organs should study the criteria for UN Membership as well as other forms of association for those micro-States (or Lilliputian States, as they had been called in the League of Nations) which would not qualify for full Membership.[25]

The United States had been concerned about the other aspect of the problem, that the future admission of a large number of mini-States might distort the voting process in the General Assembly; but to raise the matter was almost always tactless, since the move might be interpreted as a slight by countries or territories awaiting admission. In 1967, however, there was no pending applications for Membership from newly independent States, and the United States suggested that the Security Council should seek advice and assistance on the matter from the Council's Committee on the Admission of New Members, which had been inactive for almost twenty years.[26]

For eighteen months nothing much happened, although on four occasions the Council's President for the month reported that more urgent matters had prevented him from engaging in the necessary informal consultations.[27] Finally, in July and August 1969, U.S. Ambassador Yost (see p. 132) raised the matter formally with Secretary-General Thant and with the President of the Security Council, and at the end of August, the Security Council met twice to consider a U.S. proposal that the Secretary-General should be urged to raise the matter in the General Assembly.[28]

The U.S. proposal was no doubt a ploy to force a reluctant Security Council to take some action. The United States had originally suggested that the matter be referred to a Security Council committee. Month after month had gone by, and no Council meeting had been held to consider the U.S. proposal: the President for the month had either been too busy to engage in consultations, or had consulted his colleagues and made little or no progress. The United States had then discussed the matter with Secretary-General Thant, who evidently was willing to review the mini-State question in the Introductions to his Annual Reports, but not to force the issue. From the debate in the Council in August 1969, it is clear that the only matter on which there was agreement in the Council was to shunt the problem on to a siding, in the form of a committee of experts consisting of all the members of the Security Council.[29]

This Committee of Experts held eight closed meetings betweem 12 September 1969 and 10 June 1970, and then issued an interim report; three more meetings were held in 1971.[30] The United States proposed the establishment of a new class of Associate Members for exceptionally small new States. The United Kingdom suggested that very small States should enjoy the benefits of UN Membership but should be allowed to renounce voluntarily certain rights—in particular the right to vote and the right to be a candidate for membership of UN organs. Colombia later proposed a modified form of association for mini-States 'fundamentally different from the proposal made [in 1969] by one of the super-Powers [the United States]': the form of association proposed by Colombia was, in fact, similar to the proposal of the United Kingdom in 1970. It has been reported on good authority that the UN Legal Counsel advised that neither the U.S. nor the British proposal is consonant with the Charter.[31] There the matter rests: the Committee of Experts on the mini-State question has not met since 23 April 1971.

A study by the UN Institute for Training and Research in 1969 examined ninety-six States and territories with a population of one million or less.[32] To simplify the problem, one may ignore certain States and territories which were included in the UNITAR list: States which in 1969 were already Members of the United Nations; territories which have acquired independence and UN Membership since 1969; territories which seem likely in the long term to choose some form of association with other territories or States or which have already merged; territories and States which apparently do not aspire to UN Membership, and territories with populations of less than 10,000 (which are not likely to achieve conventional Statehood) or more than 100,000 (which are not mini-States). One is then left with twenty-one territories with populations as follows:

more than 50,000	16
more than 25,000	3
more than 10,000	2

It is these twenty-one territories with populations between 10,000 and 100,000 which form the crux of the mini-State question. Some very small territories which have acquired full self-government and independence have not applied for UN Membership (Western Samoa, Tonga, Nauru); the same is true of a number of small sovereign entities in Europe (Andorra, Liechtenstein, Monaco, San Marino). But UN Membership has come to be a mark of sovereignty, and it is the twenty-one potential mini-States, and a further fourteen or so territories with populations below 10,000, which are likely to be interested in some form of association with the United Nations which is less onerous than full Membership.

4. COMMISSION FOR CONVENTIONAL ARMAMENTS

The Commission for Conventional Armaments was set up by the Security Council on 13 February 1947, following a recommendation of the General Assembly the previous December. Like the Committee of Experts and several other important subsidiary organs, it consisted of all the members of the Security Council.

In the light of what we now know about the arms-control and disarmament problem, the Security Council would seem to have been rather euphoric in 1947 when, basing itself on a French draft, it instructed the Commission for Conventional Armaments to prepare proposals for 'the general regulation and reduction of armaments and armed forces . . . [and] for practical and effective safeguards . . .' within the space of '*not more than three months*'.* The Commission was not to concern itself with matters falling within the purview of the Atomic Energy Commission.[34] In 1949, the Security Council transmitted to the Commission for Conventional Armaments '*for action*' a resolution adopted by the General Assembly in 1948, which had recommended 'the Security Council . . . through the agency of the Commission . . . to obtain concrete results *as soon as possible*'.[35] By 1950, however, States had become more realistic, and the Council transmitted to the Commission '*for further study*' a resolution adopted by the General Assembly in 1949, which had urged the Council through the agency of the Commission '*to make such progress as may be possible.*'[36]

The Commission for Conventional Armaments met ten times in 1947, five times in 1948, four times in 1949, twice in 1950, and not at all during 1951 or January 1952. It submitted to the Security Council reports, resolutions, or working papers on 25 June 1947, 4 August 1949, and 10 August 1950. The Commission was dissolved on 30 January 1952, following the

* The United States strongly opposed the three-month time limit: the chief of the Division of International Security Affairs in the State Department, Joseph E. Johnson, described the situation about the time limit as 'one of the most difficult we have yet been confronted with'. The fact was that 'very little thought [had] been given to the formulation of our own [U.S.] policy on this subject' so that the United States had 'no agreed position'.[33]

Table 21

Commission for Conventional Armaments: Chronology, 1946–52

Date	*Action*	*Document ref.*
14 Dec. 1946	General Assembly recommendations	G.A. res. 41(I) and 42(I)
31 Dec. 1946–13 Feb. 1947	Security Council debate	SCOR, 2nd year, meetings 88, 90, 92, 93, 95, 98, 99, 102–5
13 Feb. 1947	Security Council establishes Commissions on Conventional Armaments.	S.C. res. 18 (S/268/Rev.1/Corr.1)
24 Mar.–25 June 1947	1st to 9th meetings of Commission	—
25 June 1947	1st report of Commission	SCOR, 2nd year, Supplement no. 14, S/387 (see also 152nd meeting, p. 1228)
8 July 1947	Security Council approves Commission's plan of work.	SCOR, 2nd year, 152nd meeting, p. 1227
16 July 1947	10th meeting of Commission	
2–12 Aug. 1947	11th to 13th meetings of Commission	—
12 Aug. 1947	Commission adopts two resolutions and decides to prepare progress report.	
17 Aug. 1947	14th and 15th meetings of Commission; progress report approved	S/C.3/32/Rev.1 and Corr.1
19 Nov. 1947	General Assembly recommendations	G.A. res. 192(III)
7–10 Feb. 1949	Security Council debate	SCOR, 4th year, 407th and 408th meetings
10 Feb. 1949	Security Council transmits General Assembly resolution 192(III) to Commission.	S.C. res. 68 (S/1252)
15 Feb.–1 Aug. 1949	16th to 19th meetings of Commission	—
4 Aug. 1949	Commission transmits second progress report, two resolutions, and working paper to Security Council.	SCOR, 4th year, Supplement for October to December 1949, pp. 1–8, S/1371 and S/1372

11 Oct. 1949	Security Councl debate	SCOR, 4th year, meeting 450
	Soviet Union vetoes U.S. proposal.	veto no. 40
	Security Council transmits Commission's report to General Assembly.	S.C. res. 77 (S/1403)
14 and 18 Oct. 1949	Security Council debate	SCOR, 4th year, meetings 451 and 452
18 Oct. 1949	Soviet Union vetoes French proposals.	vetoes nos. 41 and 42
	Security Council transmits working paper and records of discussion to General Assembly.	S.C. res. 78 (S/1410)
5 Dec. 1949	General Assembly recommendations	G.A. res. 300(IV)
13 and 17 Jan. 1950	Security Council debate	SCOR, 5th year, meeting 461 and 462
17 Jan. 1950	Security Council transmits General Assembly resolution 300 (IV) to Commission.	S.C. res. 79 (S/1455)
27 Apr. 1950	20th meeting of Commission; Soviet proposal for exclusion of 'Kuomintang Group' defeated; Soviet representative withdraws	S/C.3/42
9 Aug. 1950	21st meeting of Commission	S/C.3/43
10 Aug. 1950	Commission submits third progress report to the Security Council.	S/1690
17 Nov. 1950	General Assembly recommendations	G.A. res. 380(V)
13 Dec. 1950	General Assembly establishes Committee of Twelve to advise on co-operation of Commission on Conventional Armaments and Atomic Energy Commission.	G.A. res. 496(V)
14 Feb. 1950	Committee of Twelve holds 9 meetings; proposes establishment of new disarmament commission.	—
11 Jan. 1952	General Assembly establishes new Disarmament Commission.	G.A. res. 502(VI)
30 Jan. 1952	Commission on Conventional Armaments dissolved	S.C. res. 97(S/2506)

decision of the General Assembly to establish a new Disarmament Commission to deal with both conventional and atomic arms. The Security Council is still seized of the item 'The general regulation and reduction of armaments and information on the armed forces of the United Nations', but the Council has not considered the question of disarmament since 1950, except obliquely during five meetings in 1958 and eleven meetings in 1960 while considering Soviet complaints about flights of U.S. military aircraft.[37]

It seems not to have been fully realized in the early post-war period that disarmament cannot be achieved by adopting resolutions by majority votes supporting or demanding particular disarmament measures. The Western powers and their friends repeatedly outvoted the Soviet bloc on disarmament questions, but there was no negotiated disarmament. It was only when disarmament negotiating bodies began to proceed on the basis of consensus that progress was achieved. This is a lesson which the General Assembly seems not to have learned yet.

5. ATOMIC ENERGY COMMISSION

The Atomic Energy Commission was not technically a subsidiary organ of the Security Council, as it was set up by the General Assembly (see Table 22).[38] The Commission consisted of all members of the Security Council plus 'Canada when that State is not a member of the Security Council' (1946–1947). The Commission was instructed to submit reports and recommendations to the Security Council, and 'in matters affecting security' was 'accountable for its work to the . . . Council'. The Council was authorized 'to issue directions' to the Commission, and the Commission was asked to submit its rules of procedure for the approval of the Council.

The Commission met ten times in 1946, four times in 1947, twice in 1948, eight times in 1949, and not at all in 1950 or 1951. It issued its first report on 31 December 1946. On 15 January 1947, the Council included in its agenda the letter transmitting the first report, and the item was removed from the Summary Statement of matters of which the Security Council was seized after the adoption of Security Council resolution 20 (S/296) on 10 March 1947.

The Commission's second report was issued on 11 September

TABLE 22

Atomic Energy Commission: Chronology, 1946–52

Date	*Action*	*Document ref.*
24 Jan. 1946	General Assembly establishes Atomic Energy Commission.	G.A. res. 1(1); AECOR, 1st year, Supplement no. 1
14 June–3 July 1946	1st to 4th meetings of Commission	AECOR, meetings 1–4
5 July 1946	Commission submits provisional rules of procedure to Security Council.	SCOR, 1st year, 2nd series, Supplement no. 1, S/102; AECOR, 1st year, Supplement no. 2
10 July 1946	Security Council approves Commission's rules of procedure.	SCOR, 1st year, 2nd series, 50th meeting, pp. 1–7
18 July–30 Dec. 1946	5th to 10th meetings of the Commission	AECOR, 1st year, meetings 5–10
31 Dec. 1946	1st report of Commission	SCOR, 2nd year, Supplement no. 5, pp. 59–60, S/239; AECOR, 1st year, Special Supplement, AEC/18/Rev. 1
13 Feb.–10 Mar. 1947	Security Council debate	SCOR, 2nd year, meetings 105, 106, 108, 110, 112, 115, and 117
10 Mar. 1947	Security Council requests Commission to report to the General Assembly.	S.C. res. 20
19 Mar.–11 Sept. 1947	11th to 14th meetings of Commission	AECOR., 2nd year, meeting 11–14
11 Sept. 1947	2nd report of Commission	S/557, 17 Sept. 1947 (mimeographed); AECOR, 2nd year, Special Supplement, AEC/26
7 and 17 May 1948	15th and 16th meetings of Commission	AECOR, 3rd year, meetings 15 and 16
17 May 1948	3rd report of Commisson	SCOR, 3rd year, Supplement for June 1948, p. 7, S/812; AECOR, 3rd year, Special Supplement, AEC/31/Rev. 1
11–22 June 1948	Security Council debate	SCOR, 3rd year, meetings 318, 321, and 325
22 June 1948	Soviet Union vetoes proposal to accept the three reports of the Commission.	veto no. 27

22 June 1948	Security Council transmits the reports of the Commission to the General Assembly.	S.C. res. 52 (S/852)
4 Nov. 1948	General Assembly approves reports of Commission, and asks its permanent members to confer.	G.A. res. 191(III)
18 Feb.–29 July 1949	17th to 24th meetings of Commission	AECOR, 4th year, meetings 17–24
29 July 1949	Commission adopts two resolutions and transmits them to the Council.	SCOR, 4th year, Supplement for September to December 1949, pp. 8–10, S/1377 (AEC/42 and AEC/43)
9 Aug. 1949	Six permanent members of Commission (Canada, China, France, Soviet Union, United Kingdom, United States) begin consultations as requested by the General Assembly	—
15 and 16 Sept. 1949	Security Council debate	SCOR, 4th year, meetings 445–7
16 Sept. 1949	Security Council transmits to the General Assembly the two resolutions approved by the Commission on 29 July 1949 and the records of discussion.	S.C. res. 74 (S/1393)
13 Oct. 1949	Six permanent members of Commission conclude consultations.	GAOR, 4th session, Supplement no. 15, pp. 33–37
23 Nov. 1949	General Assembly asks six permanent members of the Commission to continue their consultations.	G.A. res. 299(IV)
20 Dec. 1949	Six permanent members of Commission resume consultations.	GAOR, 5th session, Annexes, agenda item 26, A/1253 and A/1254
19 Jan. 1950	Soviet Union declines to take part in consultations so long as the representative of the Kuomintang Group participates in them.	—
13 Dec. 1950	General Assembly establishes Committee of Twelve to advise on co-ordination of Atomic Energy Commission and Commission on Conventional Armaments.	G.A. res. 496(V)
14 Feb.–28 Sept. 1951	Committee of Twelve holds 9 meetings; proposes establishment of new disarmament commission.	GAOR, 6th session, Annexes, agenda items 66 and 16, A/1922
11 Jan. 1952	General Assembly dissolves Atomic Energy Commission and establishes new Disarmament Commission.	G.A. res. 502(VI)

1947, but this was never included in the agenda of the Security Council. The third report was issued on 17 May 1948, and on 11 June the Council included in its agenda the letter transmitting the report. The item was removed from the Summary Statement after the adoption of Security Council resolution 52 (S/852) on 22 June 1948. The Commission sent two resolutions to the Council on 29 July 1949, and the letter transmitting these was included in the Council's agenda on 15 September. After the adoption by the Council of resolution 74 (S/1393) on 16 September, the item was changed to read 'International control of atomic energy'. The Council remains seized of this item.

The General Assembly dissolved the Commission on 11 January 1952 and established a new Disarmament Commission.

6. *AD HOC* SUB-COMMITTEES ON NAMIBIA

The Security Council set up a Sub-Committee on South-West Africa (known by the United Nations as Namibia since 5 August 1968) 'in accordance with rule 28' on 30 January 1970, asking that, in consultation with the Secretary-General, it should study ways and means by which the resolutions of the Council could be effectively implemented, 'in the light of the flagrant refusal of South Africa to withdraw from Namibia . . .' The Sub-Committee was composed of all the members of the Security Council.[39] The Committee decided to hold closed meetings and to take decisions by consensus. It met seventeen times between 4 February and 7 July 1970 and issued two reports: a brief interim report (less than one page in length) was issued on 30 April 1970 and a slightly longer report on 7 July 1970 (9 pages), to which were annexed replies to requests from the Sub-Committee and extracts from the record of one of its meetings.

On 29 July 1970, the Sub-Committee was re-established by the Council with identical terms of reference, except that the requirement to consult with the Secretary-General was dropped. In October 1971, the Council asked the Sub-Committee to continue its work and, 'taking into account the need for the effective protection of Namibian interests at the international level, to study appropriate measures for the fulfilment of the responsibility of the United Nations towards Namibia'.[40]

The new Sub-Committee met once during 1970, sixteen times during 1971, and six times during 1972. Burundi was

Table 23

Ad Hoc *Sub-Committees on Namibia: Chronology, 1970–3*

Date	*Document*	*SCOR*
30 Jan. 1970	S.C. res. 276 (S/9620/Rev. 1)	
	note by President of Council	25th year, Supplement for January to March, p. 118, S/9632
30 Apr. 1970	interim report of Sub-Commmttee	25th year, Supplement for April to June, pp. 165–6, S/9771
15 May 1970	note by President of Council	25th year, Supplement for April to June, p. 184, S/9803
7 July 1970	report of Sub-Committee	25th year, Supplement for July to September, pp. 81–103, S/9863 and Add. 1/Rev. 1 (except Austria and Belgium, p. 84)
29 July 1970	S.C. res. 283 (S/9891)	—
	S.C. res. 284 (S/9892)	—
18 Aug. 1970	note by President of Council	25th year, Supplement for July to September, p. 131, S/9911
23 Sept. 1970	report of Sub-Committee	25th year, Supplement for July to September, p. 84, S/9863/Add. 1, Rev. 1 (Austria and Belgium)
23 Sept. 1971	report of Sub-Committee	26th year, Special Supplement no. 5, S/10330
20 Oct. 1971	S.C. res. 301 (S/10372/Rev. 1)	—

appointed chairman, and Finland and Nepal as vice-chairmen, the latter two being replaced by Italy and Argentina when their term on the Council ceased at the end of 1971. The Sub-Committee's work was overshadowed during 1970–3 by other UN efforts regarding Namibia, in particular the Council's request to the International Court of Justice for an Advisory Opinion and the Council's reaction to that Opinion, and then by the efforts of Secretary-General Waldheim and his representative to make progress in direct contacts with the South African Government, as well as by the work of the General Assembly's Council for Namibia. Hardly surprisingly, the Sub-Committee was disappointed at the small response to its requests for information, and it has encountered both political and procedural difficulties in performing the tasks entrusted to it by the Council.

7. COMMITTEE ESTABLISHED IN PURSUANCE OF RESOLUTION 253 (1968) CONCERNING THE QUESTION OF SOUTHERN RHODESIA

The Security Council's resolution 253 of 29 May 1968 was concerned with sanctions against the illegal regime in Rhodesia, and the Committee 'in pursuance of resolution 253' was set up 'in accordance with rule 28' to examine the Secretary-General's reports on the implementation of the resolution and to seek further information about possible violations. On 18 March 1970, the terms of reference of the Committee were extended to include the study of ways and means of making the sanctions policy more effective. Subsequent resolutions continued sanctions and authorized the Committee to change its methods so as to make its work more effective, including action which could be taken against Portugal and South Africa for their persistent refusal to implement the Security Council's mandatory policy. The United Kingdom vetoed proposals relating to Rhodesia on 17 March 1970 (with the United States), and alone on 10 November 1970, 30 December 1971, and 4 February 1972, on the ground that the proposal condemned the United Kingdom for not using force in Rhodesia, or that it called for no independence before majority African rule, or that it expressly rejected the Smith–Home agreement of November 1971 (which was later rejected by the people of Rhodesia as a whole).[41]

TABLE 24

Committee established in pursuance of resolution 253 (1968) concerning the question of Southern Rhodesia: Chronology 1968–1973

Date	*Document*	*SCOR*
29 May 1968	S.C. res. 253 (S/8601)	
13 June 1968	report of Secretary-General	23rd year, Supplement for April to June, pp. 1–92, S/7781/Add. 5
28 Aug. 1968	report of Secretary-General	23rd year, Supplement for July to September, pp. 153–216, S/8786
25 Sept. 1968	report of Secretary-General	23rd year, Supplement for July to September, pp. 216–31, S/8786/ Add. 1
10 Oct. 1968	report of Secretary-General	23rd year, Supplement for October to December, pp. 33–8, S/8786/ Add. 2
1 Nov. 1968	report of Secretary-General	23rd year, Supplement for October to December, pp. 38–45, S/8786/ Add. 3
27 Nov. 1968	report of Secretary-General	23rd year, Supplement for October to December, pp. 45–8, S/8786/ Add. 4
30 Dec. 1968	1st report of Committee	23rd year, Supplement for October to December, pp. 181–295, S/8954
30 Jan. 1969	report of Secretary-General	24th year, Supplement for January to March, pp. 32–7, S/8786/Add. 5
3 Mar. 1969	report of Secretary-General	24th year, Supplement for January to March, pp. 37–9, S/8786/Add. 6
19 Mar. 1969	report of Secretary-General	24th year, Supplement for January to March, pp. 39–48, S/8786/ Add. 7
11 Apr. 1969	report of Secretary-General	24th year, Supplement for April to June, pp. 86–8, S/8786/Add. 8
6 June 1969	report of Secretary-General	24th year, Supplement for April to June, pp. 89–91, S/8786/Add. 9
12 June 1969	2nd report of Committee	24th year, Supplement for April to June, pp. 195–329, S/9252 and Add. 1
17 June 1969	report of Secretary-General	24th year, Supplement for April to June, pp. 91–2, S/8786/Add. 10
23 Sept. 1969	report of Secretary-General	24th year, Supplement for Septembert to December, pp. 95–9, S/8786/Ass. 11
18 Mar. 1970	S.C. res. 277 (S/9709, as amended)	—

TABLE 24—*continued*

Date	*Document*	*SCOR*
15 June 1970	3rd report of Committee	25th year, Special Supplements nos. 3 and 3A, S /9844 and Add. 1, 2, 3
1 Juy 1970	report of Secretary-General	25th year, Supplement for July to September, pp. 56–71, S/9853
30 Sept. 1970	note by President of Council	25th year, Supplement for July to September, p. 147, S/9951
1 Oct. 1970	report of Secretary-General	25th year, Supplement for October to December, pp. 12–14, S/ 9853/Add.1
16 June 1971	4th report of Committee	26th year, Special Supplements nos. 2 and 2A, S/10229 and Add. 2
17 Nov. 1971	S.C. res. 288 (S/9980)	—
3 Dec. 1971	1st interim report of Committee	26th year, Supplement for October to December, pp. 78–9, S/10480
28 Feb. 1972	S.C. res. 314 (S/10541/Rev. 1 and Corr.1, as amended)	—
29 Mar. 1972	2nd interim report of Committee	27th year, Supplement for January to March, pp. 74–5, S/10680
10 Apr. 1972	3rd interim report of Committee	27th year, Supplement for April to June, p. 27, S/10593
13 Apr. 1972	note by President of Council	27th year, Supplement for April to June, pp. 29–30, S/10597
27 Apr. 1972	note by President of Council	27th year, Supplement for April to June, p. 39, S/10622
9 May 1972	1st special report of Committee	27th year, Supplement for April to June, pp. 47–9, S/10632
28 July 1972	S.C. res. 318 (S/10747)	—
29 Sept. 1972	S.C. res. 320 (S/10804/Rev. 1)	—
22 Dec. 1972	5th report of Committee	27th year, Special Supplement no. 2, S/10852/Rev.1
31 Dec. 1972	Addendum to 5th report of Committee	S/10852/Add. 1
2 Feb. 1973	Second addendum to 5th report of Committee	S/10852/Add. 2
10 Mar. 1973	S.C. res. 328 (S/10898/Rev. 1)	—
15 Apr. 1973	2nd special report of Committee	S/10920
22 May 1973	S.C. res. 333 (S/10927)	—
3, 9, and 11 Jan. 1974	6th report of Committee	S/11178 and Adds.1 and 2

The Committee was originally composed of seven members: Algeria, France, India, Paraguay, the Soviet Union,* the United Kingdom, and the United States. India ceased to be a member of the Security Council at the end of 1968 and was replaced on the Committee by Pakistan. Algeria, Pakistan, and Paraguay ceased to be members of the Council at the end of 1969, and after some delay were replaced by Sierra Leone, Nepal, and Nicaragua respectively. Later in 1970, it was decided that the Committee should consist of all the members of the Security Council.[43] The Committee met three times in 1968, twenty-two times in 1969, eleven times in 1970, twenty-seven times in 1971, fifty-three times in 1972, and sixty-six times in 1973, 182 meetings in all. All meetings except one (the 175th) have been closed (private).[44]

It was agreed in 1970 that the chairmanship should rotate on a monthly basis, as is the practice in the Security Council itself.[45] In March 1972, however, during the chairmanship of the Soviet Union, Somalia suggested that the Committee could work more effectively if the chairman held office for a full year. This was supported by eight other members, but the five Western members plus Japan opposed the idea. The United Kingdom said that if it would make things any easier, he would renounce the chairmanship for April and allow the Soviet representative to continue in office for an extra month, but this did not satisfy the critics. As deadlock had been reached, the matter was referred to the Security Council itself which had, of course, the same membership as the Committee. In the Security Council, a compromise emerged by which the Committee would appoint one chairman and two vice-chairmen for a one-year term. Sudan was elected chairman and Japan and Panama as vice-chairmen for the remainder of 1972; Guinea became chairman for 1973, with Indonesia and Yugoslavia as vice-chairmen.[46]

The Council's decision to embark on mandatory sanctions was without precedent in the United Nations, and the Committee's task has been a very difficult one. The Committee made use of trade statistics collected by the Secretariat as well as 172 alleged violations brought to its attention in 1968–73, 137 of them by the United Kingdom. The Committee also took up a

* The Security Councils annual report for 1969–70 fails to mention the Soviet Union's membership of the Committee.[42]

number of major violations, such as the decision of the U.S. Congress, adopted as an amendment to a military procurement bill, which allowed the importing of Rhodesian chrome ore. But the Committee lacked the resources to pursue its task in the relentless way which was necessary if every violation was to be exposed, and the major Western powers had no wish at that time to come into confrontation with Portugal and South Africa, which had made no secret of the fact that they were opposed to the whole sanctions venture.

8. COMMITTEE ON COUNCIL MEETINGS AWAY FROM HEADQUARTERS

The Security Council normally meets at Headquarters (Rule 5), but meetings were held in London (Jan. and Feb. 1946) and Paris (Sept. to Dec. 1948 and Nov. 1951 to Feb. 1952) when the General Assembly was meeting, to suit the convenience of Council members. Suggestions for meetings away from Headquarters for political or symbolic purposes were made in connection with the Congo in 1960 and 1961, and the Dominican Republic in 1965, but were not acted on.[47] It was not until 1972 that the Council decided to hold a series of meetings away from Headquarters expressly to demonstrate concern for the problems of a particular region.

I have reviewed on pages 31–4 of Chapter 2 the decisions of the Council to meet in Addis Ababa in 1972 and Panama City in 1973. It was in connection with these decisions that the Security Council created a committee of the whole to examine the financial, legal, and other problems involved. The Committee met eight times in 1972 and six times in 1973. Apart from the expense of meeting away from Headquarters, which amounted to $101,380 in 1972 and was estimated at $92,000 in 1973, there was uneasiness on the part of some States that if the staff and members of the Council were to be absent from New York for any considerable time, the Council would not be able to 'function continuously' as required by Article 28(1) of the Charter. The Committee decided that this objection was not insuperable, and recommended that the Secretary-General should negotiate with the host government in each year an agreement on legal aspects along the lines set out in a Secretariat working paper in 1972.[48]

TABLE 25

Work of the Committee on Council meetings away from Headquarters, 1972–3

Request	*Date of Security Council reference to Committee*	*No. of meetings held*	*Report of Committee SCOR*	*Security Council decision*	*Places and dates of meetings*
G.A. res. 2863 (XXVI), 20 Dec. 1971; S/10480, 29 Dec. 1971	11 Jan. 1972	8	27th year, Supplement for January to March 1972, pp. 20–7, S/10514	S.C. res. 308, 19 Jan. 1972	Addis Ababa, 28 Jan.–4 Feb. 1972
S/10858, 9 Jan. 1973	16 Jan. 1973	6	S/10868	S.C. res. 325, 26 Jan. 1973	Panama City, 15–21 Mar. 1973

9. OTHER SUBSIDIARY ORGANS

As indicated earlier, it is possible to classify subsidiary organs of the Council in a number of ways. The classification in Table 26 is based on composition rather than function: committees of the whole, select committees composed of a limited number of members, persons appointed individually, and field operations. These categories overlap. The *Repertory of Practice* of UN organs classifies as 'Field commissions and similar subsidiary organs' several of the organs I have described as 'select committees' (e.g. Commission for India and Pakistan, Commission for Indonesia, Sub-Committee on Laos) as well as the organs composed of persons individually appointed. Subsidiary organs can, of course, establish their own subsidiary organs, as was the case when the Commission of Investigation concerning Greek Frontier Incidents created a Subsidiary Group.

Of fifty-five subsidiary organs established by or with the authority of the Security Council during twenty-eight years, no fewer than twenty-four were created during the first three years, 1946–8. This was to some extent because standing bodies had to be established to be responsible for procedural and constitutional matters, but even more because during that period drafting and negotiating bodies were set up to deal with matters which at a later stage would be the subject of informal consultation. In the next fifteen years, 1949–63, the Council established only seven subsidiary organs; twenty-one were established in the ten years 1964–73. The number of subsidiary organs created by the Council thus averaged eight a year in 1946–48, one every *other* year in 1949–63, and seven a year in 1964–73.

Committees of the whole were used in about one-third of the

subsidiary organs created in 1946 and 1947, and select committees in the other cases. The use of select committees then became the normal practice until 1964 and after 1969, when committees of the whole again became necessary for the main on-going tasks. Of the eight select committees created in the twenty-four years 1950–73, all except two (committee on Southern Rhodesia, 1968–70, and the group on contacts with South Africa about Namibia, 1972–3) were missions sent to particular countries to collect and assess facts.

Of the persons appointed on an individual basis, there has been only one group of experts, the Group on South Africa, 1963–4. The other cases of individual appointments have been of persons given intermediary, good-offices, or fact-finding functions.

Observation or peace-keeping operations in the field have been set up by the Security Council as needed and are not concentrated in any particular period. Of ten such operations initiated by the Security Council, five are still in being: in Kashmir, between Israel and Egypt, along the cease-fire lines between Israel and Syria, along the armistice demarcation line between Israel and Lebanon, and in Cyprus.

There have been nineteen proposals to establish subsidiary organs which were not approved by the Security Council, either because the proposal was not pressed to a vote or because it was voted on and received insufficient votes or because it was vetoed. Two-thirds of these occurred in the first three years, 1946–8, and it is now unusual to make a proposal of this kind until the sponsor has already discovered in private consultations that there is adequate support.

In an article reviewing the experience of the United Nations in the collection of facts, I have recalled an experience of President Kennedy in September 1963. Feeling the need to take a fresh look at the situation in South Vietnam, Kennedy sent an experienced diplomat who had previously served as political counsellor in the Saigon embassy and the Pentagon's senior expert in counter-insurgency to see things at first-hand. Their assessments of conditions in South Vietnam were so diametrically opposed that Kennedy was moved to ask, 'You two did visit the same country, didn't you?'[51]

The trouble with facts is not that they are in short supply but

TABLE 26

Subsidiary organs established by or with the authority of the Security Council, 1946–73

(a) *Committees of the Whole*

Date authorized or established	*Res., mtg., or doc. no.*	*Title or function*	*Date of termination or fulfilment of mandate*
17 Jan. 1946	1st meeting, p. 11	Committee of Experts	—
17 May 1946	res. 6	Committee on Admission of New Members	—
19 Dec. 1946	res. 15 (S/339)	Commission of Investigation concerning Greek Frontier Incidents	15 Sept. 1947
13 Feb. 1947	res. 18 (S/268/Rev.1/Corr.1)	Commission for Conventional Armaments	30 Jan. 1952
18 Apr. 1947	res. 23 (S/330/Corr.1)	Subsidiary Group of the Commission concerning Greek Frontier Incidents	15 Sept. 1947
18 June 1964	res. 191 (S/5773)	Expert Committee on Measures concerning the Question of Race Conflict in South Africa	27 Feb. 1965
29 Aug. 1969	mtg. 1506, para. 61	Committee of Experts [on the question of mini-States]	—
30 Jan. 1970	res. 276 (S/8601)	*Ad Hoc* Sub-Committee established in pursuance of Security Council resolution 276 (Namibia)	29 July 1970
29 July 1970	res. 283 (S/9891)	*Ad Hoc* Sub-Committee on Namibia (re-established)	—
30 Sept. 1970	S/9951	Committee established in pursuance of resolution 253 (1968) concerning the question of Southern Rhodesia	—
11 Jan. 1972	P.V. 1625, pp. 33–38	Committee on Council Meetings away from Headquarters	—

(b) *Select Committees composed of a limited number of Member States*

Date of authorization or appointment	*Res., mtg., or doc. no.*	*Title or function*	*Composition*	*Date of termination or fulfilment of mandate*
26 Mar. 1946	26th mtg., p. 43	To seek agreement on a draft resolution relating to the Iranian question	France, Soviet Union, United States	27 Mar. 1946
25 Apr. 1946	37th mtg., p. 237	To seek agreement on a draft resolution relating to the Spanish question	Australia, Brazil, China, France, Poland	26 Apr. 1946
29 Apr. 1946	res. 4	To examine statements made before the Council regarding the Spanish question	Australia, Brazil, China, France Poland	6 June 1946

24 June 1946	48th mtg., p. 400	To seek agreement on a draft resolution relating to the Spanish question	Australia, Poland, United Kingdom	26 June 1946
4 Feb. 1947	99th mtg., pp. 166, 172	To seek agreement on a draft resolution relating to the general regulation and reduction of armaments	Australia, Colombia, France, Soviet Union, United States	11 Feb. 1947
27 Feb. 1947	res. 19	To examine evidence relating to the Corfu Channel question	Australia, Colombia, Poland (and Syria for one meeting only)	20 Mar. 1947
10 July 1947	155th mtg., p. 1277	To collect additional information about candidates suggested as Governor for Trieste	Australia, Colombia, Poland	10 Sept. 1947
6 Aug. 1947	res. 28	To seek agreement on a draft resolution relating to the question of Greek Frontier Incidents	Australia, Colombia, France, Soviet Union, United Kingdom, United States	12 Aug. 1947
25 Aug. 1947	res. 30 (S/525, I)	Indonesian question: Consular Commission at Batavia	Australia, Belgium, China, France, United Kingdom, United States	6 Apr. 1951
25 Aug. 1947	res. 31 (S/525, II)	Indonesian question: Committee of Good Offices	Australia, Belgium, United States	28 Jan. 1949
3 Oct. 1947	217th mtg., pp. 2716–7	To seek agreement on a draft resolution relating to the Indonesian question	Australia, Belgium, China, United States	1 Nov. 1947
20 Jan. 1948 21 Apr. 1948	res. 39 (S/654) res. 47 (S/726)	Commission for India and Pakistan	Argentina, Belgium, Colombia, Czechoslovakia, United States	17 May 1950
23 Apr. 1948	res. 48 (S/727)	Truce Commission for Palestine	Belgium, France, United States, (Syria declined membership)	11 Jan. 1949
18 June 1948	324th mtg., pp. 16–17	To meet with a committee of the Trusteeship Council on the question of the respective functions of the two Councils with regard to strategic areas	Belgium, Syria, Ukraine	7 Mar. 1949
19 Aug. 1948	355th mtg. o. 56	To approve corrections to the draft report to the General Assembly	France, Soviet Union, Ukraine, United Kingdom, United States	20 Aug. 1948

TABLE 26 (*continued*).

Date of authorization or appointment	*Res., mtg., or doc. no*	*Title or function*	*Composition*	*Date of termination or fulfilment of mandate*
29 Oct. 1948	res. 60 (S/1062)	To prepare, in consultation with the Acting Mediator, a revised draft resolution relating to the Palestine question	Belgium, China, France, Ukraine, United Kingdom	4 Nov. 1948
4 Nov. 1948	res. 61 (S/1070)	To give such advice as the Acting Mediator might require in connection with the Palestine question and, in case of non-compliance, to report on further appropriate measures	Five permanent members, plus Belgium (1948), Colombia (1948), Cuba (1949), and Norway (1949)	7 Jan. 1949
28 Jan. 1949	res. 67 (S/1234)	Commission for Indonesia	Australia, Belgium, United States	3 Apr. 1951
7 Sept. 1959	res. 132 (S/4216)	Sub-Committee on Laos	Argentina, Italy, Japan, Tunisia	5 Nov. 1959
4 June 1964	res. 189 (S/5741)	Mission to Cambodia and the Republic of [South] Viet-Nam	Brazil, Ivory Coast, Morocco	27 July 1964
29 May 1968	res. 253 (S/8601)	Situation in Southern Rhodesia	Algeria (1968 and 1969), France, India (1968), Nepal (1970), Nicaragua (1970), Pakistan (1969), Paraguay (1968 and 1969), Sierra Leone (1970), Soviet Union, United Kingdom, United States	30 Sept. 1970
23 Nov. 1970	res. 289 (S/9990/Rev. 1)	Special Mission to the Republic of Guinea	Colombia, Finland, Nepal, Poland, Zambia	3 Dec. 1970

15 July 1971	res. 294 (S/10266)	Special Mission to Senegal	Belgium, Burundi, Japan, Nicaragua, Poland, Syria	16 Sept. 1971
3 Aug. 1971	res. 295 (S/10281)	Special Mission to the Republic of Guinea	Argentina, Syria	14 Sept. 1971
4 Feb. 1972	res. 309 (S/10376/Rev. 2)	Group on contacts with the parties concerning Namibia	Argentina (1972), Peru (1973), Somalia (1972), Sudan (1973), Yugoslavia (1972 and 1973)	11 Dec. 1972
2 Feb. 1973	res. 326 (S/10876/Rev. 1)	Special Mission to Zambia	Austria, Indonesia, Peru, Sudan	5 Mar. 1973

(c) *Individuals**

Date of authorization or appointment	*Res. mtg., or doc. no.*	*Title or function*	*Date of death, resignation or, fufilment of mandate*
14 Mar. 1950 12 Apr. 1950	res. 80 (S/1469)	Representative for India and Pakistan (Sir Owen Dixon)	30 Mar. 1951
30 Mar. 1951 30 Apr. 1951	res. 91 (S/2017/Rev.1)	Representative for India and Pakistan (Frank P. Graham)	—
4 Dec. 1963	res. 182 (S/5471)	Group of Experts on South Africa (Mrs. Alva Myrdal, Sir Edward Asafu-Adjaye, Josip Djerdja, Sir Hugh Foot, Dey Ould Sidi Baba)	20 Apr, 1964
4 Mar. 1964	res. 186 (S/5575)	Mediator in Cyprus (Sakari S. Tuomioja)	9 Sept. 1964
16 Sept. 1964		Mediator in Cyprus (Galo Plaza)	31 Dec. 1965
14 May 1965	res. 203 (S/6355)	Representative of the Secretary-General in the Dominican Republic (José Antonio Mayobre)	14 Oct. 1966
5 Nov. 1965	res. 215 (S/6876)	Representative of the Secretary-General in the matter of withdrawal of troops by India and Pakistan (Brigadier-General Yulio Marambio)	28 Feb. 1966

* I have not included in this Table the Technical Committee on Berlin Currency and Trade, established on 30 Nov. 1948 'by virtue of a directive' of the President of the Security Council 'in the exercise of his powers' and composed of 'financial experts nominated by neutral members of the Security Council.' The Technical Committee issued an inconclusive report on 11 Feb. 1949.[49]

The United Nations mediator for Palestine, Count Folke Bernadotte, was appointed by the General Assembly; after Count Bernadotte's assassination, Secretary-General Lie, with the approval of the President of the Council for September 1948 (representative of the United Kingdom), appointed Ralph J. Bunche as Acting Mediator.[50]

TABLE 26 (*continued*).

Date of authorization or appointment	Res., mtg., or doc. no.	Title or function	Date of death, resignation, or fulfilment of mandate
22 Nov. 1967	res. 242 (S/8247)	Special Representative of the Secretary-General in the Middle East (Gunnar Jarring)	—
27 Sept. 1968	res. 259 (S/8825/Rev.2)	Special Representative of the Secretary-General to report on the treatment of civilians in Israel-occupied territories †	
20 Mar. 1970	S/9726	Personal Representative leading the Good Offices Mission to Bahrain (Vittorio Winspeare-Guicciardi) ‡	30 Apr. 1970
21 Dec. 1971	res. 307 (S/10465)	Special Representative for humanitarian problems in the India–Pakistan subcontinent (Vittorio Winspeare-Guicciardi)	
Security Council res. 278 (S/9792).			
(d) *Field operations*			
21 Apr. 1948	res. 47 (S/726)	Military Observer Group for India and Pakistan (UNMOGIP)	—
29 May 1948	res. 50 (S/801)	Truce Supervision Organization in Palestine (UNTSO)	—
11 June 1958	res. 128 (S/4023)	Observation Group in Lebanon (UNOGIL)	17 Nov. 1958
14 July 1960	res. 143 (S/4387)	Operation in the Congo (ONUC)	30 June 1964
11 June 1963	res. 179 (S/5331)	Observation Mission in Yemen (UNYOM)	4 Sept. 1964
4 Mar. 1964	res. 186 (S/5575)	Peace-keeping force in Cyprus (UNFICYP)	—
20 Sept. 1965	res. 211 (S/6694)	India–Pakistan Observer Mission (UNIPOM)	25 Feb. 1966
9–10 July 1967	1366th mtg., paras. 125–7 (S/8047)	Military Observers in the Suez Canal sector (under the Chief of Staff of UNTSO)	9 Oct. 1973
23 Oct 1973	res. 339 (S/11039)	Observers to supervise the cease-fire between Israel and Egypt (assimilated with UNTSO)	—
25 Oct. 1973	res 340 (S/11046/Rev. 1)	Emergency Force in the Middle East (UNEF)	—

† The Secretary-General reported on 14 October 1968 that Israel's reply to his request for co-operation did not afford him a basis, on which to dispatch the Special Representative (S/8851).

‡ Appointed by the Secretary-General with the agreement of the parties: the report of the Personal Representative was endorsed by Security Council res. 278 (S/9792).

that there is a superabundance of them. Any diplomat worth his salt knows how to select facts in order to support a weak case. Fact-finding in the UN context may consist of the painstaking collection of information using the most rigorous rules of evidence, or it may be the amassing of reports in order to bolster a predetermined political position.

It is not surprising, therefore, that there should have been different views in the Security Council on whether proposals to set up subsidiary organs with fact-finding responsibilities should be subject to veto. As Articles 28–32 come in part of the Charter with the sub-heading *Procedure*, it has been argued that all decisions taken on the basis of these articles are procedural and therefore outside the scope of the veto. A decision to establish a subsidiary organ under Article 29 would, according to this view, be a procedural one. The Soviet Union, on the other hand, has made two contrary points. First, proposals for inquiry, or investigation of any dispute or situation which might lead to friction or give rise to a dispute, arise from Article 34 of the Charter rather than Article 29. Second, the problem of fact-finding by the Security Council must be seen within the context of the 'chain of events' theory which the five major powers adumbrated at San Francisco.

The San Francisco statement on voting, which does not have the same legal authority as the Charter but expressed the views which the five permanent members of the Council held in 1945,[52] makes it clear that the setting up of such bodies or agencies as the Council deems necessary for the performance of its functions should be governed by a procedural vote. The statement goes on, however, to elaborate a 'chain of events' theory by which any proposal which initiates a chain of events which might, in the end, require the Council to invoke measures of enforcement under Chapter VII of the Charter should be subject to veto. This chain of events could be initiated at an early stage—for example, by a decision to make an investigation. 'It is to such decisions and actions that unanimity of the permanent members [the veto] applies . . .'[53]

This problem arose in the very early days. The Council was discussing the Spanish question, and Australia proposed

> in accordance with Article 34 of the Charter, to make further inquiries in order to determine whether or not . . . a situation

Table 27

Subsidiary organs proposed but not established, 1946–73

(a) *Proposal not pressed to a vote*

Date	*Item*	*Document*	*SCOR*
21/22 Aug. 1960	Congo question	S/4453	15th year, 889th meeting, paras. 141–3
23 Oct. 1962	Situation in the Caribbean	S/5182	17th year, 1022nd meeting, para. 80

(b) *Insufficient votes for adoption of proposal*

Date	*Item*	*Document*	*SCOR*
13 Feb. 1946	Indonesian question (first phase)	—	1st year, 1st series, 18th meeting, pp. 257–8
13 Feb. 1946	Indonesian question (first phase)	—	1st year, 1st series, 18th meeting, p. 263
18 Apr. 1947	Greek question	—	2nd year, 131st meeting, p. 808
4 Aug. 1947	Greek question	S/404	2nd year, 174th meeting, p. 1730
25 Aug. 1947	Indonesian question (second phase)	S/512	2nd year, 194th meeting, p. 2209
25 Aug. 1947	Indonesian question (second phase)	S/448/Add. 1	2nd year, 194th meeting, p. 2209
15 June 1948	Palestine question	S/841	3rd year, 320th meeting, p. 11
24 Dec. 1948	Indonesian question (second phase)	S/1148 and Add. 1	3rd year, 392nd meeting, pp. 41–2
13 Dec. 1949	Indonesian question (second phase)	S/1433	4th year, 456th meeting, p. 35
15 Mar. 1961	Situation in Angola	S/4769	16th year, 946th meeting, para. 165

(c) *Proposal vetoed*

Date	*Item*	*Document*	*SCOR*	*Veto no.*
20 Sept. 1946	Ukrainian complaint against Greece	—	1st year, 2nd series, 70th meeting, p. 412	9
29 July 1947	Greek frontier incicents	S/391	2nd year, 170th meeting, p. 1612	11
19 Aug. 1947	Greek frontier incidents	S/471 and Add. 1	2nd year, 188th meeting, pp. 2093–4	15
25 Aug. 1947	Indonesian question (second phase)	—	2nd year, 194th meeting, p. 2199	19
24 May 1948	Czechoslovak question (1948)	—	3rd year, 303rd meeting pp. 19, 28–9	25–6 (double veto)
12 Sept. 1950	Complaint of bombing of China	S/1752	5th year, 501st meeting, p. 28	46
26 July 1960	RB-47 incident	S/4409/Rev. 1	16th year, 883rd meeting, para. 188	92

[leading to international friction and endangering international peace and security] exists . . .

Discussion of the Spanish question was adjourned, but when it was resumed a week later, the Australian representative submitted a revised proposal.

I have cut out the idea of a formal investigation under Article 34 so as to enable the proposed body to be brought in under Article 29 as a subsidiary organ; and I call it a sub-committee instead of a committee.

The published records do not indicate why the change was made, although one assumes that the revised wording was more acceptable to the Soviet Union. The resolution finally decided

to make further studies in order to determine whether the situation in Spain has led to international friction and does endanger international peace and security . . . [and] *appoints* a sub-committee . . . to examine the statements made . . . to receive further statements and documents, and to conduct such inquiries as it may deem necessary . . .[54]

The same issue arose later in 1946 in connection with the Ukrainian complaint against Greece. The United States submitted a proposal to establish a commission of investigation 'acting under Article 34 of the Charter'. The President (the Soviet Union) stated that the U.S. proposal 'relates to the substance of the matter' and was accordingly within the scope of the veto. France suggested that, on the contrary, the U.S. proposal 'comes under the provision of Article 29 of the Charter'. The Soviet Union insisted that, in accordance with the San Francisco statement, the U.S. proposal was a question of substance, and the United States agreed. The U.S. proposal was put to the vote, and the negative Soviet vote was regarded as a veto.[55]

In 1947, the issue arose in connection with the Corfu Channel case, but it became entangled with a different question, whether the United Kingdom was a party to a dispute and therefore required to abstain from voting. The President (Belgium), supported by Britain, Colombia, Syria, and the United States, took the view that a proposal to appoint a sub-committee 'to examine all the available evidence . . . [and] to request further information' was procedural. The Soviet Union took a contrary stand but, as it was not opposed to the setting up of a sub-committee, abstained when the proposal was put to a vote.[56]

In connection with the Czechoslovak question in 1948, Chile (a non-member of the Council) proposed that a sub-committee should be set up

> in accordance with Article 34 of the Charter . . . to receive or to hear . . . evidence, statements and testimonies . . .

The United States held that the proposal was 'clearly a procedural decision. It is a decision under Article 29 . . . The use of such a subsidiary organ to assist the Security Council . . . is expressly provided for in Article 29 . . .' This view was supported by Canada and Syria. The Soviet Union, however, considered the proposal substantive, and cast a double veto.[57]

One more example may be cited. When Laos sought UN assistance in 1959, three Western members of the Council proposed that a sub-committee should be appointed 'to examine the statements made before the Security Council . . . to receive further statements and documents and to conduct such inquiries as it may determine necessary . . .' In the Western view, this was simply the establishing of a subsidiary organ for which a procedural vote was sufficient, but for the Soviet Union this was or might be the first step in a chain of events which might lead to goodness knows what. A Soviet attempt to exercise the double veto was frustrated by a Presidential ruling.[58]

There have been three other Soviet vetoes of proposals to establish subsidiary organs for investigation, observation, or conciliation (vetoes 11, 15, and 46) and one veto of a proposal to confer additional functions on a subsidiary organ (veto 16). Six vetoes and one double veto have been used to prevent the reference of questions to some other organ or agency (vetoes 2, 50, 60, 61, 92, and 93, and double veto 20–21).[59]

It is not surprising, therefore, that the authors of a standard work on the UN Charter should write that the practice of the Council regarding proposals for investigation or inquiry 'has not been consistent'.[60] All that one can say with confidence is that differences of view on the question were frequent during the first five years, diminished during the next decade, and have caused negligible difficulty since 1961.

CHAPTER 7

NEW CHARTER, NEW RULES, OR NEW NATIONAL POLICIES?

> While the final responsibility for all success or failure in diplomacy would seem to rest upon the . . . ministers at home, it is none the less true that since these ministers can only act upon information from abroad, the influence which an enlightened diplomat can exercise upon the actions and designs of the home government is very large.

I. NEW CHARTER?

I HAVE nowhere in this book expressed the view that improvements in the working of the Security Council depend upon changes in the Charter. To be sure, many of the provisions of the Charter are unsatisfactory diplomatic compromises, but we are lucky to have a United Nations. The process by which the Organization was constructed was painful, and it is astonishing that the United Nations has survived the stresses of three difficult decades. The provisions in the Charter which are most criticized—the veto, the machinery for dealing with dependent territories, and the ban on intervening in essentially domestic matters—are precisely the matters on which one or more of the permanent members would be most unyielding, and no amendment can take effect if it is not ratified by all five permanent members.

This is not to say that there will be no amendments to the Charter. Both the Security Council and the Economic and Social Council have already been enlarged, and other changes of this kind are conceivable. But the broad structure of the United Nations, the principles on which it is based, the purposes to which it is directed, are likely to remain unaltered. The challenge is not to draft a better Charter: it is to make better use of the Charter we have.

2. NEW RULES?

Although the Rules of Procedure are still only provisional, they have provided an adequate procedural framework for the Security Council. I see no advantage to be gained from substantial amendment, although certain provisions are redundant or unnecessary (the last ten words of Rule 1, Rules 4, 10, 12, the first eleven words of Rule 19, the first sentence of Rule 21, Rules 23, 24, 28, 40, the last sentence of Rule 53, and Rule 57); three Rules contain expressions which are both ambiguous and unnecessary (Rules 31–3); one Rule could with advantage be clarified (Rule 36); in one case, the English version (and possibly also the Russian) is inconsistent with other languages (Rule 30); and there is a lack of consistency in referring to 'member(s) of' and 'representative(s) on' the Council.

In the pages that follow, I review the Rules of Procedure and the Appendix, using roughly the order of subjects indicated by the Chapter headings of the Rules. I have indented below and on pp. 291, 294, 301, 302, 305, and 306 suggestions for minor changes in the Rules which might be worth considering when next they are reviewed.

It should be stressed that there is no Rule of Procedure giving effect to Article 32 of the Charter regarding the participation of parties to a dispute which are not members of the Council.

a. Meetings

The President of the Council calls a meeting at the request of any member of the Council, or if the General Assembly addresses to the Council a recommendation or refers to it a question or situation, or if the Secretary-General expressly invokes Article 99, or if a State draws the Council's attention to a dispute or situation. The President consults Council members informally and arranges the meeting to suit the wishes of members of the Council (Rules 1–3). This procedure has worked satisfactorily most of the time, and no change in the Rules would be likely to improve things.

> The phrase 'but the interval between meetings shall not exceed fourteen days', which was inserted in Rule 1 by the Committee of Experts in 1946 'to stress . . . the permanent nature of the Security Council',[1] is now redundant.

The Charter provides in Article 28(2) for 'periodic meetings at which each of [the Council's] members may, if it so desires, be represented by a member of the government or by some other specially designated representative'; Rule 4, stipulating that such 'periodic' meetings shall be held twice a year, was approved by the Security Council on 9 April 1946.[2]

> This Rule has been generally ignored, and the single 'periodic' meeting was not exactly a success (see pp. 34–9 of Chapter 2). No harm would be done if Rule 4 (and possibly also Rule 12 about the provisional agenda for a 'periodic' meeting) were now dropped.

The Council 'normally' meets at UN Headquarters, but in accordance with Article 28(3) and Rule 5, the Council may decide to meet elsewhere when it judges that this would facilitate its work. The meetings held in London and in Paris where the General Assembly was in session, were to the convenience of all and thus facilitated the Council's work; but it is doubtful if the meetings held in Ethiopia in 1972 and Panama in 1973 were so overwhelmingly successful as to suggest that the Council should in future leave New York for an annual safari (pages 31–4 and 277–8).

In the absence of a decision to the contrary, the Council meets in public. Following a recommendation of the Executive Committee of the Preparatory Commission, the Rules of Procedure require the Council to meet in private when making recommendations to the General Assembly regarding the appointment of the Secretary-General, and in practice the Council does meet in private when considering the draft of its annual report. At the close of a private meeting, a *communiqué* is issued through the Secretary-General in place of a verbatim record. The Council may decide to keep a record of a private meeting in a single copy only, and any such record is kept by the Secretary-General. Representatives of UN Members who have taken part in a private meeting have access to the record kept by the Secretary-General, and the Council may grant access to this record to the authorized representatives of other Members (Rules 48, 51, 55, and 56). Australia assumed in 1946, when these Rules were adopted, that the decision to meet in private should be taken at a public meeting. Although nobody challenged this assumption,[3] there appears to be no reason why the

Council should not continue the practice of meeting in private as a result of agreement reached in private informal consultations.

It is convenient to mention here Rule 61, which was added in 1947 after a tiresome difference of opinion about the meaning of the Statute of the International Court of Justice. The Statute refers to meetings of the Security Council and the General Assembly for the election of judges (Articles 11 and 12 of the Statute). When the first election took place in 1946, the President of the Security Council (Australia), supported by Britain and China, took the view that a meeting of the Security Council was a sitting of the Council at which one or more votes took place. But the majority of members of the Council, or a majority of those who spoke, supported by the President of the General Assembly (Paul-Henri Spaak), interpreted *meeting* to mean a vote or ballot. An *ad hoc* arrangement was resorted to in 1946, and the General Assembly and Security Council later agreed unanimously that a 'meeting' of either organ for the election of judges 'shall continue until as many candidates as are required for all the seats to be filled have obtained in one or more ballots an absolute majority of votes'.[4]

b. Agenda

The provisional agenda for each ordinary meeting of the Council is drawn up by the Secretary-General, approved by the President, and communicated to members at least three days before the meeting; but in urgent circumstances (which is usually the case) the provisional agenda may be communicated simultaneously with the notice of the meeting. The provisional agenda for a 'periodic' meeting is circulated at least twenty-one days before the meeting, and subsequent changes or additions are to be brought to the notice of members at least five days before the meeting; in urgent circumstances, the Council may add to the agenda at any time during a 'periodic' meeting. The first item of the provisional agenda is the adoption of the agenda (Rules 7–9 and 12).

The Secretary-General brings to the attention of the Council communications from named sources 'concerning any matter for the consideration of the Security Council in accordance with the provisions of the Charter' (Rule 6). The provisional agenda is composed of those items which have been brought to the Council's attention under Rule 6, or items consideration of which was not completed at a previous meeting, or matters which the Council has previously decided to defer (Rules 7 and 10).

Under Rule 11, the Secretary-General communicates to the members of the Council a weekly Summary Statement of matters of which the Council is seized and of the stage reached in their consideration. The Notification to the General Assembly of matters relative to the maintenance of international peace and security which are being dealt with by the Council, which is required by Article 12(2) of the Charter, is based on the Summary Statement. The Committee of Experts proposed Rule 11 'for the convenience of the members of the Security Council . . .'[5]

The preparation and circulation of the Summary Statement have undoubtedly met the convenience of members. Beginning on 22 August 1972, the Secretary-General has economized by reproducing the full up-to-date Summary Statement only once a year and issuing each week an addendum to the basic list, indicating any items on which further action has been taken by the Council during the week covered.[6] If the Security Council agrees to delete an item from the Summary Statement and the General Assembly is in session (as in the case of the deletion of the Indonesian question in September 1973), the Secretary-General is required by Article 12(2) of the Charter to notify the General Assembly 'immediately'; if the General Assembly is not in session, the Secretary-General notifies UN Members.

The Summary Statement now contains nearly one hundred items, and several Members of the General Assembly have suggested that the Council should delete those items which have not been actively considered recently. Of the ninety-one items of which the Council was seized on 1 March 1974, nine had not been considered since 1948, nine since 1953, fifteen since 1958, and sixteen since 1963. For all practical purposes, the Council is not actively seized of the forty-nine items not considered for more than a decade, but to attempt to delete these items would take more trouble than it is worth. The situation is untidy, but the Council has more pressing business to occupy its time than deciding which matters it is no longer concerned with.

Rule 10 provides that any item consideration of which has not been completed at a meeting of the Council shall, unless the Council decides to the contrary, 'automatically be included in the agenda of the next meeting'. This text was proposed by the Committee of Experts in 1946 to ensure that 'the continued consideration of such business as is left over from one meeting shall constitute part of the agenda of the next meeting'. The use of the word *agenda* was, according to the chairman of the Committee of Experts, used advisedly.[7] In practice, the Council has interpreted *agenda* in Rule 10 to mean the totality of the matters of which the Council is seized.

If ever this interpretation were to give rise to misunderstanding, it would be possible to amend Rule 10 to read:

> Any item of the agenda of a meeting of the Security Council, consideration of which has not been completed at that meeting, shall, unless the Security Council otherwise decides, automatically be included in the summary statement of matters of which the Security Council is seized.

c. *Representation and Credentials*

A Head of Government or Minister of Foreign Affairs of a member is entitled to sit on the Security Council without submitting credentials. The credentials of other representatives, issued by the Head of the State or of the Government or the Minister of Foreign Affairs, are to be communicated to the Secretary-General not less than twenty-four hours before he takes his seat or attends, and the Secretary-General examines the credentials and submits a report on them to the Council for approval. Pending the approval of his credentials, a representative on the Council is seated provisionally with the same rights as other representatives; any representative on the Council to whose credentials objection has been made 'within the Council' continues to sit with the same rights as other representatives until the Council has decided the matter (Rules 13–17). There is no indication in the Rules of Procedure as to the course to be followed if objection is made to the credentials of a non-member of the Council, but it would be logical to apply the procedure outlined in Rule 17, which deals with objections to the credentials of representatives on the Council.

Since 1948, the reports of the Secretary-General on credentials have been circulated to Council members and, in the absence of any request that they be considered by the Council, are regarded as approved without objection. In practice, credentials are submitted and reported on only when changes in representation are made and when non-permanent members have been newly elected.

When the representation of China was being considered in 1950, India drew attention to the fact that none of the Rules of Procedure indicates what is to be done when questions arise as to which is the recognized government of any particular State. In order to obviate a situation in which different UN organs might 'by their own majorities' reach conflicting decisions, India favoured some uniform procedure which could be adopted by all the organs. In order to 'set the ball rolling', India submitted a draft new Rule to the effect that, where the right of a person to represent a State on the Security Council is called into question on the ground that he does not represent the recognized government of that State, the President of the Council should, before submitting the question to the Council, ascertain 'by telegraph if necessary' and place before the Council the views of the governments of all other UN Members on the matter.[8] The Indian proposal was remitted to the Committee of Experts, which praised India's laudable initiative but thought that the matter should go to the General Assembly for study. On the advice of the Committee of Experts, the Security Council decided to take no decision.[9]

It was Cuba which took the matter to the General Assembly where, after a period of confused and unsatisfactory debate and diplomacy, a resolution was adopted which, in its first operative paragraph, recommended that whenever more than one authority claims to be the government entitled to represent a Member State in the United Nations, and this becomes the subject of controversy, the question should be considered 'in the light of the purposes and principles of the Charter and the circumstances of each case'.[10] This platitudinous advice was regularly recalled by the United States and its partners in connection with the Representation of China, but it may be doubted whether it throws significant light on the problem of governmental legitimacy.

d. Presidency

The presidency rotates on a monthly basis in the English alphabetical order of the members of the Security Council (Rule 18). The President represents the Council in its capacity as an organ of the United Nations, and this was 'intended to give him the requisite authority to nominate committees and to conclude agreements on behalf of the Council'.[11] He is given precedence immediately after the President of the General Assembly, in accordance with the order of principal organs named in Article 7 of the Charter.[12] The presidency is 'deemed to attach to the member State concerned and not to the person of its representative',[13] and if the President is unable to preside because of illness or for personal reasons, 'the presidency . . . [is] assumed by an accredited representative of the same State'.[14] This happened in October 1956, for example, when Louis de Guiringaud took over the presidency after Cornut-Gentille's collapse (see pp. 113 and 114).

The President presides over Council meetings (Rule 19). He performs tasks specified in the Rules of Procedure (Rules 1, 2, 3, 7, 27, 30, 36, 53, and 59) and acts in his discretion over four matters mentioned in the Rules (Rules 1, 20, 29, and 52).

The Secretariat stressed at an early stage that it would not be possible to elaborate the Rules so as to provide for 'the multitudinous variety of procedural problems that may arise'. The Secretariat suggested that, 'at least as regards the regulation of debate, certain powers [should] inhere in the office of President as such, and that he should advance rulings which shall be valid in the absence of objection'.[15] The President is guided by certain customary practices of the presiding officers of intergovernmental organs.

No Rule governs the fact that, unlike the President of the General Assembly, the President of the Security Council is also the representative of a Council member. This can lead to confusion, as happened in Panama City on 21 March 1973, and it has been suggested that this might be minimized if a new Rule were adopted to the effect that, whenever the President speaks in his capacity as representative of a member of the Council rather than as President, he shall preface his remarks with an indication to that effect. But it may be doubted whether real difficulties on this score have been sufficiently frequent or grave to warrant the adoption of a new Rule.

Rule 20 provides for the devolution of the presidential chair whenever the President deems that, for the proper fulfilment of the responsibilities of the presidency, he should not preside during consideration of a particular question with which the member he represents is 'directly connected'. All members of the Council are *concerned* about any matter which the Council decides to consider, but not all members are 'directly connected' with every such matter.

The initiative for invoking Rule 20 is to be taken by the President himself. The Committee of Experts was unanimous that the obligation to leave the chair 'was essentially a moral one', and that to leave the matter to the President's discretion 'was alone suitable for the conception which the representatives on the Security Council have of their duties'.[16] It is, of course, open to any other member of the Council, under Rule 30, to ask the President whether or not he intends to cede the presidency during the consideration of any particular question.

e. Secretariat

Chapter V of the Rules of Procedure is headed 'Secretariat', which is named in Article 7 of the Charter as one of the six principal organs of the United Nations. The staff who comprise the Secretariat are appointed by the Secretary-General, who is the Organization's chief administrative officer (Articles 97 and 101 (1) and (2)). The Rules in the Chapter headed 'Secretariat', therefore, specify tasks which are to be performed under the authority of the Secretary-General.

In addition to the other rights and duties of the Secretary-General arising from the Charter, the Rules of Procedure require the Secretary-General to 'act in that capacity' in all meetings of the Security Council (Article 98 and Rule 21) and to provide from the Secretariat the staff required by the Council (Article 101 (2) and Rule 24). The first sentences of Rule 21 and Rule 24 merely repeat the provisions of the Charter, but the second sentence of Rule 21 permits the Secretary-General to authorize a deputy to act in his place at Council meetings, and Rule 23 allows the Secretary-General's deputy to make oral or written statements. This deputy is not the deputy Secretary-

General but the Secretary-General's personal representative at those meetings of the Security Council from which he is unavoidably absent. The Security Council may invite any member of the Secretariat 'to supply it with information or to give other assistance . . .' (Rule 39).

Other duties of the Secretary-General are specified in the Rules of Procedure (nos. 6–8, 11, 13–15, 25, 26, 50, 51, and 55–9), as are three matters on which the Secretary-General acts at his own discretion (Rules 5, 21, and 22). The third of these discretionary rules allows the Secretary-General or his deputy 'acting on his behalf' to make oral or written statements concerning any question under consideration by the Council, and the Committee of Experts agreed unanimously in 1946 that the Secretary-General or his deputy 'should have the same power in relation to [committees, commissions, or other subsidiary organs of the Council] unless the Council should decide otherwise'.[17]

Rule 23, which is probably unnecessary but harmless, states that the Secretary-General 'may be appointed . . . as rapporteur for a specified question'. The crucial aspect, on which the Committee of Experts made a unanimous comment in its report in 1946 but did not translate its comment into a Rule, is that 'such an appointment should clearly be subject to the consent of the Secretary-General in each case'.[18]

The Appendix to the Rules of Procedure provides that 'the Secretariat' shall, if requested, give to any representative on the Council a copy of any communication from a private individual or a non-governmental body relating to a matter of which the Council is seized.

f. Conduct of Business and Voting

Fourteen Rules deal with the conduct of business and voting. Three are concerned with the participation of non-members (37–9), two with the order of speakers (27 and 29), one with points of order (30), five with procedural motions and draft resolutions (31–5), one with amendments (36), one with certain subsidiary organs (28), and one directly, and several indirectly, with voting (40, also 32–8).

The Charter and Rules of Procedure provide in specified circumstances for the participation of UN Members which are not members of the Security Council, of non-Members of the United Nations, of members of the Secretariat, and of 'other persons' competent to give information or other assistance. Under Articles 31 and 35(1) of the Charter and Rule 37, UN Members which are not members of the Council *may* be invited to participate without vote whenever the Council considers that the interests of that Member are specially affected or when that Member has brought to the attention of the Council a dispute or a situation which might lead to international friction or give rise to a dispute.

So far so good. But in two circumstances the Charter provides that a UN Member not a member of the Council *shall* be invited to participate although there is no Rule of Procedure which expressly gives effect to the Charter provisions: 'in the discussion' relating to any dispute to which the Member is a party (Article 32), and 'in the decisions' if the Council calls upon a Member to provide armed forces (Article 44). In the case of a party to a dispute (Article 32), the Committee of Experts reported in 1946 that it 'did not consider it advisable to provide in [Rule 37] for Members invited in accordance with Article 32 of the Charter because the invitation to a Member under this Article is mandatory.'[29] The Council thus obtains the participation of parties to a dispute under Article 32 by regarding the party to a dispute as a Member whose interests are specially affected and thus covered by Rule 37, or by regarding the representative of the party to a dispute as a person competent to supply information or give other assistance and thus covered by Rule 39.

In the case of a Member called upon to provide armed forces (Article 44), which will arise only after agreements to make armed forces available to the Security Council have been made under Article 43, the Council could regard the Member's participation in the decisions as an application of Rule 40, which states *inter alia* that voting shall be in accordance with the relevant Articles of the Charter.

A State which is not a Member of the United Nations *shall* be invited to participate without vote in the discussion of any dispute to which it is a party, which it has brought to the attention of the Security Council, provided that it accepts for the purpose of that dispute the Charter obligations of pacific settlement (Articles 32 and 35(2)). There is no specific provision in the Charter or the Rules of Procedure for the participation of a non-UN Member *except when it is a party to a dispute.*[20] Presumably the Council has considered the representative of a non-UN Member which is not a party to a dispute as a person competent to supply it with information or to give other assistance, and therefore within the scope of Rule 39.

Rule 39, which was inserted by the Preparatory Commission in face of U.S. opposition,[21] provides for the participation of members of the Secretariat and other persons considered competent to supply information or give other assistance 'in examining matters within [the Council's] competence'.

Differences of view about the participation of non-members of the Council are likely to occur from time to time, and no changes in the Rules would be likely to obviate such differences or to make it easier to reconcile them. *But it should be recognized that Rule 37 is discretionary in character and limited in scope, and that there is no Rule of Procedure giving effect to Article 32 of the Charter concerning the mandatory participation of parties to a dispute under consideration by the Council; and, further, that neither the Charter nor the Rules of Procedure provide for the participation of non-UN Members which are not parties to a dispute, except in the catch-all wording of Rule 39 concerning persons competent to give information or other assistance.*

The order of speakers is governed by Rule 27, which states that the President shall call upon representatives in the order in which they signify their desire to speak, and by Rule 29, which allows the President to accord precedence to any rapporteur appointed by the Council or to the chairman of a commission or committee who has to explain a report to the Council. These two Rules have to be applied in the light of the customary practice of the Council, which is that, in the absence of a decision to the contrary, the usual order of speakers is Member(s) requesting the meeting, other parties to the question, situation, or dispute, members of the Council, President of the Council (in his capacity as representative), non-members of the Council.

Rule 30 provides for the raising of points of order, for immediate presidential rulings, and for decisions by the Council in the event of challenges to presidential rulings: UN procedural committees have found it impossible to devise comprehensive definitions of what constitute legitimate points of order, although the General Assembly has provided in paragraph 79 of Annex V to its Rule of Procedure some recommendations about the raising of points of order, drafted by a committee on rationalizing the Assembly's procedures and organization. But however carefully or rigidly a point of order is defined, astute representatives will find ways of making substantive comments in the guise of raising points of order.

If ever it should be found necessary to amend the Rules of Procedure, occasion should certainly be taken to make consistent the differing versions of the second sentence of Rule 30 in the five languages of the Council. In English and French, this sentence reads

If [the ruling] is challenged, the President shall submit his ruling to the Security Council for immediate decision and it shall stand unless overruled.	*S'il y a contestation, le Président en réfère au Conseil de sécurité pour une décision immédiate, et la règle qu'il a proposée est maintenue, à moins qu'elle ne soit annulée.*

In English, the President submits his ruling (*règle*) for the decision of the Council; in French, the *contestation* (challenge). If the Council is divided eight votes to seven, the motion of challenge fails to secure nine votes whichever language of Rule 30 is used. If the English version is used, the President's ruling fails and is overruled, even though there were not nine votes to overrule. In the more logical French version, the challenge fails and so the President's ruling stands.

> As the result can be different depending on the language it used, would be sensible, and indeed overdue, to bring the English version (and, if necessary, the Russian) into line with the other languages.

Procedure for dealing with motions and proposals is provided for in Rules 31–35: Rule 31 requiring that motions and proposals (and amendments) shall 'normally' be submitted in writing, Rule 34 stating that motions and proposals do not need to be seconded before being put to the vote, Rule 35 providing for the withdrawal of motions and proposals, the first sentence of Rule 32 and Rule 33 dealing with the order of voting on motions and proposals (and the introduction of amendments), and the second sentence of Rule 32 providing for voting separately on parts of a motion or proposal.

The main defect of these Rules is the inconsistency of the language and the uncertainty as to the meaning of 'substantive motions' in Rule 31 and of 'principal motions' in Rules 32 and 33. Motions deal with procedure, proposals (proposed or draft resolutions) with other matters; the original proposal is a proposal to which amendments have been submitted.

> The expressions 'substantive motions' used in Rule 31 and 'principal motions' used in Rules 32 and 33 only cause confusion; if these Rules cannot be amended, the doubtful expressions are best forgotten.

An amendment is 'normally' to be placed before members of the Council in writing (Rule 31), and its introduction takes precedence in accordance with the order stated in Rule 33. If more than one amendment is submitted, the order of voting is governed by Rule 36. To the extent that differences of view about the order of voting on amendments can be resolved by reference to a Rule of Procedure, Rule 36 has served a useful purpose.

I suggest, nevertheless, for the reasons indicated on pp. 192–5 of Chapter 4, that this Rule would be clearer if it were to read as follows:

> If two or more amendments to a motion or proposal are submitted, the President shall rule on the order in which they are to be voted upon. [If the ruling is challenged, the President shall submit the challenge to the Security Council for its decision.*]
>
> In making his ruling, the President shall bear in mind that ordinarily, when an amendment adds to or deletes from the text of a motion or proposal, that amendment shall be voted on first, and that in other cases the Council shall first vote on the amendment furthest removed in substance from the original proposal, and then on the amendment next furthest removed, until all amendments have been put to the vote.

The first version of Rule 28, as drafted by the Committee of Experts, read platitudinously: 'The Security Council may appoint a rapporteur for a specified question.'[22] When this draft came before the Council, Sir Alexander Cadogan of the United Kingdom (see pp. 118 and 119) questioned whether the

* This sentence to be included only if the English version of Rule 30 on points of order is made consistent with the other languages.

rule was necessary, but thought that, if it were being retained, it should be made consistent with the second paragraph of the next rule.[23] It was therefore amended to read: 'The Security Council may appoint a commission or committee or rapporteur for a specified question.' This is a partial application of Article 29 of the Charter, which authorizes the Security Council to establish such subsidiary organs as it deems necessary for the performance of its functions. In 1950, the Council approved the basic principles of a proposal of the General Assembly, which had originated with the British delegation after study of the experience of the League of Nations, for the appointment of a rapporteur or conciliator for a situation or dispute brought to the Council's attention. According to Ambassador Chauvel of France (see p. 112), at that time President of the Council, the rapporteur or conciliator might be the President himself or any other member of the Council. Once appointed, he should carry out his work 'independently of his office, if he is President, and . . . even independently of his membership of the Council' (see pages 102–3).[24]

The Committee of Experts was of the opinion in 1946 that, in principle, only a representative on the Council or the Secretary-General was likely to be appointed rapporteur, but the Committee did not want to exclude the possibility that, in exceptional circumstances, the Council might appoint some other specially qualified person as rapporteur.[25]

Rule 40 is perhaps the most unnecessary Rule of them all. Although it consists of only twenty-six words, it comprises the whole of Chapter VII of the Rules of Procedure. It was first drafted by the Executive Committee of the Preparatory Commission, with the comment that certain delegations were doubtful 'whether the provisions of the Charter relating to voting would by themselves prove adequate'. The prevailing view, however, was that it was undesirable to elaborate additional rules regarding voting at that time (November 1945).[26] The draft rule was approved by the Preparatory Commission itself in December 1945 and by the Committee of Experts in February 1946. There then ensued a struggle between the United States and the Soviet Union, as mentioned on pp. 14–15 of Chapter 1. The Soviet Union wanted to entrench both the veto and the double veto in the Rules of Procedure, whereas the

United States would have liked to get rid of the double veto altogether, even though its legitimacy had been recognized in the San Francisco Statement of the five permanent members of the Security Council on 8 June 1945.[27] In the end, the Committee of Experts submitted a revised version of the Rules of Procedure on 13 May 1946 with this rule unaltered 'for the time being' pending further study. The Committee reported that there had been 'a full and free exchange of views on this subject', which evidently meant that things had got pretty difficult, and that some members had taken the view that the Rules 'should contain detailed provisions covering the mechanics of the vote and the majorities by which various decisions . . . should be taken'.[28] Three days later, the Council approved the text without debate.

Rule 40 can thus be regarded as not only the most unnecessary of all the Rules, but also as the most provisional. Neither the Committee of Experts nor the Security Council has yet resumed the 'further study' which the Committee of Experts decided 'to postpone' nearly thirty years ago, other than in the context of inconclusive exchanges of view concerning the veto.

g. Languages and Records

Now that the distinction between official and working languages has disappeared, Rules 41–7 are simpler. The five languages of the Security Council are Chinese, English, French, Russian, and Spanish.* Speeches made in any of the five languages are interpreted into the other four, and verbatim records, resolutions, and other documents are issued in the five languages (Rules 41, 42, 45, and 46). A representative speaking in a language other than one of the five languages of the Council shall himself provide interpretation into one of those languages, and the Council can decide to publish any of its documents in a language other than one of the languages of the Council (Rules 44 and 47). Rule 43, which was only necessary when the Council distinguished between official and working languages, has been deleted.

A provisional verbatim record of each Council meeting is available in mimeographed form by 10 a.m. of the first working day following the meeting. Representatives who have taken part

* Pressure to add Arabic seems to be on the increase.

in the meeting may suggest corrections which they wish to have made, within two working days if the meeting was held in public and within ten days if the meeting was in private. The longer period allowed for suggesting corrections to the record of a private meeting is because of 'the difficulty of consulting the record in those instances when the Council has decided that only a single copy . . . shall be kept'.[29] The Committee of Experts took the view in 1946 'that . . . in principle, the formal approval of records is the prerogative of the Security Council itself, but that it would be appropriate to delegate this power to the President except when a major difficulty necessitates an exchange of views within the Council'.[30] The Rules therefore provide that the President may refer 'sufficiently important' corrections to representatives on the Council, who then have the right to submit any comments they wish to make within two working days (Rules 49–52).

When no corrections have been requested, or when the President is of the opinion that corrections are not 'sufficiently important' to be referred to the Council, or if corrections are referred to the Council but do not give rise to comments, or when agreement is reached after the submission of comments, the provisional record is considered as approved and thereupon becomes 'the official record'. The official record is then published in the five languages 'as soon as possible' (Rules 52–4). In practice, there is a delay of between two and a half and four years in the publication of the printed record of Council meetings.

From the earliest days, the President has not signed the corrected record, as required by the last sentence of Rule 53, and nothing would be lost if this sentence were deleted.

The Secretary-General brings to the attention of the Council communications 'concerning any matter for the consideration of the Security Council in accordance with . . . the Charter', if the communication is from a State, a UN organ, or from the Secretary-General himself (Rule 6). In the case of communications from private individuals or non-governmental bodies relating to matters of which the Council is seized, a list of communications is circulated to members of the Council, and the Secretariat gives a copy of any particular communication to a member of the Council who so requests (Appendix to the Rules of Procedure). When presenting the text of this Appendix, the chairman of the Committee of Experts said that the intention was to exclude frivolous communications.[31] The Secretariat suggested in 1946 that 'the standard practice should be for communications to be addressed to the Secretary-General',[32] but this advice has not been consistently followed.

Each year, the Secretary-General is supposed to notify members of the Council of records and documents which up to that time have been considered confidential, and the Council should then decide which shall be made public, which shall be available on a limited or restricted basis to UN Members only, and which shall remain confidential (Rule 57).

This Rule has never been applied, and it is unlikely that it will be applied in the future.

h. Admission of new Members

The Executive Committee of the Preparatory Commission drafted three simple rules relating to applications for UN Membership. A State wishing to become a Member was to submit to the Secretary-General an application, together with a declaration of its readiness to accept the obligations contained in the Charter. This application would be placed before the Security Council, which would decide whether the applicant is a peace-loving State and is able and willing to carry out the Charter obligations. If the Security Council should make a favourable recommendation, this should be placed before the General Assembly. These rules were approved by the Preparatory Commission in December 1945 and by the Committee of Experts in February 1946.

In a revision submitted by the Committee of Experts in May 1946, two additions were made. First, unless the Security Council should decide otherwise, the President should refer each application to a committee composed of all the members of the Security Council. Secondly, the Council should in normal circumstances transmit its recommendations to the General Assembly not less than twenty-five days before a regular session or four days before a special session; but in 'special circumstances' the Council might disregard the time limits.[33] The amended rules were duly approved by the Council.

Australia reserved its position on these rules in the Committee of Experts on the ground that the procedure failed to accord a proper role to the General Assembly in dealing with applications for Membership, but a proposal to defer approval of the draft rules until after consultation with the General Assembly secured only the Australian vote in the Council.[34]

Two changes to the Rules of Procedure were made in 1947, following consultations between the General Assembly and the Security Council. First, Rule 58 was amended to provide that an applicant's acceptance of the obligations of the Charter should be 'made in a formal instrument'. Second, two new paragraphs were inserted in Rule 60 to the effect that the Council should submit to the General Assembly with its recommendation 'a complete record of the discussion'; in cases where the Council did not make a favourable recommendation, it should also submit 'a special report . . .' The opportunity was taken to make a minor verbal correction to the English text of what is now paragraph 4 of Rule 60.[35]

The procedure for dealing with applications for Membership has been satisfactory since the revival of the Council's Committee on Admission of New Members.

Two other procedural matters have been considered by the Committee of Experts without a rule being recommended. The first was the question of a quorum. Some members thought that the adoption of a special rule on this subject 'might raise difficulties', and so the Committee of Experts took no decision.[36]

The other matter considered by the Committee of Experts was the closure of debates, to which the United States attached special importance. The Committee of Experts reported that this matter involved 'the very important problem of the limitation of the right of each representative to give full expression to his point of view', and the question was postponed to a later date. Ambassador Stettinius (see pp. 124–5) raised the matter again in the Security Council. He believed that it would be possible to devise a rule which, while not preventing freedom of expression, would contribute to orderly procedure, and he expressed the hope that the Committee of Experts would take the matter up again 'at an early date'. The Committee of Experts did not take the hint, however, presumably because of a general view that the provisions in Rule 33 for adjourning the meeting or postponing discussion were sufficient for terminating debate.[37]

3. NEW NATIONAL POLICIES?

If the Charter is to remain unamended in major respects, and if only a marginal improvement in the working of the Security Council is likely to follow from changes in its Rules of Procedure, in which direction should we look for a panacea to improve the effectiveness of the Security Council in its primary task of maintaining world peace?

Alas, there is no panacea, nor ever likely to be; but we can, nevertheless, work for a more effective Security Council through changes in national attitudes and national policies, as States review their perceptions of national interest in the light of the national interests of others. All States and all regions stand to gain from a firmer and more humane international order in which short-term national advantage is not pursued to the limit if to do so frustrates the universal common good. The obligation to relate short-term to long-term considerations, the national to the global interest, is needed for prudential as well as for ethical reasons. Most governments recognize these interrelationships part of the time; but at moments of crisis the short-term and national tends to swamp the long-term and universal.

Let me close this book, then, by suggesting ten areas of concern in which adjustments of national policies might help the Security Council to become a more effective instrument for achieving world peace, security, and relative justice.

1. The Charter does not impair the right of regional consultation or self-defence. Agencies for collective self-defence have been created because States were not confident that the United Nations Organization had the will or the means to keep the peace. As tension and conflict have oscillated, so have the functions of alliances. Originally created as instruments of collective self-defence, some alliances have in recent years also been used to co-ordinate policies of détente.

Such regional activities do not detract from the authority or primary responsibility of the Security Council. The Charter requires that the Council be informed immediately of measures taken in exercise of the right of self-defence (Article 51) and of activities 'undertaken *or in contemplation* . . . by regional agencies for the maintenance of international peace and security' (Article 54, my italics). The obligation to report to the Security Council under Article 51 of the UN Charter has been expressly included in the Rio Inter-American Pact (Article 5), the North Atlantic Treaty (Article 5), the Arab Joint Defence Treaty (Article 2), SEATO (Article IV), and the Warsaw Pact (Article 4). The Rio Pact also includes the obligation to report to the Security Council under that part of the UN Charter which deals with regional agencies or arrangements (Article 5). There is no express requirement to report to the Security Council in the CENTO Treaty.

These obligations under the UN Charter and the different treaties have largely remained dead letters. A more scrupulous regard for the obligation to keep the Security Council fully and immediately informed of other activities to maintain peace would enhance the Council's authority.

2. Election to the Security Council is not a reward for faithful diplomatic service nor something to be bargained for in log-rolling in the *couloirs*. The criteria for election are clearly stated in the Charter: 'due regard being specially paid, in the first instance, to the contribution of Members of the United Nations to the maintenance of international peace and security and to the other purposes of the Organization, and also to equitable geographical distribution' (Article 23(1)).

3. If the Secretary-General is to have an informed opinion as to matters which may threaten the maintenance of international peace and security which he may bring to the Council's attention, he should be encouraged to exercise to the full his implied fact-finding and diplomatic powers under Article 99 of the Charter.

4. While it has always been inconceivable that the Security Council would apply enforcement measures under Chapters VII or VIII against one of its permanent members, the Council is likely, as in the past, to need military forces for observation, peace-keeping, or provisional or preventive measures. A favourable opportunity should be sought to make a renewed attempt to conclude special agreements under Article 43 of the Charter

for making appropriate forces and facilities available to the Council.

5. According to Article 103, obligations under the UN Charter prevail over other international obligations. An explicit condition of UN Membership is a readiness to accept and carry out the decisions of the Security Council in accordance with the Charter (Article 25), since the Council carries out its duties on behalf of all the Members (Article 24(1)). Members are under a treaty obligation to carry out the mandatory decisions of the Council, and should also accord full respect to the Council's recommendations.

6. The five permanent members of the Security Council have a special responsibility, in part under Article 106, for upholding the authority of the Council, and should exercise restraint in the use of the veto, particularly in connection with the admission of new Members, the appointment of the Secretary-General, and the peaceful settlement of disputes.

7. When a greater measure of agreement on the organization of UN peace-keeping has been reached, an attempt should be made to resuscitate the Military Staff Committee so that it can advise and assist the Council on the requirements for the maintenance of international peace and security, and possibly also on 'the regulation of armaments, and possible disarmament' (Article 47(1)). Renewed consideration should also be given to the establishment of regional subcommittees of the Military Staff Committee 'after consultation with appropriate regional agencies' (Article 47(4)).

8. The Security Council should use to the full those methods of fact-finding, peace-making, peace-keeping, judicial settlement, or advisory legal opinions which are provided for in the Charter, or not expressly excluded by it (Articles 33, 34, 36(3), and 96(1) *inter alia*). The Office of the Secretary-General should be used as a centre for harmonizing the actions of the Council in seeking to attain the purposes of the United Nations.

9. In cases where the Council has for many years been seized of disputes which are likely to endanger world peace or of situations of like nature, the Council should not hesitate to exercise its powers under Articles 36(1) and 37(2) by which it may recommend 'appropriate procedures or methods of adjustment' or 'such terms of settlement as it may consider appropriate', or,

if the parties to a dispute so request, 'make recommendations . . . with a view to a pacific settlement of the dispute' under Article 38.

10. The Charter refers to 'a system for the regulation of armaments' (Article 26) and to 'the regulation of armaments, and possible disarmament' (Article 47(1)). The problem of controlling arms is now more necessary than these cautious words suggest. Indeed, the whole UN edifice for maintaining peace and security could collapse if it is not reinforced by a balanced system for the control and progressive reduction of arms, forces, and military budgets.

I hope to examine aspects of these areas of concern in greater depth in a future volume.

APPENDICES

APPENDIX 1

(a) EXTRACTS FROM THE UN CHARTER

WE THE PEOPLES
OF THE UNITED NATIONS
DETERMINED

to save succeeding generations from the scourge of war, which twice in our lifetime has brought untold sorrow to mankind, and

to reaffirm faith in fundamental human rights, in the dignity and worth of the human person, in the equal rights of men and women and of nations large and small, and

to establish conditions under which justice and respect for the obligations arising from treaties and other sources of international law can be maintained, and

to promote social progress and better standards of life in larger freedom,

AND FOR THESE ENDS

to practice tolerance and live together in peace with one another as good neighbours, and

to unite our strength to maintain international peace security, and

to ensure, by the acceptance of principles and the institution of methods, that armed force shall not be used, save in the common interest, and

to employ international machinery for the promotion of the economic and social advancement of all peoples,

HAVE RESOLVED TO
COMBINE OUR EFFORTS TO
ACCOMPLISH THESE AIMS.

Accordingly, our respective Governments, through representatives assembled in the city of San Francisco, who have exhibited their full powers found to be in good and due form, have agreed to the present Charter of the United Nations and do hereby establish an international organization to be known as the United Nations.

Chapter I

PURPOSES AND PRINCIPLES

Article 1

The Purposes of the United Nations are:

1. To maintain international peace and security, and to that end: to take effective collective measures for the prevention and removal of threats to the peace, and for the suppression of acts of aggression or other breaches of the peace, and to bring about by peaceful means, and in conformity with the principles of justice and international law, adjustment or settlement of international disputes or situations which might lead to a breach of the peace;

2. To develop friendly relations among nations based on respect for the principle of equal rights and self-determination of peoples, and to take other appropriate measures to strengthen universal peace;

3. To achieve international cooperation in solving international problems of an economic, social, cultural, or humanitarian character, and in promoting and encouraging respect for human rights and for fundamental freedoms for all without distinction as to race, sex, language, or religion; and

4. To be a center for harmonizing the actions of nations in the attainment of these common ends.

Article 2

The Organization and its Members, in pursuit of the Purposes stated in Article 1, shall act in accordance with the following Principles.

1. The Organization is based on the principle of the sovereign equality of all its Members.

2. All Members, in order to ensure to all of them the rights and benefits resulting from membership, shall fulfil in good faith the obligations assumed by them in accordance with the present Charter.

3. All Members shall settle their international disputes by peaceful means in such a manner that international peace and security, and justice, are not endangered.

4. All Members shall refrain in their international relations from the threat or use of force against the territorial integrity or political independence of any state, or in any other manner inconsistent with the Purposes of the United Nations.

5. All Members shall give the United Nations every assistance in

any action it takes in accordance with the present Charter, and shall refrain from giving assistance to any state against which the United Nations is taking preventive or enforcement action.

6. The Organization shall ensure that states which are not Members of the United Nations act in accordance with these Principles so far as may be necessary for the maintenance of international peace and security.

7. Nothing contained in the present Charter shall authorize the United Nations to intervene in matters which are essentially within the domestic jurisdiction of any state or shall require the Members to submit such matters to settlement under the present Charter; but this principle shall not prejudice the application of enforcement measures under Chapter VII.

Chapter II

MEMBERSHIP

. . .

Article 4

1. Membership in the United Nations is open to all . . . peace-loving states which accept the obligations contained in the present Charter and, in the judgment of the Organization, are able and willing to carry out these obligations.

2. The admission of any such state to membership in the United Nations will be effected by a decision of the General Assembly upon the recommendation of the Security Council.

Article 5

A Member of the United Nations against which preventive or enforcement action has been taken by the Security Council may be suspended from the exercise of the rights and privileges of membership by the General Assembly upon the recommendation of the Security Council. The exercise of these rights and privileges may be restored by the Security Council.

Article 6

A Member of the United Nations which has persistently violated the Principles contained in the present Charter may be expelled from the Organization by the General Assembly upon the recommendation of the Security Council.

CHAPTER III
ORGANS

Article 7

1. There are established as the principal organs of the United Nations: a General Assembly, a Security Council, an Economic and Social Council, a Trusteeship Council, an International Court of Justice, and a Secretariat.

2. Such subsidiary organs as may be found necessary may be established in accordance with the present Charter.

Article 8

The United Nations shall place no restrictions on the eligibility of men and women to participate in any capacity and under conditions of equality in its principal and subsidiary organs.

CHAPTER IV
THE GENERAL ASSEMBLY

. . .

Functions and Powers

Article 10

The General Assembly may discuss any questions or any matters within the scope of the present Charter or relating to the powers and functions of any organs provided for in the present Charter, and, except as provided in Article 12, may make recommendations to the Members of the United Nations or to the Security Council or to both on any such questions or matters.

Article 11

1. The General Assembly may consider the general principles of cooperation in the maintenance of international peace and security, including the principles governing disarmament and the regulation of armaments, and may make recommendations with regard to such principles to the Members or to the Security Council or to both.

2. The General Assembly may discuss any questions relating to the maintenance of international peace and security brought before it by any Member of the United Nations, or by the Security Council, or by a state which is not a Member of the United Nations in

accordance with Article 35, paragraph 2, and, except as provided in Article 12, may make recommendations with regard to any such questions to the state or states concerned or to the Security Council or to both. Any such question on which action is necessary shall be referred to the Security Council by the General Assembly either before or after discussion.

3. The General Assembly may call the attention of the Security Council to situations which are likely to endanger international peace and security.

4. The powers of the General Assembly set forth in this Article shall not limit the general scope of Article 10.

Article 12

1. While the Security Council is exercising in respect of any dispute or situation the functions assigned to it in the present Charter, the General Assembly shall not make any recommendation with regard to that dispute or situation unless the Security Council so requests.

2. The Secretary-General, with the consent of the Security Council, shall notify the General Assembly at each session of any matters relative to the maintenance of international peace and security which are being dealt with by the Security Council and shall similarly notify the General Assembly, or the Members of the United Nations if the General Assembly is not in session, immediately the Security Council ceases to deal with such matters.

Article 13

1. The General Assembly shall initiate studies and make recommendations for the purpose of:

a. promoting international cooperation in the political field and encouraging the progressive development of international law and its codification;

b. promoting international cooperation in the economic, social, cultural, educational, and health fields, and assisting in the realization of human rights and fundamental freedoms for all without distinction as to race, sex, language, or religion.

2. The further responsibilities, functions and powers of the General Assembly with respect to matters mentioned in paragraph 1(b) above are set forth in Chapters IX and X.

Article 14

Subject to the provisions of Article 12, the General Assembly may recommend measures for the peaceful adjustment of any situation, regardless of origin, which it deems likely to impair the general welfare or friendly relations among nations, including situations resulting from a violation of the provisions of the present Charter setting forth the Purposes and Principles of the United Nations.

Article 15

1. The General Assembly shall receive and consider annual and special reports from the Security Council; these reports shall include an account of the measures that the Security Council has decided upon or taken to maintain international peace and security.

. . .

Article 17

1. The General Assembly shall consider and approve the budget of the Organization.

2. The expenses of the Organization shall be borne by the Members as apportioned by the General Assembly.

. . .

Voting

Article 18

1. Each member of the General Assembly shall have one vote.

2. Decisions of the General Assembly on important questions shall be made by a two-thirds majority of the members present and voting. These questions shall include: recommendations with respect to the maintenance of international peace and security, the election of the non-permanent members of the Security Council, the election of the members of the Economic and Social Council, the election of members of the Trusteeship Council in accordance with paragraph 1(c) of Article 86, the admission of new Members to the United Nations, the suspension of the rights and privileges of membership, the expulsion of Members, questions relating to the operation of the trusteeship system, and budgetary questions.

3. Decisions on other questions, including the determination of additional categories of questions to be decided by a two-thirds majority, shall be made by a majority of the members present and voting.

Article 19

A Member of the United Nations which is in arrears in the payment of its financial contributions to the Organization shall have no vote in the General Assembly if the amount of its arrears equals or exceeds the amount of the contributions due from it for the preceding two full years. The General Assembly may, nevertheless, permit such a Member to vote if it is satisfied that the failure to pay is due to conditions beyond the control of the Member.

Procedure

Article 20

The General Assembly shall meet in regular annual sessions and in such special sessions as occasion may require. Special sessions shall be convoked by the Secretary-General at the request of the Security Council or of a majority of the Members of the United Nations.

. . .

Chapter V

THE SECURITY COUNCIL

Composition

Article 23

1. The Security Council shall consist of fifteen Members of the United Nations. The Republic of China, France, the Union of Soviet Socialist Republics, the United Kingdom of Great Britain and Northern Ireland, and the United States of America shall be permanent members of the Security Council. The General Assembly shall elect ten other Members of the United Nations to be non-permanent members of the Security Council, due regard being specially paid, in the first instance to the contribution of Members of the United Nations to the maintenance of international peace and security and to the other purposes of the Organization, and also to equitable geographical distribution.

2. The non-permanent members of the Security Council shall be elected for a term of two years . . . A retiring member shall not be eligible for immediate re-election.

3. Each member of the Security Council shall have one representative.

Functions and Powers

Article 24

1. In order to ensure prompt and effective action by the United Nations, its Members confer on the Security Council primary responsibility for the maintenance of international peace and security, and agree that in carrying out its duties under this responsibility the Security Council acts on their behalf.

2. In discharging these duties the Security Council shall act in accordance with the Purposes and Principles of the United Nations. The specific powers granted to the Security Council for the discharge of these duties are laid down in Chapters VI, VII, VIII, and XII.

3. The Security Council shall submit annual and, when necessary, special reports to the General Assembly for its consideration.

Article 25

The Members of the United Nations agree to accept and carry out the decisions of the Security Council in accordance with the present Charter.

Article 26

In order to promote the establishment and maintenance of international peace and security with the least diversion for armaments of the world's human and economic resources, the Security Council shall be responsible for formulating, with the assistance of the Military Staff Committee referred to in Article 47, plans to be submitted to the Members of the United Nations for the establishment of a system for the regulation of armaments.

Voting

Article 27

1. Each member of the Security Council shall have one vote.

2. Decisions of the Security Council on procedural matters shall be made by an affirmative vote of nine members.

3. Decisions of the Security Council on all other matters shall be made by an affirmative vote of nine members including the concurring votes of the permanent members; provided that, in decisions under Chapter VI, and under paragraph 3 of Article 52, a party to a dispute shall abstain from voting.

Procedure

Article 28

1. The Security Council shall be so organized as to be able to function continuously. Each member of the Security Council shall for this purpose be represented at all times at the seat of the Organization.

2. The Security Council shall hold periodic meetings at which each of its members may, if it so desires, be represented by a member of the government or by some other specially designated representative.

3. The Security Council may hold meetings at such places other than the seat of the Organization as in its judgment will best facilitate its work.

Article 29

The Security Council may establish such subsidiary organs as it deems necessary for the performance of its functions.

Article 30

The Security Council shall adopt its own rules of procedure, including the method of selecting its President.

Article 31

Any Member of the United Nations which is not a member of the Security Council may participate, without vote, in the discussion of any question brought before the Security Council whenever the latter considers that the interests of that Member are specially affected.

Article 32

Any Member of the United Nations which is not a member of the Security Council or any state which is not a Member of the United Nations, if it is a party to a dispute under consideration by the Security Council, shall be invited to participate, without vote, in the discussion relating to the dispute. The Security Council shall lay down such conditions as it deems just for the participation of a state which is not a Member of the United Nations.

Chapter VI

PACIFIC SETTLEMENT OF DISPUTES

Article 33

1. The parties to any dispute, the continuance of which is likely to endanger the maintenance of international peace and security, shall, first of all, seek a solution by negotiation, enquiry, mediation, conciliation, arbitration, judicial settlement, resort to regional agencies or arrangements, or other peaceful means of their own choice.

2. The Security Council shall, when it deems necessary, call upon the parties to settle their dispute by such means.

Article 34

The Security Council may investigate any dispute, or any situation which might lead to international friction or give rise to a dispute, in order to determine whether the continuance of the dispute or situation is likely to endanger the maintenance of international peace and security.

Article 35

1. Any Member of the United Nations may bring any dispute, or any situation of the nature referred to in Article 34, to the attention of the Security Council or of the General Assembly.

2. A state which is not a Member of the United Nations may bring to the attention of the Security Council or of the General Assembly any dispute to which it is a party if it accepts in advance, for the purposes of the dispute, the obligations of pacific settlement provided in the present Charter.

3. The proceedings of the General Assembly in respect of matters brought to its attention under this Article will be subject to the provisions of Articles 11 and 12.

Article 36

1. The Security Council may, at any stage of a dispute of the nature referred to in Article 33 or of a situation of like nature, recommend appropriate procedures or methods of adjustment.

2. The Security Council should take into consideration any procedures for the settlement of the dispute which have already been adopted by the parties.

3. In making recommendations under this Article the Security Council should also take into consideration that legal disputes should as a general rule be referred by the parties to the International Court of Justice in accordance with the provisions of the Statute of the Court.

Article 37

1. Should the parties to a dispute of the nature referred to in Article 33 fail to settle it by the means indicated in that Article, they shall refer it to the Security Council.

2. If the Security Council deems that the continuance of the dispute is in fact likely to endanger the maintenance of international peace and security, it shall decide whether to take action under Article 36 or to recommend such terms of settlement as it may consider appropriate.

Article 38

Without prejudice to the provision of Articles 33 to 37, the Security Council may, if all the parties to any dispute so request, make recommendations to the parties with a view to a pacific settlement of the dispute.

Chapter VII

ACTION WITH RESPECT TO THREATS TO THE PEACE, BREACHES OF THE PEACE, AND ACTS OF AGGRESSION

Article 39

The Security Council shall determine the existence of any threat to the peace, breach of the peace, or act of aggression and shall make recommendations, or decide what measures shall be taken in accordance with Articles 41 and 42, to maintain or restore international peace and security.

Article 40

In order to prevent an aggravation of the situation, the Security Council may, before making the recommendations or deciding upon the measures provided for in Article 39, call upon the parties concerned to comply with such provisional measures as it deems necessary or desirable. Such provisional measures shall be without prejudice to the rights, claims, or position of the parties concerned. The Security Council shall duly take account of failure to comply with such provisional measures.

Article 41

The Security Council may decide what measures not involving the use of armed force are to be employed to give effect to its decisions, and it may call upon the Members of the United Nations to apply such measures. These may include complete or partial interruption of economic relations and of rail, sea, air, postal, telegraphic, radio, and other means of communication, and the severance of diplomatic relations.

Article 42

Should the Security Council consider that measures provided for in Article 41 would be inadequate or have proved to be inadequate, it may take such action by air, sea, or land forces as may be necessary to maintain or restore international peace and security. Such action may include demonstrations, blockade, and other operations by air, sea, or land forces of Members of the United Nations.

Article 43

1. All Members of the United Nations, in order to contribute to the maintenance of international peace and security, undertake to make available to the Security Council, on its call and in accordance with a special agreement or agreements, armed forces, assistance, and facilities, including rights of passage, necessary for the purpose of maintaining international peace and security.

2. Such agreement or agreements shall govern the numbers and types of forces, their degree of readiness and general location, and the nature of the facilities and assistance to be provided.

3. The agreement or agreements shall be negotiated as soon as possible on the initiative of the Security Council. They shall be concluded between the Security Council and Members or between the Security Council and groups of Members and shall be subject to ratification by the signatory states in accordance with their respective constitutional processes.

Article 44

When the Security Council has decided to use force it shall, before calling upon a Member not represented on it to provide armed forces in fulfillment of the obligations assumed under Article 43, invite that Member, if the Member so desires, to participate in the decisions of the Security Council concerning the employment of contingents of that Member's armed forces.

Article 45

In order to enable the United Nations to take urgent military measures, Members shall hold immediately available national air-force contingents for combined international enforcement action. The strength and degree of readiness of these contingents and plans for their combined action shall be determined, within the limits laid down in the special agreement or agreements referred to in Article 43, by the Security Council with the assistance of the Military Staff Committee.

Article 46

Plans for the application of armed force shall be made by the Security Council with the assistance of the Military Staff Committee.

Article 47

1. There shall be established a Military Staff Committee to advise and assist the Security Council on all questions relating to the Security Council's military requirements for the maintenance of international peace and security, the employment and command of forces placed at its disposal, the regulation of armaments, and possible disarmament.

2. The Military Staff Committee shall consist of the Chiefs of Staff of the permanent members of the Security Council or their representatives. Any Member of the United Nations not permanently represented on the Committee shall be invited by the Committee to be associated with it when the efficient discharge of the Committee's responsibilities requires the participation of that Member in its work.

3. The Military Staff Committee shall be responsible under the Security Council for the strategic direction of any armed forces placed at the disposal of the Security Council. Questions relating to the command of such forces shall be worked out subsequently.

4. The Military Staff Committee, with the authorization of the Security Council and after consultation with appropriate regional agencies, may establish regional subcommittees.

Article 48

1. The action required to carry out the decisions of the Security Council for the maintenance of international peace and security shall be taken by all the Members of the United Nations or by some of them, as the Security Council may determine.

2. Such decisions shall be carried out by the Members of the United Nations directly and through their action in the appropriate international agencies of which they are members.

Article 49

The Members of the United Nations shall join in affording mutual assistance in carrying out the measures decided upon by the Security Council.

Article 50

If preventive or enforcement measures against any state are taken by the Security Council, any other state, whether a Member of the United Nations or not, which finds itself confronted with special economic problems arising from the carrying out of those measures shall have the right to consult the Security Council with regard to a solution of those problems.

Article 51

Nothing in the present Charter shall impair the inherent right of individual or collective self-defence if an armed attack occurs against a Member of the United Nations, until the Security Council has taken measures necessary to maintain international peace and security. Measures taken by Members in the exercise of this right of self-defense shall be immediately reported to the Security Council and shall not in any way affect the authority and responsibility of the Security Council under the present Charter to take at any time such action as it deems necessary in order to maintain or restore international peace and security.

CHAPTER VIII

REGIONAL ARRANGEMENTS

Article 52

1. Nothing in the present Charter precludes the existence of regional arrangements or agencies for dealing with such matters relating to the maintenance of international peace and security as are appropriate for regional action, provided that such arrangements or agencies and their activities are consistent with the Purposes and Principles of the United Nations.

2. The Members of the United Nations entering into such arrangements or constituting such agencies shall make every effort to achieve pacific settlement of local disputes through such regional arrangements or by such regional agencies before referring them to the Security Council.

3. The Security Council shall encourage the development of pacific settlement of local disputes through such regional arrangements or by such regional agencies either on the initiative of the states concerned or by reference from the Security Council.

4. This Article in no way impairs the application of Articles 34 and 35.

Article 53

1. The Security Council shall, where appropriate, utilize such regional arrangements or agencies for enforcement action under its authority. But no enforcement action shall be taken under regional arrangements or by regional agencies without the authorization of the Security Council, with the exception of measures against any enemy state, as defined in paragraph 2 of this Article, provided for

pursuant to Article 107 or in regional arrangements directed against renewal of aggressive policy on the part of any such state, until such time as the Organization may, on request of the Governments concerned, be charged with the responsibility for preventing further aggression by such a state.

2. The term enemy state as used in paragraph 1 of this Article applies to any state which during the Second World War has been an enemy of any signatory of the present Charter.

Article 54

The Security Council shall at all times be kept fully informed of activities undertaken or in contemplation under regional arrangements or by regional agencies for the maintenance of international peace and security.

CHAPTER IX

INTERNATIONAL ECONOMIC AND SOCIAL COOPERATION

Article 55

With a view to the creation of conditions of stability and well-being which are necessary for peaceful and friendly relations among nations based on respect for the principle of equal rights and self-determination of peoples, the United Nations shall promote:

a. higher standards of living, full employment, and conditions of economic and social progress and development;

b. solutions of international economic, social, health, and related problems; and international cultural and educational co-operation; and

c. universal respect for, and observance of, human rights and fundamental freedoms for all without distinction as to race, sex, language, or religion.

Article 56

All Members pledge themselves to take joint and separate action in cooperation with the Organization for the achievement of the purposes set forth in Article 55.

. . .

CHAPTER X

ECONOMIC AND SOCIAL COUNCIL

Article 65

The Economic and Social Council may furnish information to the Security Council and shall assist the Security Council upon its request.

. . .

CHAPTER XI

DECLARATION REGARDING NON-SELF-GOVERNING TERRITORIES

Article 73

Members of the United Nations which have or assume responsibilities for the administration of territories whose peoples have not yet attained a full measure of self-government recognize the principle that the interests of the inhabitants of these territories are paramount, and accept as a sacred trust the obligation to promote to the utmost, within the system of international peace and security established by the present Charter, the well-being of the inhabitants of these territories, and, to this end:

. . .

c. to further international peace and security;

. . .

CHAPTER XII

INTERNATIONAL TRUSTEESHIP SYSTEM

Article 76

The basic objectives of the trusteeship system, in accordance with the Purposes of the United Nations laid down in Article 1 of the present Charter, shall be:

a. to further international peace and security;

. . .

Article 77

1. The trusteeship system shall apply to such territories in the following categories as may be placed thereunder by means of trusteeship agreements:

a. territories now held under mandate;

b. territories which may be detached from enemy states as a result of the Second World War; and

c. territories voluntarily placed under the system by states responsible for their administration.

2. It will be a matter for subsequent agreement as to which territories in the foregoing categories will be brought under the trusteeship system and upon what terms.

. . .

Article 82

There may be designated, in any trusteeship agreement, a strategic area or areas which may include part or all of the trust territory to which the agreement applies, without prejudice to any special agreement or agreements made under Article 43.

Article 83

1. All functions of the United Nations relating to strategic areas, including the approval of the terms of the trusteeship agreements and of their alteration or amendment, shall be exercised by the Security Council.

. . .

3. The Security Council shall, subject to the provisions of the trusteeship agreements and without prejudice to security considerations, avail itself of the assistance of the Trusteeship Council to perform those functions of the United Nations under the trusteeship system relating to political, economic, social, and educational matters in the strategic areas.

Article 84

It shall be the duty of the administering authority to ensure that the trust territory shall play its part in the maintenance of international peace and security. To this end the administering authority may make use of volunteer forces, facilities, and assistance from the trust territory in carrying out the obligations towards the Security Council undertaken in this regard by the administering authority, as well as for local defence and the maintenance of law and order within the trust territory.

. . .

Chapter XIII

THE TRUSTEESHIP COUNCIL

Composition

Article 86

1. The Trusteeship Council shall consist of the following Members of the United Nations:

a. those Members administering trust territories;

b. such of those Members mentioned by name in Article 23 as are not administering trust territories; and

c. as many other Members elected for three-year terms by the General Assembly as may be necessary to ensure that the total number of members of the Trusteeship Council is equally divided between those Members of the United Nations which administer trust territories and those which do not.

. . .

Functions and Powers

Article 87

The General Assembly and, under its authority, the Trusteeship Council, in carrying out their functions, may:

a. consider reports submitted by the administering authority;

b. accept petitions and examine them in consultation with the administering authority;

c. provide for periodic visits to the respective trust territories at times agreed upon with the administering authority; and

d. take these and other actions in conformity with the terms of the trusteeship agreements.

Article 88

The Trusteeship Council shall formulate a questionnaire on the political, economic, social, and educational advancement of the inhabitants of each trust territory, and the administering authority for each trust territory within the competence of the General Assembly shall make an annual report to the General Assembly upon the basis of such questionnaire.

. . .

Chapter XIV

THE INTERNATIONAL COURT OF JUSTICE

Article 92

The International Court of Justice shall be the principal judicial organ of the United Nations. It shall function in accordance with the annexed Statute, which is based upon the Statute of the Permanent Court of International Justice and forms an integral part of the present Charter.

Article 93

1. All Members of the United Nations are *ipso facto* parties to the International Court of Justice.

2. A state which is not a Member of the United Nations may become a party to the Statute of the International Court of Justice on conditions to be determined in each case by the General Assembly upon the recommendation of the Security Council.

Article 94

1. Each Member of the United Nations undertakes to comply with the decision of the International Court of Justice in any case to which it is a party.

2. If any party to a case fails to perform the obligations incumbent upon it under a judgment rendered by the Court, the other party may have recourse to the Security Council, which may, if it deems necessary, make recommendations or decide upon measures to be taken to give effect to the judgment.

Article 95

Nothing in the present Charter shall prevent Members of the United Nations from entrusting the solution of their differences to other tribunals by virtue of agreements already in existence or which may be concluded in the future.

Article 96

1. The General Assembly or the Security Council may request the International Court of Justice to give an advisory opinion on any legal question.

. . .

Chapter XV
THE SECRETARIAT

Article 97

The Secretariat shall comprise a Secretary-General and such staff as the Organization may require. The Secretary-General shall be appointed by the General Assembly upon the recommendation of the Security Council. He shall be the chief administrative officer of the Organization.

Article 98

The Secretary-General shall act in that capacity in all meetings of the General Assembly, of the Security Council, of the Economic and Social Council, and of the Trusteeship Council, and shall perform such other functions as are entrusted to him by these organs. The Secretary-General shall make an annual report to the General Assembly on the work of the Organization.

Article 99

The Secretary-General may bring to the attention of the Security Council any matter which in his opinion may threaten the maintenance of international peace and security.

Article 100

1. In the performance of their duties the Secretary-General and the staff shall not seek or receive instructions from any government or from any other authority external to the Organization. They shall refrain from any action which might reflect on their position as international officials responsible only to the Organization.

2. Each Member of the United Nations undertakes to respect the exclusively international character of the responsibilities of the Secretary-General and the staff and not to seek to influence them in the discharge of their responsibilities.

Article 101

1. The staff shall be appointed by the Secretary-General under regulations established by the General Assembly.

2. Appropriate staffs shall be permanently assigned to the Economic and Social Council, the Trusteeship Council, and, as required, to other organs of the United Nations. These staffs shall form a part of the Secretariat.

3. The paramount consideration in the employment of the staff

and in the determination of the conditions of service shall be the necessity of securing the highest standards of efficiency, competence, and integrity. Due regard shall be paid to the importance of recruiting the staff on as wide a geographical basis as possible.

. . .

Chapter XVI

MISCELLANEOUS PROVISIONS

. . .

Article 103

In the event of a conflict between the obligations of the Members of the United Nations under the present Charter and their obligations under any other international agreement, their obligations under the present Charter shall prevail.

. . .

Chapter XVII

TRANSITIONAL SECURITY ARRANGEMENTS

Article 106

Pending the coming into force of such special agreements referred to in Article 43 as in the opinion of the Security Council enable it to begin the exercise of its responsibilities under Article 42, the parties to the Four-Nation Declaration, signed at Moscow, October 30, 1943, and France, shall, in accordance with the provisions of paragraph 5 of that Declaration, consult with one another and as occasion requires with other Members of the United Nations with a view to such joint action on behalf of the Organization as may be necessary for the purpose of maintaining international peace and security.

Article 107

Nothing in the present Charter shall invalidate or preclude action, in relation to any state which during the Second World War has been an enemy of any signatory to the present Charter, taken or authorized as a result of that war by the Governments having responsibility for such action.

Chapter XVIII

AMENDMENTS

Article 108

Amendments to the present Charter shall come into force for all Members of the United Nations when they have been adopted by a vote of two thirds of the members of the General Assembly and ratified in accordance with their respective constitutional processes by two thirds of the Members of the United Nations, including all the permanent members of the Security Council.

Article 109

1. A General Conference of the Members of the United Nations for the purpose of reviewing the present Charter may be held at a date and place to be fixed by a two-thirds vote of the members of the General Assembly and by a vote of any nine members of the Security Council. Each Member of the United Nations shall have one vote in the conference.

2. Any alteration of the present Charter recommended by a two-thirds vote of the conference shall take effect when ratified in accordance with their respective constitutional processes by two thirds of the Members of the United Nations including all the permanent members of the Security Council.

3. If such a conference has not been held before the tenth annual session of the General Assembly following the coming into force of the present Charter, the proposal to call such a conference shall be placed on the agenda of that session of the General Assembly, and the conference shall be held if so decided by a majority vote of the members of the General Assembly and by a vote of any seven members of the Security Council.

. . .

(b) EXTRACTS FROM THE STATUTE OF THE INTERNATIONAL COURT OF JUSTICE

Article 1

The International Court of Justice established by the Charter of the United Nations as the principal judicial organ of theUnited Nations shall be constituted and shall function in accordance with the provisions of the present Statute.

. . .

Article 2

The Court shall be composed of a body of independent judges, elected regardless of their nationality from among persons of high moral character, who possess the qualifications required in their respective countries for appointment to the highest judicial offices, or are jurisconsults of recognized competence in international law.

Article 3

1. The Court shall consist of fifteen members, no two of whom may be nationals of the same state.

. . .

Article 4

1. The members of the Court shall be elected by the General Assembly and by the Security Council from a list of persons nominated by the national groups in the Permanent Court of Arbitration, in accordance with the following provisions.

. . .

3. The conditions under which a state which is a party to the present Statute but is not a Member of the United Nations may participate in electing the members of the Court shall, in the absence of a special agreement, be laid down by the General Assembly upon recommendation of the Security Council.

. . .

Article 7

1. The Secretary-General shall prepare a list in alphabetical order of all the persons thus nominated. Save as provided in Article 12, paragraph 2, these shall be the only persons eligible.

2. The Secretary-General shall submit this list to the General Assembly and to the Security Council.

Article 8

The General Assembly and the Security Council shall proceed independently of one another to elect the members of the Court.

Article 9

At every election, the electors shall bear in mind not only that the persons to be elected should individually possess the qualifications required, but also that in the body as a whole the representation of the main forms of civilization and of the principal legal systems of the world should be assured.

Article 10

1. Those candidates who obtain an absolute majority of votes in the General Assembly and in the Security Council shall be considered as elected.

2. Any vote of the Security Council, whether for the election of judges or for the appointment of members of the conference envisaged in Article 12, shall be taken without any distinction between permanent and non-permanent members of the Security Council.

3. In the event of more than one national of the same state obtaining an absolute majority of the votes both of the General Assembly and of the Security Council, the eldest of these only shall be considered as elected.

Article 11

If, after the first meeting held for the purpose of the election, one or more seats remain to be filled, a second and, if necessary, a third meeting shall take place.

Article 12

1. If, after the third meeting, one or more seats still remain unfilled, a joint conference consisting of six members, three appointed by the General Assembly and three by the Security Council, may be formed at any time at the request of either the General Assembly or the Security Council, for the purpose of choosing by the vote of an absolute majority one name for each seat still vacant, to submit to the General Assembly and the Security Council for their respective acceptance.

2. If the joint conference is unanimously agreed upon any person who fulfills the required conditions, he may be included in its list, even though he was not included in the list of nominations referred to in Article 7.

3. If the joint conference is satisfied that it will not be successful in procuring an election, those members of the Court who have already been elected shall, within a period to be fixed by the Security Council, proceed to fill the vacant seats by selection from among those candidates who have obtained votes either in the General Assembly or in the Security Council.

4. In the event of an equality of votes among the judges, the eldest judge shall have a casting vote.

. . .

Article 35

1. The Court shall be open to the states parties to the present Statute.

2. The conditions under which the Court shall be open to other states shall, subject to the special provisions contained in treaties in force, be laid down by the Security Council, but in no case shall such conditions place the parties in a position of inequality before the Court.

3. When a state which is not a Member of the United Nations is a party to a case, the Court shall fix the amount which that party is to contribute towards the expenses of the Court. This provision shall not apply if such state is bearing a share of the expenses of the Court.

. . .

Article 41

1. The Court shall have the power to indicate, if it considers that circumstances so require, any provisional measures which ought to be taken to preserve the respective rights of either party.

2. Pending the final decision, notice of the measures suggested shall forthwith be given to the parties and to the Security Council.

. . .

Article 65

1. The Court may give an advisory opinion on any legal question at the request of whatever body may be authorized by or in accordance with the Charter of the United Nations to make such a request.

. . .

Article 69

Amendments to the present Statute shall be effected by the same procedure as is provided by the Charter of the United Nations for amendments to that Charter, subject however to any provisions which the General Assembly upon recommendation of the Security Council may adopt concerning the participation of states which are parties to the present Statute but are not Members of the United Nations.

. . .

APPENDIX 2

PROVISIONAL RULES OF PROCEDURE OF THE SECURITY COUNCIL, AS AMENDED 17 JANUARY 1974

CHAPTER I. MEETINGS

Rule 1

Meetings of the Security Council shall, with the exception of the periodic meetings referred to in rule 4, be held at the call of the President at any time he deems necessary, but the interval between meetings shall not exceed fourteen days.

Rule 2

The President shall call a meeting of the Security Council at the request of any member of the Security Council.

Rule 3

The President shall call a meeting of the Security Council if a dispute or situation is brought to the attention of the Security Council under Article 35 or under Article 11 (3) of the Charter, or if the General Assembly makes recommendations or refers any question to the Security Council under Article 11 (2), or if the Secretary-General brings to the attention of the Security Council any matter under Article 99.

Rule 4

Periodic meetings of the Security Council called for in Article 28 (2) of the Charter shall be held twice a year, at such times as the Security Council may decide.

Rule 5

Meetings of the Security Council shall normally be held at the seat of the United Nations.

Any member of the Security Council or the Secretary-General may propose that the Security Council should meet at another place. Should the Security Council accept any such proposal, it shall decide upon the place, and the period during which the Council shall meet at such place.

CHAPTER II. AGENDA

Rule 6

The Secretary-General shall immediately bring to the attention of all representatives on the Security Council all communications from States, organs of the United Nations, or the Secretary-General concerning any matter for the consideration of the Security Council in accordance with the provisions of the Charter.

Rule 7

The provisional agenda for each meeting of the Security Council shall be drawn up by the Secretary-General and approved by the President of the Security Council.

Only items which have been brought to the attention of the representatives on the Security Council in accordance with rule 6, items covered by rule 10, or matters which the Security Council has previously decided to defer, may be included in the provisional agenda.

Rule 8

The provisional agenda for a meeting shall be communicated by the Secretary-General to the representatives on the Security Council at least three days before the meeting, but in urgent circumstances it may be communicated simultaneously with the notice of the meeting.

Rule 9

The first item of the provisional agenda for each meeting of the Security Council shall be the adoption of the agenda.

Rule 10

Any item of the agenda of a meeting of the Security Council, consideration of which has not been completed at that meeting, shall, unless the Security Council otherwise decides, automatically be included in the agenda of the next meeting.

Rule 11

The Secretary-General shall communicate each week to the representatives on the Security Council a summary statement of matters of which the Security Council is seized and of the stage reached in their consideration.

Rule 12

The provisional agenda for each periodic meeting shall be circulated to the members of the Security Council at least twenty-one days before the opening of the meeting. Any subsequent change in or addition to the provisional agenda shall be brought to the notice of the members at least five days before the meeting. The Security Council may, however, in urgent circumstances, make additions to the agenda at any time during a periodic meeting.

The provisions of rule 7, paragraph 1, and of rule 9, shall apply also to periodic meetings.

CHAPTER III.

REPRESENTATION AND CREDENTIALS

Rule 13

Each member of the Security Council shall be represented at the meetings of the Security Council by an accredited representative. The credentials of a representative on the Security Council shall be communicated to the Secretary-General not less than twenty-four hours before he takes his seat on the Security Council. The credentials shall be issued either by the Head of the State or of the Government concerned or by its Minister of Foreign Affairs. The Head of Government or Minister of Foreign Affairs of each member of the Security Council shall be entitled to sit on the Security Council without submitting credentials.

Rule 14

Any Member of the United Nations not a member of the Security Council and any State not a Member of the United Nations, if invited to participate in a meeting or meetings of the Security Council, shall submit credentials for the representative appointed by it for this purpose. The credentials of such a representative shall be communicated to the Secretary-General not less than twenty-four hours before the first meeting which he is invited to attend.

Rule 15

The credentials of representatives on the Security Council and of any representive appointed in accordance with rule 14 shall be examined by the Secretary-General who shall submit a report to the Security Council for approval.

Rule 16

Pending the approval of the credentials of a representative on the Security Council in accordance with rule 15, such representative shall be seated provisionally with the same rights as other representatives.

Rule 17

Any representative on the Security Council, to whose credentials objection has been made within the Security Council, shall continue to sit with the same rights as other representatives until the Security Council has decided the matter.

CHAPTER IV. PRESIDENCY

Rule 18

The presidency of the Security Council shall be held in turn by the members of the Security Council in the English alphabetical order of their names. Each President shall hold office for one calendar month.

Rule 19

The President shall preside over the meetings of the Security Council and, under the authority of the Security Council, shall represent it in its capacity as an organ of the United Nations.

Rule 20

Whenever the President of the Security Council deems that for the proper fulfilment of the responsibilities of the presidency he should not preside over the Council during the consideration of a particular question with which the member he represents is directly connected, he shall indicate his decision to the Council. The presidential chair shall then devolve, for the purpose of the consideration of that question, on the representative of the member next in English alphabetical order, it being understood that the provisions of this rule shall apply to the representatives on the Security Council called upon successively to preside. This rule shall not affect the representative capacity of the President as stated in rule 19, or his duties under rule 7.

CHAPTER V. SECRETARIAT

Rule 21

The Secretary-General shall act in that capacity in all meetings of the Security Council. The Secretary-General may authorize a deputy to act in his place at meetings of the Security Council.

Rule 22

The Secretary-General, or his deputy acting on his behalf, may make either oral or written statements to the Security Council concerning any question under consideration by it.

Rule 23

The Secretary-General may be appointed by the Security Council, in accordance with rule 28, as rapporteur for a specified question.

Rule 24

The Secretary-General shall provide the staff required by the Security Council. This staff shall form a part of the Secretariat.

Rule 25

The Secretary-General shall give to representatives on the Security Council notice of meetings of the Security Council and of its commissions and committees.

Rule 26

The Secretary-General shall be responsible for the preparation of documents required by the Security Council and shall, except in urgent circumstances, distribute them at least forty-eight hours in advance of the meeting at which they are to be considered.

CHAPTER VI. CONDUCT OF BUSINESS

Rule 27

The President shall call upon representatives in the order in which they signify their desire to speak.

Rule 28

The Security Council may appoint a commission or committee or a rapporteur for a specified question.

Rule 29

The President may accord precedence to any rapporteur appointed by the Security Council.

The Chairman of a commission or committee, or the rapporteur appointed by the commission or committee to present its report, may be accorded precedence for the purpose of explaining the report.

Rule 30

If a representative raises a point of order, the President shall immediately state his ruling. If it is challenged, the President shall submit his ruling to the Security Council for immediate decision and it shall stand unless overruled.

Rule 31

Proposed resolutions, amendments and substantive motions shall normally be placed before the representatives in writing.

Rule 32

Principal motions and draft resolutions shall have precedence in the order of their submission.

Parts of a motion or of a draft resolution shall be voted on separately at the request of any representative, unless the original mover objects.

Rule 33

The following motions shall have precedence in the order named over all principal motions and draft resolutions relative to the subject before the meeting:

1. To suspend the meeting;
2. To adjourn the meeting;
3. To adjourn the meeting to a certain day or hour;
4. To refer any matter to a committee, to the Secretary-General or to a rapporteur;
5. To postpone discussion of the question to a certain day or indefinitely; or
6. To introduce an amendment.

Any motion for the suspension or for the simple adjournment of the meeting shall be decided without debate.

Rule 34

It shall not be necessary for any motion or draft resolution proposed by a representative on the Security Council to be seconded before being put to a vote.

Rule 35

A motion or draft resolution can at any time be withdrawn so long as no vote has been taken with respect to it.

If the motion or draft resolution has been seconded, the representative on the Security Council who has seconded it may require that it be put to the vote as his motion or draft resolution with the same right of precedence as if the original mover had not withdrawn it.

Rule 36

If two or more amendments to a motion or draft resolution are proposed, the President shall rule on the order in which they are to be voted upon. Ordinarily, the Security Council shall first vote on the amendment furthest removed in substance from the original proposal and then on the amendment next furthest removed until all amendments have been put to the vote, but when an amendment adds to or deletes from the text of a motion or draft resolution, that amendment shall be voted on first.

Rule 37

Any Member of the United Nations which is not a member of the Security Council may be invited, as the result of a decision of the Security Council to participate, without vote, in the discussion of any question brought before the Security Council when the Security Council considers that the interests of that Member are specially affected, or when a Member brings a matter to the attention of the Security Council in accordance with Article 35 (1) of the Charter.

Rule 38

Any Member of the United Nations invited in accordance with the preceding rule, or in application of Article 32 of the Charter, to participate in the discussions of the Security Council may submit proposals and draft resolutions. These proposals and draft resolutions may be put to a vote only at the request of a representative on the Security Council.

Rule 39

The Security Council may invite members of the Secretariat or other persons, whom it considers competent for the purpose, to supply it with information or to give other assistance in examining matters within its competence.

CHAPTER VIII. VOTING

Rule 40

Voting in the Security Council shall be in accordance with the relevant Articles of the Charter and of the Statute of the International Court of Justice.

CHAPTER VIII. LANGUAGES

Rule 41

Chinese, English, French, Russian and Spanish shall be both the official and the working languages of the Security Council.

Rule 42

Speeches made in any of the five languages of the Security Council shall be interpreted into the other four languages.

Rule 43

[Deleted]

Rule 44

Any representative may make a speech in a language other than the languages of the Security Council. In this case, he shall himself provide for interpretation into one of those languages. Interpretation into the other languages of the Security Council by the interpreters of the Secretariat may be based on the interpretation given in the first such language.

Rule 45

Verbatim records of meetings of the Security Council shall be drawn up in the languages of the Council.

Rule 46

All resolutions and other documents shall be published in the languages of the Security Council.

Rule 47

Documents of the Security Council shall, if the Security Council so decides, be published in any language other than the languages of the Council.

CHAPTER IX. PUBLICITY OF MEETINGS, RECORDS

Rule 48

Unless it decides otherwise, the Security Council shall meet in public. Any recommendation to the General Assembly regarding the appointment of the Secretary-General shall be discussed and decided at a private meeting.

Rule 49

Subject to the provisions of rule 51, the vertabim record of each meeting of the Security Council shall be made available to the representatives on the Security Council and to the representatives of any other States which have participated in the meeting not later than 10 a.m. of the first working day following the meeting.

Rule 50

The representatives of the States which have participated in the meeting shall, within two working days after the time indicated in rule 49, inform the Secretary-General of any corrections they wish to have made in the verbatim record.

Rule 51

The Security Council may decide that for a private meeting the record shall be made in a single copy alone. This record shall be kept by the Secretary-General. The representatives of the States which have participated in the meeting shall, within a period of ten days, inform the Secretary-General of any corrections they wish to have made in this record.

Rule 52

Corrections that have been requested shall be considered approved unless the President is of the opinion that they are sufficiently important to be submitted to the representatives on the Security Council. In the latter case, the representatives on the Security Council shall submit within two working days any comments they may wish to make. In the absence of objections in this period of time, the record shall be corrected as requested.

Rule 53

The verbatim record referred to in rule 49 or the record referred to in rule 51, in which no corrections have been requested in the period of time required by rules 50 and 51, respectively, or which has been corrected in accordance with the provisions of rule 52, shall be considered as approved. It shall be signed by the President and shall become the official record of the Security Council.

Rule 54

The official record of public meetings of the Security Council, as well as the documents annexed thereto, shall be published in the official languages as soon as possible.

Rule 55

At the close of each private meeting the Security Council shall issue a *communiqué* through the Secretary-General.

Rule 56

The representatives of the Members of the United Nations which have taken part in a private meeting shall at all times have the right to consult the record of that meeting in the office of the Secretary-General. The Security Council may at any time grant access to this record to authorized representatives of other Members of the United Nations.

Rule 57

The Secretary-General shall, once each year, submit to the Security Council a list of the records and documents which up to that time have been considered confidential. The Security Council shall decide which of these shall be made available to other Members of the United Nations, which shall be made public, and which shall continue to remain confidential.

CHAPTER X. ADMISSION OF NEW MEMBERS

Rule 58

Any State which desires to become a Member of the United Nations shall submit an application to the Secretary-General. This application shall contain a declaration made in a formal instrument that it accepts the obligations contained in the Charter.

Rule 59

The Secretary-General shall immediately place the application for membership before the representatives on the Security Council. Unless the Security Council decides otherwise, the application shall be referred by the President to a committee of the Security Council upon which each member of the Security Council shall be represented. The committee shall examine any application referred to it and report its conclusions thereon to the Council not less than thirty-five days in advance of a regular session of the General Assembly or, if a special session of the General Assembly is called, not less than fourteen days in advance of such session.

Rule 60

The Security Council shall decide whether in its judgement the applicant is a peace-loving State and is able and willing to carry out the obligations contained in the Charter and, accordingly, whether to recommend the applicant State for membership.

If the Security Council recommends the applicant State for membership, it shall forward to the General Assembly the recommendation with a complete record of the discussion.

If the Security Council does not recommend the applicant State for membership or postpones the consideration of the application, it shall submit a special report to the General Assembly with a complete record of the discussion.

In order to ensure the consideration of its recommendation at the next session of the General Assembly following the receipt of the application, the Security Council shall make its recommendation not less than twenty-five days in advance of a regular session of the General Assembly, nor less than four days in advance of a special session.

In special circumstances, the Security Council may decide to make a recommendation to the General Assembly concerning an application for membership subsequent to the expiration of the time limits set forth in the preceding paragraph.

CHAPTER XI. RELATIONS WITH OTHER UNITED NATIONS ORGANS

Rule 61

Any meeting of the Security Council held in pursuance of the Statute of the International Court of Justice for the purpose of the election of members of the Court shall continue until as many candidates as are required for all the seats to be filled have obtained in one or more ballots an absolute majority of votes.

APPENDIX

Provisional procedure for dealing with communications from private individuals and non-governmental bodies

A. A list of all communications from private individuals and non-governmental bodies relating to matters of which the Security Council is seized shall be circulated to all representatives on the Security Council.

B. A copy of any communication on the list shall be given by the Secretariat to any representative on the Security Council at his request.

APPENDIX 3

MATTERS OF WHICH THE SECURITY COUNCIL WAS SEIZED ON 1 MARCH 1974

The full titles of items 1 to 72 are given in Appendix 4 of my *Voting in the Security Council* (Indiana University Press, 1969), pp. 136–53. The date shown after each item indicates when it was first included in the agenda.

1. The Iranian question, 25 Jan. 1946
2. Special agreements under Article 43 of the Charter and the organization of the armed forces to be made available to the Security Council, 17 Jan. 1946
3. Rules of procedure of the Security Council, 17 Jan. 1946
4. Statute and rules of procedure of the Military Staff Committee, 17 Jan. 1946
5. The general regulation and reduction of armaments and information on the armed forces of the United Nations, 31 Dec. 1946 and 7 Jan. 1947
6. Appointment of a Governor for the Free Territory of Trieste, 20 June 1947
7. The Egyptian question, 17 July 1947
8. Voting procedure in the Security Council, 27 Aug. 1947
9. Reports on the strategic Trust Territory of the Pacific Islands pursuant to resolution 70 (S/1280) of the Security Council of 7 Mar. 1949
10. Admission of new Members, 28 Jan. 1946*
11. The Palestine question, 9 Dec. 1947
12. The India–Pakistan question, 6 Jan. 1948†
13. The Czechoslovak question, 17 Mar. 1948
14. The question of the Free Territory of Trieste, 4 Aug. 1948
15. The Hyderabad question, 16 Sept. 1948
16. Identical notifications dated 29 Sept. 1948 from the Governments of the French Republic, the United Kingdom, and the

* From 28 Nov. 1947 to 22 Aug. 1972, this item was entitled 'Application for membership'.

† This item was originally entitled 'The Kashmir and Jammu question' (226th meeting, 6 Jan. 1948), but was later changed to 'The India–Pakistan question' (231st meeting, 22 Jan. 1948).

United States to the Secretary-General [The situation in Berlin], 5 Oct. 1948

17. International control of atomic energy, 15 Jan. 1947, 11 June 1948, and 15 Sept. 1949*
18. Complaint of armed invasions of Taiwan (Formosa), 29 Aug. 1950
19. Complaint of bombing by air forces of the Territory of China, 31 Aug. 1950
20. Complaint of failure by the Iranian Government to comply with provisional measures indicated by the International Court of Justice in the Anglo-Iranian Oil Company Case, 1 Oct. 1951
21. Question of an appeal to States to accede to and ratify the Geneva Protocol of 1925 for the prohibition of the use of bacterial weapons, 18 June 1952
22. Question of a request for investigation of alleged bacterial warfare, 23 June 1952
23. Letter dated 29 May 1954 from the acting representative of Thailand addressed to the President of the Security Council [The Thailand question], 3 June 1954
24. Cablegram dated 19 June 1954 from the Minister of External Relations of Guatemala addressed to the President of the Security Council [The Guatemalan question], 20 June 1954
25. Letter dated 8 Sept. 1954 from the representative of the United States addressed to the President of the Security Council [Alleged attack on a US Navy aircraft], 10 Sept. 1954
26. Letter dated 28 Jan. 1955 from the representative of New Zealand addressed to the President of the Security Council concerning the question of hostilities in the area of certain islands off the coast of the mainland of China; letter dated 30 Jan. 1955 from the representative of the USSR addressed to the President of the Security Council concerning the question of acts of aggression by the United States of America against the People's Republic of China in the area of Taiwan and other islands of China, 31 Jan. 1955
27. Situation created by the unilateral action of the Egyptian Government in bringing to an end the system of international operation of the Suez Canal which was confirmed and com-

* The letter transmitting the First Report of the Atomic Energy Commission was included in the agenda of the 92nd meeting (15 Jan. 1947). The letter transmitting the Third Report of the AEC was included in the agenda of the 318th meeting (11 June 1948). A letter from the Chairman of the AEC dated 29 July 1949 was included in the agenda of the 444th meeting (15 Sept. 1949). On 11 Jan. 1952, the General Assembly dissolved the AEC and established a new Disarmament Commission.

pleted by the Suez Canal Convention of 1888 [Complaint by France and the United Kingdom against Egypt], 26 Sept. 1956

28. Actions against Egypt by some Powers, particularly France and the United Kingdom, which constitute a danger to international peace and security and are serious violations of the Charter of the United Nations [The Suez Canal], 26 Sept. 1956
29. The situation in Hungary, 28 Oct. 1956
30. Military assistance rendered by the Egyptian Government to the rebels in Algeria, 29 Oct. 1956
31. Letter dated 30 Oct. 1956 from the representative of Egypt addressed to the President of the Security Council [Complaint by Egypt against France and the United Kingdom], 30 Oct. 1956
32. Letter dated 13 Feb. 1958 from the Permanent Representative of Tunisia to the President of the Security Council concerning: 'Complaint by Tunisia in respect of an act of aggression committed against it by France on 8 Feb. 1958 at Sakiet-Sidi-Youssef', 18 Feb. 1958 (see items 36 and 48)
33. Letter dated 14 Feb. 1958 from the Permanent Representative of France to the President of the Security Council concerning: 'Situation resulting from the aid furnished by Tunisia to rebels enabling them to conduct operations from Tunisian territory directed against the integrity of French territory and the safety of persons and property of French nationals', 18 Feb. 1958 (see item 37)
34. Letter dated 20 Feb. 1958 from the representative of the Sudan addressed to the Secretary-General [complaint of massed concentrations of Egyptian troops], 21 Feb. 1958
35. Complaint of the representative of the USSR in a letter to the President of the Security Council dated 18 Apr. 1958 entitled: 'Urgent measures to put an end to flights by United States military aircraft with atomic and hydrogen bombs in the direction of the frontiers of the Soviet Union', 21 Apr. 1958
36. Letter dated 29 May 1958 from the representative of Tunisia to the President of the Security Council concerning: 'Complaint by Tunisia in respect of acts of armed aggression committed against it since 19 May 1958 by the French military forces stationed in its territory and in Algeria', 2 June 1958 (see items 32 and 48)
37. Letter dated 29 May 1958 from the representative of France to the President of the Security Council concerning: (a) 'The complaint brought by France against Tunisia on 14 February 1958'; and (b) 'The situation arising out of the disruption, by Tunisia, of the *modus vivendi* which had been established since

Feb. 1958 with regard to the stationing of French troops at certain points in Tunisian territory', 2 June 1958 (see item 33)

38. Report by the Secretary-General on the letter received from the Minister of Foreign Affairs of the Royal Government of Laos, transmitted on 4 Sept. 1959 by a note from the Permanent Mission of Laos, 7 Sept. 1949
39. Letter dated 25 Mar. 1960 from the representatives of Afghanistan, Burma, Cambodia, Ceylon [Sri Lanka], Ethiopia, Federation of Malaya [Malaysia], Ghana, Guinea, India, Indonesia, Iran, Iraq, Japan, Jordan, Laos, Lebanon, Liberia, Libya, Morocco, Nepal, Pakistan, Philippines, Saudi Arabia, Sudan, Thailand, Tunisia, Turkey, the United Arab Republic [Egypt and Syria], and Yemen addressed to the President of the Security Council [Question relating to the situation in South Africa], 30 Mar. 1960 (see item 56)
40. Cable dated 18 May 1960 from the Minister for Foreign Affairs of the USSR addressed to the President of the Security Council [The U-2 incident], 23 May 1960
41. Letter dated 23 May 1960 from the representatives of Argentina, Ceylon, Ecuador, and Tunisia addressed to the President of the Security Council [Question of relations between the great Powers], 26 May 1960
42. Letter dated 13 July 1960 from the Secretary-General of the United Nations addressed to the President of the Security Council [The Congo question], 13 July 1960
43. Letter dated 11 July 1960 from the Minister for Foreign Affairs of Cuba addressed to the President of the Security Council, 18 July 1960
44. Letter dated 31 Dec. 1960 addressed to the President of the Security Council by the Minister for External Affairs of Cuba, 4 Jan. 1961
45. Letter dated 20 Feb. 1961 from the representative of Liberia addressed to the President of the Security Council [Complaint relating to Angola] (see item 46)
46. Letter dated 26 May 1961 addressed to the President of the Security Council by the representatives of Afghanistan, Burma, Cambodia, Cameroon, Central African Republic, Ceylon, [Sri Lanka], Chad, Congo (Brazzaville), Congo (Leopoldville) [Zaire], Cyprus, Dahomey, Ethiopia, Federation of Malaysia, Gabon, Ghana, Guinea, India, Indonesia, Iran, Iraq, Ivory Coast, Japan, Jordan, Laos, Lebanon, Liberia, Libya, Madagascar, Mali, Morocco, Nepal, Nigeria, Pakistan, Philippines, Saudi Arabia, Senegal, Somalia, Sudan, Togo, Tunisia,

United Arab Republic [Egypt and Syria], Upper Volta, Yemen, and Yugoslavia [Question relating to Angola], 6 June 1961 (see item 45)

47. Complaint by Kuwait in respect of the situation arising from the threat by Iraq to the territorial independence of Kuwait, which is likely to endanger the maintenance of international peace and security; complaint by the Government of the Republic of Iraq in respect of the situation arising out of the armed threat by the United Kingdom to the independence and security of Iraq, which is likely to endanger the maintenance of international peace and security, 2 July 1961
48. Telegram dated 20 July 1961 addressed to the President of the Security Council by the Secretary of State for Foreign Affairs of the Republic of Tunisia; letter dated 20 July 1961 from the Permanent Representative of Tunisia addressed to the President of the Security Council, 21 July 1961 (see items 32 and 36)
49. Letter dated 21 Nov. 1961 from the Permanent Representative of Cuba addressed to the President of the Security Council [Question relating to the Dominican Republic], 22 Nov. 1961
50. Letter dated 18 Dec. 1961 from the Permanent Representative of Portugal addressed to the President of the Security Council [Question relating to Goa], 18 Dec. 1961
51. Letter dated 22 Oct. 1962 from the Permanent Representative of the United States of America addressed to the President of the Security Council; letter dated 22 Oct. 1962 from the Permanent Representative of Cuba addressed to the President of the Security Council; letter dated 23 Oct. 1962 from the Deputy Permanent Representative of the USSR addressed to the President of the Security Council [Question relating to the situation in the Caribbean], 23 Oct. 1962
52. Complaints by Senegal [of violation of airspace by Portuguese aircraft], 17 Apr. 1963
53. Telegram dated 5 May 1963 from the Minister for Foreign Affairs of the Republic of Haiti to the President of the Security Council [complaint of aggression and interference by the Dominican Republic], 8 May 1963
54. Reports by the Secretary-General to the Security Council concerning developments relating to Yemen, 10 June 1963
55. Question concerning the situation in Territories under Portuguese administration: letter dated 11 July 1963 addressed to the President of the Security Council by the representatives of 32 Member States, 22 July 1963
56. The question of race conflict in South Africa resulting from the

policies of *apartheid* of the Government of the Republic of South Africa, 22 July 1963 (see item 39)

57. Question concerning the situation in Southern Rhodesia, 9 Sept. 1963
58. Letter dated 26 Dec. 1963 from the Permanent Representative of Cyprus to the President of the Security Council, 27 Dec. 1963
59. Letter dated 10 Jan. 1964 from the Permanent Representative of Panama addressed to the President of the Security Council [Question relating to the Panama Canal Zone], 10 Jan. 1964
60. Letter dated 1 April 1964 from the Deputy Permanent Representative of Yemen, *Charge d'affaires a.i.*, addressed to the President of the Security Council [complaint of British acts of aggression], 2 April 1964
61. Complaint concerning acts of aggression [by US and South Viet-Namese forces] against the territory and civilian population of the Khmer Republic (Cambodia), 19 May 1964
62. Letter dated 4 Aug. 1964 from the Permanent Representative of the United States of America addressed to the President of the Security Council [Question concerning incidents in the Gulf of Tonkin], 5 Aug. 1964 [See item 69]
63. Letter dated 3 Sept. 1964 from the Permanent Representative of Malaysia addressed to the President of the Security Council [Question of relations between Malaysia and Indonesia], 9 Sept. 1964
64. Letter dated 5 Sept. 1964 from the Permanent Representative of Greece addressed to the President of the Security Council, and letter dated 8 Sept. 1964 from the Permanent Representative of Greece addressed to the President of the Security Council [Question of relations between Greece and Turkey], 11 Sept. 1964 (see item 65)
65. Letter dated 6 Sept. 1964 from the Permanent Representative of Turkey addressed to the President of the Security Council [Question of relations between Greece and Turkey], 11 Sept. 1964 (see item 64)
66. Letter dated 1 Dec. 1964 addressed to the President of the Security Council from the representatives of Afghanistan, Algeria, Burundi, Cambodia, Central African Republic, Congo (Brazzaville), Dahomey, Ethiopia, Ghana, Guinea, Indonesia, Kenya, Malawi, Mali, Mauritania, Somalia, Sudan, United Republic of Tanzania, Uganda, United Arab Republic [Egypt], Yugoslavia, and Zambia [Questions concerning the Democratic Republic of the Congo], 9 Dec. 1964 (see item 67)
67. Letter dated 9 Dec. 1964 from the Permanent Representative

of the Democratic Republic of the Congo addressed to the President of the Security Council, 9 Dec. 1964 (see item 66)

68. Letter dated 1 May 1965 from the Permanent Representative of the USSR addressed to the President of the Security Council [The situation in the Dominican Republic], 3 May 1965
69. Letter dated 21 Jan. 1966 from the Permanent Representative of the United States of America addressed to the President of the Security Council [Question concerning Viet Nam], 2 Feb. 1966 (See item 62)
70. Letter dated 2 Aug. 1966 from the Deputy Permanent Representative of the United Kingdom addressed to the President of the Security Council [Question relating to the Yemen-South Arabian Federation Frontier], 4 Aug. 1966
71. Complaints by the Democratic Republic of the Congo [of provocation and aggression by Portugal], 30 Sept. 1966 and 8 Nov. 1967
72. The situation in the Middle East, 24 May 1967
73. The situation in Namibia (South West Africa).* Letter dated 24 Jan. 1968 addressed to the President of the Security Council by the representatives of Afghanistan, Algeria, Burundi, Cambodia, Cameroon, the Central African Republic, Chad, Congo (Brazzaville), Congo (Democratic Republic of) [Zaire], Dahomey, Ethiopia, Ghana, Guinea, India, Indonesia, Iran, Iraq, Ivory Coast, Jordan, Kenya, Liberia, Libya, Madagascar, Malaysia, Mali, Mauritania, Morocco, Nepal, Niger, Nigeria, Pakistan, the Philippines, Saudi Arabia, Senegal, Sierra Leone, Singapore, Somalia, Sudan, Syria, Thailand, Togo, Turkey, Uganda, the United Arab Republic [Egypt], the United Republic of Tanzania, Upper Volta, Yemen, Yugoslavia, and Zambia; letter dated 23 Jan. 1968 addressed to the President of the Security Council by the President of the United Nations Council for Namibia [South West Africa], 25 Jan. 1968
74. Letter dated 25 Jan. 1968 from the Permanent Representative of the United States of America addressed to the President of the Security Council [complaint by the United States of America concerning the U.S.S. *Pueblo*], 26 Jan. 1968
75. Letter dated 21 May 1968 from the Permanent Representative *ad interim* of Haiti addressed to the President of the Security Council [complaint of armed aggression against Haiti], 27 May 1968

* This item was originally entitled 'The question *of* South West Africa'. Since the 1464th meeting held on 20 Mar. 1969, the item has been entitled 'The situation *in* Namibia' (my italics).

76. Letter dated 12 June 1968 from the Permanent Representative of the USSR, the United Kingdom, and the United States of America addressed to the President of the Security Council [Question relating to measures to safeguard non-nuclear-weapon States parties to the Treaty on the Non-Proliferation of Nuclear Weapons], 17 June 1968
77. Letter dated 21 Aug. 1968 from the representatives of Canada, Denmark, France, Paraguay, the United Kingdom, and the United States of America [Question concerning Czechoslovakia], 21 Aug. 1968
78. Letter dated 15 July 1969 from the Permanent Representative of Zambia addressed to the President of the Security Council [complaint of Portuguese violations of territorial integrity of Zambia], 18 July 1969
79. Letter dated 18 Aug. 1969 from the Permanent Representative of the United States of America addressed to the President of the Security Council [The question of 'micro-States'], 27 Aug. 1969
80. Letter dated 4 Dec. 1969 from the *Charge d'affaires ad interim* of Guinea addressed to the President of the Security Council [complaint of aggression by the Portuguese colonial army], 15 Dec. 1969
81. The question of Bahrain: (a) letter dated 4 May 1970 from the Permanent Representative of Iran addressed to the President of the Security Council; (b) letter dated 5 May 1970 from the Permanent Representative of the United Kingdom addressed to the President of the Security Council; (c) note by the Secretary-General, 11 May 1970
82. The question of initiating periodic meetings of the Security Council in accordance with Article 28, paragraph 2, of the Charter: letter dated 5 June 1970 from the Permanent Representative of Finland addressed to the President of the Security Council, 12 June 1970
83. The situation created by increasing incidents involving the hijacking of commercial aircraft: (a) letter dated 9 Sept. 1970 from the Permanent Representative of the United States of America addressed to the President of the Security Council; (b) letter dated 9 Sept. 1970 from the Permanent Representative of the United Kingdom addressed to the President of the Security Council, 9 Sept. 1970
84. The situation in the India/Pakistan subcontinent, 4 Dec. 1971.
85. Letter dated 3 Dec. 1971 from the Permanent Representatives of Algeria, Iraq, the Libyan Arab Republic, and the People's Democratic Republic of Yemen addressed to the President of

the Security Council [Question concerning the Island of Abu Musa, the Greater Tunb and the Lesser Tunb], 9 Dec. 1971.

86. Request of the Organization of African Unity concerning the holding of meetings of the Council in an African capital (operative paragraph 2 of General Assembly resolution 2863 (XXVI)), 11 Jan. 1972.
87. Consideration of questions relating to Africa with which the Security Council is currently seized and implementation of its relevant resolutions, 28 Jan. 1972.
88. Consideration of measures for the maintenance and strengthening of international peace and security in Latin America in conformity with the provisions and principles of the Charter, 15 March 1973.
89. Complaint by Cuba, 17 Sept. 1973.
90. Arrangements for the proposed Peace Conference on the Middle East, 15 Dec. 1973
91. Complaint by Iraq concerning incidents on the frontier with Iran, 15 Feb. 1974.

APPENDIX 4

MATTERS OF WHICH THE SECURITY COUNCIL WAS NO LONGER SEIZED ON 1 MARCH 1974

The date immediately following the item indicates when it was first included in the agenda.

A. *Matters disposed of by resolution or other decision*

Item	*Disposed of*		
	Meeting no.	*Date*	*Resolution no.*
1. Recommendation regarding the Secretary-General, 17 Jan. 1946	4	29 Jan. 1946	—
	510	12 Oct. 1950	—
	513	21 Oct. 1950	—
	515	25 Oct. 1950	—
	516	30 Oct. 1950	—
	613	13 Mar. 1953	—
	614	19 Mar. 1953	—
	617	31 Mar. 1953	—
	792	26 Sept. 1957	—
	972	3 Nov. 1961	168 (S/4972)
	1026	30 Nov. 1962	—
	1301	29 Sept. 1966	—
	1311	28 Oct. 1966	227
	1329	2 Dec. 1966	229
	1618	17 Dec. 1971	—
	1619	20 Dec. 1971	—
	1620	21 Dec. 1971	306
2. Questions relating to the International Court of Justice:			
(a) Election of members, 17 Jan. 1946	9	6 Feb. 1946	—
	369, 371	22 Oct. 1948	—
	548	29 May 1951	94 (S/2174)

	567	6 Dec. 1951	—
	618	12 Aug. 1953	99
	644	27 Nov. 1953	—
	677	28 July 1954	105 (S/3274)
	681	7 Oct. 1954	—
	733	6 Sept. 1956	117 (S/3643)
	760	11 Jan. 1957	—
	794	1 Oct. 1957	—
	840	25 Nov. 1958	130 (S/4118)
	849	29 Sept. 1959	—
	864	31 May 1960	137 (S/4331)
	909	16 Nov. 1960	—
	910	17 Nov. 1960	—
	1071, 1072	21 Oct. 1963	—
	1236	10 Aug. 1965	208
	1262	16 Nov. 1965	—
	1315	2 Nov. 1966	—
	1318	3 Nov. 1966	—
	1515	27 Oct. 1969	—
	1671	30 Oct. 1972	—
(b) Conditions under which the Court shall be open to States not parties to the Statute, 10 July 1946	76	15 Oct. 1946	9 (S/169)
(c) Applications to become parties to the Statute of the Court, 30 Oct. 1946	80	15 Nov. 1946	11 (S/191)
	432	27 July 1949	71 (S/1342)
	645	3 Dec. 1953	102 (S/3146), 103 (S/3147)
(d) Conditions under which a State which is a party to the Statute of the Court but is not a member of the United Nations may participate in electing members of the Court, 28 Sept. 1948	360	28 Sept. 1948	58 (S/969)
(e) Participation of States parties to the Statute of the Court but not members of the United Nations in amendments to the Statute, 23 Oct. 1969	1514	23 Oct. 1969	272

Item	Meeting no.	Disposal of Date	Resolution no.
3. Letter from the Acting Head of the USSR delegation to the President of the Security Council dated 21 Jan. 1946 [The Greek question], 25 Jan. 1946	10	6 Feb. 1946	—
4. Letter from the Chairman of the Council of Foreign Ministers to the Secretary-General, received 20 Dec. 1946, concerning the Statute of the Free Territory of Trieste, 7 Jan. 1947	91	10 Jan. 1947	16 (S/233, as amended)
5. Letter dated 10 Jan. 1947 from the representative of the United Kingdom addressed to the Secretary-General concerning incidents in the Corfu Channel, 20 Jan. 1947	127	9 Apr. 1947	22 (S/324)
6. Letter from the representative of the United States to the Secretary-General dated 17 Feb. 1947 and draft trusteeship agreement for the former Japanese mandated islands, 26 Feb. 1947	124	2 Apr. 1947	21 (S/318)
7. Letter dated 17 June 1949 from the representatives of Australia, Belgium, Colombia, and France to the President of the Security Council concerning travelling expenses and subsistence allowances of alternate representatives on Security Council commissions, 27 July 1949	448	27 Sept. 1949	75 (S/1401)
8. Cablegram dated 5 Aug. 1949 from the Consular Commission at Batavia to the Secretary-General requesting that the United Nations assume future costs of military observers in Indonesia, 16 Sept. 1949	449	5 Oct. 1949	76 (S/1404)
9. Letter dated 13 May 1949 from the Secretary-General to the President of the Security Council transmitting resolution 268B (III) adopted by the General Assembly at its 199th meeting on 28 Apr. 1949, containing a recommendation with regard to the appointment of a rapporteur or conciliator for a situation or dispute brought to the attention of the Security Council, 24 May 1950	472	14 May 1950	81 (S/1486)
10. Proposal to call a General Conference of the Members of the United Nations for the purpose of reviewing the Charter (Article 109 of the Charter): letter dated 12 Dec. 1955 from the Secretary-General addressed to the President of the Security Council, 16 Dec. 1955	707	16 Dec. 1955	110 (S/3504)

	Meeting no.	Date	Resolution no.
11. Letter dated 5 Sept. 1960 from the First Deputy Minister for Foreign Affairs of the USSR addressed to the President of the Security Council [Question relating to the Dominican Republic], 8 Sept. 1960	895	9 Sept. 1960	156 (S/4491)
12. Request of Panama concerning the holding of meetings of the Security Council in Panama City: letter dated 9 Jan. 1973 from the Minister of Foreign Affairs of Panama addressed to the President of the Security Council, 16 Jan. 1973.	1684 1685 1686	16 Jan. 1973 16 Jan. 1973 26 Jan. 1973	325 (S/10868), para. 23

B. *Matters disposed of by rejection of all proposals*

	Rejected	
	Meeting no.	*Date*
13. Letter from the Head of the Ukrainian SSR delegation to the President of the Security Council dated 21 Jan. 1946 [The Indonesian question], 25 Jan. 1946	18	13 Feb. 1946
14. Letter from the Heads of the Lebanese and Syrian delegations to the Secretary-General dated 4 Feb. 1946 [The Syrian and Lebanese question], 7 Feb. 1946	23	16 Feb. 1946
15. Draft resolution submitted by the representative of the USSR at the 459th meeting . . . (S/1443) [The question of Chinese representation], 12 Jan. 1950	461 462	13 Jan. 1950 17 Jan. 1950
16. Telegrams dated 13 July 1960 from the Minister for Foreign Affairs of the USSR addressed to the Secretary-General [The RB-47 incident], 22 July 1960	883	26 July 1960
17. Telegram dated 8 Sept. 1960 from the Prime Minister of the Republic of the Congo [Zaire] addressed to the Secretary-General, 9/10 Sept. 1960	896	9 Sept. 1960
18. Letter dated 8 Mar. 1962 from the Permanent Representative of Cuba [to the United Nations] addressed to the President of the Security Council [Question concerning the Punta del Este decisions], 14 Mar. 1962	998	23 Mar. 1962

C. *Matters disposed of by decision to delete item, or by rejection of proposal to retain item*

		Deleted or deletion requested	
	Meeting no.	*Date*	*Resolution no.*
19. Letter dated 8 Apr. 1946 from the representative of Poland addressed to the Secretary-General [The Spanish question], 15 Apr. 1946	79	4 Nov. 1946	10
20. Telegram from the Minister of Foreign Affairs of the Ukrainian SSR to the Secretary-General, dated 24 Aug. 1946 [Ukrainian complaint against Greece], 3 Sept. 1946	70	20 Sept. 1946	—

Item	*Deleted or deletion requested* *Meeting no.*	*Date*	*Resolution no.*
21. Letter from the Acting Chairman of the delegation of Greece to the Secretary-General dated 3 Dec. 1946 and memorandum concerning the situation in northern Greece [Greek frontier incidents], 10 Dec. 1946	202	15 Sept. 1947	34 (S/555)
22. Letter dated 30 July 1947 from the acting representative of Australia on the Security Council to the Secretary-General (S/449); letter dated 30 July 1947 from the Permanent Liaison Officer of India addressed to the President of the Security Council (S/447) [The Indonesian question]	—	24 Sept. 1973	—
23. Complaint of aggression upon the Republic of Korea: (a) Letter dated 25 June 1950 from the representative of the United States addressed to the Secretary-General transmitting a communication to the President of the Security Council concerning an act of aggression upon the Republic of Korea; (b) Cablegram dated 25 June 1950 from the United Nations Commission on Korea addressed to the Secretary-General concerning aggression upon the Republic of Korea, 25 June 1950	531	31 Jan. 1951	90S/1995)
24. Letter dated 22 May 1958 from the representative of Lebanon addressed to the President of the Security Council concerning 'Complaint by Lebanon in respect of a situation arising from the intervention of the United Arab Republic [Egypt and Syria] in the eternal affairs of Lebanon, the continuance of which is likely to endanger the maintenance of international peace and security', 27 May 1958	840	25 Nov. 1958	—
25. Letter dated 17 July 1958 from the representative of Jordan addressed to the President of the Security Council concerning 'Complaint by the Hashemite Kingdom of Jordan of interference in its domestic affairs by the United Arab Republic' [Egypt and Syria], 17 July 1958	—	10 June 1964	—
26. Letter dated 15 June 1960 from the representative of Argentina addressed to the President of the Security Council [Question relating to the case of Adolf Eichmann] 22 June 1960 '	—	12 July 1965	—

APPENDIX 5

OPINIONS BY THE UN LEGAL COUNSEL ON THE PRACTICE OF THE UNITED NATIONS REGARDING RELATIONS BETWEEN THE GENERAL ASSEMBLY AND THE SECURITY COUNCIL

(a) 10 September 1964*

(A) Relevant provisions of the Charter

1. The following provisions of the Charter are relevant to the question of simultaneous consideration by the General Assembly and the Security Council of the same agenda item:

'Article 12

'1. While the Security Council is exercising in respect of any dispute or situation the functions assigned to it in the present Charter, the General Assembly shall not make any recommendation with regard to that dispute or situation unless the Security Council so requests.

'2. The Secretary-General, with the consent of the Security Council, shall notify the General Assembly at each session of any matters relative to the maintenance of international peace and security which are being dealt with by the Security Council and shall similarly notify the General Assembly, or the Members of the United Nations if the General Assembly is not in session, immediately the Security Council ceases to deal with such matters.'

'Article 10

'The General Assembly may discuss any questions or any matters within the scope of the present Charter or relating to the powers and functions of any organs provided for in the present Charter, and, except as provided in Article 12, may make recommendations to the Members of the United Nations or to the Security Council or to both on any such questions or matters.'

'Article 11

'2. The General Assembly may discuss any questions relating to the maintenance of international peace and security brought before

* *Juridical Yearbook 1964*, pp. 228–37.

it by any Member of the United Nations, or by the Security Council, or by a state which is not a Member of the United Nations in accordance with Article 35, paragraph 2, and, except as provided in Article 12, may make recommendations with regard to any such questions to the state or states concerned or to the Security Council or to both. Any such question on which action is necessary shall be referred to the Security Council by the General Assembly either before or after discussion.'

'Article 35

'1. Any Member of the United Nations may bring any dispute, or any situation of the nature referred to in Article 34, to the attention of the Security Council or of the General Assembly.

. . .

'3. The proceedings of the General Assembly in respect of matters brought to its attention under this Article will be subject to the provisions of Articles 11 and 12.'

(B) Practice of the United Nations

2. Since the inception of the United Nations, there have been many occasions on which a question was considered both by the General Assembly and by the Security Council. These instances may be grouped for the purpose of presentation into two general categories: questions which were first considered by the Security Council and then by the General Assembly and questions which were first considered by the General Assembly and then by the Security Council.

(*i*) *Items originally submitted to the Security Council and later considered by the General Assembly*

(1) *Consideration by the General Assembly at the request of the Security Council*

3. The Security Council had requested the convening of *emergency special sessions* of the General Assembly in accordance with rule 8(*b*) of the rules of procedure of the Assembly pursuant to Assembly resolution 377 A (V) ('Uniting for Peace') in the following cases: (1) the question of the invasion of Egypt; (2) the question of Hungary; (3) the question of Lebanon and Jordan and (4) the situation in the Congo.* In each of these cases, the request was made in the form of a resolution adopted by the Security Council on the ground that the Security Council was unable to exercise its

* There was an emergency special session of the General Assembly on the Middle East in 1967 convered at the request of the Soviet Union. S.D.B.

primary responsibility for the maintenance of international peace and security because of the lack of unanimity among its permanent members.

4. The Security Council has also requested the convening of a *special session* of the General Assembly in accordance with rule 8 (*a*) of the Assembly's rules of procedure. Thus, on 1 April 1948, the Council adopted a resolution requesting the Secretary-General to convoke a special session of the General Assembly 'to consider further the question of the future government of Palestine'.[13]

5. The Security Council had also sent to the General Assembly questions which were considered at *regular sessions* of the Assembly. This was done by removal of the question from the list of matters of which the Security Council was seized. For example, on 4 November 1946, the Security Council resolved 'that the situation in Spain is to be taken off the list of matters of which the Council is seized, and that all records and documents of the case be put at the disposal of the General Assembly'. The Council requested 'the Secretary-General to notify the General Assembly of this decision.' In the case of the Greek frontier incidents question, the Security Council, on 15 September 1947, '(*a*) [*resolved*] that the dispute between Greece, on the one hand, and Albania, Yugoslavia and Bulgaria, on the other, be taken off the list of matters of which the Council is seized; and (*b*) [*requested*] that the Secretary-General be instructed to place all records and documents in the case at the disposal of the Assembly General.' In another case, a proposal to defer consideration of an item (Complaint of armed invasion of Taiwan (Formosa), 1950) before the Council when a similar item was to be discussed by the General Assembly was adopted by the Council.

6. Although no decision had been taken by the Security Council to request the General Assembly to make recommendations in respect of a matter of which the Council remained seized, the possibility for the Council to make such a request is clearly set forth in Article 12, paragraph 1, of the Charter. On several occasions, a request of this nature had been formulated in draft resolutions submitted to the Security Council. Thus, in connection with the Greek

[13] It may be noted that the Palestine question was first submitted to the General Assembly which referred certain aspects falling within the scope of Chapter VII of the Charter to the Security Council for consideration. It may also be noted that in the course of the discussion which led to the adoption of the above-mentioned resolution, the representative of Belgium expressed the following opinion: '. . . the convoking of the General Assembly would not prevent the Council from considering, in the meantime, any substantive proposals which it might be in a position to submit to the General Assembly.'

frontier incidents question considered by the Council in September 1947, a draft resolution was proposed by the United States which read as follows:

> '*The Security Council*, pursuant to Article 12 of the Charter,
>
> '(*a*) *Requests* the General Assembly to consider the dispute between Greece on the one hand and Albania, Yugoslavia and Bulgaria on the other, and to make any recommendations with regard to that dispute which it deems appropriate under the circumstances;
>
> '(*b*) *Instructs* the Secretary-General to place all records and documents in the case at the disposal of the General Assembly.'

In connexion with the question of Southern Rhodesia, considered by the Council in September 1963, a three-power draft resolution was submitted which, after inviting the United Kingdom Government to take certain actions, would request 'the General Assembly to continue its examination of the question . . . with a view to securing a just and lasting settlement.' Both draft resolutions referred to above failed of adoption owing to the negative vote of a permanent member. In the first case, the objection was made on the ground that a request to the Assembly for recommendation would mean an abdication by the Council of its primary responsibility for the maintenance of international peace and security under the Charter. In the second case, the objection was made to the effect that the question was one of domestic jurisdiction and neither the Security Council nor the General Assembly was competent to deal with it. The rejection of the draft resolutions is, therefore, not to be construed as a denial of the power of the Security Council to request the General Assembly for recommendations as provided for in Article 12, paragraph 1, of the Charter.

(2) *Consideration by the General Assembly at the request of Member States*

The Indonesian question

7. The Indonesian question as submitted by Australia in July 1947 was considered by the Security Council in the years 1947, 1948 and 1949. By a letter dated 30 and 31 March 1949, the delegations of India and Australia requested that the Indonesian question be placed on the agenda of the second part of the third regular session of the General Assembly. On 12 April, during the consideration by the General Assembly of adoption of this agenda item, the representative of the Netherlands, supported by the representatives of Norway and Belgium, invoked Article 12, paragraph 1 of the Charter as a ground for objecting to the inclusion of

the item in the agenda. They stated that the General Assembly could not make recommendations on the subject unless it was so requested by the Security Council and that a discussion in the General Assembly could in no way lead to any conclusion. On the other hand, the representative of Iraq, while recognizing the existence of procedural difficulties, considered that as long as paragraph 2 of Article 11 of the Charter remained in effect, the General Assembly had a right to discuss any question and any dispute which was before the Security Council.[14] After the General Assembly had voted in favour of inclusion of the item on its agenda, a resolution was adopted to defer further consideration of the item to the fourth regular session of the Assembly (resolution 274 (III)).

8. At the Assembly's fourth session, two draft resolutions were submitted in the *ad hoc* Political Committee. The first draft resolution provided that the General Assembly should 'welcome' the announcement that an agreement had been reached at the Round-Table Conference, 'commend' the parties concerned and the United Nations Commission for Indonesia for their contributions thereto and 'welcome' the forthcoming establishment of the Republic of the United States of Indonesia as an independent sovereign State. The second draft resolution contained provisions for the withdrawal of the Netherlands forces, the establishment of a United Nations commission to observe the implementation of such measures and to investigate the activities of the Netherlands authorities, as well as instructions to the commission regarding its work. During the discussion, the Chairman drew the attention of the Committee to the provisions of Article 12, paragraph 1, of the Charter. Pointing out that the Security Council was still seized of the question, he stated that, before putting each of the draft resolutions to the vote, he would ask the Committee to pronounce itself on whether its terms constituted a recommendation within the meaning of Article 12, paragraph 1. The *ad hoc* Political Committee decided by 42 votes to one with 6 abstentions, that the first draft resolution did not constitute a recommendation within the meaning of Article 12,

[14] In this connection, the representative of Iraq stated at the 190th plenary meeting that 'The right of the General Assembly to discuss any situation or dispute already before the Security Council had been thoroughly considered at the San Francisco Conference. Some delegations had thought that the General Assembly should have the right to discuss questions of any kind, even if they were before the Security Council, and to make recommendations with regard to them. Other delegations had opposed the granting of such a right to the General Assembly. A compromise had finally been reached whereby the General Assembly could consider a question which was on the agenda of the Security Council but could not make recommendations upon it.'

paragraph 1, and by 42 votes to 5 with 4 abstentions, that the second draft resolution did constitute a recommendation. The first draft resolution was then adopted and the second rejected.[15]

The Tunisian question

9. On 20 July 1961, Tunisia requested a meeting of the Security Council as a matter of extreme urgency to consider its complaint against France 'for acts of aggression infringing the sovereignty and security of Tunisia and threatening international peace and security.' On 22 July, the Council adopted a resolution which (1) called for an immediate cease-fire and a return of all armed forces to their original position and (2) decided to continue the debate. On 29 July, three draft resolutions dealing with implementation of the earlier resolution were rejected by the Council.

10. On 7 August, a number of delegations requested the convening of a special session of the General Assembly 'to consider the grave situation in Tunisia obtaining since 19 July 1961, in view of the failure of the Security Council to take appropriate action'. On the receipt of the concurrence of a majority of the Members on 10 August, the Secretary-General summoned, in accordance with rule 8 (*a*) of the Assembly's rules of procedure, the third special session of the General Assembly to meet on 21 August. In its resolution 1622 (S-III) adopted on 25 August, the Assembly, while noting that the Security Council had failed to take further appropriate action, reafirmed the Security Council's interim resolution, urged the Government of France to implement fully the provisions of the operative paragraph I of that resolution, recognized the sovereign right of Tunisia to call for the withdrawal of all French armed forces present on its territory without its consent, and called upon the Governments of France and Tunisia to enter into immediate negotiations to devise peaceful and agreed measures for the withdrawal of French armed forces from Tunisian territory.

The situation in Angola

11. The question of Angola was first submitted to the Security Council in February 1961. On 15 March, the Council failed to

[15] A similar situation arose at the first emergency special session of the General Assembly in connexion with two draft resolutions, submitted by the United States. Objection to those draft resolutions were raised on the ground that the first draft resolution which dealt with the Palestine question in general and the second which dealt with the Suez Canal question were matters of which the Security Council was actually seized. The emergency session had been convened to consider the situation arisen from the invasion of Egypt and not another question. The two draft resolution were subsequently withdrawn.

adopt a draft resolution which would call upon Portugal to implement General Assembly resolution 1514 (XV) (containing the declaration on ending colonialism) and propose to establish a sub-committee to examine the question and report to the Council. On 20 March, 39 delegations requested the inclusion of the question in the Assembly's agenda. Opposition to consideration of the question by the Assembly was based on Article 2, paragraph 7, of the Charter. During the discussion, a number of delegations proposing the item stated that because of the failure of the Security Council to take action, it had become necessary to refer the question to the General Assembly, which should take immediate measures to bring about a solution of the problem. A draft resolution identical in terms with that submitted to the Security Council, except that the proposed sub-committee would examine statements before the Assembly (rather than the Council) and report to the Assembly, was adopted as resolution 1603 (XV) on 20 April 1961.

(*ii*) *Items submitted to the General Assembly and later also considered by the Security Council*

(1) *By decision of the General Assembly*

12. The Palestine question was originally submitted to the General Assembly. In its resolution 181 (II), the Assembly recommended to Members the adoption and implementation of a plan of partition with economic union and *requested the Security Council* to take the necessary measures provided for in the plan and to consider, if circumstances during the transitional period required such consideration, whether the situation in Palestine constituted a threat to the peace. Since then the Palestine question had continued to be on the agenda of both the General Assembly and the Security Council, with the latter dealing generally with security and military aspects of the question and the former with political, economic and social aspects.

(2) *At the request of Member States*

13. Only in one case had the Security Council rejected the request by a Member State for inclusion in its agenda of an item which was before the General Assembly and in respect of which arguments based on Article 12, paragraph 1, of the Charter were advanced. This was the case of a USSR request dated 5 November 1956 for consideration by the Council of an item entitled 'Non-compliance by the United Kingdom, France and Israel with the decision of the emergency special session of the General Assembly of the United Nations of 2 November 1956 and immediate steps to halt the agression of the aforesaid States against Egypt.' On the one hand it was

argued that just as the General Assembly could not consider a question of which the Security Council was seized, so the Security Council could not logically consider a question pending before the General Assembly, particularly one referred to the Assembly by the Council itself. On the other hand it was contended that the fact that the General Assembly was taking action on a question did not relieve the Security Council of the obligation to act if the circumstances demanded it. The USSR request was rejected by 3 votes in favour, 4 against with 4 abstentions.

14. In the more recent cases dealt with below, whether the questions were originally submitted to the General Assembly or the Security Council, concurrent consideration by the two organs of those questions took place and in most cases both organs adopted substantive resolutions without reference to Article 12, paragraph 1, of the Charter.

The situation in the Congo, 1960–1961

15. At its fourth emergency special session convened at the request of the Security Council (resolution adopted on 16/17 September 1960) to consider the situation in the Congo, the General Assembly adopted, on 20 September 1960, resolution 1474 (ES-IV) which took note of the resolutions previously adopted by the Security Council and requested Member States to take certain actions. By a letter dated 16 September 1960, the USSR requested the inclusion of the Congo question as an additional item in the agenda of the fifteenth regular session of the General Assembly. On 28 September, the General Committee decided to include the item in the agenda of the Assembly. On 6 December 1960, the USSR proposed that the question of the situation in the Congo and the steps to be taken on the matter should be examined at the earliest possible date by the Security Council and the General Assembly. The Council met from 7 to 14 December but failed to adopt three draft resolutions before it. On 16 December, the General Assembly resumed consideration of the situation in the Congo and had before it two draft resolutions (one submitted by 7 Afro-Asian States and Yugoslavia, and the other by the United States and the United Kingdom), both containing provisions requiring specific action. The two draft resolutions were rejected by vote, but Article 12, paragraph 1, of the Charter was not referred to during the discussion. On 20 December, the Assembly adopted resolution 1592 (XV) to keep the item on the agenda of its resumed fifteenth session.

16. The Security Council met again from 12 to 14 January and from 1 to 21 February 1961 to consider the Congo question at the

request of the USSR. These meetings resulted in the adoption by the Council, on 21 February, of a resolution dealing with the situation. Consideration of the Congo question by the General Assembly at its resumed fifteenth session resulted in the adoption, on 15 April 1961, of resolutions 1599 (XV) calling upon States to take certain action and 'deciding' on the complete withdrawal and evacuation of military personnel and political advisers not under the United Nations Command, 1600 (XV) establishing a Commission of Conciliation and 1601 (XV) establishing a Commission of Investigation. At no time was Article 12, paragraph 1, of the Charter invoked as a limitation of the competence of the Assembly to make recommendations.

The situation in Angola, 1961–1962

17. After the General Assembly adopted on 20 April 1961 resolution 1603 (XV) to establish a sub-committee (*see* paragraph 11 above), a group of States, by a letter dated 26 May 1961, requested consideration by the Security Council of the Angolan question. On 9 June, the Council adopted a resolution reaffirming the Assembly resolution, calling upon Portugal to desist from repressive measures and requesting the sub-committee to report both to the Security Council and to the Assembly.

18. By a letter dated 19 July 1961 addressed to the Secretary-General, a group of States considered the situation in Angola as endangering international peace and security and reserved the right to ask for 'effective remedial action to be taken either by the Security Council or by the General Assembly.' The item entitled 'The situation in Angola: report of the Sub-committee established by General Assembly resolution 1603 (XV)' was placed on the provisional agenda of the sixteenth session of the Assembly. Portugal objected to the inclusion of this agenda item on ground of Article 2, paragraph 7, of the Charter. On 30 January 1962, the Assembly adopted resolution 1742 (XVI) by which it decided to continue the Sub-Committee, requested Member States to take certain actions and recommended 'the Security Council, in the light of the Council's resolution of 9 June 1961 and of the present resolution, to keep the matter under constant review.'

The apartheid *question, 1960–1963*

19. Beginning with its twelfth session, the General Assembly has adopted at each regular session a resolution on the question of race conflict in South Africa resulting from the policies of *apartheid* of the Government of South Africa. Resolution 1375 (XIV) on this ques-

tion was adopted by the Assembly on 17 November 1959. On 25 March 1960, 29 Asian-African States requested an urgent meeting of the Security Council to consider the situation arising out of the large-scale killings of unarmed and peaceful demonstrators against racial discrimination and segregation in the Union of South Africa. They considered that the situation endangered international peace and security. The question was taken up by the Council on 30 March. On 1 April, the Council adopted a resolution calling upon the Union Government to initiate measures to bring about racial harmony and to abandon its policies of *apartheid* and racial discrimination. Subsequently, the Assembly adopted the following resolutions on the *apartheid* question: 1598 (XV) of 13 April 1961, 1663 (XVI) of 28 November 1961, and 1761 (XVII) of 6 November 1962. In the last-mentioned resolution, the Assembly decided to establish a Special Committee on *apartheid*, invited Member States to inform the General Assembly at its eighteenth session regarding actions taken, separately or collectively, in dissuading the Government of South Africa from pursuing its policies of *apartheid*, and requested 'the Security Council to take appropriate measures, including sanctions, to secure South Africa's compliance with the resolutions of the General Assembly and of the Security Council on this subject and, if necessary, to consider action under Article 6 of the Charter.'

20. On 11 July 1963, 32 African States requested a meeting of the Security Council to consider the explosive situation in South Africa which constituted a serious threat to international peace and security. Meanwhile, the Special Committee on *apartheid* had submitted its reports both to the General Assembly and to the Security Council. On 7 August, the Council adopted a resolution calling upon the Government of South Africa to abandon its policies of *apartheid* and to liberate prisoners, calling upon all States to cease forthwith the sale and shipment of arms and ammunition of all types and requesting the Secretary-General to keep the situation in South Africa under observation and to report to the Security Council by 30 October 1963.

21. In accordance with Assembly resolution 1761 (XVII) (*see* paragraph 19 above), the item 'The policies of *apartheid* of the Government of the Republic of South Africa: reports of the Special Committee . . . and replies by Member States under General Assembly resolution 1761 (XVII)' was included in the agenda of the Assembly's eighteenth session. On 11 October 1963, the Assembly adopted resolution 1881 (XVIII) requesting once more the Government of South Africa to release political prisoners, requesting all

Member States to make all necessary efforts to ensure compliance by the Government of South Africa with the Assembly's request, and requesting the Secretary-General 'to report to the General Assembly and the Security Council, as soon as possible during the eighteenth session', on the implementation of the resolution.

22. On 23 October, 32 States requested a meeting of the Security Council to consider the report submitted by the Secretary-General pursuant to Council resolution of 7 August. On 4 December, the Council adopted a resolution which reaffirmed in essence the provisions of its previous resolution and requested the Secretary-General to establish a group of experts to examine methods of resolving the situation.

23. Meanwhile, a report of the Secretary-General pursuant to Assembly resolution 1881 (XVIII) of 11 October (*see* paragraph 21 above) was circulated to the General Assembly on 19 November. After consideration, the Assembly adopted, on 16 December 1963, resolution 1978 (XVIII) appealing again to all States to take appropriate measures and requesting the Special Committee to continue its work and submit reports to the General Assembly and to the Security Council whenever appropriate. In the same resolution the Assembly further requested the Secretary-General to provide relief and assistance, through appropriate international agencies, to the families of all persons persecuted by the Government of South Africa and to report thereon to the Assembly at its nineteenth session.

24. In the course of the practically simultaneous consideration of the *apartheid* question in the Security Council and in the General Assembly, no reference was made to Article 12, paragraph 1 of the Charter.

The question relating to Territories under Portuguese Administration, 1962–1963

25. By resolution 1699 (XVI) of 19 December 1961, the General Assembly established a Special Committee on Territories under Portuguese Administration to report on the question. In its resolution 1807 (XVII) of 14 December 1962, the Assembly, noting the opinion of the Special Committee concerning the implications of the supply of military equipment to the Portuguese Government, urged Portugal to give effect to the recommendations of the Special Committee, requested the Special Committee on the Situation with regard to the Implementation of the Declaration on the Granting of Independence to Colonial Countries and Peoples to examine the situation, called upon Member States to use their influence to induce Portugal to carry out its obligations under Chapter XI of the

Charter, requested all States to refrain from offering Portugal assistance and to prevent the sale and supply of arms and military equipment to the Portuguese Government, and requested 'the Security Council, in case the Portuguese Government should refuse to comply with the present resolution and previous General Assembly resolutions on this question, to take all appropriate measures to secure the compliance of Portugal with its obligations as a Member State.'

26. On 4 April 1963, the Special Committee on the Situation with regard to the Implementation of the Declaration on the Granting of Independence to Colonial Countries and Peoples adopted a resolution drawing the immediate attention of the Security Council to the situation in the Territories under Portuguese administration, with a view to the Council taking appropriate measures, including sanctions, to secure the compliance by Portugal of the relevant resolutions of the General Assembly and of the Security Council. The text of this resolution and the report of the Special Committee were transmitted to the Council.

27. On 11 July 1963, the President of the Security Council received a request from 32 African States to convene a meeting of the Council. On 31 July, the Council adopted a resolution by which it called upon Portugal to take certain action, requested all States to prevent sale and supply of arms and military equipment to the Portuguese Government and requested the Secretary-General to report to the Country by 31 October.

28. On 3 December, the General Assembly adopted resolution 1913 (XVIII) by which the Assembly, recalling the resolutions previously adopted by the Assembly and the Council on the question and in particular the provisions of Council resolution of 31 July, and noting with regret and concern the continued refusal of the Portuguese Government to implement those resolutions, requested 'the Security Council to consider immediately the question of Territories under Portuguese administration and to adopt necessary measures to give effect to its own decisions, particularly those contained in the resolution of 31 July 1963' and decided to maintain the question on the agenda of its eighteenth session.

29. Prior to the adoption by the General Assembly of resolution 1913 (XVIII), 29 African States requested the convening of the Security Council to consider the report of the Secretary-General submitted in pursuance of Council resolution of 31 July 1963. The Council began consideration of the question on 6 December. On 11 December, the Council adopted a resolution which, *inter alia*, called upon all States to comply with Council resolution of 31 July

and requested the Secretary-General to continue his efforts and report to the Council not later than 1 June 1964.

30. During the discussion of the question in the Assembly and the Council the provisions of Article 12, paragraph 1, of the Charter were not mentioned. Objection to the competence of the two organs to deal with the question was raised by Portugal on ground of Article 2, paragraph 7.

The question of Southern Rhodesia, 1962–1963

31. By resolution 1755 (XVII) of 12 October 1962, the General Assembly urged the Government of the United Kingdom to take measures to secure the release of political prisoners and to lift the ban on the Zimbabwe African Peoples Union. In its resolution 1760 (XVII) of 31 October, the Assembly, *inter alia,* requested the Government of the United Kingdom to take certain measures including the convening of a constitutional conference on Southern Rhodesia, requested the Acting Secretary-General to lend his good offices to promote conciliation and decided to keep the question on the agenda of its seventeenth session.

32. On 2 and 30 August 1963, requests were made by a number of African States for a meeting of the Security Council to consider the question of Southern Rhodesia. The Council met from 9 to 13 September but failed to adopt a draft resolution submitted by Ghana, Morocco and the Philippines, owing to the negative vote of a permanent member.

33. On 18 July 1963, a group of States requested the inclusion of the question of Southern Rhodesia in the agenda of the eighteenth session of the General Assembly. After consideration of the question, the Assembly adopted two resolutions. By resolution 1883 (XVIII) of 14 October, the Assembly invited the Government of the United Kingdom not to take certain actions relating to the status of Southern Rhodesia, on the one hand, and to put into effect the previous Assembly resolutions concerning the question, on the other. By resolution 1889 (XVIII) of 6 November, the Assembly, *inter alia,* invited once more the United Kingdom to hold a constitutional conference, urged all Member States to use their influence with a view to ensuring the realization of the legitimate aspirations of the people of Southern Rhodesia, requested the Secretary General to continue to use his good offices and decided to keep the question on the agenda of its eighteenth session.

(C) Conclusions

34. Without a detailed legal analysis being undertaken, the following brief observations may be made on the basis of the text

of the Charter provisions and of the survey of the past practice of the General Assembly and the Security Council as summarized in this note.

(*i*) A request by the Government of a Member State to have a question of which the Security Council is seized placed on the provisional agenda or the supplementary list of items for a regular session of the General Assembly would have to be complied with by the Secretary-General. The General Assembly itself, acting on the basis of a recommendation by the General Committee, would decide whether it wishes to include the item in the agenda of the session.

(*ii*) In the event the Security Council removes the question from the list of matters of which is seized or in the event the Security Council specifically requests the General Assembly to consider the question, the Assembly could perform in regard to that question its functions under the Charter without any special limitations as to the nature and scope of its recommendations.

(*iii*) Even if the Security Council remains seized of the question, Article 12 of the Charter would not bar the General Assembly from considering and discussing the question as it is only 'recommendations' which are prohibited by the Article.

(*iv*) The above summary of the practice contains instances in which the General Assembly recognized the distinction for purposes of Article 12 between 'recommendations' and resolutions which were not recommendatory. In the latter category, for example, were resolutions welcoming steps taken by the parties to the dispute and commending Member States or United Nations organs for their contributions to the settlement.

(*v*) The most interesting feature of the practice is that the General Assembly, beginning in 1960, adopted several resolutions clearly containing recommendations in cases of which the Security Council was then seized and could reasonably be regarded as exercising its functions in regard to that question. Six such cases have been found in which the General Assembly appears to have departed from the actual text of Article 12. In none of these cases, however, did a Member object to the recommendation on the ground of Article 12.

(*vi*) Although Article 12 has not been invoked in these cases, it would be difficult to maintain that it is legally no longer in effect. A Member may therefore argue in the General Assembly that Article 12 forbids the adoption of a recommendation in the case, and the point, if pressed, may have to be decided by the General Assembly.

(*vii*) Finally, it is to be noted that Governments may argue that the phrase 'recommendation with regard to that dispute or situation', used in Article 12, is not applicable to certain types of resolutions, such as a confirmation by the General Assembly of a Security Council resolution, or a resolution reminding Member States to comply with certain Charter principles. There may, of course, be disagreement as to whether such resolutions contain implied recommendations and, if raised, this issue would have to be determined by the General Assembly, either by explicit decision or implicity in its action on the proposed resolution.

(b) 12 December 1968*

The Legal Counsel replied to [a] question put by the representative of Peru who had asked whether the adoption of measures of the kind provided for in operative paragraph 7 of . . . draft resolution [A/C.3/L.1637/Rev. 2] [by which the General Assembly would call upon all States to sever all relations with South Africa, Portugal and the illegal minority régime in Southern Rhodesia and to scrupulously refrain from giving any military or economic assistance to these régimes] was within the competence of the Third Committee. Article 10 of the United Nations Charter stated that the General Assembly might discuss any question or any matters within the scope of the Charter or relating to the powers and functions of any organs provided for in the Charter, and, except as provided in Article 12, might make recommendations to the Members of the United Nations or to the Security Council. Article 12 provided that, while the Security Council was exercising in respect of any dispute or situation the functions assigned to it in the Charter, the General Assembly should not make any recommendation with regard to that dispute or situation unless the Security Council so requested. The matters relating to South Africa, Southern Rhodesia and the Territories under Portuguese rule were on the agenda of the Security Council and, in principle, the General Assembly could not make any recommendations. However, the Assembly had interpreted the words 'is exercising' as meaning 'is exercising at this moment'; consequently, it had made recommendations on other matters which the Security Council was also considering. Thus, in accordance with that practice followed by the General Assembly, there were no obstacles to the recommending of measures of the kind provided for in draft resolution A/C.3/L.1637/Rev. 2.

* *Juridical Yearbook 1968*, p. 185 (footnote omitted).

SELECT BIBLIOGRAPHY

BAILEY, SYDNEY D., *Voting in the Security Council*, Bloomington, Ind., and London, Indiana University Press, 1970.

BENNETT, A. LEROY, 'The Rejuvenation of the Security Council—Evidence and Reality', *Midwest Journal of Political Science*, vol. 9 (1965), pp. 361–75.

BOYD, ANDREW, *Fifteen Men on a Powder Keg*, London, Methuen, 1971.

CHAI, F. Y., *Consultation and Consensus in the Security Council*, New York and Geneva, UN Institute for Training and Research, 1971.

CLAUDE, INIS L., 'The Security Council' in *The Evolution of International Organization*, edited by Evan Luard, London, Thames and Hudson, 1966.

CONFORTI, BENEDETTO, 'The Legal Effect of Non-Compliance with Rules of Procedure in the U.N. General Assembly and Security Council', *American Journal of International Law*, vol. 63 (1969), pp. 479–89.

GILMOUR, DAVID R., 'Article 2(7) of the United Nations Charter and the Practice of the Permanent Members of the Security Council', *Australian Yearbook of International Law*, London, Butterworth, 1970, pp. 153–210.

GOODRICH, LELAND M., 'The UN Security Council', *International Organization*, vol. xii, no. 3 (1958), pp. 273–87.

GREEN, L. C., 'Representation in the Security Council—A Survey', *Indian Year Book of International Affairs*, University of Madras, 1962, pp. 48–75.

HIGGINS, ROSALYN, 'The Place of International Law in the Settlement of Disputes in the Security Council', *American Journal of International Law*, vol. 64, no. 1 (1970), pp. 1–18.

JIMÉNEZ DE ARÉCHAGA, EDUARDO, *Voting and the Handling of Disputes in the Security Council*, New York, Carnegie Endowment for International Peace, 1950.

KAHNG, TAE JIN, *Law, Politics, and the Security Council*, The Hague, Nijhoff, 1964.

KELSEN, HANS, 'Organization and Procedure of the Security Council of the United Nations', *Harvard Law Review*, vol. 59 (1946), pp. 1087–1121.

LALL, ARTHUR, *The Security Council in a Universal United Nations*, New York, Carnegie Endowment for International Peace, 1971.

MURTI, B. S. N., 'Periodic Meetings of the Security Council: Article 28, paragraph 2 of the UN Charter', *Indian Journal of International Law*, vol. 10 (1970), pp. 283–99.

PADELFORD, NORMAN J., 'Politics and Change in the Security Council', *International Organization*, vol. xiv, no. 3 (1960), pp. 38–1401.

PETERSEN, KEITH S., 'The Business of the United Nations Security Council: History (1946–1963) and Prospects', *Journal of Politics*, vol. 27 (1965), pp. 818–38.

PRANDLER, ÁRPÁD, 'Rules of Procedure of the Security Council' *Questions of International Law*, Budapest, Hungarian Branch of the International Law Association, 1971, pp. 147–78.

RUSSELL, RUTH B., assisted by Muther, Jeanette E., *A History of the United Nations Charter*, Washington, D.C., Brookings: London, Faber, 1958.

SCHACHTER, OSCAR, 'The Quasi-Judicial Role of the Security Council and the General Assembly', *American Journal of International Law*, vol. 58, no. 4 (1964), pp. 959–66.

TEJA, JASKARAN S., 'Expansion of the Security Council and its Consensus Procedure', *Nederlands Tijdschrift voor International Recht*, vol. 16, no. 4 (1969), pp. 349–63.

WERNERS, S. E., *The Presiding Officers of the United Nations*, Haarlem, Bohn, 1967.

ABBREVIATIONS

Add.	Addendum (addition of text to the main document)
AEC	Atomic Energy Commission
AECOR	Official Records of the Atomic Energy Commission
Corr.	Corrigendum (to correct errors, revise wording, or reorganize text, whether for substantive or technical reasons)
ECOSOC	Economic and Social Council
FRUS	Foreign Relations of the United States
G.A. res.	General Assembly resolution
GAOR	General Assembly Official Records
ICJ	International Court of Justice
PC	Document of the Preparatory Commission of the United Nations
PC/EX	Document of the Executive Committee of the Preparatory Commission
PV.	Provisional Verbatim Record (Procès-Verbal) (mimeo.)
Rev.	Revision (new text superseding and replacing a previously issued document)
S.C. res.	Security Council resolution
SCOR	Security Council Official Records
UNCIO	Documents of the United Nations Conference on International Organization, 1945
UNEF	UN Emergency Force
UNTS	UN Treaty Series

REFERENCES
for pp. 1–16

CHAPTER 1

1. PC/20, 23 Dec. 1945, pp. 24–7; SCOR, 1st year, 1st series, 1st meeting (17 Jan. 1946), pp. 1–2.
2. GAOR, 27th session, Supplement no. 1A, A/8701/Add. 1, pp. 1–2.
3. Speech on 28 Oct. 1969, printed in *UN Monthly Chronicle*, vol. vi, no. 10 (Nov. 1969), p. 85.
4. Árpád Prandler, 'Rules of Procedure of the Security Council', *Questions of International Law 1970*, Budapest, Hungarian Branch of the International Law Association, 1971, p. 177.
5. Hearings before the Committee on Foreign Relations, United States Senate: submission of the Vietnam Conflict to the United Nations, 90th Congress, first session, 26 Oct. 1967, p. 50.
6. Robert E. Riggs, 'Overselling the UN Charter—Fact and Myth', *International Organization*, vol. xiv, no. 2 (Spring 1960), pp. 277–90.
7. *The Papers of Adlai E. Stevenson, vol. ii, 1941–1948*, edited by Walter Johnson and Carol Evans, Boston, Mass., Little Brown, 1973 (hereafter cited as 'Stevenson'), pp. 306–8.
8. *Foreign Relations of the United States, 1946*, vol. i, Washington, D.C., Government Printing Office, 1972, pp. 314, 342, 352; ibid., *1947*, vol. i, 1973, p. 69; Paul-Henri Spaak, *The Continuing Battle*, translated by Ray Steding and Henry Fox, London, Weidenfeld and Nicolson, 1971, p. 109.
9. SCOR, 1st year, 1st series, 9th meeting (6 Feb. 1946), p. 148.
10. *The General Assembly of the United Nations*, second edition, 1964, New York, Praeger: London, Pall Mall, p. 111.
11. SCOR, 1st year, 1st series, 9th meeting (6 Feb. 1946), p. 143.
12. Prandler, p. 147.
13. A/9128, 25 Oct. 1973 (mimeo.), pp. 3–4.
14. See Benedetto Conforti, 'The legal effect of non-compliance with the Rules of Procedure of the UN General Assembly and Security Council', *American Journal of International Law*, vol. 63 (July 1969), pp. 479–89.
15. PC/EX/113/Rev. 1, 12 Nov. 1945, p. 45; see also SCOR, 1st year, 1st series, Supplement no. 2, p. 42, S/88.
16. PC/20, 23 Dec. 1945, pp. 25–7.
17. Ibid., pp. 125–9.
18. SCOR, 1st year, 1st series, 1st meeting (17 Jan. 1946), p. 11.
19. Ibid., Supplement no. 2, pp. 1–8, S/6.
20. Ibid., pp. 8–15.
21. Ibid., 31st meeting (9 Apr. 1946), pp. 100–18.
22. FRUS, 1946, vol. 1, pp. 251–92; SCOR, 1st year, 1st series, Supplement no. 2, p. 23, S/57.
23. Ibid., 41st meeting (16 May 1946), pp. 253–69; 42nd meeting (17 May 1946), pp. 270–8; 44th meeting (6 June 1946), p. 311; 48th meeting (24 June 1946), p. 382.
24. SCOR, 2nd year, 138th meeting (4 June 1947), pp. 949–52; 222nd meeting

(9 Dec. 1947), p. 2771; S.C. res. 26 (S/368), 4 June 1947; S.C. res. 37 (S/612), 9 Dec. 1947.

25. SCOR, 5th year, 462nd meeting (17 Jan. 1950), pp. 10–13; 468th meeting (28 Feb. 1950), pp. 9–11.
26. S.C. res. 263 (S/8976), 24 Jan. 1969; 345 (S/11192), 17 Jan. 1974.

CHAPTER 2

1. A/AC. 154/23, 4 March 1974 (mimeo.), para. 21.
2. A/AC. 18/SC.4 (mimeo), 18 May 1948, para. 4.
3. *Repertoire of the Practice of the Security Council 1946–1951* (ST/PSCA/1), 1954, p. 8. Six volumes of the *Repertoire* have been issued, and will be cited as follows:

form of citation	*period covered*	*UN doc ref*	*year of publication*
Repertoire I	1946–51	ST/PSCA/1	1954
Repertoire II	1952–5	ST/PSCA/1/Add. 1	1957
Repertoire III	1956–8	ST/PSCA/1/Add. 2	1959
Repertoire IV	1959–63	ST/PSCA/1/Add. 3	1965
Repertoire V	1964–5	ST/PSCA/1/Add. 4	1968
Repertoire VI	1966–8	ST/PSCA/1/Add. 5	1971

4. SCOR, 4th year, 424th meeting (10 May 1949), pp. 2 and 8.
5. SCOR, 11th year, 746th meeting (28 Oct. 1956), paras. 1–4; 752nd meeting (2 Nov. 1956), paras. 3–5; 22nd year, 1341st meeting (24 May 1967), para. 1.
6. SCOR, 14th year, Supplement for July to Sept. 1959, pp. 6–8, S/4212, S/4213; 847th meeting(7 Sept. 1959), paras. 5, 14–22, and 30; 848th meeting (7 Sept. 1959), paras. 12 and 22.
7. SCOR, 20th year, 1237th meeting (4 Sept, 1965), paras. 5–10 and 19–63.
8. The following are examples of meetings called by different Presidents without the agreement of all Council members:

the Soviet representative	SCOR, 16th year, 973rd meeting (13 Nov. 1961), paras. 17–19;
the Malaysian representative	SCOR, 20th year, 1208th meeting (14 May 1965), paras. 2–4;
the Dutch representative	SCOR, 20th year, 1220th meeting (3 June 1965), paras. 8–24.

9. SCOR, 24th year, Supplement for July to September 1969, p. 159, S/9394; 1503rd meeting (20 Aug. 1969).
10. SCOR, 3rd year, 390th meeting (23 Dec. 1948), pp. 5 and 17.
11. SCOR, 21st year, Supplement for April to June 1966, pp. 29–33, S/7237, S/7238, S/7240, S/7241; 1276th meeting (9 April 1966), paras. 10, 11, 14, 38–41, 82–5; 1277th meeting (9 April 1966), paras. 5–10, 36–9. Also oral communications from diplomats and officials.
12. SCOR, 21st year, Supplement for April to June 1966, pp. 46–9 and 62–3, S/7261 and S/7272.
13. *Repertoire VI*, pp. 5–6.
14. Keith S. Petersen, 'The Business of the United Nations Security Council: history (1946–1963) and prospects', *Journal of Politics*, vol. 27 (1965), p. 821.
15. SCOR, 26th year, 1601st meeting (24 Nov. 1971), para. 128.
16. S/540, 2 Sept. 1947 (mimeo.).
17. SCOR, 2nd year, 90th meeting (9 Jan. 1947), pp. 21–4; 92nd meeting (15 Jan. 1947), pp. 63–4.

18. SCOR, 3rd year, 356th meeting (30 Aug. 1948), pp. 1–10.
19. SCOR, 3rd year, 387th meeting (20 Dec. 1948), p. 5; 385th meeting (17 Dec. 1948), pp. 18–19; 386th meeting (17 Dec. 1948), pp. 19–23, and 37.
20. SCOR, 4th year, 454th meeting (18 Nov. 1949).
21. SCOR, 15th year, 911th meeting, (3/4 Dec. 1960), paras. 3–98.
22. SCOR, 24th year, 1503rd meeting (20 Aug. 1969).
23. SCOR, 3rd year, 365th meeting (14 Oct. 1948), pp. 1–4.
24. SCOR, 9th year, 657th meeting (4 Feb. 1954), paras. 3–114.
25. SCOR, 15th year, Supplement for July to September 1960, p. 145, S/4486; 896th meeting (9/10 Sept. 1960), paras. 9–81; 16th year, 941st meeting (20 Feb. 1961), paras. 23–4; 942nd meeting (20/1 Feb. 1961), paras. 246–7.
26. SCOR, 20th year, 1225th meeting (16 June 1965), paras. 107–20; 1226th meeting (18 June 1965), paras. 11, 30–32, 68–70, 85.
27. G. A. res. 2863 (XXVI), 20 Dec. 1971; SCOR, 27th year, Supplement for January to March 1972, p. 23, S/10514, Annex 1; S.C. res. 308 (S/10514), 19 Jan. 1972.
28. SCOR, 27th year, Supplement for January to March 1972, p. 38, S/10525.
29. Ibid., pp. 80–2, S/10602/Rev. 2, S/10604, S/10605; S/PV. 1630, 31 Jan. 1972, pp. 3–7; S/PV. 1632, 1 Feb. 1972, p. 17; S/PV. 1633, 1 Feb. 1972, p. 8; S/PV. 1634, 2 Feb. 1972, p. 2.
30. S.C. res. 309 (S/10376/Rev. 2); 310 (S/10608/Rev. 1); 311 (S/10609/Rev. 1); 312 (S/10607/Rev. 1); S/10535; all dated 4 Feb. 1972.
31. SCOR, 27th year, Supplement for January to March 1972, pp. 82–3, S/10606.
32. A/8775, 5 Oct. 1972, pp. 31–2; A/8847, 8 Dec. 1972, p. 2; A/8847/Add. 1, 12 Dec. 1972, pp. 10–11; A/PV. 2205, 18 Dec. 1973, pp. 68, 77 (all mimeo.).
33. S/PV. 1631, 31 Jan. 1972, pp. 3–16.
34. S/10858, 9 Jan. 1973; S/10859, 9 Jan. 1973; S/10872, 30 Jan. 1973; S/10878, 2 Feb. 1973 (all mimeo.).
35. S/10868, 25 Jan. 1973 (mimeo.); S.C. res. 325, 26 Jan. 1973.
36. S/10931/Rev. 1, 21 March 1973 (mimeo.); S.C. res. 330, 21 March 1973.
37. Press Feature no. 214, July 1971 (mimeo.), p. 11.
38. See B.S.N. Murti, 'Periodic Meetings of the Security Council, Article 28, paragraph 2 of the UN Charter', *Indian Journal of International Law*, vol. 10 (1970), pp. 283–98.
39. *Voting in the Security Council*, Indiana University Press, 1969, pp. 26–62. See also Andrew Boyd, *Fifteen men on a powder keg*, London, Methuen: New York, Stein and Day, 1971, pp. 62–3, 66–9, 83–5, 96–7.
40. Leland M. Goodrich, 'The UN Security Council', *International Organization*, vol. xii, no. 3 (Summer 1958), p. 283.
41. GAOR, 5th session, Supplement no. 1, A/1287, pp. xii-xiii; Annexes, Agenda item 60, pp. 1–4, A/1304; 6th session, Supplement no. 1A, A/1844/Add. 1, p. 6; Trygve Lie, *In the cause of peace*, London and New York, Macmillan, 1954, pp. 279, 431; GAOR, 10th session, Supplement no. 1, A/2911, p. xii; 14th session, Supplement no. 1A, A/4132/Add. 1, p. 3; 22nd session, Supplement no 1A, A/6701/Add. 1, paras. 157–60; 23rd session, Supplement no. 1A, A/7201/Add. 1, para. 169; *UN Monthly Chronicle*, vol. vii, no. 8 (Aug–Sept. 1970), p. 90; GAOR, 25th session, Supplement no. 1A, A/8001/Add. 1, para. 64; A/8431, 24 Sept. 1971 (mimeo.), p. 4, para. 9: GA res. 494 (V), 20 Nov. 1950; 503B(VI), 12 Jan. 1952; 817(IX), 23 Nov. 1954; 2606(XXIV), 16 Dec. 1969. See also Goodrich, p. 287.
42. S/PV. 1247, 25 Oct. 1965, p. 81; SCOR, 20th year, 1247th meeting (25 Oct. 1965), para. 141.
43. Ibid., 1257th-1263rd meetings (12–17 Nov. 1965).

44. This meeting was not numbered; the verbatim record is contained in a Supplement to the Council's official records, SCOR, 24th year, Supplement for April to June 1969, pp. 331–4, S/9259.
45. SCOR, 13th year, Supplement for July to September 1958, pp. 97–110, S/4071–4075.
46. GAOR, 24th session, Annexes, Agenda item 103, p. 2, A/7654; G.A. res. 2606(XXIV), 16 Dec. 1969.
47. SCOR, 25th year, Supplement for April to June 1970, pp. 153–6 and 207, S/9799 and S/9824.
48. SCOR, 25th year, 1544th meeting (12 June 1970), paras. 19–89; A/7922, 15 May 1970 (mimeo.), pp. 50–1, 62, 70, 88; A/7922/Add. 1, 4 June 1970 (mimeo.), pp. 5, 16; A/7922/Add. 2, 1 July 1970 (mimeo.), p. 3.
49. SCOR, 25th year, 1544th meeting (12 June 1970), para. 2; Supplement for April to June 1970, p. 210, S/9835.
50. SCOR, 25th year, 1555th meeting (21 Oct. 1970).
51. G.A. res. 2734(XXV), 16 Dec. 1970.
52. GAOR 26th session, Supplement no. 1A, A/8401/Add. 1, para. 99. See also A/8431, 24 Sept. 1971 (mimeo.), p. 4.
53. A/8847, 8 Dec. 1972 (mimeo.), p. 2 and Annex, pp. 3, 10, 11, and 18; A/8847/Add. 1, 12 Dec. 1972 (mimeo.), pp. 9–10; A/9128, 25 Oct. 1973 (mimeo.), pp. 9, 23; A/9143, 30 Nov. 1973 (mimeo.), pp. 10, 21; see also A/PV. 2205, 18 Dec. 1973, p. 72.
54. Spaak, p. 102.
55. *The First Assembly*, edited by Oliver Brett, London, Macmillan, 1921, p. 239.
56. Goodrich, p. 287.
57. *Repertoire I*, p. 218.
58. SCOR, 5th year, 510th meeting (12 Oct. 1950); Lie, pp. 376–7.
59. SCOR, 8th year, 613th meeting (13 Mar. 1953); Lie, p. 415.
60. S/PV. 1620, 21 Dec. 1971.
61. S/PV. 1752, 27 Oct. 1973, pp. 1–5, 17, 21, 22, and personal communication.
62. S/PV. 1759, 14 Dec. 1973, p. 86; S/PV. 1760, 15 Dec. 1973, pp. 2 and 17; S.C. res. 344 (S/11156), 15 Dec. 1973.
63. SCOR, 11th year, 739th–741st meetings (9, 11, and 12 Oct. 1956); S.C. res. 118 (S/3675), 13 Oct. 1956. See also Brian Urquhart, *Hammarskjold*, New York, Knopf: London, Bodley Head, 1973, pp. 165–8.
64. SCOR, 1st year, 1st series, 31st meeting (9 Apr. 1946), p. 101.
65. Ibid., pp. 109–10.
66. SCOR., 2nd series, 77th meeting (16 Oct. 1946), p. 483; 2nd year, 202nd meeting (15 Sept. 1947), pp. 2405–6.
67. The notification for 1973 was issued on 18 Sept. as doc. A/9158 (mimeo.).
68. SCOR, 1st year, 1st series, Supplement no. 2, pp. 46–7, S/30.
69. Ibid., Supplement no. 1, pp. 16–17, Annex 2A.
70. S.C. res. 2, 30 Jan. 1946; res. 3, 4 April 1946.
71. SCOR, 1st year, 1st series, Supplement no. 2, p. 47, S/33; 32nd meeting (15 Apr. 1946), pp. 122–3.
72. Ibid., 33rd meeting (16 Apr. 1946), pp. 142–3.
73. Ibid., pp. 143–5, S/39.
74. Lie, pp. 79–80.
75. Ibid., pp. 80–3.
76. SCOR, 1st year, 1st series, 33rd meeting (16 Apr. 1946), p. 145.
77. ICJ Reports 1971, paras. 24 and 26.
78. SCOR, 1st year, 1st series, Supplement no. 2, pp. 47–50, S/42.
79. Ibid., 36th meeting (23 Apr. 1946), pp. 213–14.

80. S.C. res. 5, 8 May 1946.
81. SCOR, 1st year, 1st series, Supplement no. 2, pp. 52–4, S/66 and S/68.
82. Ibid., 43rd meeting (22 May 1946), p. 305.
83. SCOR, 13th year, 840th meeting (25 Nov. 1958), paras. 22–6.
84. GAOR, 19th session, Annex no. 1, p. 3; S/11185, 7 Jan. 1974 (mimeo.), p. 1.
85. Vratislav Pechota, *Complementary Structures of third party settlement of International Disputes*, UNITAR (PS 3), 1971, p. 22.
86. SCOR, 5th year, 473rd meeting (25 June 1950), pp. 1–2.
87. SCOR, 7th year, 577th meeting (18 June 1952), paras. 2–89.
88. See, for example, SCOR, 3rd year, 231st meeting (22 Jan. 1948), pp. 143–64; 19th year, 1127th meeting (8 June 1964), paras. 1–2. Since 5 Aug. 1968, South West Africa has been known as Namibia in official documents of the Security Council; the title of the agenda item was changed at the 1464th meeting of the Council on 20 Mar. 1969.
89. SCOR, 1st year, 2nd series, 59th meeting (3 Sept. 1946), pp. 175–6.
90. See, for example, SCOR, 3rd year, 268th meeting (17 Mar. 1948), p. 100; 6th year, 559th meeting (1 Oct. 1951), para. 5; 7th year, 574th meeting (4 Apr. 1952), paras. 46, 51, and 96; 575th meeting (10 April 1952), para. 25; 576th meeting (14 Apr. 1952), para. 29; 11th year, 730th meeting (26 June 1956), paras. 14–15; 17th year, 991st meeting (27 Feb. 1962) para. 65.
91. David R. Gilmour, 'Article 2(7) of the United Nations Charter and the Practice of the Permanent Members of the Security Council', *Australian Yearbook of International Law 1967*, London, Butterworth, 1970, p. 162.
92. SCOR, 3rd year, 361st meeting (4 Oct. 1948), pp. 16–17.
93. Ibid., 357th meeting (16 Sept. 1948), p. 8.
94. SCOR, 2nd year, 171st meeting (31 July 1947), p. 1617.
95. SCOR, 3rd Year, 357th meeting (16 Sept. 1948), p. 10.
96. Ibid., p. 4.
97. Rules of Procedure of the General Assembly, nos. 81 and 122.
98. S/Agenda/1651, 18 July 1972 (mimeo.).
99. S.C. res. 316 (S/10722), 26 June 1972.
100. S/Agenda/1651, 18 July 1972 (mimeo.).
101. S/PV. 1651, 18 July 1972, pp. 3–27.
102. SCOR, 3rd year, 356th meeting (30 Aug. 1948), pp. 7–10; 5th year, 502nd meeting (18 Sept. 1950), pp. 11–14. See also SCOR, 3rd year, 327th meeting (25 June 1948), p. 6.
103. S/PV. 1651, 18 July 1972, pp. 27–58 (mimeo.). For other examples of difficulties over formulating the agenda when the Council is convened to consider the situation in the Middle East, see SCOR, 21st year, 1288th meeting (25 July 1966), paras. 6–45; 1305th meeting (14 Oct. 1966), paras. 1–131; 22nd year, 1365th meeting (8 July 1967), paras. 4–53.
104. SCOR, 24th year, Supplement for April to June 1969, pp. 331–4, S/9259.
105. S/PV. 1703, 21 March 1973.
106. SCOR, 1st year, 1st series, 31st meeting (9 Apr. 1946), pp. 101–2.
107. *Repertoire III*, p. 47; *Repertoire IV*, p. 28; *Repertoire V*, p. 47; *Repertoire VI*, p. 38.
108. SCOR, 3rd year, 383rd meeting (2 Dec. 1948), pp. 2–7.
109. SCOR, 5th year, 480th meeting (1 Aug. 1950), pp. 12–21; 481st meeting (2 Aug. 1950), pp. 1–7, 10–18; 482nd meeting (3 Aug. 1950), pp. 1–23; 504th meeting (27 Sept. 1950), pp. 1–3; 7th year, 594th meeting (2 Sept. 1952), paras. 6–26; 16th year, 973rd meeting (13 Nov. 1961), paras. 2–16.
110. See, for example, SCOR, 7th year, 599th meeting (12 Sept. 1952), paras. 2–3, 6–11, 26–31; 21st year, 1305th meeting (14 Oct. 1966), paras. 94 and 121.

111. SCOR, 9th year, 676th meeting (25 June 1954), paras. 140 and 195.
112. SCOR, 1st year, 2nd series, 71st meeting (23 Sept. 1946), pp. 426–8; 72nd meeting (24 Sept. 1946), pp. 453–5; 12th year, 783rd meeting (20 Aug. 1957), paras. 32 and 58.
113. SCOR, 7th year, 574th meeting (4 Apr. 1952), paras. 27 and 34; see also SCOR, 12th year, 783rd meeting (20 Aug. 1957), paras. 35 and 50; 784th meeting (20 Aug. 1957), para. 22.
114. SCOR, 1st year, 2nd series, 71st meeting (23 Sept. 1946), p. 425; 72nd meeting (24 Sept. 1946), pp. 448–9; 7th year, 574th meeting (4 Apr. 1952), para. 34; 575th meeting (10 April 1952), paras. 9, 11, 18, 58–62, 68; 576th meeting (14 Apr. 1952), paras. 58 and 63; 8th year, 620th meeting (27 Aug. 1953), paras. 26–7; 621st meeting (31 Aug. 1953), paras. 7–8; 623rd meeting (2 Sept. 1953), para. 18; 11th year, 730th meeting (26 June 1956), paras. 48–9, 57, 84; 755th meeting (5 Nov. 1956), paras. 28–9, 56; 17th year, 991st meeting (27 Feb. 1962), paras. 15 and 19; 24th year, 1503rd meeting (20 Aug. 1969), paras. 8 and 10.
115. SCOR, 3rd year, 327th meeting (25 June 1948), p. 3; 6th year, 559th meeting (1 Oct. 1951), paras. 2–4, 9–10; 8th year, 619th meeting (26 Aug. 1953), paras. 5–6, 24–8; 620th meeting (27 Aug. 1953), paras. 16–23; 623rd meeting (2 Sept. 1953), paras. 11–12, 29; 624th meeting (3 Sept. 1953), paras. 12–15; 11th year, 729th meeting (26 June 1956), paras. 29, 95–101; 730th meeting (26 June 1956), paras. 36–40, 52–3, 60–5; 12th year, 783rd meeting (20 Aug. 1957), paras. 57, 64, 73–7; 784th meeting (20 Aug. 1957), para. 30; 24th year, 1503rd meeting (20 Aug. 1969), paras. 2–9.
116. See, for example, SCOR, 1st year, 2nd series, 71st meeting (23 Sept. 1946), p. 425; 17th year, 991st meeting (27 Feb. 1962), paras. 2–3, 94–5, 100.
117. Gilmour, p. 175.
118. A. Leroy Bennett, 'The Rejuvenation of the Security Council—Evidence and Reality', *Midwest Journal of Political Science*, vol. 9 (Nov. 1965), pp. 363–5.
119. G.A. res. 2479(XXIII), 21 Dec. 1968; S.C. res. 263 (S/8976), 24 Jan. 1969.
120. G.A. res. 3189(XXVIII), 18 Dec. 1973; S.C. res. 345 (S/11192), 17 Jan. 1974.
121. H. A. L. Fisher, *An International Experiment*, Oxford, Clarendon Press, 1921, p. 25.
122. GAOR, 2nd session, plenary meetings, Annex 4, A/388 (23 Sept. 1947), paras. 27–30 (my italics).
123. SCOR, 7th year, 575th meeting (10 Apr. 1952), para. 13.
124. GAOR, 22nd session, Annexes, Agenda item 82, pp. 8–10, A/6860, paras. 45–56.
125. G.A. res. 2359B(XXII), 19 Dec. 1967; 2480B(XXIII), 21 Dec. 1968; 2539(XXIV), 11 Dec. 1969; 2736A(XXV), 17 Dec. 1970.
126. SCOR, 1st year, 1st series, Supplement no. 1, pp. 19–24, S/1.
127. SCOR, 25th year, Supplement for October to December 1970, p. 54, S/10000.
128. *Information for Delegations* (ST/CS/23), September 1973, pp. 19–20.
129. SCOR, 5th year, 524th meeting (17 Nov. 1950), p. 2. The statement is in ibid., 523rd meeting (16 Nov. 1950), pp. 27–30, S/1902.
130. SCOR, 7th year, 576th meeting (14 Apr. 1952), paras. 5–13.
131. See, for example, SCOR, 12th year, Supplement for January to March 1957, pp. 12–20 (S/PV. 761/Add. 1) and 21–82 (S/PV. 762/Add. 1); 23rd year, 1326th meeting (23 Nov. 1966), Annex; 1408th meeting (26 Mar. 1968) p. 13; 1418th meeting (1 May 1968), paras. 124–5; 1421st meeting (3 May 1968), paras. 52, 174–5; S/PV. 1421/Adds. 1 and 2, 6 May and 24 June 1968.
132. SCOR, 26th year, 1589th meeting (6 Oct. 1971), paras. 2–43.
133. SCOR, 1st year, 1st series, 31st meeting (9 Apr. 1946), pp. 117–18.

134. See, for example, the communication from the Zimbabwe African People's Union about the Rhodesian question, circulated at the request of Algeria, SCOR, 21st year, Supplement for April to June 1966, p. 102, S/7313.
135. See, for example, SCOR, 11th year, 742nd meeting (13 Oct. 1956), paras. 5–6.
136. See, for example, SCOR, 3rd year, Supplement for September 1948, pp. 5–7, S/986, S/998, S/1000; 4th year, 409th meeting (15 Feb. 1949), pp. 12–15, 18, S/1247 and S/1256.
137. SCOR, 2nd year, Supplement no. 1, pp. 1–2, S/224; 143rd meeting (20 June 1947), p. 1043, S/374; 3rd year, Supplement for August 1948, pp. 79–84, S/927.
138. SCOR, 13th year, Supplement for January to March 1958, pp. 12–13, S/3951.
139. SCOR, 27th year, Supplement for April to June 1972, pp. 44–7, S/10631 (text also in *U.S. Department of State Bulletin*, vol. 66, pp. 750–1).
140. SCOR, 6th year, 550th meeting (1 Aug. 1951), paras. 34–42; 553rd meeting (16 Aug. 1951), para. 60.
141. SCOR, 13th year, 827th meeting (15 July 1958), para. 84; 833rd meeting (18 July 1958), para. 10; 836th meeting (22 July 1958), para. 7.
142. SCOR, 22nd year, 1347th meeting (5 June 1967), paras. 30–2, 134; S/PV. 1736, 13 Aug. 1973, p. 96.
143. SCOR, 17th year, 995th meeting (20 Mar. 1962), para. 59.
144. SCOR, 15th year, 920th meeting (13/14 Dec. 1960), para. 78.
145. SCOR, 16th year, Supplement for July to September 1961, pp. 52–7, S/4908–S/4911/Adds. 1 and 2.
146. Ibid., 976th meeting (17 Nov. 1961), paras. 114–17; Supplement for October to December 1961, pp. 135–6, S/4988.
147. SCOR, 18th year, Supplement for January to March 1963, pp. 116–29, S/5259, paras. 9, 13, 17, and 60.
148. Ibid., pp. 130–2, 141–7, S/5260, S/5264, S/5266, S/5268, S/5271, S/5272.
149. Ibid., pp. 133, 143–145, 147, S/5262, S/5267, S/5269, S/5273.
150. SCOR, 22nd year, Supplement for January to March 1967, pp. 233–4, S/7822.
151. Ibid., Supplement for April to June 1967, pp. 103–4, S/789 1. See also GAOR, 26th session, Supplement no. 1A, A/8401/Add. 1, para. 101.
152. SCOR, 22nd year, Supplement for April to June 1967, pp. 98–9, S/7888.
153. SCOR, 23rd year, 1445th meeting (24 Aug. 1968), paras. 3–157.
154. SCOR, 24th year, Supplement for July to September 1969, p. 186, S/9455; Supplement for October to December 1969, pp. 95–6, S/9486; p. 104, S/9498; pp. 117–18, S/9515.
155. Ibid., 1514th meeting (23 Oct. 1969), paras. 22, 32, 35, 38.
156. Ibid., Supplement for October to December 1969, p. 165, S/9759; 25th year, Supplement for January to March 1970, pp. 115 and 149, S/9624 and S/9674.
157. Ibid., Supplement for July to September 1970, pp. 130–1, S/9909; Supplement for October to December 1970, pp. 36 and 85, S/9974 and S/10042.
158. SCOR, 26th year, Supplement for October to December 1971, pp. 34–5, S/10389.
159. SCOR, 27th year, Supplement for January to March 1972, pp. 63–4, 72–3, 80–81, S/10563, S/10577, S/10603; Supplement for April to June 1972, pp. 50 and 69, S/10637 and S/10660.
160. Ibid., p. 139, S/10718.
161. Ibid., Supplement for October to December 1972, pp. 31–2, S/10831.
162. SCOR, 23rd year, 1445th meeting (24 Aug. 1968), paras. 16–19, 23–34.

163. SCOR, 25th year, Supplement for January to March 1970, pp. 151–2, 163, 170–1, 173, S/9680, S/9704, S/9718, S/9723.
164. SCOR, 26th year, Supplement for January to March 1971, p. 61, S/10104.
165. SCOR, 27th year, Supplement for July to September 1972, pp. 94–5, S/10774.
166. A/8987, 18 Dec. 1972; A/8991, 4 Jan. 1973; A/9037, 23 Jan. 1973; A/9040, 30 Jan. 1973; A/9047, 21 Feb. 1973; A/9115, 7 Aug. 1973; A/9118, 10 Aug. 1973; A/9210, 10 Dec. 1973; see also A/9052, 29 March 1973 (all mimeo.).

CHAPTER 3

1. GAOR, 5th session, 289th plenary meeting (28 Sept. 1950), para. 40.
2. SCOR, 11th year, 751st meeting (31 Oct. 1956), para. 1.
3. Ibid., 754th meeting (4 Nov. 1956), para. 76.
4. SCOR, 14th year, 847th meeting (7 Sept. 1959), para. 12.
5. SCOR, 15th year, 873rd meeting (13/14 July 1960), para. 26. For Hammarskjold's understanding of Art. 99, see Urquhart pp. 254–5, 310, 343, 396–7, 533, 538.
6. SCOR, 23rd year, Supplement for April to June 1968, pp. 167–9, S/8592 and S/8593.
7. Press Release SG/SM/1516, 2 Aug. 1971, later reproduced in SCOR, 26th year, Supplement for October to December 1971, p. 80, S/10410, para. 3; Press Release SG/SM/1530, 14 Sept. 1971, p. 15.
8. For U Thant's own explanation of his role in 1971, see GAOR, 26th year, Supplement no. 1A, A/8401/Add. 1, paras. 187–8. See also Vratislav Pechota, *The Quiet Approach*, New York, UNITAR (PS 6), 1972, pp. 47–8, 58.
9. Address at the annual luncheon of the Dag Hammarskjold Memorial Scholarship Fund on 16 Sept. 1971, printed in *UN Monthly Chronicle*, vol. viii, no. 9 (Oct. 1971), p. 184.
10. SCOR, 1st year, 2nd series, 70th meeting (20 Sept. 1946), p. 404.
11. GAOR, 15th session, 5th Committee, 769th meeting (18 Oct. 1960), paras. 10 and 17.
12. SCOR, 16th year, 964th meeting (28 July 1961), paras. 86; see also A/9128, 25 Oct. 1973 (mimeo.), p. 9.
13. GAOR, 26th session, Supplement no. 1A, A/8401/Add. 1, para. 126.
14. SCOR, 3rd year, 331st meeting (7 July 1948), pp. 32–4; 338th meeting (15 July 1948), pp. 63–5. The resolution of the General Assembly was no. 186 (S–2), 14 May 1948.
15. SCOR, 13th year, 837th meeting (22 July 1958), paras. 10–16.
16. S.C. res. 203 (S/6355), 14 May 1965; SCOR, 20th year, 1209th meeting (14 May 1965), paras. 56–7; 1227th meeting (18 June 1965), paras. 4–5.
17. S/PV. 1755, 12 Nov. 1973, pp. 2–3.
18. 'A Quiet United Nations Road to Accord', *UN Monthly Chronicle*, vol. vii, no. 7 (July 1970), pp. 122–31. See also GAOR, 22nd session, Supplement no. 1A, A/6701/Add. 1, para. 156; 24th session, Supplement no. 1A, A/7601/Add. 1, paras. 176–86; 26th session, Supplement no. 1A/ A/8401/Add. 1, paras. 129–35.
19. A/3934/Rev. 1, 29 Sept. 1958 (mimeo.), paras. 26–38.
20. GAOR, 15th session, Supplement no. 1, A/4390, p. 23.
21. SCOR, 22nd year, Supplement for July to September 1967, pp. 199–209, S/8124; Supplement for October to December 1967, pp. 80–154, S/8158.
22. Ibid., Supplement for July to September 1967, p. 195, S/8121; pp. 232–86, S/8146.
23. SCOR, 25th year, Supplement for January to March 1970, pp. 175–6,

S/9726; Supplement for April to June, pp. 143, 166–70, 175, 178, S/9737, S/9738, S/9772, S/9779, S/9783.

24. SCOR, 11th year, Supplement for January to March 1956, pp. 20–1, S/3561 and S/3562.
25. Ibid., 720th meeting (3 Apr. 1956), para. 9. Eisenhower was under the impression that 'the Soviets supported Arab opposition' to Hammarskjold's trip, and he also gives the date of the Security Council decision as March rather than April, Dwight D. Eisenhower, *Waging Peace 1956–1961*, New York, Doubleday, 1965: London, Heinemann, 1966, pp. 28–9.
26. SCOR, 11th year, 722nd meeting (4 Apr. 1956), paras. 36–46; S.C. res. 113 (S/3575), 4 April 1956. See also Urquhart, pp. 138–53.
27. Note no. 1243, 27 Feb. 1956; SCOR, 11th year, 722nd meeting (4 Apr. 1956), para. 51; Note no. 1265, 5 April 1956.
28. E. L. M. Burns, *Between Arab and Israeli*, London, Harrap, 1962, p. 141; *Markings*, translated by Leif Söjberg and W. H. Auden, London, Faber: New York, Knopf, 1964, p. 111.
29. SCOR, 11th year, Supplement for April to June 1956, pp. 27–66, S/3594 and S/3596. See also Supplement for July to September 1956, pp. 48–70, S/3658 and S/3659.
30. S.C. res. 114 (S/3605), 4 June 1956.
31. GAOR, 26th session, Supplement no. 1A, A/8401/Add. 1, para. 127; Pechota, *The Quiet Approach*, p. 10.
32. GAOR, 23rd session, Supplement no. 1A, A/7201/Add. 1, paras. 201–4; 24th session, Supplement no. 1A, A/7601/Add. 1, para. 205; 27th session, Supplement no. 1, A/8701, pp. 75–6; Pechota, pp. 67, 77; Vratislav Pechota, *Complementary structures of third party settlement of international disputes*.
33. Conor Cruise O'Brien (and Feliks Topolski), *The United Nations: sacred drama*, London, Hutchinson, 1968, p. 122.
34. Press Release SG/SM/567, 19 Sept. 1966, pp. 4 and 8.
35. SCOR, 21st year, 1329th meeting (2 Dec. 1966), p. 2.
36. Note no. 3075, 24 Feb. 1965, p. 5.
37. SCOR, 18th year, Supplement for April to June 1963, p. 51, S/5236; 1038th meeting (11 June 1963), paras. 15–22; 1039th meeting (11 June 1963), paras. 17–25.
38. SCOR, 20th year, 1247th meeting (25 Oct. 1965), para. 243; 1251st meeting (5 Nov. 1965), paras. 83–7.
39. SCOR, 21st year, Supplement for July to September 1965, pp. 108–9, S/7478.
40. SCOR, 24th year, Supplement for January to March 1969, pp. 106–10, 115–16, 132–3, S/9053 and Adds. 1–6, S/9054, S/9055, S/9066, S/9101.
41. S.C. res. 221 (S/7236/Rev. 1), 9 April 1966.
42. SCOR, 21st year, Supplement for April to June 1966, pp. 59–62, 89–90, S/7271, S/7294.
43. ICJ Reports 1971, p. 22.
44. SCOR, 21st year, Supplement for April to June 1966 pp. 208–9, S/7373.
45. Ibid., Supplement for July to September 1966, pp. 16–17, S/7392.
46. Ibid., pp. 67–9, S/7445; SCOR, 22nd year, Supplement for January to March 1967, pp. 113–16, S/7781 (S/7735/Rev. 1); p. 204, S/7798. See also 23rd year, Supplement for January to March 1968, pp. 276–7, S/8481; 24th year, Supplement for January to March 1969, pp. 88–90, S/9026, S/9027; 25th year, Supplement for July to September 1970, pp. 65–6, S/9853 (S/9753).
47. A/9052, 29 March 1973; see also A/9079, 28 June 1973 and A/9085, 2 July 1973 (all mimeo.).

48. A/9065, 18 May 1973 (mimeo.).
49. See my article 'UN fact-finding and human rights complaints', *International Affairs*, vol. 48, no. 2 (Apr. 1972), esp. pp. 257–9.
50. S.C. res. 237 (S/7969/Rev. 3), 14 June 1967; G.A. res. 2252 (ES–V), 4 July 1967; Commission on Human Rights res. 6 (XXIV), 27 Feb. 1968.
51. SCOR, 22nd year, Supplement for April to June 1967, pp. 199–209, S/8124; Supplement for October to December 1967, pp. 80–154, S/8158.
52. SCOR, 23rd year, Supplement for April to June 1968, pp. 126–33, S/8553; Supplement for July to September 1968, pp. 73–95, S/8699.
53. A/8997, 28 Dec. 1972; A/9036, 19 Jan. 1973 (both mimeo.).
54. S. E. Werners, *Presiding Officers in the United Nations*, Haarlem (Netherlands), De Erven F. Bohn, 1967, pp. 41–3.
55. PC/EX/113/Rev. 1 (12 Nov. 1945), p. 46.
56. SCOR, 1st year, 1st series, 31st meeting (9 Apr. 1946), pp. 115–16.
57. PC/EX/113/Rev. 1 (12 Nov. 1945), pp. 24 and 40.
58. SCOR, 1st sear, 1st series, 1st meeting (17 Jan. 1946), p. 4.
59. SCOR, 1st year, 2nd series, 84th meeting (16 Dec. 1946), pp. 585–7; S.C. res. 14 (S/212), 16 Dec. 1946.
60. PC/EX/113/Rev. 1, 12 Nov. 1945, p. 45; SCOR, 1st year, 1st series, Supplement no. 2, p. 42, S/88.
61. SCOR, 5th year, 461st meeting (13 Jan. 1950), pp. 11–16; 462nd meeting (17 Jan. 1950), pp. 1–3, 13–16; 6th year, 566th meeting (10 Nov. 1951), paras. 1–3; 10th year, 700th meeting (8 Sept. 1955), paras. 1–5.
62. SCOR, 13th year, 814th meeting (29 Apr. 1958), paras. 2–15.
63. SCOR, 15th year, 912th meeting (7 Dec. 1960), paras. 3–122.
64. SCOR, 3rd year, 354th meeting (19 Aug. 1948), p. 29.
65. PC/EX/113/Rev. 1, (12 Nov. 1945), p. 46.
66. F. Y. Chai, *Consultation and consensus in the Security Council*, UNITAR (PS 4), 1971, pp. 13–27. Examples of draft resolutions being submitted by or for the President include S.C. res. 233 (S/7935), 6 June 1967; 235 (S/7960), 9 June 1967; 240, 25 Oct. 1967; 251, 2 May 1968; 258, 18 Sept. 1968; 266, 10 June 1969; 270, 26 Aug. 1969; 274, 11 Dec. 1969; 278, 11 May 1970; 281, 9 June 1970; 286, 9 Sept. 1970; 291 (S/10036), 10 Dec. 1970; 293 (S/10209), 26 May 1971; 305 (S/10441), 13 Dec. 1971; 315 (S/10699), 15 June 1972; 324 (S/10847), 12 Dec. 1972.
67. Prandler, p. 166.
68. See, for example, SCOR, 16th year, 963rd meeting (22 July 1961), paras. 142–4; 23rd year, 1412th meeting (4 Apr. 1968), para. 122.
69. G.A. res. 268B(111), 28 April 1949; S.C. res. 81 (S/1486), 24 May 1950.
70. SCOR, 3rd year, 387th meeting (20 Dec. 1948), pp. 3–5.
71. SCOR, 1st year, 1st series, 48th meeting (24 June 1946), p. 400; S.C. res. 47 (S/726), 21 April 1948; SCOR, 3rd year, 289th meeting (7 May 1948), p. 8; S.C. res. 276 (S/9620/Rev. 1), 30 Jan. 1970; SCOR, 25th year, Supplement for March to July 1970, p. 148, S/9748; S.C. res. 283 (S/9891), 29 July 1970; SCOR, 25th year, Supplement for July to September 1970, p. 147, S/9951.
72. SCOR, 2nd year, 174th meeting (4 Aug. 1947), pp. 1717–18; S.C. res. 289 (S/9990/Rev. 1), 23 Nov. 1970; res. 294 (S/10266, 15 July 1971; res. 295 (S/10281), 3 Aug. 1971.
73. SCOR, 16th year, 960th meeting (7 July 1961), para. 82; 962nd meeting (22 July 1961), para. 62; 19th year, 1086th meeting (10 Jan. 1964), paras. 59–60, 104–5; 1143rd meeting (9/11 Aug. 1964), paras. 11–14; 21st year, 1300th meeting (16 Aug. 1966), para. 2; 22nd year, 1383rd meeting (24/25

Nov. 1967), para. 151; 23rd year, 1448th meeting (8/9 Sept. 1968), para. 37.
74. SCOR, 3rd year, 229th meeting (17 Jan. 1948), pp. 125–8; 230th meeting (20 Jan. 1948), pp. 132–3; 235th meeting (24 Jan. 1948), pp. 259, 262–4; 277th meeting (1 Apr. 1948), pp. 2 and 36–41; 282nd meeting (15 Apr. 1948), p. 2; 4th year, 457th meeting (17 Dec. 1949), pp. 4–8; 458th meeting (29 Dec. 1948), pp. 4–22.
75. SCOR, 19th year, 1140th meeting (5 Aug. 1964), paras. 88–91; 1141st meeting (7 Aug. 1964), paras. 22–3.
76. S.C. res. 290 (S/10030), 8 Dec. 1970; res. 298 (S/10337, S/10338/Add. 1), 25 Sept. 1971; res. 302 (S/10395, as amended), 24 Nov. 1971; res. 317 (S/10742), 21 July 1972.
77. SCOR, 3rd year, 226th meeting (6 Jan. 1948), pp. 4–5, S/636.
78. S.C. res. 43 (S/714, 1), 1 April 1948; SCOR, 3rd year, 282nd meeting (15 Apr. 1948), pp. 2–4; S.C. res. 46 (S/723), 17 April 1948.
79. GAOR, 4th session, Supplement no. 1, A/930, pp. 17–18; Supplement no. 2, A/945, p. 65; S/1182, 4 Jan. 1948 (mimeo.); Press Release SC/908, 15 March 1949 (mimeo.); Lie, p. 216.
80. S.C. res. 132 (S/4216), 7 Sept. 1959.
81. SCOR, 12th year, 768th meeting (15 Feb. 1957) to 773rd meeting (20 Feb. 1957), para. 126; Supplement for January to March 1957, pp. 7–8, S/3787 and S/3789.
82. Ibid., 773rd meeting (20 Feb. 1957), paras. 127–53; 774th meeting (21 Feb. 1957), paras. 1–82; S.C. res. 123 (S/3793), 21 Feb. 1957; Supplement for April to June 1957, pp. 12–16, S/3821.
83. Ibid., 797th meeting (25 Oct. 1957), paras. 1, 25, 45, 55; 798th meeting (29 Oct. 1957), paras. 1, 14, 24, 45.
84. UNCIO, 1945, vol. XI, pp. 710–14.
85. See my *Voting in the Security Council*, pp. 48–50, 112–35.
86. G.A. res. 1619(XV), 21 April 1961; 1732(XVI), 20 Dec. 1961; 1854B(XVII), 19 Dec. 1962; 1874 (S–IV), 27 June 1963; 2053B(XX), 15 Dec. 1965.
87. FRUS, 1947, vol. i, p. 511.
88. *The Diaries of Sir Alexander Cadogan*, 1938–1945, edited by David Dilks, London, Cassell: New York, Putnam, 1971, pp. 318 and 86.
89. Lie, p. 260; *The Memoirs of Lord Gladwyn*, London, Wiedenfeld and Nicolson: New York, Weybright, 1972, p. 233.
90. Personal communication to the author.
91. FRUS, 1947, vol. i, p. 315.
92. Personal communication.
93. See, for example, S/PV. 1748, 23 Oct. 1973, p. 21.
94. Personal communication.
95. Lie, p. 259; Gladwyn, pp. 232–3; personal communication.
96. Lie, p. 51; Urquhart, p. 78.
97. Personal communication.
98. Dean Acheson, *Present at the Creation*, London, Hamish Hamilton: New York, Norton, 1969, pp. 34 and 78; Stevenson, p. 262 (see also p. 301); Gladwyn, p. 147; FRUS, 1946, vol. 1, pp. 404, 422, 667, 692; 1947, vol. 1, p. 110; Lie, p. 171.
99. Cadogan, pp. 656, 659, 749; Gladwyn, p. 147.
100. Ibid., p. 232.
101. James J. Wadsworth, *The Glass House*, London and New York, Praeger, 1966, pp. 146–7.
102. Gladwyn, pp. 232, 237; personal communication.
103. In *As we knew Adlai*, edited by Edward P. Doyle, New York, Harper and Row,

1966, p. 265, and *Memoirs of Lester Pearson, 1948–1957: the International Years*, edited by John A. Munro and Alex I. Inglis, London: Gollancz, 1974, pp. 333–4.

104. Ibid., pp. 122–3; Lie, p. 31; Acheson, p. 34; Cadogan, p. 708, fn.; Gladwyn, pp. 184, 232; Robert Murphy, *Diplomat among Warriors*, London, Collins: New York, Doubleday, 1964, p. 366; Wadsworth, p. 212; Spaak, p. 111; personal communication; see also Stevenson, p. 413.
105. Lie, pp. 46, 208; Cadogan, p. 749; Gladwyn, p. 147; FRUS, 1945, vol. 1, 1967, p. 1089; Urquhart, p. 316; personal communication; Henry Cabot Lodge, *The Storm has many eyes*, New York, Norton, 1973, p. 140.
106. SCOR, 23rd year, 1433rd meeting (19 June 1968), para. 123.
107. Personal communication.
108. Personal communication.
109. Lie, p. 182; Personal communication.
110. Cadogan, pp. 787, 789, 790.
111. Stevenson, p. 345; FRUS, 1946, vol. 1, pp. 167 and 180.
112. Gladwyn, pp. 234, 248, 383–402; Acheson, p. 510; Lie, p. 341; personal communication; Paul Gore-Booth, *With Great Truth and Respect*, London, Constable, 1974, p. 153.
113. Cadogan, pp. 33, 95.
114. Personal communication.
115. Anthony Eden, *Full Circle*, London, Cassell: Boston, Mass., Houghton Mifflin, pp. 219, 531; Cadogan, p. 530 (see also p. 549).
116. Lodge, p. 131.
117. Piers Dixon, *Double Diploma*, London and New York, Hutchinson, 1968, pp. 266, 277–8.
118. Personal communications; Harold Macmillan, *Riding the Storm, 1956–1959*, London, Macmillan, 1971, p. 561.
119. Ibid., pp. 665 and 692; Hugh Foot, *A Start in Freedom*, London, Hodder and Stoughton: New York, Harper and Row, 1964.
120. Personal communication.
121. SCOR, 22nd year, 1353rd meeting (9 June 1967), para. 228.
122. Lester Pearson, *Through Diplomacy to Politics*, London, Gollancz (publishdd in the United States under the title *Mike: the memoirs of . . . Vol. I, 1897–1948*, New York, Quadrangle Books), 1973, pp. 224, 274; Acheson, p. 89; Cadogan, pp. 617–18; Charles E. Bohlen, *Witness to History*, New York, Norton, 1973, p. 166.
123. Lie, p. 30; Gladwyn, p. 147; Cordell Hull, *Memoirs*, vol. ii, London, Hodder and Stoughton: New York, Macmillan, 1948, p. 1256; Acheson, p. 89; Cadogan, pp. 617, 624; Arthur H. Vandenberg, Jr., with the collaboration of Joe Alex Morris (editors), *The Private Papers of Senator Vandenberg*, Boston, Mass., Houghton Mifflin, 1952, pp. 167 and 191.
124. ICJ Reports 1966, pp. 323–442.
125. Personal communication.
126. Harry S. Truman, *Memoirs, Vol. ii: Years of Trial and Hope*, London, Hodder and Stoughton: New York, Doubleday, 1956, p. 129.
127. Lie, p. 203; Bohlen, p. 281; personal communication.
128. Truman, p. 164.
129. Murphy, p. 366.
130. Philip C. Jessup, 'The Berlin Blockade and the Use of the United Nations', *Foreign Affairs*, vol. 50, No. 1 (Oct. 1971), p. 169; personal communications.
131. Stevenson, p. 362; Lie, pp. 118, 171; Pearson, vol. 1, p. 224; Murphy, p. 366; Gladwyn, p. 232.

132. Wadsworth, pp. 166–7; Pearson, vol. 1, p. 224.
133. Dwight D. Eisenhower, *Mandate for Change, 1953–1956*, London, Heinemann: New York, Doubleday, 1963, p. 89; Lodge, p. 129.
134. Ibid., p. 129.
135. Ibid., p. 129; Murphy, pp. 366–7; personal communications.
136. Murphy, pp. 367, 368, 374 (my italics).
137. Gladwyn, p. 255; personal communication.
138. SCOR, 9th year, 676th meeting (25 June 1954), paras. 36–7.
139. Dwight D. Eisenhower, *Waging Peace, 1956–1961*, p. 478; Lodge, p. 147.
140. Stevenson, pp. 237 and 382; Hermon Dunlop Smith and Francis T. P. Plimpton, in Doyle, pp. 33 and 254; Lie, pp. 2, 10, 13, 61–2; Gladwyn, pp. 177–8.
141. Arthur M. Schlesinger, Jr., *A Thousand Days*, London, Deutsch: Boston, Mass., Houghton Mifflin, p. 411; Francis T. P. Plimpton, in Doyle, p. 258.
142. Ibid., pp. 245–7; Pierre Salinger, *With Kennedy*, London, Cape, 1967: New York, Doubleday, 1966, pp. 145–9, 191; Barbara Ward, Harry S. Ashmore, Francis T. P. Plimpton, and Jane Warner Dick, in Doyle, pp. 225, 233, 263–6, 286–7; Murphy, p. 368; Richard Walton, *Remnants of Power*, New York, Howard McCann, 1968, pp. 168–72.
143. Schlesinger, pp. 125–6, 409–10; Mary McGrory, in Doyle, p. 178.
144. Acheson, p. 686.
145. Barbara Ward, in Doyle, p. 224; Lie, pp. 10, 50–1; Gladwyn, p. 178; Arnold Beichman, *The 'Other' State Department*, London and New York, Basic Books, 1968, p. 163, fn. 23; personal communication.
146. SCOR, 17th year, 1025th meeting (25 Oct. 1962), paras. 35, 49–51, 77, 90.
147. Lyndon Baines Johnson, *The Vantage Point*, London, Weidenfeld and Nicolson, 1972; New York, Holt, Rinehart, and Winston, 1971, pp. 322, 543–4; personal communication.
148. S.C. res. 217 (S/6955, as amended), 20 Nov. 1965 (my italics).
149. Beichman, pp. 94, 98, 99, 115, 145, 172.
150. SCOR, 22nd year, 1355th meeting (10 June 1967), para. 147; 1356th meeting (10/11 June 1967), para. 71; Beichman, pp. 174–5, fn. 9.
151. Beichman, pp. 130, 133.
152. Schlesinger, p. 411.
153. Personal communication.
154. Salinger, pp. 271, 274–9; Robert Kennedy, *Thirteen Days*, Pan Books, 1969, pp. 90–1.
155. G.A. res. 1991A(XVIII), 17 Dec. 1963.
156. Ruth B. Russell, assisted by Jeanette E. Muther, *A History of the United Nation Charter*, Washington, D.C., Brookings Institution: London, Faber, 1958, p. 444.
157. Ibid., pp. 648–9.
158. FRUS, 1946, vol. 1, pp. 117–250.
159. GAOR, 1st session, Part 1, 4th and 5th plenary meetings (12 January 1946).
160. FRUS, 1947, vol. 1, pp. 135, 154, 157.
161. L. C. Green, 'Representation in the Security Council—a survey', *Indian Year Book of International Affairs*, University of Madras, 1962, pp. 48–75.
162. GAOR, 8th session, 450th plenary meeting (5 Oct. 1953), para. 19. See also 4th session, 231st plenary meeting (20 Oct. 1949), para. 10; 6th session, 353rd plenary meeting (7 Dec. 1951), paras. 10–13; 11th session, 612th plenary meeting (7 Dec. 1956), paras. 17–22; SCOR, 20th year, Supplement for January to March 1965, pp. 264–5, S/6264.
163. FRUS, 1947, vol. 1, pp. 102–65.

164. GAOR, 2nd session, 109th plenary meeting (13 Nov. 1947), p. 750.
165. GAOR, 10th session, 551st plenary meeting (6 Dec. 1955), para. 64.
166. Ibid., 559th plenary meeting (16 Dec. 1955), paras. 197–201.
167. Ibid., paras. 271, 301–2.
168. GAOR, 11th session, Annexes, Agenda item 68, A/3332.
169. Ibid., 612th plenary meeting (7 Dec. 1956), paras. 18–22.
170. GAOR, 14th session, 857th plenary meeting (12 Dec. 1959), paras. 301–6.
171. G.A. res. 1991(XVIII), 17 Dec. 1963.
172. GAOR, 18th session, Annexes, Agenda items 82 and 12, A/5686, paras. 18–21.
173. GAOR, 20th session, Annexes, Agenda items 15 and 16, A/6019, pp. 1–3.
174. SCOR, 18th year, Supplement for July to September 1963, pp. 6–10, S/5347.
175. This first occurred during the Congo debate in February 1961; see SCOR, 16th year, 934th meeting (15 Feb. 1961), para. 14; see also 19th year, 1171st meeting (10 Dec. 1964), para. 3; S/PV. 1745, 11 Oct. 1973, p. 2; S/PV. 1746, 12 Oct. 1973, pp. 2–5; S/PV. 1747, 21 Oct. 1973, p. 2; S/PV. 1748, 23 Oct. 1973, p. 2; S/PV. 1749, 24 Oct. 1973, p. 2; S/PV. 1750, 25 Oct. 1973, p. 2; S/PV. 1751, 26 Oct. 1973, p. 2; S/PV. 1752, 27 Oct. 1973, p. 2; S/PV. 1754, 2 Nov. 1973, p. 2; S/PV. 1763, 20 Feb. 1974, p. 2; S/PV. 1764, 28 Feb. 1974, pp. 2–5.
176. *Repertoire I*, p. 101.
177. See, for example, SCOR, 2nd year, 96th meeting (28 Jan. 1947), p. 133; 171st meeting (31 July 1947), p. 1619; 5th year, 520th meeting (8 Nov. 1950), p. 9.
178. SCOR, 3rd year, 231st meeting (22 Jan. 1948), paras. 144–64.
179. SCOR, 24th year, Supplement for July to September 1969, p. 159, S/9394; 1503rd meeting (20 Aug. 1969).
180. SCOR, 21st year, 1312th meeting (28 Oct. 1966), paras. 125–6, 133, 135, 139.
181. SCOR, 2nd year, 192nd meeting (22 Aug. 1947), p. 2152. See also 11th year, 746th meeting (28 Oct. 1956), paras. 39–41.
182. SCOR, 6th year, 540th meeting (2 April 1951), paras. 10–13; 16th year, 962nd meeting (22 July 1961), para. 57; 19th year, 1142nd meeting (8 Aug. 1964), para. 50; 20th year, 1247th meeting (25 Oct. 1965), paras. 77–86, 102–9, 112–21, 129–35, 138–40; S/PV. 1613, 13 Dec. 1971, pp. 51, 53–5, 63.
183. SCOR, 6th year, 558th meeting (1 Sept. 1951), paras. 7–11; 8th year, 643rd meeting (25 Nov. 1953), paras. 1–13; 9th year, 664th meeting (29 March 1954), paras. 117–37.
184. SCOR, 3rd year, 278th meeting (6 April 1948), pp. 1–7; 5th year, 520th meeting (8 Nov. 1950), p. 8; 10th year, 260th meeting (31 Jan. 1955), para. 143; 15th year, 851st meeting (30 March 1960), paras. 80–1; 887th meeting (21 Aug. 1960), paras. 1–2; 18th year, 1040th meeting (22 July 1963), paras. 10–12; 1041st meeting (23 July 1960), para. 89; 1050th meeting (31 July 1960), paras. 5–6; 19th year, 1141st meeting (7 Aug. 1964), para. 22; 21st year, 1248th meeting (27 Oct. 1965), paras. 1–8; 1261st meeting (15 Nov., 1965) paras. 63–4; 1262nd meeting (16 Nov. 1965), para. 35.
185. See Richard F. Pedersen, 'National Representation in the United Nations', *International Organization*, vol. xv, no. 2 (Spring 1961), pp. 256–66.
186. General Assembly res. 257A(III), 3 Dec. 1948.
187. UNTS, vols. 1, p. 15; 11, p. 11; and 500, p. 108.
188. A/INF/159, para. 2, 17 Dec. 1973.
189. Address to the Students Association, Copenhagen, SG/812, 1 May 1959, p. 2; GAOR, 14th session, Supplement no. 1A, A/4132/Add. 1, p. 2.
190. General Assembly res. 1990(XVIII) and 1991A(XVIII), 17 Dec. 1963.

191. Journal No. 5203, 1 July 1971, p. 4.
192. S/7298, 16 May 1966; S/9872, 16 July 1970 (both mimeo.).
193. SCOR, 22nd year, Supplement for July to September 1967, p. 212, S/8127; 23rd year, Supplement for January to March 1968, p. 263, S/8459.
194. SCOR, 21st year, 1307th meeting (14/15 Oct. 1966), para. 3.
195. S/10859, 9 Jan. 1973 (mimeo.).
196. S/10889, 26 Feb. 1973 (mimeo.).
197. Stevenson, p. 342.
198. SCOR, 1st year, 1st series, Supplement no. 2, Annex 1a, pp. 2 and 4, S/6.
199. Ibid., 31st meeting (9 Apr. 1946), pp. 111–15.
200. SCOR, 5th year, Supplement January to May 1950, pp. 2–3 and 16–18, S/1447 and S/1457 and Corr. 1; 468th meeting (28 Feb. 1950), pp. 9–11.
201. The Secretary-General's report on credentials for the five non-permanent members of the Council elected on 15 Oct. 1973 was issued as S/11166, 20 Dec. 1973 (mimeo.).
202. See, for example, SCOR, 2nd year, 171st meeting (31 July 1947), p. 1618; 181st meeting (12 Aug. 1947), p. 1940; 184th meeting (14 Aug. 1947), p. 1980; see also Juridical Yearbook 1971, p. 194.
203. SCOR, 11th year, 752nd meeting (2 Nov. 1956), paras. 7–44.
204. SCOR, 13th year, 827th meeting (15 July 1958), paras. 1–29; 834th meeting (18 July 1958), paras. 2–42; Supplement for July to September, pp. 54–6 and 124–5, S/4060, S/4080, and S/4081; 838th meeting (7 Aug. 1958), para. 1.
205. SCOR, 15th year, 899th meeting (14 Sept. 1960), paras. 5–38; 900th meeting (14 Sept. 1960), paras. 53–87.
206. SCOR, 20th year, 1207th meeting (13 May 1965), paras. 4–109; 1209th meeting (14 May 1965), paras. 3–49; Supplement for April to June 1965, pp. 118–22, S/6353.
207. SCOR, 23rd year, Supplement for January to March 1968, pp. 143–5, S/8365 and Corr. 1, paras. 2–3.
208. Ibid., 1387th meeting (25 Jan. 1968), paras. 11–37.
209. Ibid., Supplement for January to March 1968; pp. 143–5, S/8365 and Corr. 1, para. 5.
210. See my monograph *Chinese Representation in the Security Council and the General Assembly of the United Nations*, Brighton, Institute for the Study of International Organization, 1970.
211. SCOR, 23rd year, Supplement for January to March 1968, pp. 143–5, S/8365, and Corr. 1, para. 4.
212. A/1123, 21 Nov. 1949 (mimeo.).
213. GAOR, 4th session, 227th plenary meeting (24 Sept. 1950), p. 48.
214. SCOR, 4th year, 458th meeting (29 Dec. 1949), pp. 1–3.
215. S/1462, 24 Feb. 1950 (mimeo.), p. 2; SCOR, 5th year, 459th meeting (10 Jan. 1950), pp. 1–4.
216. SCOR, 5th year, 460th meeting (12 Jan. 1950) and 461st meeting (13 Jan. 1950), pp. 1–10.
217. S/1462, 24 Feb. 1950 (mimeo.), pp. 2–3.
218. Lie, p. 254.
219. Ibid., pp. 254–5, 258–60.
220. Ibid., pp. 256–7, 261; SCOR, 5th year, Supplement for January to May 1950, pp. 18–23, S/1466.
221. Ibid., pp. 23–6, S/1470. See also Lie, pp. 249–74.
222. SCOR, 5th year, Supplement for January to May 1950, pp. 23–6, S/1470.
223. Ibid., 459th meeting (10 Jan. 1950), pp. 8–9; 460th meeting (12 Jan. 1950), pp. 6–7; 462nd meeting (17 Jan. 1950), pp. 1–12; Supplement for January

to May 1950, pp. 2–3, and 16–18, S/1447 and S/1457 and Corr. 1, paras. 4–12; 468th meeting (28 Feb. 1950), paras. 9–11.

224. Ibid., 480th meeting (1 Aug. 1950), pp. 1–12; 481st meeting (2 Aug. 1950); 482nd meeting (3 Aug. 1950), pp. 1–22.

225. SCOR, 6th year, 566th meeting (10 Nov. 1951), p. 1; 10th year, 689th meeting (31 Jan. 1955), paras. 1–27; 700th meeting (8 Sept. 1955), paras. 1–5; 22nd year, 1341st meeting (24 May 1967), paras. 8–59.

226. SCOR, 26th year, 1565th meeting (9 Feb. 1971), paras. 51–101.

227. General Assembly res. 2758(XXVI), 25 Oct. 1971.

228. A/PV. 1983, 15 Nov. 1971, pp. 87–101.

229. SCOR, 5th year, 525th meeting (27 Nov. 1950), p. 20; 526th meeting (28 Nov. 1950), p. 2; 527th meeting (28 Nov. 1950), pp. 1–26; 528th meeting (29 Nov. 1950), pp. 8 and 11; 529th meeting (30 Nov. 1950), p. 1; 530th meeting (30 Nov. 1950), pp. 1 and 19–20.

230. S/10378, 26 Oct. 1971 (mimeo.); S/10382, 2 Nov. 1971 (mimeo.); S/10391, 19 Nov. 1971 (mimeo.); SCOR, 26th year, 1599th meeting (23 Nov. 1971), paras. 1–94.

231. See, for example, SCOR, 23rd year, 1417th meeting (27 Apr. 1968), paras. 71–2; 25th year, 1530th meeting (6 Mar. 1970), para. 5.

232. *Guardian*, 9 Aug. 1973.

233. Richard A. Falk, 'The United Nations: Various Systems of Operation', in *The United Nations in World Politics*, edited by Leon Gordenker, Princeton University Press, 1971, p. 209, fn. 64; Arthur Lall, *The Security Council in a Universal United Nations*, New York, Carnegie Endowment for International Peace, 1971, pp. 30, 31, 34.

234. Lall, p. 34.

235. Falk, p. 209, fn. 64; Neil H. Jacoby, *Center Report*, Santa Barbara, Calif. Center for the Study of Democratic Institutions, vol. iv, no. 4, Oct. 1971, pp. 10, 12; Lall, pp. 31–2.

236. Falk, p. 209, fn. 64; Jacoby, pp. 10, 12; Lall, p. 30; Lie, p. 433.

237. Jacoby, p. 12; Lall, pp. 9, 31.

238. Lall, pp. 31, 34.

239. Lall, p. 34.

240. Falk, p. 209, fn. 64; T. C. Rhee, 'Japan: "security" and "militarism"', *World Today*, vol. 27, no. 9 (Sept. 1971), p. 390; Jacoby pp. 10, 12; Lall, pp. 30, 34; Alastair Buchan, 'A World Restored?', *Foreign Affairs*, vol. 50, no. 4 (July 1972), pp. 657–8;* UN doc. A/8746, 22 Aug. 1972, p. 36; Osamu Miyoshi, 'The Nixon Doctrine in Asia' and Alastair Buchan, 'The End of Bipolarity',* *Adelphi Paper no. 91*, London, International Institute for Strategic Studies, 1972, pp. 19 and 26–7 respectively; Richard Ellingworth, 'Japanese Economic Policies and Security', *Adelphi Paper no. 90*, 1972, p. 5; UN doc. A/8847, 8 Dec. 1972, p. 14; Kei Wakaizumi, 'Japan's Role in a New World Order', *Foreign Affairs*, vol. 51, no. 2 (Jan. 1973), p. 323; 'Japanese Security and the United States' *Adelphi Paper no. 95*, 1973, p. 32; A/PV. 2124 (24 Sept. 1973), p. 31.

241. *Report of the President's Commission for the observance of the twenty-fifth anniversary of the United Nations*, Washington, D.C., Government Printing Office, 1971 (hereafter cited as *Report of President's Commission*), p. 44; Evan Luard, *The United Nations in a new era*, London, Fabian Society, 1972, p. 16.

242. Lall, pp. 31–2, 34, 38–9; Alastair Buchan, 'A World Restored?', *Foreign Affairs*, vol. 50, no 4 (July 1972), p. 658.

* Alastair Buchan's support for permanent membership of the Security Council for Japan seems to have decreased marginally between July and September 1972.

243. Lall, pp. 3, 18, 19.
244. Lall, pp. 4–11, 36, 42.
245. SCOR, 22nd year, 1342nd meeting (24 May 1967), paras. 25, 81–4, 90–7.
246. Lall, pp. 10–11, 21, 23, 30, 35, 39.
247. Lall, pp. 34–5.
248. A/8746, 22 Aug. 1972 (mimeo.); GAOR, 27th session, 2050th plenary meeting (3 Oct. 1972); A/8847, 8 Dec. 1972 (mimeo.), p. 25.
249. Lall, p. 36.
250. *Report of President's Commission*, p. 44; *The United Nations in the 1970s*, New York, United Nations Association, 1971, pp. 22–3; A/8746, 22 Aug. 1972, pp. 30, 36; A/8847, 8 Dec. 1972 (mimeo.), p. 14; A/9128, 25 Oct. 1973 (mimeo.), pp. 8–9; A/9143, 30 Nov. 1973 (mimeo.), pp. 3 and 9.

CHAPTER 4

1. SCOR, 27th year, Supplement for April to June 1972, pp. 32–3, S/10611, S/10612.
2. SCOR, 19th year, 1136th meeting (18 June 1964), para. 16.
3. SCOR, 21st year, 1316th meeting (3 Nov. 1966), paras. 3–4.
4. SCOR, 19th year, 1136th meeting (18 June 1964), para. 15.
5. SCOR, 22nd year, 1355th meeting (10 June 1967), paras. 47–8; 1373rd meeting (9/10 Nov. 1967), paras. 15, 34, 45; S/PV. 1748, 23 Oct. 1973, p. 58.
6. S/PV. 1744, 9 Oct. 1973, pp. 48–50.
7. SCOR, 5th year, 519th meeting (8 Nov. 1950), pp. 1–14.
8. SCOR, 3rd year, 357th meeting (16 Sept. 1948), pp. 11–18.
9. SCOR, 5th year, 525th meeting (27 Nov. 1950), pp. 21–2; 526th meeting (28 Nov. 1950), pp. 2–10.
10. SCOR, 19th year, 1095th meeting (18 Feb. 1964), paras. 2–32.
11. SCOR, 22nd year, 1373rd meeting (9/10 Nov. 1967), paras. 5–45.
12. SCOR, 3rd year, 330th meeting (7 July 1948), pp. 6, 10–11; 15th year, 893th meeting (8 Sept. 1960), para. 71; 22nd year, 1373rd meeting (9/10 Nov. 1967), para. 8; S/PV. 1749, 24 Oct. 1973, pp. 51 and 62.
13. SCOR, 9th year, 656th meeting (22 Jan. 1954), para. 19.
14. SCOR, 17th year, 1025th meeting (25 Oct. 1962), paras. 49, 51.
15. SCOR, 11th year, 753rd meeting (3 Nov. 1956), paras. 15, 23–31; 22nd year, 1355th meeting (10 June 1967), paras. 18–58.
16. SCOR, 15th year, 874th meeting (18 July 1960), paras. 4–5; 893rd meeting (8 Sept. 1960), paras. 27, 71; 16th year, 975th meeting (16 Nov. 1961), paras. 122, 124–30; 20th year, 1263rd meeting (17 Nov. 1965), paras. 22–4.
17. SCOR, 19th year, 1142nd meeting (8 Aug. 1964), paras. 8–46.
18. SCOR, 20th year, 1210th meeting (18 May 1965), para. 5.
19. Cited in my *The General Assembly of the United Nations*, 2nd edition, 1964, p. 121.
20. SCOR, 2nd year, 185th meeting (15 Aug. 1947), p. 2024.
21. GAOR, 26th session, Supplement no. 26, A/8426, p. 44, para. 229(a) (Reference inserted by the author).
22. Ibid., p. 45, para. 229(d).
23. SCOR, 1st year, 2nd series, 67th meeting (16 Sept. 1946), p. 338.
24. SCOR, 17th year, 989th meeting (30 Jan. 1962), paras. 32–41, 45, 49.
25. Ibid., paras. 54–5, 62, 67–74. For an exception to this practice, see SCOR, 23rd year, 1448th meeting (8/9th Sept. 1968), paras. 67–72.
26. GAOR, 26th session, Supplement no. 26, A/8426, pp. 44–5, paras. 229(a) and (c).

27. Ibid., para. 229(c).
28. SCOR, 11th year, 751st meeting (31 Oct. 1956), paras. 126–7.
29. *Repertoire I*, p. 32, fn. 22.
30. For an exception, see SCOR, 17th year, 998th meeting (23 Mar. 1962), paras. 154–6.
31. GAOR, 26th session, Supplement no. 26, A/8426, p. 45, para. 229(c).
32. SCOR, 1st year, 2nd series, 67th meeting (16 Sept. 1946), pp. 336–8; 5th year, 525th meeting (27 Nov. 1950), pp. 20–1.
33. SCOR, 2nd year, 202nd meeting (15 Sept. 1947), p. 2402; 20th year, 1247th meeting (25 Oct. 1965), paras. 78, 102–9, 112–19; 21st year, 1295th meeting (3 Aug. 1966), para. 133.
34. SCOR, 2nd year, 213rd meeting (22 Oct. 1947), pp. 2619–20.
35. SCOR, 3rd year, 329th meeting (6 July 1948), pp. 20–1.
36. See, for example, SCOR, 5th year, 480th meeting (1 Aug. 1950), p. 1.
37. SCOR, 1st year, 1st series, Supplement no. 2, p. 22, S/57.
38. Ibid., 41st meeting (16 May 1946), p. 257.
39. Ibid., pp. 255, 257 (my italics).
40. Ibid., 7th meeting (4 Feb. 1946), pp. 123–4.
41. For discussion of the application of Rule 31, see SCOR, 3rd year, 328th meeting (1 July 1948), p. 25; 329th meeting (6 July 1948), pp. 27–30; 337th meeting (15 July 1948), p. 42; 9th year, 655th meeting (21 Jan. 1954), paras. 76, 79, 83, 85; 16th year, 942nd meeting (20/21 Feb. 1961), para. 170; 966th meeting (29 July 1961), paras. 62–3.
42. See, for example, SCOR, 10th year, 690th meeting (31 Jan. 1955), para. 138; 20th year, 1214th meeting (21 May 1965), paras. 64–7.
43. SCOR, 2nd year, 194th meeting (25 Aug. 1947), pp. 2193–6; 3rd year, 381st meeting (16 Nov. 1948), pp. 50–1; 4th year, 408th meeting (10 Feb. 1949), pp. 16–19; 447th meeting (16 Sept. 1949), pp. 22–3; 8th year, 653rd meeting (22 Dec. 1953), paras. 65–76.
44. See, for example, SCOR, 5th year, 492nd meeting (29 Aug. 1950), pp. 15–16; 497th meeting (7 Sept. 1950), pp. 27–9; 501st meeting (12 Sept. 1950), pp. 2–13; 10th year, 702nd meeting (10 Dec. 1955), paras. 17, 22–6; 703rd meeting (13 Dec. 1955), paras. 62–6.
45. Ibid., 709th meeting (22 Dec. 1955), para. 43; 11th year, Supplement for January to March 1956, pp. 1–2, S/3528; 715th meeting (19 Jan. 1956), paras. 120–30.
46. SCOR, 4th year, 405th meeting (27 Jan. 1949), pp. 31–2.
47. GAOR, 26th session, Supplement no. 26, A/8426, p. 45, para. 229(b).
48. For examples of the correct procedure (by the Soviet Union, Tunisia, and the United States respectively), see SCOR, 11th year, 746th meeting (28 Oct. 1956), paras. 47–8; 15th year, 897th meeting (10 Sept. 1960), paras. 78–9; 898th meeting (12 Sept. 1960), paras. 7–8.
49. SCOR, 1st year, 1st series, Supplement no. 2, p. 22, S/57; 41st meeting (16 May 1946), pp. 259–60.
50. SCOR, 2nd year, 160th meeting (17 July 1947), p. 1387; 193rd meeting (22 Aug. 1947), pp. 2172–3; 9th year, 656th meeting (22 Jan. 1954), paras. 14–22.
51. SCOR, 1st year, 1st series, 8th meeting (5 Feb. 1946), p. 133; 9th meeting (6 Feb. 1946), pp. 136–63.
52. SCOR, 1st year, 2nd series, 57th meeting (29 Aug. 1946), pp. 113–15.
53. SCOR, 7th year, 591st meeting (9 July 1952), para. 43; 8th year, 653rd meeting (22 Dec. 1953), para. 38; 10th year, 706th meeting (15 Dec. 1955), para. 123; 12th year, 788th meeting (6 Sept. 1957), paras. 54 and 67.

54. SCOR, 16th year, 982nd meeting (24 Nov. 1961), paras. 87–94.
55. SCOR, 19th year, 1143rd meeting (9/11 Aug. 1964), paras. 144, 149–50, 169–70, 180.
56. See, for example, SCOR, 25th year, 1247th meeting (25 Oct. 1965), paras. 91, 110–11; 21st year, 1277th meeting (9 April 1966), paras. 138, 143; 1340th meeting (16 Dec. 1966), paras. 99, 106, 109; 22nd year, 1342nd meeting (24 May 1967), paras. 85–6; 23rd year, 1448th meeting (8/9 Sept. 1968), paras. 63–72.
57. SCOR, 22nd year, 1349th meeting (7 June 1967), paras. 23–43; 1350th meeting (7 June 1967), p. 1.
58. SCOR, 5th year, 507th meeting (29 Sept. 1950), pp. 15–17.
59. SCOR, 22nd year, 1358th meeting (13 June 1967), paras. 329–33, and 334.
60. SCOR, 17th year, 989th meeting (30 Jan. 1962), paras. 30–75.
61. Conforti, p. 485.
62. SCOR, 1093rd meeting (17 Feb. 1964), paras. 4, 16, 22; 1104th meeting (17 Mar. 1964), paras. 2–89; 1105th meeting (20 Mar. 1964), paras. 2–51.
63. SCOR, 15th year, 898th meeting (12 Sept. 1960), paras. 16–26.
64. SCOR, 11th year, 714th meeting (18 Jan. 1956), paras. 107–27.
65. See, for example, SCOR, 2nd year, 121st meeting (21 July 1947), p. 590; 122nd meeting (25 Mar. 1947, pp. 609–11; 5th year, 459th meeting (10 Jan. 1950), p. 10; 17th year, 989th meeting (30 Jan. 1962), paras. 30–75.
66. SCOR, 1st year, 2nd series, 57th meeting (29 Aug. 1946), p. 113; 11th year, 714th meeting (18 Jan. 1956), para. 110; 22nd year, 1349th meeting (7 June 1967), para. 23.
67. SCOR, 1st year, 1st series, 19th meeting (14 Feb. 1946), p. 278; 2nd year, 93rd meeting (15 Jan. 1947), p. 82.
68. SCOR, 1st year, 2nd series, 55th meeting (28 Aug. 1946), p. 55.
69. Ibid., 57th meeting (29 Aug. 1946), p. 116; 3rd year, 384th meeting (15 Dec. 1948), p. 14.
70. SCOR, 8th year, 651st meeting (21 Dec. 1953), para. 30; 12th year, 790th meeting (9 Sept. 1957), paras. 45, 47.
71. SCOR, 11th year, 746th meeting (28 Oct. 1956), paras. 48–53.
72. SCOR, 2nd year, 132nd meeting (30 Apr. 1947), pp. 818–21.
73. SCOR, 12th year, 788th meeting (6 Sept. 1957), para. 97.
74. SCOR, 7th year, 577th meeting (18 June 1952), para. 138; 582nd meeting (25 June 1952), paras. 96–8; 583rd meeting (26 June 1962), para. 6.
75. SCOR, 1st year, 1st series, 19th meeting (14 Feb. 1946), pp. 275–81.
76. SCOR, 1st year, 2nd series, 55th meeting (28 Aug. 1946), pp. 55, 68; 57th meeting (29 Aug. 1946), pp. 117–19, 125–7, 135–6, 138; see also FRUS, 1947, vol. 1, pp. 236, 238–46, 252.
77. See, for example, SCOR, 2nd year, 93rd meeting (15 Jan. 1947), pp. 83, 85–6; 95th meeting (20 Jan. 1947), pp. 122–3; 3rd year, 384th meeting (15 Dec. 1948), pp. 13–14, 22, 28; 5th year, 506th meeting (29 Sept. 1950), p. 5; 6th year, 565th meeting (19 Oct. 1951) paras. 10–16, 19–26, 28–9, 34, 47–8, 62; 7th year, 590th meeting (9 July 1952), paras. 38–58, 77; 591st meeting (9 July 1952), paras. 1–96; 8th year, 628th meeting (20 Oct. 1953), paras. 4–5, 43–9, 79–82, 90, 131–3; 634th meeting (2 Nov. 1953), paras. 14, 20, 53, 56, 88–9; 641st meeting (23 Nov. 1953), paras. 6–8, 54, 77, 101; 647th meeting (14 Dec. 1943), paras. 3–5, 9–10, 40–3; 13th year, 820th meeting (2 June 1958), para. 109; 821st meeting (4 June 1958), para. 62.
78. SCOR, 2nd year, 90th meeting (9 Jan. 1947), p. 24.
79. SCOR, 10th year, 689th meeting (31 Jan. 1955), paras. 2–26.
80. *Voting in the Security Council*, pp. 25, 108.

81. SCOR, 5th year, 484th to 488th meetings (8 to 17 Aug. 1950).
82. See, for example, SCOR, 1st year, 2nd series, 55th meeting (28 Aug. 1946), p. 62; 2nd year, 132nd meeting (30 April 1947), pp. 820–1.
83. SCOR, 3rd year, 330th meeting (7 July 1948), pp. 2–9; 4th year, 443rd meeting (13 Sept. 1949), pp. 22–7; 5th year, 480th meeting (1 Aug. 1950), p. 9; 482nd meeting (3 Aug. 1950), pp. 18–20; 494th meeting (1 Sept. 1950), pp. 2–11; 7th year, 581st meeting (25 June 1952), paras. 31–4; 9th year, 676th meeting (25 June 1954), paras. 29–63; 17th year, 989th meeting (30 Jan. 1962), paras. 32–74; 998th meeting (23 Mar. 1962), paras. 145–56; 19th year, 1143rd meeting (9 to 11 Aug. 1964), paras. 174–7.
84. SCOR, 5th year, 484th meeting (8 Aug. 1950), p. 16; 492nd meeting (29 Aug. 1950), pp. 15–16.
85. SCOR, 1st year, 1st series, 49th meeting (26 June 1946), pp. 410–13.
86. Ibid., 41st meeting (16 May 1946), p. 260; 49th meeting (26 June 1946) p. 411.
87. SCOR, 2nd year, 169th meeting (29 July 1947), pp. 1585–95.
88. SCOR, 10th year, Supplement for October to December 1955, pp. 20 and 22, S/3502 and S/3506.
89. Ibid., 704th meeting (13 Dec. 1955), paras. 24–48.
90. SCOR, 1st year, 1st series, 17th meeting (12 Feb. 1946), pp. 251–3; 18th meeting (13 Feb. 1946), p. 257; 7th year, 590th meeting (9 July 1952), paras. 38–43, 56–8; 591st meeting (9 July 1952), paras. 10, 25–34, 38.
91. SCOR, 27th year, Supplement for April to June 1972, pp. 132–3, S/10709.
92. SCOR, 15th year, 863rd meeting (27 May 1960), paras. 43, 45–6.
93. SCOR, 2nd year, 131st meeting (18 Apr. 1947), p. 807.
94. SCOR, 17th year, 998th meeting (23 Mar. 1962), paras. 113–58.
95. SCOR, 2nd year, 206th meeting (1 Oct. 1947), pp. 2465, 2469; 9th year, 655th meeting (21 Jan. 1954), paras. 58, 87–8; 656th meeting (22 Jan. 1954), paras, 107–35; 11th year, 715th meeting (19 Jan. 1956), paras. 140–1; 722nd meeting (4 April 1956), para. 43; 749th meeting (30 Oct. 1956), para. 124; 21st year, 1319th meeting (4 Nov. 1966), paras. 52–4.
96. See, for example, SCOR, 3rd year, 286th meeting (21 Apr. 1948), pp. 39–40.
97. SCOR, 2nd year, 170th meeting (29 July 1947), p. 1612; 174th meeting (4 Aug. 1947), pp. 1723–6; 9th year, 670th meeting (4 May 1954), paras. 72–3.
98. SCOR, 2nd year, 174th meeting (4 Aug. 1947), p. 1724.
99. SCOR, 5th year, 530th meeting (30 Nov. 1950), pp. 24–5.
100. SCOR, 17th year, 998th meeting (23 Mar. 1962), paras. 78–110.
101. SCOR, 1st year, 1st series, 16th meeting (11 Feb. 1946), pp. 223–32; 18th meeting (13 Feb. 1946), p. 258.
102. SCOR, 2nd year, 206th meeting (1 Oct. 1947), pp. 2465–75.
103. SCOR 10th year, 706th meeting (15 Dec. 1955), paras. 90, 99, 119.
104. GAOR, 5th session, Annexes, Agenda item 49, A/1356, paras. 23–4 (paragraph no. omitted, my italics).
105. *Repertoire I*, p. 2. This information is repeated in abbreviated form in later volumes of the *Repertoire*.
106. *Resolutions and Decisions of the Security Council* . . . (published annually), p. 2.
107. ICJ Reports 1962, p. 163.
208. S.C. res. 146 (S/4426), 9 Aug. 1960, para. 5.
109. S.C. res. 232 (S/7621/Rev. 1, as amended), 16 Dec. 1966, paras. 3 and 6.
110. S.C. res. 253 (S/8601), 29 May 1968, paras. 11–12.
111. S.C. res. 288 (S/9980), 17 Nov. 1970, para. 4.

112. S.C. res. 314 (S/10541/Rev. 1 and Corr. 1, as amended), 28 Feb. 1972, para. 2; 320 (S/10804/Rev. 1), 29 Sept. 1972, para. 2.
113. S.C. res. 269 (S/9384), 12 Aug. 1969, preamble.
114. S.C. res. 246 (S/8429), 14 Mar. 1968.
115. *Repertoire VI*, p. 217.
116. See, for example, S.C. res. 67 (S/1234), 28 Jan. 1949; 91 (S/2017/Rev. 1), 30 March 1951; 144 (S/4395), 19 July 1960.
117. ICJ Reports 1971, pp. 52–4.
118. SCOR, 2nd year, 162nd meeting (22 July 1947), p. 1419.
119. Ibid., 134th meeting (16 May 1947), p. 843.
120. Ibid., 162nd meeting (22 July 1947), p. 1422.
121. Ibid., 167th meeting (25 July 1947), p. 1530.
122. Ibid., 135th meeting (20 May 1947), p. 875.
123. Ibid., 156th meeting (11 July 1947), p. 1280.
124. Ibid., 160th meeting (17 July 1947), pp. 1379, 1383.
125. Ibid., 167th meeting (25 July 1947), pp. 1541–2.
126. SCOR, 3rd year, 293rd meeting (17 May 1948), p. 2; 296th meeting (19 May 1948), pp. 2–12, 22; 298th meeting (20 May 1948), pp. 14–15, 32.
127. SCOR, 12th year, 767th meeting (8 Feb. 1957), paras. 92–3; 774th meeting (21 Feb. 1957), para. 31; 805th meeting (21 Nov. 1957), para. 52.
128. S.C. res. 145 (S/4405), 22 July 1960, para. 3.
129. S.C. res. 146 (S/4426), 9 Aug. 1960, para. 5.
130. SCOR, 15th year, Supplement for July to September 1960, pp. 139–40, S/4482/Add. 1; Supplement for October to December 1960, pp. 100–3, S/4599; 16th year, Supplement for January to March 1961, pp. 261–5, S/4775, section I.
131. S.C. res. 161 (S/4741), 21 Feb. 1961, paras. 1 and 5.
132. SCOR, 16th year, Supplement for January to March 1961, pp. 178–9, S/4752, Annex I; pp. 182–3, S/4752, Annex III; pp. 190–7, S/4752/Add. 1; pp. 269–71, S/4775, section IV.
133. GAOR, 16th session, Supplement no. 1A, A/4800/Add. 1, p. 4; U Thant expressed a similar view in a speech on 28 October 1969, see *UN Monthly Chronicle*, vol. VI, no. 10 (Nov. 1969), p. 86.
134. SCOR, 23rd year, Supplement for January to March 1968, pp. 284–7, S/8495.
135. SCOR, 26th year, 1588th meeting (5 Oct. 1971), para. 18; 1594th meeting (14 Oct. 1971), para. 51; 1589th meeting (6 Oct. 1971), paras. 51–3.
136. Ibid., para. 116.
137. Rosalyn Higgins, 'The Advisory Opinion on Namibia', *International and Comparative Law Quarterly*, vol. 21 (Apr. 1972), pp. 281–2.

CHAPTER 5

1. GAOR, 4th session, Supplement no. 1, A/930, p. 46.
2. SCOR, 1st year, 1st series, Supplement no. 1, pp. 2 and 3; 2nd meeting (25 Jan. 1946), pp. 12–14; S.C. res. 1, 25 Jan. 1946.
3. S/10, 14 Feb. 1946 (restricted). There is some uncertainty as to the precise date on which the Military Staff Committee held its first meeting. Some UN documents give 4 Feb. 1946 (GAOR, 1st session, 2nd part, A/65, p. 9; *Repertoire I*, p. 239); see also FRUS, 1946, vol. 1, p. 734, fn. 46. The first report of the Security Council, however, gives 3 Feb. (GAOR, 1st session, Supplement no. 1, A/93, p. 84).
4. SCOR, 1st year, 1st series, 23rd meeting (16 Feb. 1946), p. 369; 25th meeting (16 Mar. 1946), p. 10.

5. FRUS, 1946, vol. 1, pp. 790, 895, 914–15, 931, 1036; 1947, vol. 1, p. 447.
6. S/124 and Corr. 1 and Add. 1, 8 Aug. 1946 (restricted).
7. S/115, 1 Aug. 1946 (restricted). There is again some uncertainty about dates, some documents giving 1 Aug. (*Repertoire I*, p. 238), others giving 24 July (Ibid., p. 191; GAOR, 2nd session, Supplement no. 2, A/366, p. 103). The document which presumably gives the correct date (S/115) is restricted.
8. S/165, 20 Sept. 1946; S/187, 28 Oct. 1946; S/325, 9 April 1947; S/356, 19 May 1947 (all restricted).
9. S/421, 17 July 1947 (restricted).
10. G.A. res. 41(1) and 42(1), 14 Dec. 1946; S.C. res. 18 (S/268/Rev. 1/Corr. 1), 13 Feb. 1947.
11. SCOR, 2nd year, Special Supplement no. 1, S/336.
12. FRUS, 1947, vol. 1, p. 468, fn. 3, and p. 495. A convenient annotated text of the principles approved by the Security Council, with alternative formulations of the articles not agreed, is in *Repertory II*, pp. 396–408; Lie, pp. 95–8.
13. Inis L. Claude, Jr., 'The United Nations and the use of force', *International Conciliation*, no. 532 (March 1961), pp. 346–55; see also Professor Claude's 'United Nations use of military force', *Journal of Conflict Resolution*, vol. 7, no. 2 (June 1963), pp. 117–29.
14. SCOR, 2nd year, 142nd meeting (18 June 1947), pp. 1027–41, 143rd meeting (20 June 1947), pp. 1053–4, 1061–2; 145th meeting (24 June 1947), pp. 1078–91; 146th meeting (25 June 1947), pp. 1104–13; 149th meeting (30 June 1947), pp. 1158 and 1175–9; 154th meeting (10 July 1947), p. 1267; Special Supplement no. 13, pp. 133–40, S/394.
15. Ibid., 141st meeting (16 June 1947), pp. 1018–19.
16. S/879, 2 July 1948 (mimeo.).
17. GAOR, 4th session, Supplement no. 2, A/945, p. 95; MS/417, 6 Aug. 1948; MS/420, 16 Aug. 1948.
18. GAOR, 5th session, Supplement no. 2, A/1361, p. 62; 6th session, Supplement no. 2, A/1873, p. 88.
19. GAOR, 19th session, Annexes, item 21, A/5721, section 3; 5th special session, Annexes, Agenda item 8, A/6654, paras. 117, 119–20, 130.
20. ICJ Reports 1950, p. 10.
21. Goodrich, pp. 276, 279, 283–4.
22. Speech on 28 October 1969, published in *UN Monthly Chronicle*, vol. vi, no. 10 (November 1969), p. 86.
23. GAOR, 26th session, Supplement no. 1A, A/8401/Add. 1, para. 96.
24. Russell, pp. 154–5; Hull, p. 1684.
25. GAOR, 25th session, Supplement no. 2, A/8002, p. 1.
26. GAOR, 24th session, Annexes, Agenda item 11, p. 1, A/L. 580. See also A/9143, 30 Nov. 1973 (mimeo.), p. 10.
27. GAOR, 24th session, 1837th plenary meeting (17 Dec. 1969), paras. 56–83.
28. Ibid., paras. 84–94; G.A. res. 2619(XXIV), 17 Dec. 1969.
29. G.A. res. 2864(XXVI), 20 Dec. 1971.
30. A/PV. 2027, 20 Dec. 1971, pp. 117–26.
31. A/PV. 2111, 15 Dec. 1972, pp. 11–15.
32. Ibid., pp. 22–6.
33. Ibid., pp. 26–32; G.A. res. 2991(XXVII), 15 Dec. 1972.
34. A/PV. 2205, 18 Dec. 1973, pp. 61–71, 76–8.
35. Ibid., pp. 71–5.
36. G.A. res. 3186(XXVIII), 18 Dec. 1973 (paragraph numbers and footnote omitted).

37. G.A. res. 181(II); SCOR, 2nd year, Supplement no. 20, p. 172, S/614; 222nd meeting (9 Dec. 1947), pp. 2776–88.
38. G.A. res. 268B(III), 28 April 1949; S/1323, 13 May 1949 (mimeo.); S.C. res. 81 (S/1486), 24 May 1950.
39. G.A. res. 1(I), 24 Jan. 1946; 41(I), 14 Dec. 1946; 42(I), 14 Dec. 1946; 191(III), 4 Nov. 1948; 192(III), 19 Nov. 1948; 299(IV), 23 Nov. 1949; 300(IV), 5 Dec. 1949; 502(VI), 11 Jan. 1952.
40. A/9158, 18 Sept. 1973 (mimeo.); S/11185, 7 Jan. 1974 (mimeo.), p. 1; GAOR, 19th session, Annex no. 1, p. 3; A/5980, 20 Sept. 1965 (mimeo.), p. 7.
41. SCOR, 5th year, 503rd meeting (26 Sept. 1950), pp. 29–33; 504th meeting (27 Sept. 1950), pp. 5–6; 505th meeting (28 Sept. 1950), p. 22; 506th meeting (29 Sept. 1950), pp. 4–5.
42. *Juridical Yearbook 1964*, p. 229, 237; *Juridical Yearbook 1968*, p. 185.
43. SCOR, 1st year, 2nd series, 79th meeting (4 Nov. 1956), p. 498.
44. S.C. res. 34 (S/555), 15 Sept. 1947.
45. S.C. res. 87 (S/1836), 29 Sept. 1950.
46. S.C. res. 90 (S/1995), 31 Jan. 1955.
47. S.C. res. 44 (S/714, II), 1 April 1948.
48. S.C. res. 119 (S/3721), 31 Oct. 1956.
49. S.C. res. 120 (S/3733), 4 Nov. 1956.
50. S.C. res. 129 (S/4083), 7 Aug. 1958.
51. S.C. res. 157 (S/4526), 17 Sept. 1960.
52. SCOR, 1st year, 1st series, 48th meeting (24 June 1946), p. 398.
53. SCOR, 1st year, 2nd series, 79th meeting (4 Nov. 1956), p. 497.
54. *Juridical Yearbook 1964*, p. 237.
55. *Juridical Yearbook 1968*, p. 185 (I have changed the verbs to the present tense).
56. G.A. res. 377(V), 3 Nov. 1950.
57. FRUS, 1947, vol. 1, p. 201; ICJ Reports 1962, pp. 155, 163–5; see also I.C.J. Reports 1971, p. 50.
58. G.A. res. 34(I), 9 Nov. 1946; 35(I) and 36(I), 19 Nov. 1946; 113(II), 17 Nov. 1947; 197(III), 8 Dec. 1948; 296(IV), 22 Nov. 1949; 495(V), 4 Dec. 1950; 506(VI), 1 Feb. 1951; 620(VII), 21 Dec. 1952; 718(VIII), 23 Oct. 1953; 816(IX) and 817(IX), 23 Nov. 1954; 917(X) and 918(X), 8 Dec. 1955; 1017(XI), 23 Feb. 1957; 1144(XII), 23 Oct. 1957; see also res. 550(VI), 7 Dec. 1951.
59. SCOR, 20th year, 1244th meeting (22 Sept. 1965), para. 30.
60. GAOR, 19th session, Annexes, Item 11, p. 1, A/5844; SCOR, 20th year, Supplement for January to March 1965, pp. 20–2, S/6157.
61. A/5861, 25 Jan. 1965 (mimeo.); *Juridical Yearbook, 1966*, pp. 222–3; SCOR, 20th year, Supplement for January to March 1965, pp. 73 and 174–5, S/6202 and S/6229; 1190th meeting (15 March 1965), para. 128; Supplement for April to June 1965, pp. 6–8 and 124–6, S/6269 and S/6356.
62. Ibid., 1190th meeting (15 March 1965), para. 113; Supplement for January to March 1965, pp. 264–5, S/6264.
63. SCOR, 21st year, Supplement for July to September 1966, p. 127, S/7498; *Juridical Yearbook, 1966*, p. 223; GAOR, 21st session, 1420th plenary meeting (28 Sept. 1966), paras. 1–8.
64. *General Assembly of the United Nations*, pp. 221–38.
65. SCOR, 18th year, 1039th meeting (11 June 1963), paras. 19–25; 19th year, 1102nd meeting (4 March 1964), para. 11; 20th year, 1247th meeting (25 Oct. 1965), para. 243.
66. S/PV. 1750, 25 Oct. 1973, pp. 26–7, 48, 57.

67. S/11052/Rev. 1, 27 Oct. 1973 (mimeo.), para. 7; S.C. res. 341 (S/11054), 27 Oct. 1973; A/9314, 14 Nov. 1973 (mimeo.), paras. 3–4; A/9428, 10 Dec. 1973 (mimeo.); G.A. res. 3101(XXVIII), 11 Dec. 1973.
68. See ECOSOC res. 214B(viii), 16 Feb. 1949, concerning human rights in Palestine, circulated to the Security Council as S/1291, 14 March 1949 (mimeo.); SCOR, 3rd year, 354th meeting (19 Aug. 1948), pp. 55–6 (Palestine refugees); S.C. res. 85 (S/1657), 31 July 1950, para. 4 (relief and support for the civilian population of Korea).
69. A/8775/Add. 4, 19 Dec. 1972 (mimeo.).
70. S.C. res. 330 (S/10932/Rev. 2), 21 March 1973.
71. SCOR, 2nd year, 113th meeting (26 Feb. 1947), p. 410.
72. S.C. res. 21 (S/318), 2 April 1947; see also FRUS, 1947, vol. 1, pp. 258–78.
73. SCOR, 2nd year, 220th meeting (15 November 1947), p. 2763.
74. S.C. res. 70 (S/1280), 7 March 1949. The President of the Trusteeship Council's interpretation of the procedure, also approved by the Security Council on 7 March 1949, is in SCOR, 4th year, Supplement for March 1949, pp. 1–3, S/916.
75. See my *General Assembly of the United Nations*, pp. 176–84 and 'The Future Composition of the Trusteeship Council', *International Organization*, vol. xiii No. 3 (Summer 1959), pp. 412–21.
76. UNCIO, 1945, vol. iii, pp. 600 and 619.
77. PC/EX/TC/4, 15 Sept. 1945 (mimeo.), para. 5.
78. SCOR, 23rd year, Supplement for January to March 1968, pp. 71–2, S/8355 and Add. 1 and 2.
79. G.A. res. 2145(xxi), 25 Jan. 1968.
80. S.C. res. 245, 25 Jan. 1968; 246 (S/8429), 14 March 1968.
81. S.C. res. 264 (S/9100), 20 March 1969.
82. S.C. res. 269 (S/9384), 12 Aug. 1969; 276 (S/9620/Rev. 1), 30 Jan. 1970; 283 (S/9891) and 284 (S/9892), 29 July 1970; 301 (S/10372/Rev. 1), 20 Oct. 1971; 309 (S/10376/Rev. 2) and 310 (S/10608/Rev. 1), 4 Feb. 1972; 319 (S/10750, as amended), 1 Aug. 1972; 323 (S/10846, as amended), 6 Dec. 1972; 342 (S/11152/Rev. 1), 11 Dec. 1973.
83. pp. 84–9.
84. SCOR, 1st year, 2nd series, Supplement no. 1, pp. 8–12, S/99; 50th meeting (10 July 1946), pp. 7–8; Supplement no. 6, pp. 153–6, S/169; 76th meeting (15 Oct. 1946), pp. 466–82.
85. S.C. res. 9, 15 Oct. 1946.
86. SCOR, 1st year, 2nd series, Supplement no. 7, S/185; 78th meeting (30 Oct. 1946), pp. 485–7.
87. Ibid., Supplement No. 8, S/191.
88. S.C. res. 11, 15 Nov. 1946.
89. SCOR, 4th year, Supplement for April 1949, p. 6, S/1298 and Corr. 1; 423rd meeting (8 Apr. 1949), pp. 16–17; Supplement for July 1949, pp. 2–3, S/1342; 432nd meeting (27 July 1949), pp. 1–6; 8th year, Supplement for October to December 1953, pp. 37, 56–7, 72–3, S/3126, S/3137, S/3146, S/3147; 641st meeting (23 Nov. 1953), pp. 1–2; 645th meeting (3 Dec. 1953), pp. 2–4.
90. SCOR, 3rd year, Supplement for September 1948, pp. 1–2, S/947.
91. SCOR, 1st year, 2nd series, Supplement no. 8, p. 161, S/191, para. 7.
92. SCOR, 3rd year, Supplement for September 1948, pp. 3–4, S/969; S.C. res. 58, 28 Sept. 1948.
93. G.A. res. 264(111), 8 Oct. 1948.
94. SCOR, 1st year, 1st series, 9th meeting (6 Feb. 1946), pp. 156–60; 2nd year,

194th meeting (24 Aug. 1947), p. 2193; 3rd year, 334th meeting (13 July 1948), pp. 52–3; 17th year, 992nd meeting (14 March 1962), paras. 111–22.

95. S.C. res. 276 (S/9620/Rev. 1), 30 Jan. 1970; 284 (S/9892), 29 July 1970.
96. SCOR, 25th year, 1550th meeting (29 July 1970), paras. 132, 145–7, 186–93.
97. ICJ Reports 1971, p. 58.
98. S.C. res. 301 (S/10372/Rev. 1), 20 Oct. 1971.
99. SCOR, 26th year, 1589th meeting (6 Oct. 1971), paras. 57–9; Higgins, p. 282.
100. SCOR, 2nd year, 189th meeting (20 Aug. 1947), p. 2115; 3rd year, 363rd meeting (6 Oct. 1948), p. 10; 9th year, 679th meeting (10 Sept. 1954), paras. 38–9.
101. SCOR, 2nd year, Supplement no. 3, pp. 35–50, S/247, S/250; Supplement no. 6; 95th meeting (20 Jan. 1947), pp. 123–4; S.C. res. 19, 27 Feb. 1947; SCOR, 2nd year, Supplement no. 10, pp. 77–118, S/300, S/298, S/304; 122nd meeting (25 Mar. 1947), p. 609; 127th meeting (9 Apr. S.C. res. 22 (S/324), 9 April 1947.
102. ICJ Reports 1951, p. 100.
103. SCOR, 6th year, Supplement for October to December 1951, pp. 1–5, S/2357, S/2358 and Revs. 1 and 2.
104. Shabtai Rosenne, *The Law and Practice of the International Court of Justice*, Leyden, Sijthoff, 1965, vol. I, pp. 156, 157.
105. SCOR, 6th year, 559th meeting (1 Oct. 1951), paras. 16, 94; 560th meeting (15 Oct. 1951), paras. 58, 60.
106. Ibid., 559th meeting (1 Oct. 1951), paras. 9–10; 561st meeting (16 Oct. 1951), paras, 68–74, 79–80; 562nd meeting (17 Oct. 1951), paras. 24–6, 38–40; 565th meeting (19 Oct. 1951), paras. 27, 29, 48–50, 63.

CHAPTER 6

1. SCOR, 1st year, 1st series, 1st meeting (1 Feb. 1946), p. 11.
2. SCOR, 2nd year, 138th meeting (4 June 1947), pp. 950–1; 3rd year, 305th meeting (26 May 1948), p. 35; Supplement for May 1948, p. 99, S/782.
3. SCOR, 1st year, 1st series, 31st meeting (9 Apr. 1946), pp. 100–2, 110, 115–16, 117–18; 41st meeting (16 May 1946), pp. 253–4, 255, 256, 260; 42nd meeting (17 May 1946), p. 270; 44th meeting (6 June 1946), pp. 310–11; 1st year, 2nd series, 76th meeting (15 Oct. 1946), p. 466; 80th meeting (15 Nov. 1946), p. 502; 2nd year, 197th meeting (27 Aug. 1947), p. 2256; 3rd year, 320th meeting (15 June 1948), p. 13; 4th year, 432nd meeting (27 July 1949), pp. 1–2; 5th year, 468th meeting (28 Feb. 1950), pp. 9–11.
4. SCOR, 1st year, 1st series, Supplement no. 1, pp. 5–6.
5. Ibid., Supplement no. 2, S/57, pp. 25, 38–9.
6. Ibid., 41st meeting (16 May 1946), pp. 261–267; 42nd meeting (17 May 1946), pp. 275–7.
7. Ibid., p. 277 see also FRUS, 1946, vol. 1, pp. 386–454.;
8. *Repertoire I*, p. 261; SCOR, 2nd year, Supplement no. 19, pp. 157–62, S/520; 197th meeting (27 Aug. 1947), pp. 2256–64; GAOR, 2nd session, First Committee, pp. 550–1, A/384, 12 Sept. 1947; ICJ Reports, 1950, p. 10.
9. SCOR, 2nd year, Supplement no. 19, pp. 164–5, S/520/Add. 1; FRUS, 1947, vol. 1, pp. 236–47; SCOR, 2nd year, 197th meeting (27 Aug. 1047); 222nd meeting (9 Dec. 1947), p. 2771.
10. SCOR, 7th year, 598th meeting (10 Sept. 1952), paras. 48, 84, 95; 599th meeting (12 Sept. 1952), paras. 63–4, 104–87.
11. SCOR, 2nd year, 206th meeting (1 Oct. 1947), pp. 2461–4, 2476.
12. Ibid., 186th meeting (18 Aug. 1947), pp. 2029–30.

13. SCOR, 4th year, 410th meeting (16 Feb. 1949), p. 15.
14. FRUS, 1946, vol. V, 1969, p. 1077; A/8746, 22 Aug. 1972 (mimeo.), p. 14.
15. *Repertoire I*, p. 272. A comprehensive survey of the practice of United Nations organs regarding the admission of new Members can be found in A/C. 64/L.1, 22 April 1953 (mimeo.).
16. SCOR, 3rd year, Supplement for December 1948, S/1110 and Corr. 1, pp. 119–20.
17. SCOR, 4th year, Supplement for September to December 1949, S/1382, pp. 10–12.
18. SCOR, 25th year, Supplement for April to June 1970, pp. 210–1, S/9836, para. 5; 1554th meeting (10 Oct. 1970).
19. Ibid. 1565th meeting (9 Feb. 1971), para. 126.
20. GAOR, 5th year, Supplement no. 2, A/1361, p. 48; 26th year, Supplement no. 2, A/8402, p. 57.
21. SCOR, 1st year, 2nd series, 54th meeting (28 Aug. 1946), pp. 39–40; 2nd year, 186th meeting (18 Aug. 1947), pp. 2030–1; 3rd year, 279th meeting (10 Apr. 1948), pp. 2–3; 351st meeting (18 Aug. 1948), p. 351.
22. SCOR, 26th year, 1587th meeting (30 Sept. 1971), paras. 86–106.
23. S.C. res. 99 (S/10345, para. 4), 30 Sept. 1971; G.A. res. 2754(XXVI), 7 Oct. 1971.
24. SCOR, 27th year, Supplement for July to September 1972, pp. 85–6, 90–2, 93–5, S/10759, S/10766, S/10768, S/10771, S/10773, S/10774; S/PV. 1660, 25 Aug. 1972, p. 47; G.A. res. 2937(XXVII), 29 Nov. 1972.
25. GAOR, 22nd session, Supplement no. 1A, A/6701/Add. 1, paras. 163–6. See also GAOR, 23rd session, Supplement no. 1A, A/7201/Add. 1, para. 172; 24th session, Supplement no. 1A, A/7601/Add. 1, para. 187; 25th session, Supplement no. 1A, A/8001/Add. 1, para. 163; 26th session, Supplement no. 1A, A/8401/Add. 1, para. 105.
26. SCOR, 22nd year, Supplement for October to December 1967, pp. 321–2, S/8296.
27. Ibid., p. 333, S/8316; 23rd year, Supplement for January to March 1968, pp. 156 and 208, S/8376 and S/8437; Supplement for April to June 1968, pp. 108–9, S/8520.
28. SCOR, 24th year, Supplement for July to September 1969, pp. 124, 159–60, and 164, S/9327, S/9397, and S/9414.
29. Ibid., 1505th and 1506th meetings, 27 and 29 Aug. 1969.
30. SCOR, 25th year, Supplement for April to June 1970, pp. 210–11, S/9836; GAOR, 27th session, Supplement no. 2, A/8702, p. 134.
31. SCOR, 25th year, Supplement for April to June 1970, pp. 210–11, S/9836 Annexes I and II; A/8746, 22 Aug. 1972 (mimeo.), pp. 15–16; A/8746/Add. 1, 13 Sept. 1972 (mimeo.), p. 14; Stephen M. Schwebel, 'Mini-States and a More Effective United Nations', *American Journal of International Law*, vol. 67, No. 1 (Jan. 1973), pp. 110 and 112.
32. *Status and Problems of Very Small States and Territories*, UN Institute for Training and Research, 1969, pp. 58–76; see also Patricia Wohlgemuth Blair, *The Ministate Dilemma*, New York, Carnegie Endowment for International Peace, 1967.
33. FRUS, 1946, vol. 1, p. 901; 1947, vol. 1, pp. 330, 338, 395–415, 450, 560–1, 566, 584–5, 643.
34. S.C. res. 18 (S/268/Rev. 1/Corr. 1), 13 Feb. 1947; S/C. 3/32, 14 Aug. 1948 (my italics).
35. S.C. res. 68 (S/1252), 10 Feb. 1949; G.A. res. 192(111), 19 Nov. 1948 (my italics).

36. S.C. res. 79 (S/1455), 17 Jan. 1950; G.A. res. 300(IV) (my italics).
37. SCOR, 13th year, 813th to 817th meetings (21 Apr. to 2 May 1958); 15th year, 857th to 863rd meetings (23–6 May 1960); 880th to 883rd meetings (22–6 July 1960).
38. G.A. res. 1(1), 17 Jan. 1946.
39. S.C. res. 276 (S/9620/Rev. 1), 30 Jan. 1970; SCOR, 25th year, Supplement for January to March 1970, p. 118, S/9632.
40. S.C. res. 283 (S/9891), 29 July 1970; 301 (S/10372/Rev. 1), 20 Oct. 1971.
41. SCOR, 25th year, Supplement for January to March 1970, pp. 160–1, S/9696; Supplement for October to December 1970, pp. 36–7, S/9976; 26th year, Supplement for October to December 1971, pp. 129–30, S/10489; 27th year, Supplement for January to March 1972, pp. 82–3, S/10606.
42. GAOR, 25th session, Supplement no. 2, A/8002, p. 67.
43. SCOR, 23rd year, Supplement for July to September 1968, pp. 71–2, S/8697; 24th year, Supplement for January to March 1969, p. 32, S/8697/Rev. 1; 25th year, Supplement for April to June 1970, p. 148, S/9748; Supplement for September to December 1970, p. 147, S/9951.
44. S/11178, 3 Jan. 1974 (mimeo.), para. 4.
45. S/AC,. 17/SR. 2, 9 March 1970 (mimeo.), p. 2.
46. SCOR, 27th year, Supplement for January to March 1972, pp. 69–70, 73, S/10571, S/10578; Special Supplement no. 2, S/10852, paras. 64–5; S/11178, 3 Jan. 1974 (mimeo.), para. 2.
47. SCOR, 15th year, Supplement for July to September 1960, p. 145, S/4486; 16th year, 941st meeting (20 Feb. 1961), para. 23; 20th year, 1225th meeting (16 June 1965), paras. 107–9.
48. SCOR, 27th year, Supplement for January to March 1972, pp. 20–7, S/10514; S/10868, 25 Jan. 1973 (mimeo.).
49. GAOR, 4th session, Supplement no. 1, A/930, pp. 17–19; Supplement no. 2, A/945, p. 65; S/1182, 4 Jan. 1948 (mimeo.); Press Release SC/908, 15 March 1949 (mimeo.); Lie, p. 216.
50. G.A. res. 186 (S–2), 14 May 1948; SCOR, 3rd year, 358th meeting (18 Sept. 1948).
51. 'UN fact-finding and human rights complaints', *International Affairs*, pp. 250–66.
52. FRUS, 1946, vol. 1, pp. 294, 303, 305, 339.
53. UNCIO, 1945, vol. XI, pp. 710–14. The full text of the San Francisco statement is printed in my *Voting in the Security Council*, pp. 105–8.
54. SCOR, 1st year, 1st series, 35th meeting (18 April 1946), p. 198; 37th meeting (25 April 1946), p. 216; S.C. res. 4, 29 April 1946.
55. SCOR, 1st year, 2nd series, 70th meeting (20 Sept. 1946), pp. 396, 410–12. The full text of the vetoed proposal is in *Voting in the Security Counil*. p. 161.
56. SCOR, 2nd year, 114th meeting (27 Feb. 1947), pp. 425–32; S.C. res. 19, 27 Feb. 1947. For further discussion of the procedural confusion on this occasion, see *Voting in the Security Council*, pp. 20–1 and 65–6.
57. SCOR, 3rd year, 288th meeting (29 Apr. 1948), pp. 19–23; 303rd meeting (24 May 1948), pp. 4–29; full text of vetoed proposal in *Voting in the Security Council*, p. 168; see also pp. 22–3.
58. SCOR, 14th year, 848th meeting (7 Sept. 1959); see also Urquhart, pp. 329–67.
59. *Voting in the Security Council*, pp. 21, 23, 45, 160–6, 168, 173–6, 179–80, and 187–8.
60. Leland M. Goodrich, Eduard Hambro, and Anne Patricia Simons, *Charter of*

the United Nations: commentary and documents, third edition, Columbia University Press, 1969, p. 224.

CHAPTER 7

1. SCOR, 1st year, 1st series, Supplement no. 2, p. 2, S/6.
2. Ibid., 31st meeting (9 Apr. 1946), pp. 103–6.
3. Ibid., 41st meeting (16 May 1946), p. 261.
4. G.A. res. 88(I), 19 Nov. 1946; S.C. res. 26 (S/368), 4 June 1947.
5. SCOR, 1st year, 1st series, 31st meeting (9 Apr. 1946), p. 101.
6. S/10770, 22 Aug. 1972 (mimeo.), p. 1.
7. SCOR, 1st year, 1st series, 31st meeting (9 Apr. 1946), pp. 101–2.
8. SCOR, 5th year, Supplement for January to May 1950, pp. 2–3, S/1447.
9. Ibid., pp. 16–18, S/1457 and [in English only] Corr. 1; 462nd meeting (17 Jan. 1950), pp. 10–13; 468th meeting (28 Feb. 1950), pp. 9–11.
10. G.A. res. 396(V), 14 Dec. 1950.
11. PC/EX/113/Rev. 1, 12 Nov. 1945, p. 45.
12. *Yearbook of the International Law Commission, 1968*, vol. ii, p. 164 (A/CN. 4/L. 129, 3 July 1968).
13. PC/EX/113/Rev. 1, 12 Nov. 1945, p. 45.
14. SCOR, 1st year, 1st series, Supplement no. 2, p. 42, S/88.
15. Ibid., p. 8.
16. Ibid., p. 42, S/88.
17. Ibid., p. 39, S/71.
18. Ibid., pp. 39–40, S/71.
19. Ibid., p. 22, S/57.
20. Ibid., p. 13.
21. FRUS, 1945, vol. 1, 1967, p. 1495.
22. SCOR, 1st year, 1st series, Supplement no. 2, p. 25, Rule 25; 41st meeting (16 May 1946), pp. 254–5.
23. S.C. res. 81 (S/1486), 24 May 1950.
24. SCOR, 5th year, 472nd meeting (24 May 1950), p. 4.
25. GAOR, 1st session, 1st part, Supplement no. 1, A/93, p. 88.
26. PC/EX/113/Rev. 1, 12 Nov. 1945, p. 45.
27. FRUS, 1946, vol. I, pp. 251–74, The Soviet proposal is in Ibid., p. 284, the ideas of the United States on pp. 287–8.
28. SCOR, 1st year, 1st series, Supplement no. 2, p. 23, S/57.
29. Ibid., p. 24, S/57.
30. Ibid.
31. Ibid., 31st meeting (9 Apr. 1946), p. 118.
32. Ibid., Supplement no. 2, p. 10.
33. Ibid., pp. 38–9, S/57.
34. Ibid., 41st meeting (16 May 1946), pp. 261–7; 42nd meeting (17 May 1946) pp. 270–7.
35. SCOR, 2nd year, Supplement no. 19, pp. 157–60, S/520; 222nd meeting (9 Dec. 1947), p. 2771.
36. SCOR, 1st year, 1st series, Supplement no. 2, p. 23, S/57.
37. Ibid., p. 22; 41st meeting (16 May 1946), pp. 259–60.

INDEX